Deals and Development

Deals and Development

The Political Dynamics of Growth Episodes

Edited by
Lant Pritchett, Kunal Sen, and Eric Werker

OXFORD
UNIVERSITY PRESS

OXFORD
UNIVERSITY PRESS

Great Clarendon Street, Oxford, OX2 6DP,
United Kingdom

Oxford University Press is a department of the University of Oxford.
It furthers the University's objective of excellence in research, scholarship,
and education by publishing worldwide. Oxford is a registered trade mark of
Oxford University Press in the UK and in certain other countries

Published in the United States of America by Oxford University Press
198 Madison Avenue, New York, NY 10016, United States of America

British Library Cataloguing in Publication Data
Data available

Library of Congress Control Number: 2017939763

ISBN 978-0-19-880164-1

Printed and bound by
CPI Group (UK) Ltd, Croydon, CR0 4YY

Links to third party websites are provided by Oxford in good faith and
for information only. Oxford disclaims any responsibility for the materials
contained in any third party website referenced in this work.

Foreword

This foreword is written on a plane between Juba in South Sudan and Addis Ababa in Ethiopia—short in distance, but vastly distinct in recent economic and development experience. Ethiopia's economy has grown by over 6 per cent per person per year for the last twelve years, and its population has experienced progress in extreme poverty reduction, better health, and improving education. South Sudan's elite has squandered its oil wealth in only a few years in patronage-based opulence since its independence in 2011, and has descended into conflict with the most extreme form of food insecurity—famine—being declared in two parts of the country. Even though neither South Sudan's nor Ethiopia's experience is discussed here, this book is an important contribution to the quest to make sense of how tomorrow's South Sudan could experience the period of fast growth and development we are currently seeing in Ethiopia, and why it presently does not. And it helps to understand why Ethiopian growth could accelerate or may not last if mishandled.

Within much of the community of development policy advisors, there is at last an increased understanding of the importance of institutions and politics for successful development. Many will now routinely refer to *Why Nations Fail* by Acemoglu and Robinson (Crown Business, 2012) or similarly the clear expositions of historical experience in institutional development. Former Prime Minister David Cameron even once named *Why Nations Fail* as his favourite book, and not just because the historical United Kingdom is used as the leading example of successful institution building.

However, those who have to turn to such books for policy advice about what to do *now* in terms of building institutions in some of the poorest and most conflict-affected states have found less than they had hoped for. The advice may be summarized as 'get yourself a good history rather than the bad one you seem to have suffered'; this may be truthful but not quite the helpful advice to nations that are trying not to fail.

This book, based on wholly independent but nevertheless DFID-funded research, is different. It still has as its focus the importance of politics and institutions in economic development, and focuses not on long-term growth, but developing countries' growth spells: why some countries may experience extended periods of fast growth or slow growth as have characterized many developing countries, rather than the slow but persistent growth characteristic of most successful Western economies. Gone is the exclusive focus on the underlying institutions, determined by long-term historical forces. It is not that history does not matter, but the analysis focuses on the reality of politics and the way political actors interact with economic actors, or, indeed at times morph into one. The authors put forward a framework that offers insights about when the political economy is favourable to growth-enhancing reforms and when it is not.

It is a book rich in detail, using ten country case studies. All of them had periods of faster and slower growth, some stagnated or even collapsed over the time periods considered. In none of these cases can the growth histories be explained as temporary technocratic policy successes or mistakes around a long-term, institutionally determined trend. The chapters and the underlying conceptual framework suggest that politics mattered here to start and sustain growth or to stifle it: the nature of the political elite's bargain with each other, whether the dominant political forces sought legitimacy from economic progress, and how different political and business interests shaped as well as benefited from these political bargains. The framework used is careful, imaginative, insightful, and with imaginative metaphors—as one would expect from the designers of the framework, and editors of this book.

Economists are often expected to act like technocrats, identifying the best possible growth-enhancing policies and projects. There is nothing wrong with this—indeed it is important—but, in my experience, policy advice is useless or bound to fail if the political incentives to act are not well understood. As this book highlights, understanding why economic growth could take off, and be sustained or not, requires an understanding of the nature of political deals, and the way they shape and are shaped by economic actors. Economists in policymaking would do well to take this seriously, and make it part of how they think about their advice—and not just something they reserve to discussing over beer and pizza late at night in the bars of the capitals of the world.

The book's analysis and framework is not just helpful for the cases discussed. For example, one interpretation of Ethiopia's take-off to higher growth within this book's framework can be understood in ways related to Rwanda. As the authors write, Rwanda's success was shaped by a government that came to power after conflict and economic chaos, and embarked on a (relatively inclusive) growth-oriented strategy as a mechanism to legitimize the regime and prevent a return to political instability and economic chaos. Ethiopia can be seen in a similar light. Political will is key, and even if 'technically' errors can still be made in the policies, the actual strategy will still require coherence with the political approach.

The contrast with South Sudan cannot be starker: emerging out of conflict, the political bargain of 2011 created economic chaos, with a state focused on seeking legitimacy through redistribution of its new oil wealth among the small political elite. A collapsing oil price made the deal unsustainable, leading to elite behaviour increasingly focused on predation rather than production. The rent-sharing deal collapsed, allowing South Sudan to descend into a vicious cycle of national and local conflict.

A book like this also makes one think about what to do about all this—is there anything the proverbial people-of-good-will in the world can do about it? Can a development agency play any role in this? It is to this book's credit that many of the case studies try to answer what ought to come next in each of the countries, without hiding behind the benefit of hindsight. Furthermore, the concluding chapter just doesn't bash the development agencies and their no doubt many failures. Instead, it tries to generalize on what to do: how can one try to foster better political and economic deals that are better for starting and sustaining growth and development, at least for relatively long periods of time?

Of course this is daring—and involves researchers sticking their neck out by trying to speculate on how what they have learned about the past can be helpful for the future. In 2008, Nobel Prize winner Michael Spence led a commission that published a report on how to be successful at growth as a country. It stated that we know the ingredients but not the recipe. The concluding chapter in this book courageously suggests that it is searching for a recipe to foster a period of high growth and development, and even offers suggestions regarding what development actors could do. It is unlikely to be the 'right' recipe, but in many ways that does not matter; the 'right' recipe will definitely have to include a substantial dose of understanding how politics and the economy interact. As we know so little about this, it is worth trying this recipe out.

Stefan Dercon
Professor of Economic Policy, University of Oxford
Chief Economist, UK Department for
International Development (DFID)

Acknowledgements

This volume owes a lot to the efforts of several key individuals and organizations. Thanks are due to those who enhanced the intellectual content of the volume, those who provided us with editorial support, and those whose financial support made the entire venture possible.

Starting with intellectual content, we acknowledge the insightful comments of two anonymous referees as well as the commissioning editor of Oxford University Press, Adam Swallow, which greatly improved the clarity of the arguments as well as the exposition. Besides the chapter authors, Jasmina Beganovich, Ishac Diwan, Nick Lea, Aldo Musacchio, Andrew Myburgh, Sophus Reinert, Nicholas Waddell, and Lou Wells provided valuable feedback and suggestions. We have presented the conceptual framework of the volume in different academic and policy forums and the comments we have received in these places have helped us to improve the framework. We would like to thank participants and guests at seminars that we have given at the UK Department for International Development (DFID), Harvard Kennedy School, International Growth Centre, National University of Mongolia, Otgontenger University, Paris Dauphine University, University of Manchester, and USAID, for extremely helpful comments and questions.

We have also received stellar editorial support from Karishma Banga, Kat Bethell, Julia Brunt, Clare Degenhardt, and Philip Reed. Without their meticulous and painstaking work in editing the different chapters and putting the entire manuscript together, this volume would not have been possible.

Finally, we would like to acknowledge the generous financial support of the Effective States and Inclusive Development (ESID) Research Centre and DFID. We are deeply grateful for this support.

Lant Pritchett, Kunal Sen, and Eric Werker

20 February 2017

This document is an output from a project funded by UK Aid from the UK government for the benefit of developing countries. However, the views expressed and information contained in it are not necessarily those of, or endorsed by, the UK government, which can accept no responsibility for such views or information or for any reliance placed on them.

Contents

Contents

List of Figures

List of Tables

List of Abbreviations

2G	second generation
ACET	African Centre for Economic Transformation
ADMARC	Agricultural Development and Marketing Corporation (Malawi)
AFC	Asian financial crisis
AIDS	acquired immuno-deficiency syndrome
AL	Awami League (Bangladesh)
AR	Acemoglu–Robinson
ASM	artisanal and small-scale mining
BA	Barisan Alternatif (Malaysia)
BACAR	Banque Continentale Africaine du Rwanda
BANCOR	Banque à la Confiance d'Or (Rwanda)
BCDI	Bank of Commerce, Development, and Industry (Rwanda)
BCR	Banque Commerciale du Rwanda
BGMEA	Bangladesh Garments Manufacturing and Exporters' Association
BJP	Bharatiya Janata Party (India)
BK	Bank of Kigali (Rwanda)
BKMEA	Bangladesh Knitwear Manufacturing and Exporters Association
BLD	Bharatiya Lok Dal
BN	Barisan Nasional (Malaysia)
BNP	Bangladesh Nationalist Party
BOI	Board of Investment (Thailand)
BPR	Banque Populaire du Rwanda SA
BRAC	Building Resources Across Communities
BRD	Development Bank of Rwanda
CAG	Comptroller and Auditor General (India)
CDC	Council for the Development of Cambodia
CNRP	Cambodia National Rescue Party
CPB	Crown Property Bureau (Thailand)

CPP	Cambodian People's Party
CPP	Convention People's Party (Ghana)
CTG	caretaker government
CVL	Crystal Ventures Ltd (Rwanda)
DAP	Democratic Action Party (Malaysia)
DFID	Department for International Development (UK)
DoT	Department of Telecommunications (India)
DPP	Democratic Progressive Party (Malawi)
DRC	Democratic Republic of the Congo
ECI	Economic Complexity Index
ECOMOG	Economic Community of West African States' Monitoring Group
ELC	Economic Land Concession (Cambodia)
EPZ	export-processing zone
ERP	Economic Recovery Programme
ESID	Effective States and Inclusive Development Research Centre
FASMEC	Federation of Small and Medium Enterprises (Cambodia)
FDA	Forestry Development Authority (Liberia)
FDI	foreign direct investment
FECOMIRWA	Fédération des Coopératives Minières au Rwanda
FELDA	Federal Land Development Agency (Malaysia)
FUNCINPEC	Front Uni National pour un Cambodge Indépendant, Neutre, Pacifique et Coopératif (Cambodia)
GDP	gross domestic product
GDPPC	gross domestic product per capita
GLC	government-linked corporation
GMAC	Garment Manufacturers' Association of Cambodia
GNI	gross national income
G-PSF	Government-Private Sector Forum (Cambodia)
HICOM	Heavy Industry Corporation of Malaysia
HIV	human immuno-deficiency virus
ICRG	International Country Risk Guide
ICT	information and communications technology
IMF	International Monetary Fund
INC	Indian National Congress
JAGODOL	Jatiyatabadi Gonotantrik Dal (Bangladesh)
JD	Janata Dal (India)

JP	Janata Party (India)
JP	Jatiya Party (Bangladesh)
JPPCC	Joint Public and Private Sector Consultative Committee (Thailand)
KACITA	Kampala City Traders' Association
KPRP	Kampuchean People's Revolutionary Party (Cambodia)
LAOs	limited access orders
LSE	London School of Economics
MAFF	Ministry of Agriculture, Forestry, and Fisheries (Cambodia)
MCA	Malaysian Chinese Association
MCCCI	Malawi Confederation of Chambers of Commerce and Industry
MCP	Malawi Congress Party
MDR	Republican Democratic Movement (Rwanda)
MFA	Multi-Fibre Agreement
MICE	Meetings, Incentives, Conferences, and Events (Rwanda)
MINAGRI	Ministry of Agriculture and Animal Husbandry (Rwanda)
MINECOFIN	Ministry of Finance and Economic Planning (Rwanda)
MINIRENA	Ministry of Natural Resources (Rwanda)
MOJA	Movement for Justice in Africa (Liberia)
MPNOs	mobile phone network operators (Uganda)
NDC	National Democratic Congress (Ghana)
NEP	New Economic Policy (Malaysia)
NESDB	National Economic and Social Development Board (Thailand)
NGOs	non-governmental organizations
NLC	National Liberation Council (Ghana)
NPD	Nyarutarama Property Developers
NPP	New Patriotic Party (Ghana)
NPV	net present value
NRA	National Resistance Army (Uganda)
NRM	National Resistance Movement (Uganda)
NWW	North–Wallis–Weingast
OAOs	open access orders
OCIR	Office des Cultures Industrielles du Rwanda
OECD	Organisation for Economic Co-operation and Development
OSF	Open Society Foundation
PAL	Progressive Alliance of Liberia
PAS	Pan-Malaysian Islamic Party

PKR	National Justice Party (Malaysia)
PNB	Permodalan Nasional Bhd (Malaysia)
PNDC	Provisional National Defence Council (Ghana)
ppa	per cent per annum
PPP	purchasing power parity
PRK	People's Republic of Kampuchea (Cambodia)
PSF	Private Sector Foundation (Uganda)
REDEMI	Régie d'Exploitation et de Développement des Mines (Rwanda)
RFCC	Rwandan Farmers' Coffee Company
RMG	ready-made garments
RPF	Rwanda Patriotic Front
RPMs	revolutions per minute
RTC	Rwanda Trading Company
RwF	Rwandan francs
SAP	structural adjustment programme
SEC	US Securities and Exchange Commission
SMEs	small and medium-sized enterprises
SPLA	Sudan People's Liberation Army
ST	structural transformation
TRAFIPRO	Travail, Fidélité, Progrès
TRT	Thai-Rak-Thai
UGX	Uganda shilling
UIA	Uganda Investment Authority
UMA	Uganda Manufacturers' Association
UMNO	United Malays National Organization
UP	United Party (Ghana)
UPC	Uganda People's Congress
URA	Uganda Revenue Authority
USAID	US Agency for International Development
UTL	United Telecoms Limited
VPI	vertical political integration
WTO	World Trade Organization

List of Contributors

Charles Ackah is a Senior Research Fellow and Head of the Economics Division at the Institute of Statistical, Social and Economic Research (ISSER), University of Ghana. He is a development economist with research interests in trade policy, private sector development, financial sector development, gender, and entrepreneurship. Dr Ackah is External Research Fellow at the Centre for Research in Economic Development and International Trade (CREDIT) based in the University of Nottingham, UK. Prior to joining ISSER, he worked as a Research Analyst at the World Bank. He has consulted for numerous government agencies and international organizations.

Pritish Behuria is an LSE Fellow in the Department of International Development at the London School of Economics and Political Science. He completed his PhD in Development Studies at SOAS, University of London, in 2015. His current research focuses on the political economy of development with reference to political settlements, developmental states, industrial policy, and technology acquisition during clean energy transitions. He has published articles in *Journal of Modern African Studies*, *Journal of Eastern African Studies*, and *Review of African Political Economy*. He is currently working on a book examining the developmental state in Rwanda.

Badru Bukenya is a Uganda-based policy analyst and development practitioner. He currently works as a Lecturer in the Department of Social Work and Social Administration, Makerere University Kampala. Badru's research focuses on the politics of health service delivery, public sector reforms, social protection, and the politics of state–civil society engagement. In all his research endeavours, Badru proficiently employs mixed methods research approaches and has expertise in qualitative software packages such as Nvivo. His most recent publication is entitled 'From Social Accountability to a New Social Contract? The Role of NGOs in Protecting and Empowering PLHIV in Uganda', *Journal of Development Studies*.

Michael Danquah is a Senior Lecturer at the Department of Economics, University of Ghana, Legon. Previously, he worked as a Development Policy Analyst at the National Development Planning Commission, Ghana. His research has focused on inclusive growth, informality and tax reforms, economics of education, and national efficiency. Michael's authored articles have appeared in *Economic Modelling*, *Empirical Economics*, and *Review of Development Economics*. In 2014, he was awarded the Most Promising Young Scholar at the School of Social Sciences, University of Ghana, Legon. Michael was interviewed on aid and poverty reduction on a BBC World Service programme in 2015.

George Domfe is a Development Economist and a Research Fellow at the Centre for Social Policy Studies (CSPS) at the College of Humanities, University of Ghana. He holds a PhD in Development Studies and MPhil and BA (Hons) in Economics from the University of Ghana. His research focus is on poverty analysis, public sector economics, and gender and development. He is a member of the Canadian Economics Association (CEA) and a visiting lecturer of the Partnership for African Social and Governance Research (PASGR) affiliated universities in Africa.

Tom Goodfellow is a Senior Lecturer in the Department of Urban Studies and Planning at the University of Sheffield, and a Fellow of the Sheffield Institute for International Development. His research concerns the political economy of urban development in Africa, with a particular focus on Rwanda, Uganda, and Ethiopia. His work has been published in leading journals including *Development and Change*, *African Affairs*, *Comparative Politics*, *Urban Studies*, *Journal of Development Studies*, *Geoforum*, and *Oxford Development Studies*, for which he was awarded the Sanjaya Lall Prize in 2014. He is co-author of *Cities and Development* (Routledge, 2016).

Mirza Hassan is a political economist based at the BRAC Institute of Governance and Development (BIGD), BRAC University, Bangladesh. His research focuses on political settlements, private sector development, state–business relations, and national and local governance. Mirza has carried out consultancy work for UNDP, the Asia Foundation, the World Bank, DFID, CARE, in Bangladesh and in countries in North Africa and the Asia Pacific. His recent work is on the political economy of tax reform in Bangladesh, published in the *Journal of Development Studies*. He is currently leading a programme on social accountability in public procurement process for the government of Bangladesh.

Seiha Heng was a research fellow at the Cambodia Development Resource Institute (CDRI) in Phnom Penh, Cambodia, from 2009 to 2015. His wider research interests include democratic decentralization, political settlements theory, and youth and politics.

Sam Hickey is Professor of Politics and Development in the Global Development Institute, University of Manchester, and Joint Research Director of the DFID-UK-funded Effective States and Inclusive Development (ESID) Research Centre. His recent work on the politics of development has been published in *African Affairs*, *Journal of Development Studies*, and *World Development*. He has edited or co-edited six collections, the most recent being *The Politics of Inclusive Development: Interrogating the Evidence* (Oxford University Press, 2015, with Kunal Sen and Badru Bukenya).

Sabyasachi Kar is Professor at the Institute of Economic Growth, India, and an Honorary Senior Research Fellow at the University of Manchester. He has written a number of books and academic articles on macroeconomics, growth, and development economics, with a particular focus on the Indian economy. In the past, he has worked extensively for the Perspective Planning Division of the Indian Planning Commission, and provided them with inputs for successive five-year plans of the Indian government. He has also worked on projects sponsored by the World Bank, the Global Development Network (GDN), the European Commission, and DFID.

Tim Kelsall is a Senior Research Fellow at the Overseas Development Institute (ODI) in London and an Honorary Research Fellow at the University of Manchester. Prior to joining ODI he taught politics and development studies at Oxford and Newcastle Universities, edited the journal *African Affairs*, and worked freelance for several research and development organizations. He has published extensively on issues of politics and development in Africa and Asia, his latest book being *Business, Politics, and the State in Africa: Rethinking the Orthodoxies on Growth and Transformation* (Zed Books, 2013).

Robert Darko Osei is an Associate Professor in the Institute of Statistical, Social and Economic Research (ISSER), University of Ghana, Legon, and also the Vice Dean for the School of Graduate Studies at the University of Ghana. Robert's main areas of research include evaluative poverty and rural research, macro and micro implications of fiscal policies, aid effectiveness, and other economic development policy concerns. He is currently involved in a number of research projects in Ghana, Niger, Burkina Faso, and Mali.

Lant Pritchett is Professor of the Practice of Economic Development at the Harvard Kennedy School at Harvard University and is a Senior Fellow of the Center for Global Development. He has authored (either alone or with one of his fifty co-authors) over a hundred articles, with over 25,000 citations on development-related topics ranging from economic growth to education to population to social capital to health to migration to state capability. His most recent books are *Building State Capability: Evidence, Analysis, Action* (with Matt Andrews and Michael Woolcock, Oxford University Press, 2017) and *The Rebirth of Education: Schooling Ain't Learning* (Centre for Global Development, 2013).

Selim Raihan is Professor at the Department of Economics, University of Dhaka, Bangladesh and the Executive Director of the South Asian Network on Economic Modeling (SANEM). He holds a PhD from the University of Manchester. His research interests include trade policy, economic growth, political economy, labour markets, and poverty. He is the author and co-author of more than a hundred publications consisting of refereed journal articles, books and edited volumes, book chapters, working papers, and policy reports. Dr Raihan has worked for several national and international organizations.

Jagadish Prasad Sahu is a PhD candidate at the Centre for Economic Studies and Planning, Jawaharlal Nehru University, New Delhi, India. Previously, he has worked as a senior research analyst at the Institute of Economic Growth, Delhi. He holds an MPhil in economics from the Delhi School of Economics, University of Delhi. His research interests include macroeconomics and development economics. He has published several articles in peer-reviewed journals.

Jonathan Said is the Country Manager of the Africa Governance Initiative (AGI) in Liberia and the Head of AGI's Private Sector Development Practice. He is an economic and governance advisor to the government of Liberia and formerly served as an economic advisor to the governments of Malawi and Guyana. He is a practitioner whose work centres on helping low-income governments develop poverty-reducing market systems and the inclusive economy. His research has largely focused on the analysis of these economies. Jonathan also worked as an economics consultant and analyst on the UK economy.

Kunal Sen is Professor of Development Economics in the Global Development Institute, University of Manchester, and Joint Research Director of the DFID-UK-funded Effective States and Inclusive Development (ESID) Research Centre. His current research is on the political economy of development. Kunal's recent authored books are *The Political Economy of India's Growth Episodes* (Palgrave Macmillan, 2016) and *Out of the Shadows? The Informal Sector in Post-Reform India* (Oxford University Press, 2016). He has won the Sanjaya Lall Prize in 2006 and Dudley Seers Prize in 2003 for his publications.

Khwima Singini is a development economist based in Malawi specializing in private sector development and public sector policymaking. He is currently working with Imani Consultants Limited. He is also an Economic Consultant for Foster Lewis. He was the economic advisor for ABWNet and Graca Machel Trust in Malawi. He also coordinates and manages the AIRBO project under the African Entrepreneurship Hub in Malawi funded by the IDRC. He was the Local Research Consultant for Management Systems International (MSI-Washington) conducting the USAID Southern Africa Trade Hub Project. He has also worked with the AFIDEP and Dartmouth College (USA) as a lead researcher.

Matthew Tyce is undertaking a PhD in Development Policy and Management at the University of Manchester's Global Development Institute. Investigating the political dynamics of growth and structural transformation in Kenya since independence, his project looks at the nature of deal-making in key economic sectors such as horticulture, textiles and apparel, mining, and banking.

Eric Werker is Associate Professor in the Beedie School of Business at Simon Fraser University (SFU) and academic lead from SFU to the Canadian International Resources and Development Institute. He researches how less developed countries can build more thriving and inclusive private sectors, particularly when they are rich in natural resources, and how international actors can play a positive role in creating successful societies. In previous roles, Eric was on the faculty of Harvard Business School, ran the International Growth Centre Liberia program, and worked as a consulting economist at Conservation International and the Millennium Challenge Corporation.

1

Deals and Development

An Introduction to the Conceptual Framework

Lant Pritchett, Kunal Sen, and Eric Werker

1.1 Introduction

Why are there such significant and persistent differences in living standards across countries? This is one of the most important and challenging areas of development thinking and policy. Much of the focus in the academic and policy literature on 'growth' has been on steady-state or long-run average rate of growth of output per capita or, equivalently, comparing *levels* of income. But the focus on *one single* growth rate for a country misses the point that most countries observe dramatic changes in growth of per capita income. Economic growth in developing countries is episodic—massive discrete changes in growth are common, with most developing countries experiencing distinct growth episodes, and growth accelerations and decelerations or collapses as transitions between those episodes (Easterly et al., 1993; Ben-David and Papell, 1998; Pritchett, 2000; Jones and Olken, 2008). For individual countries, the change in living standards due to these growth episodes over a relatively short period of time can be staggering. For example, India was known for its 'Hindu' rate of growth till the late 1980s. Economic growth accelerated in 1993, and then again in 2002, and the cumulative income gain from these two growth accelerations was 3.7 *trillion* purchasing power parity (PPP) dollars (Pritchett et al., 2016). In contrast, after fourteen years of rapid economic growth, the growth deceleration in Malawi that began in 1978 and ended in 2002 cost each person cumulatively almost 10,000 dollars (Pritchett et al., 2016).[1]

---

[1] Average growth in gross domestic product (GDP) per capita in Malawi was 6.6 per cent per annum in 1964–78 and −2.2 per cent per annum in 1978–2002.

Why do some countries successfully initiate *episodes* of rapid growth, while others suffer extended stagnation? Why are some countries able to sustain growth episodes over many decades of rapid (or steady) growth, while other growth episodes end in reversion to stagnation or collapse? The purpose of this book is to create and then apply an analytical model that is capable of generating both transitory and sustained episodes of accelerated growth. A key feature is a feedback loop from existing economic conditions to the pressures on policy-implementing 'institutions'. This feedback loop can be positive (with economic growth leading to improved institutions for inclusive growth) or negative (with economic growth leading to worse conditions for further growth by shutting off the inclusiveness of growth and limiting economic opportunity to existing successes). Whether economic elites use their influence on political and bureaucratic elites to create more possibilities for structural transformation or, conversely, use their power to entrench their privileged position, will, to a significant extent, determine whether episodes of rapid growth can be sustained or will peter out, or even be reversed.

In this introductory chapter,[2] we begin with a fresh look at the 'stylized facts' of economic growth. We identify an important limitation in the past literature on economic growth, in that its focus on rates of *average* growth of per capita income has obscured the fact that most countries observe dramatic changes in growth of per capita income over time. Most developing countries tend to observe stop–go growth episodes, with growth accelerations followed by growth decelerations or collapses (and vice versa). We argue that an understanding of the political drivers of economic growth needs an explanation of the political dynamics around the transition from one growth phase to another—that is, the political determinants of growth accelerations, growth maintenance, and growth declines/collapses. We then propose a conceptual framework to understand the political channels of economic growth around the transitions from one growth phase to another. In developing this framework, we argue that the political drivers of growth accelerations are different from the political drivers of growth maintenance. In the rest of the book, we apply this framework to ten countries, which are at various stages of economic development. These countries are Bangladesh, Cambodia, Ghana, India, Liberia, Malawi, Malaysia, Rwanda, Thailand, and Uganda.

---

[2] This chapter builds on, while drawing heavily from, Pritchett and Werker (2012)—'The guts of a GUT (Grand Unified Theory): Elite commitment and economic growth', which was the framework chapter posed to the case study authors at the time of the first draft of their research. This chapter, as well as subsequent drafts of the country case studies, has benefited from extensive discussion and debate among all of the authors.

1.2 What Are the Basic Facts About Growth that a Theory of Growth Should Explain?

Before discussing any theory of growth, we review the facts that a theory of growth ought to be capable of explaining. Many current growth theories achieve elegance and apparent parsimony by attempting to explain only certain features of the process of economic growth. We wish to emphasize the *dynamics* of growth over the 'medium' run (longer than business cycle), rather than just 'steady-state' properties. What preoccupies policymakers and business people is not the infinite horizon level, but the immediate (quarter to quarter) and medium-run (five to ten year) growth—and, as we see, the medium run and the steady-state have completely different dynamics.

1.2.1 *Fact 1: Steady, Moderate, Constant Growth for a Century or More*

First, nearly all of the currently rich countries are rich because they grew at a modest pace for more than a hundred years. The GDP per capita (GDPPC) in OECD (Organisation for Economic Co-operation and Development) countries typically grew at around 2 per cent per annum from 1870 to today. The reason behind the differing *levels* of economic success across countries such as Denmark and Somalia is not due to Denmark having grown particularly fast, but just that Denmark has grown steadily for a long time.

One of the most striking economic facts is that one can predict OECD countries' *level* of income one hundred years ahead with remarkable accuracy. Figure 1.1 shows that, using just data from 1890 to 1901, one can predict Danish GDPPC in 2003 to within a few percentage points. One important implication is that Denmark's growth has not *accelerated* or *decelerated* in over one hundred years—its average annual growth from 1870 to 2003 was 1.94 per cent, from 1890 to 1915 it was 1.93 per cent, and from 1980 to 2003 it was 1.91 per cent. This lack of long-run growth acceleration across a century is true of the (old) OECD countries.[3]

This fact of long-run stable growth of the rich countries itself rules out models that explain steady-state growth as a linear function of anything that has increased in scale steadily over time. For example, levels of technology and education have increased steadily in rich countries over time, yet average growth rates in these countries have remained the same. As Jones (1995) pointed out early in the debate over endogenous growth, the fact that

[3] By 'old' OECD we mean the OECD before the recent additions (e.g. South Korea and Mexico). We use OECD to represent 'developed' countries, which we take to mean having attained: high productivity economies with prosperous citizens; capable institutions and organizations generally, but including a high-capability state, stable democracy and freedoms; and practised social equality.

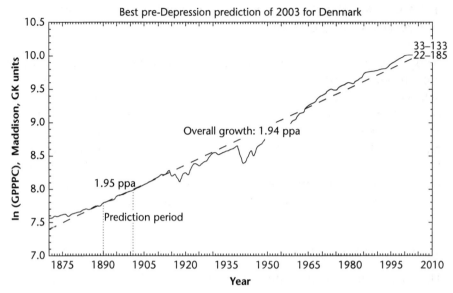

Figure 1.1. Rich countries have had stable growth rates for more than one hundred years—with neither deceleration or acceleration—Denmark, for example

Source: Authors' calculations with Maddison (2009) data. <http://www.ggdc.net/maddison/oriindex. htm>.

Note: GK units = Geary–Khamis dollar units.

measures of education or research and development have grown many-fold while growth has been stable, rules out many 'first generation' endogenous growth models and makes any positive impact of scale on long-run growth problematic (Jones, 1999; Jones, 2005).

1.2.2 *Fact 2: Poverty (or 'Low-Growth') Traps*

The second big fact is that there is a set of countries that are, even today, very near the lowest level that income per capita ever was in all of history (a level that could be called 'subsistence'). This low level of income today implies that the *long-run* average rate of their growth must be very low, well below the long-run rate of the developed economies. This growth differential caused the massive historical divergence in per capita incomes (Pritchett, 1997).

1.2.3 *Fact 3: Accelerations to Spectacularly Rapid, Extended Periods of Growth, Rarely*

Third, a very small number of countries have improved their economy very fast by historical or cross-sectional standards. South Korea's GDPPC was similar to Ghana's in 1960, but had reached Portugal's by 2005. But since South Korea was so poor in 1960, its *cumulative* historical growth rate up to 1960 must have been slow. So a theory of South Korea's growth (or that of other countries that begin episodes of rapid growth from low levels of income) must invoke something that caused an *acceleration* in growth rates from a previously low level, an acceleration to a very high level which then *persisted* for decades (as opposed to the long-run persistence of moderate growth of the OECD countries).

1.2.4 *Fact 4: Non-persistent Growth with Episodes of Boom, Stagnation, and Bust*

The principal fact about the growth rates of many countries over the medium run is *volatility* in the growth rate—with acceleration and deceleration—and hence a lack of persistence (Easterly et al., 1993; Ben-David and Papell, 1998). There is massive 'regression to the mean' in growth rates, such that a country growing fast in one decade is expected to *decelerate* substantially towards the average growth rate. There is some, but little, predictive value for a country's growth in the next decade from this decade's growth.[4]

Over the medium to long run, most countries' growth is *episodic* and has many, apparently discrete, transitions between periods of high growth, periods of negative growth, and periods of stagnation (Pritchett, 2000; Hausmann et al., 2005; Jones and Olken, 2008). For instance, Hausmann et al. (2005) examine cases of 'growth acceleration' for countries that experienced a growth episode at least seven years long: (a) that was at least 2.5 per cent per annum *faster* than previous growth; (b) in which growth after the acceleration was positive (to rule out 'accelerations' that are just slowing the pace of collapse); and (c) which led to a higher level of output than the previous peak (to rule out accelerations that were only recoveries). They find that there are many accelerations, but with very different outcomes. As Jones and Olken (2008: 582) point out:

> almost all countries in the world have experienced rapid growth lasting a decade or longer, during which they converge towards income levels in the United States. Conversely, nearly all countries have experienced periods of abysmal growth. Circumstances or policies that produce ten years of rapid economic growth appear easily reversed, often leaving countries no better off than they were prior to the expansion.

Therefore, long-run growth averages within countries often mask distinct periods of growth success and growth failure, and 'the instability of growth

---

[4] The conventional wisdom of course nearly always gets this exactly wrong and extrapolates a country's current growth rate into the (far) future.

rates makes the talk of *the* growth rate almost meaningless' (Pritchett, 2000: 247). Growth experiences differ over time within a country almost as much as they differ among countries, and identical average growth rates can mask very distinct growth paths (Jerzmanowski, 2006).

1.2.5 *The Empirics of Growth States*

To illustrate our key points about the nature of economic growth in non-OECD countries, we provide some country examples in this section. Suppose that there are just six discrete 'states' of growth, like gears of a car (reverse, neutral, first, second, third, fourth). In any given period, a country is in one of those states of growth. Thus a country's average growth is the share of time spent in each state multiplied by the growth while in that state. But a country's 'average' growth rate is not a particularly enlightening summary statistic of its underlying growth process. Countries with exactly the same rate of average growth over thirty years may have had completely different growth dynamics, in the sense of being in different growth states.

To illustrate the dynamic nature of growth episodes, we calculate five-year growth rates for every country and then 'bin' these episodes into six categories of growth rates, from collapse ($g < -2$ per cent per annum, or ppa) to negative stagnation ($-2 < g < 0$) up to rapid growth ($g > 6$ ppa). This produces a histogram with an average of around 2 per cent and a standard deviation of around two percentage points (so those in collapse or rapid growth episodes are more than two standard deviations from the cross-national mean). We then compare a given country's distribution of growth episodes to the distribution of growth rates of all countries in the world.

Figure 1.2 shows five-year growth episodes for the United Kingdom. All of the episodes are concentrated in two categories: slow growth, and moderate growth. This is typical of OECD country growth rates, nearly all steady growth with no boom or bust (just some business cycles). This is dramatically more centred than the world distribution, which shows countries with booms and collapses.

Figure 1.3 shows the same graph for Ghana. It is striking that Ghana has more variation in its growth episodes than the variation in growth rates across all countries in the world. Ghana spent more time in super-rapid growth (the right-most category, growth above 6 ppa) *and* more time in collapse (growth less than negative 2 ppa).

Figure 1.4 shows that the *average* growth of the UK and Ghana from 1950 to 2007 is almost exactly the same, but with entirely different dynamics. The UK grew quite steadily. Ghana experienced a massive boom from 1965 to 1972, followed by a massive collapse in the mid-1970s, followed by an extended stagnation, followed by reasonably rapid growth since 1999.

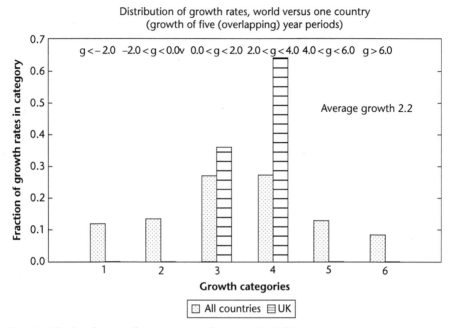

Figure 1.2. Steady growth—most growth concentrated in a narrow range
Source: Authors' calculations with PWT6.3 data (Heston et al., 2009).

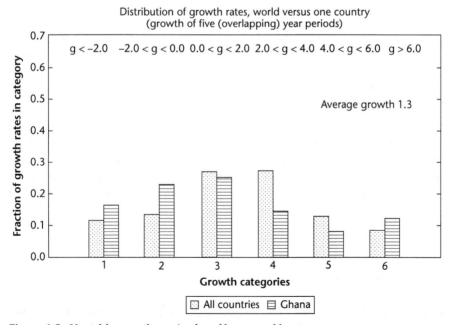

Figure 1.3. Unstable growth—episodes of boom and bust
Source: Authors' calculations with PWT6.3 data (Heston et al., 2009).

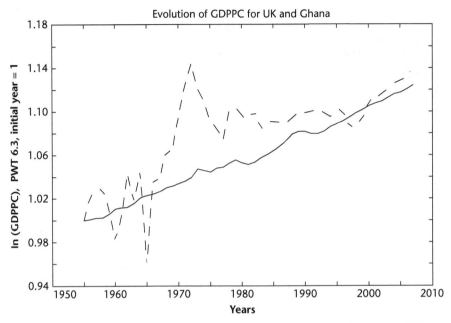

Figure 1.4. Countries may have the same average growth rate but very different dynamics

Source: Authors' calculations with PWT6.3 data (Heston et al., 2009).

Note: PWT = Penn World Tables.

This comparison between the UK and Ghana, showing that similar growth rates when averaged over long periods of time can be the result of very different underlying dynamic patterns of growth, holds more generally. As Kar et al. (2013a) document, most developing countries, with the exception of East Asia, tend to see 'boom and bust' growth—that is, periods of growth accelerations followed by periods of growth decelerations. Later in the chapter, we develop an analytical framework grounded in political economy that can explain why only a few countries see prolonged periods of strong growth, while most others witness growth that is highly episodic. But first we review two other recent theories of growth that have influenced both the intellectual understanding and practice of development.

1.3 Institutions and Rents

Our framework for understanding growth, and our focus on growth episodes, acceleration, and maintenance, emerges from—and is in response to—the evolving understanding of the political economy and institutional causes of economic development. The most powerful intellectual current, epitomized by Acemoglu and Robinson (2008, 2012) and North et al. (2009), does not focus on intermediate variables like savings rates or technological progress, but instead seeks to determine the political basis for growth-friendly institutions. We argue that these contributions provide powerful insights into why some developing countries stagnate while others observe strong economic growth, which we will build on in our own framework to explain episodic growth. However, neither of these two contributions provides an adequate understanding of why growth accelerations and decelerations occur, and why rapid growth is very difficult to maintain in a developing country. Our hope is that by focusing on episodic growth, we can put forward a framework grounded in political economy, like these other contributions, but with more actionable levers to allow policymakers the chance to influence their countries' growth trajectories.

1.3.1 *Acemoglu–Robinson*

Acemoglu and Robinson's (AR) starting point is the premise that institutions, defined as 'the rules of the game' (North, 1990) are the fundamental cause of economic growth. The set of institutions that matter for broad-based economic growth, according to AR, are inclusive economic institutions and inclusive political institutions (Acemoglu and Robinson, 2008, 2012). Inclusive economic institutions are: secure property rights for the majority of the population (such as smallholder farmers and small firms); law and order; markets that are open to relatively free entry of new businesses; state support for markets (in the form of public goods provision, regulation, and enforcement of contracts); and access to education and opportunity for the great majority of citizens. Inclusive political institutions are political institutions that allow broad participation of the citizens of the country, uphold the rule of law, and place constraints and checks on politicians along with the rule of law. AR argue that along with political pluralism, some degree of political centralization is also necessary for states to be able to enforce law and order effectively. In contrast to the growth-enhancing effects of inclusive economic and political institutions, AR argue that extractive economic institutions, such as insecure property rights and regulations that limit entry to markets, and extractive political institutions that concentrate power in the hands of a few with limited checks and balances, are not likely to lead to broad-based and sustained economic growth (that is, growth can occur for some time under these institutions, but is not likely to last and will benefit a narrow set of elites rather than the majority of the population).

But what determines the set of economic and political institutions prevailing in the country at a particular point of time? AR argue that economic institutions are politically determined, as the prevalent power relations will determine which set of economic institutions is more likely to emerge. Economic institutions determine the aggregate growth potential of the economy, as well as the distribution of resources. Political institutions are determined by the power of different groups in society. Political power can be both de jure and de facto. De jure political power refers to power that originates from the political institutions in society (such as whether the political system is democratic or autocratic). De facto political institutions, on the other hand, originate from the possibility that important social and political groups which hold political power may not find the distributions of benefits allocated by de jure political institutions and by economic institutions acceptable to them, and may use both legal and extra-legal means to impose their wishes on society and try to change these institutions (for example, they may revolt, use arms, co-opt the military, or undertake protests).

AR argue that the degree of de facto political power originates from the ability of some groups to solve their collective action problem and from the economic resources available to the group (which determines their capacity to use force against other groups). In the ultimate analysis, therefore, the initial distribution of economic resources and the nature of de jure political institutions determine both de jure and de facto political power; these in turn determine the set of economic institutions and political institutions that are likely to emerge in the economy, which in turn determine economic performance and the distribution of resources that are compatible with the distribution of political power. This can be seen in the schematic representation in Figure 1.5.

AR introduce the concept of 'political equilibrium' as a way of understanding how political factors determine the form and functioning of economic institutions and, in so doing, affect economic growth. A political equilibrium is the set of political and economic institutions compatible with the balance of de facto political power between groups. It is the political equilibrium that determines the institutional arrangements in society and the manner in which economic institutions function. Therefore, AR argue that: 'making or imposing specific institutional reforms may have little impact on the general

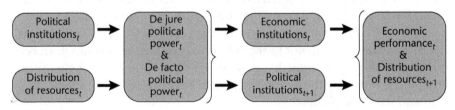

Figure 1.5. Evolution of political and economic institutions in Acemoglu–Robinson
Source: Acemoglu and Robinson (2008).

structure of economic institutions or performance if they leave untouched the underlying political equilibrium' (Acemoglu and Robinson, 2008: 13). An important implication of AR's theory is that a political equilibrium that leads to poor economic performance may persist over time, and economic growth may stagnate in a country for many years as a consequence. Political elites who hold power will always have an incentive to maintain the political institutions that give them political power, and the economic institutions that distribute resources to them. Therefore, there will be a persistence of extractive economic and political institutions in societies with such institutions, since the elites who benefit from these institutions would not be incentivized to change them. Conversely, inclusive and political institutions will be more likely to prevail (at least after a period of consolidation), since once they emerge, strong economic performance will be likely to result, reinforcing the welfare-enhancing effects of these institutions and allowing states to become more credible via greater legitimacy to the commitment of these institutions.

These possibilities are shown in Figure 1.6. As the figure makes clear, while the combination of politically and economically inclusive institutions is stable and the combination of politically and economically extractive institutions is stable, the 'off diagonal' combinations of extractive political institutions with inclusive economies, or extractive economies with political inclusive institutions, are not stable.

The 'off diagonal' instability can be resolved, either through progress (e.g. one set of institutions becomes inclusive) or deterioration.

Empirical evidence from the last six decades does not support the conjecture that the presence of extractive political institutions (at least as commonly measured) will be a cause of prolonged economic stagnation. In fact, some of the most rapid growth episodes have occurred in autocracies (Sen et al., 2016). A theoretical framework that seeks to explain episodes of rapid growth

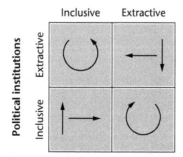

Figure 1.6. Dynamics of 'why nations fail'
Source: Acemoglu (2011).

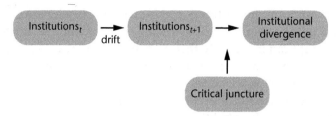

Figure 1.7. Institutional change in Acemoglu–Robinson
Source: Acemoglu and Robinson (2012).

needs to allow for the possibility that autocracies may have growth-enhancing characteristics, as well as elucidate the causal mechanisms that explain why this is the case. We will do so when we develop our framework in Section 1.4.

As we will see from the country case studies later in this chapter, a convincing theory of economic growth must be able to explain why countries move from periods of stagnation to periods of rapid growth. AR argue that while bad political equilibrium tends to persist change is possible. With time, institutional drift may occur, leading to a 'critical juncture' where there may be persistent institutional divergence. This is shown in Figure 1.7.

According to AR, many factors can contribute to this divergence. For example, new economic elites may emerge who challenge the existing balance of power, and demand change in economic institutions from extractive to more inclusive institutions. There is also the possibility of revolt from citizens excluded from current political institutions, and the elite may respond with greater political pluralism. AR view these critical junctures as 'stochastic' and, therefore, to a large extent, exogenous, and they state that it is not clear 'under what circumstance political equilibria that lead to economic growth will arise' (Acemoglu and Robinson, 2008: 10). While it is possible to argue that a country will maintain rapid growth once its economic institutions are inclusive—so AR may provide a theory of growth maintenance, particularly for OECD countries—AR do not explain why growth accelerations and decelerations occur (Sen, 2013).

1.3.2 North–Wallis–Weingast

Similar to AR, North, Wallis, and Weingast (NWW) take success in economic development as primarily about improving institutions (North et al., 2009). However, they depart from conventional thinking about institutional development in developing countries, which posits that developing countries should emulate the institutions of the most successful high-income countries of the OECD. NWW start with the premise that all societies must deal with violence, and that 'in most developing societies, individuals and organisations actively use or threaten to use violence to gather wealth and resources' (North et al., 2013: 1). Therefore, for economic development to occur, violence must be restrained. NWW argue that developing societies limit violence through the manipulation of economic interests by the political system, in order to create rents so that powerful groups and individuals find it in their interest to refrain from using violence (North et al., 2013: 3).

NWW call such societies *limited access orders* (LAOs), which are social arrangements that discourage the use of violence by organizations. In LAOs, members of the dominant coalition (who are primarily the economic and political elites) use their privileged positions to create rents and, in so doing, ensure the cooperation of all the elites that constitute the dominant coalition. The primary source of rents within the coalition is the ability to use the coalition to enforce arrangements within the organizations of the coalition members, and the rents are the glue that holds together the institutional arrangements between members of the dominant coalition. Thus, as NWW argue, the creation and structuring of rents is the logic of LAOs, and provides the mechanism by which the possibility of violence is kept in check.

NWW distinguish between three types of LAO, depending on their level of economic and political development. The first type is the *fragile* LAO, where the dominant coalition 'can barely maintain itself in the face of internal and external violence' (North et al., 2013: 11), and violence capacity itself is the principal determinant of the distribution of rents and resources. Examples of fragile LAOs are Afghanistan, Iraq, the Democratic Republic of the Congo, Syria, and several other conflict-affected societies in the Middle East and sub-Saharan Africa. The second type of LAO is the *basic* LAO, where the government is well established in comparison with fragile LAOs and is the main durable organization, though non-governmental organizations may exist within the framework of the dominant coalition. In this type of LAO, elite privileges and organizations are closely identified with the coalition and often with the government, as members of the elite and non-elite are reluctant to create economically significant private organizations, for fear of expropriation. Examples of basic LAOs are Myanmar, Cuba, North Korea, and many countries in the Arab world and in sub-Saharan Africa. The final type of LAO is the *mature* LAO, where the dominant coalition supports a variety of organizations from outside the government, as well as within it. However, the coalition limits access to organizations that the government allows and supports, thereby limiting competition and creating rents to maintain itself and prevent violence. Examples of mature LAOs include most of Latin America, China, India, and South Africa.

While most developing countries belong to one of the three types of LAO, NWW categorize the social order that characterizes developed countries as *open access orders* (OAOs). NWW argue that 'OAOs are sustained by institutions that support open access and competition: political competition to maintain open access in the economy and economic competition to maintain open access in the polity' (North et al., 2013: 16). In OAOs, the government has a monopoly on violence, potential or actual, through its control of the military and the police, while the presence of strong constitutional institutions also allows strong private organizations to check the use of military and police force by the government. The defining feature of OAOs, as compared with LAOs, is that interactions between different elite groups, as well as between elites and non-elites, take place through impersonal institutions, and that the rule of law is enforced impartially for all citizens. In contrast, exchanges between elites in LAOs take place through personalized interactions. Therefore, for an LAO to transition to an OAO (that is, for a developing country to join the ranks of developed countries), elites need to find it in their interest to expand impersonal exchange and, by doing so, incrementally increase access to the organizations that create and sustain rents in the society. NWW identify three doorstep conditions that make impersonal relationships among elites possible: (i) rule of law for elites; (ii) support for perpetually lived organizations, both private and public; and (iii) consolidated political control of the organizations with violence capacity. Very few traditionally defined developing countries have met the three doorstep conditions and made the transition to OAOs; among those few are Chile and South Korea.[5]

NWW's framework provides a powerful account of how economic and political development occurs in the developing world, as developing countries make the transition from a fragile to a basic LAO, and then from a basic to a mature LAO, with the aspiration to meet the doorstep conditions, so as to make the final transition to an OAO. NWW are clear that this movement is not unidirectional and that developing countries often regress from basic to fragile, or from mature to basic LAOs. NWW's insight that rent creation and sustenance within the dominant coalition is essential in understanding how LAOs manage to limit violence that may otherwise destabilize the country is an important one, as it shows that rents can play a positive role in economic development, in contrast to the negative role of directly unproductive rent-seeking activities on economic development that have been emphasized by economists such as Krueger (1974) and Bhagwati (1982). Further, the central role that personalized institutions play in organizing economic activity in developing countries in NWW's framework, in contrast to the importance of rule-based institutions in developed countries, highlights the difference in the nature of economic institutions between developing and developed countries.

---

[5] The fact that only two developing countries, according to NWW, have reached OAO status, suggests that much of the dynamics of growth and development are within LAOs.

We build on these two insights—the role of rents both in maintaining polit-ical stability and driving economic activity, and the importance of informal institutions in economic exchange in developing countries—in the frame-work we develop in Section 1.4 to explain the onset and duration of growth episodes.

However, NWW's framework in itself cannot explain the stylized facts of growth that we described in Section 1.2—that is, what explains the acceler-ations and decelerations in economic growth, and why some growth episodes last longer than others.[6] In particular, while NWW argue that developing countries move back from different types of LAOs, it is not apparent from their framework what the political drivers are of the movements from growth acceleration episodes to growth deceleration episodes within and across coun-tries. As we show later in this chapter and elsewhere in the book, episodes of rapid growth can occur even for fragile or basic LAOs (e.g. Cambodia and Ghana since the 1990s). It is not clear from NWW's approach why such episodes are sustained for some fragile or basic LAOs, leading to positive movements along the spectrum of LAOs and not in others. Similarly, episodes of growth decelerations can also occur in mature LAOs (e.g. Malaysia and Thailand since the late 1990s). Why do these growth deceleration episodes occur in such mature LAOs, which are seemingly close to the doorstep condi-tions for transition to OAOs?

Further, NWW do not differentiate between different types of economic actors, and what specific interests they may have in either maintaining closed access to the institutional arrangements that underpin the structure of rents in the economy, or opening up access to these institutions. In our framework, feedback loops from the process of growth to economic and political institutions are central to answering the question of why growth episodes begin and end. These feedback loops can explain why some coun-tries at similar levels of economic and political development are stuck in growth stagnation, while some countries see growth accelerate, or why growth can decelerate after an onset of rapid growth. Our framework also makes clear that whether a developing country moves further along the sort of continuum that NWW describe depends on the bargaining power of different types of economic elites, and the nature of the institutional arrangements that characterize state–business relations. We now turn to an exposition of our framework.

---

[6] North et al. (2009: 4–6) state that the reasons why countries become rich is that they are able to limit the possibility of episodes of negative growth, while observing more frequent occurrences of episodes of positive growth. This view of economic growth matches with the stylized facts presented in Section 1.2. However, NWW do not explain why such episodes of positive and negative growth occur.

1.4 A Conceptual Framework for Understanding Boom and Bust Growth

A unified growth theory would seek an encompassing model capable of explaining the dynamics of growth rates, both the persistence and the transitions. Most accounts of growth seek to answer the question: Why are some countries poor and others rich? In such attempts, the theory ends up invoking determinants that are themselves persistent characteristics of those countries. It is like trying to answer why some people are left-handed, and thus searching for traits, like genetics, which are as stable as the outcome. Yet we also want to be able to answer the question: Why are some countries with similar income levels growing, while others are stagnating or collapsing? What is their current *condition*—which is unlikely to be explained by permanent characteristics alone? This is more like trying to answer why Mary has the flu today. Some people might be more genetically susceptible to the flu than others, but this almost certainly does little to explain any of the existing variations in who has the flu today.

Let us return to the car analogy. We are searching for a model with 'phase transitions' across 'growth states', in which countries not only shift their growth rate, but in which the relationship between their growth rate and various determinants of growth can also shift. One might think that the speed of the motor has a tight link with the speed of the car and hence that causal mechanisms connected to RPMs (revolutions per minute)—like pressing the accelerator pedal—explain speed. However, engine speed only results in vehicle speed as intermediated by a transmission, which provides our 'phase transitions'. When a car is in neutral, no amount of pressing on the accelerator pedal will increase speed (even though it affects engine RPMs). If a car is in reverse, then pressing the pedal will affect car speed, but in exactly the opposite direction to if the car is in first gear, since they are different 'growth states'. An empirical study that showed a close correlation between accelerator pedal position, engine RPMs, and car speed would work well in some circumstances—really well if all the measurements happened to be done with cars in the same gear. But this empirical relationship between accelerator pedal pressure and speed would not provide any guidance for a car with its transmission in neutral, since the average determinants of speed do not apply in this state.

A look at the ability of institutional quality—a 'characteristic' of countries, since it is rather slow to change—to explain growth exemplifies this point. Figure 1.8 shows the R-squared of simple bi-variate relationships between: (a) level of GDPPC and the level of various institutional variables; (b) *growth* of GDPPC and the level of the institutional variable; and (c) growth of GDPPC and the *change* in the institutional variable. What is remarkable is that institutions do a good job of explaining the level of income (why are people left-handed?); they do a poor job of explaining the growth in income tomorrow

Dynamics	Different measures of 'good institutions'				
	Bureaucratic quality	Control of corruption	Law and order	Democratic accountability	Average across indicators
	R-squared of regressing either level or growth in GDPPC 1985–2005 on the level or change in 'institutions'				
Level of income on level of 'institutions'	0.457	0.434	0.464	0.476	0.472
Growth of GDPPC on *initial level* of 'institutions'	0.094	0.064	0.077	0.058	0.074
Growth of GDPPC on changes in 'institutions'	0.027	0.001	0.014	0.016	0.016
Number of countries (non-oil)	92	92	89	89	–
Initial year	1985	1985	1985	1985	–
Duration	20	20	20	20	–

Figure 1.8. Strong correlation between the *level* of income and 'institutions' but almost no connection *of* growth and institutions and even less of growth and changes in institutions, even over a twenty-year period

Source: GDPPC data from *Penn World Tables 6.3*, ICRG rankings for 'institutions'.

from today's quality of institutions (why does Mary have the flu today?); and they do a terrible job of predicting the growth in income based on the improvement in institutions (what happens to vehicle speed when I step on the accelerator?). Another way to state our goal is that we wish to go beyond AR and NWW and be able to explain the divergent economic growth outcomes of countries with similarly bad institutions.

To fix our ideas on transition paths around growth episodes, we provide a simple sketch of these transition paths in Figure 1.9. We classify growth episodes into four categories: miracle growth, stable growth, stagnation, and crisis. Figure 1.9 makes clear that a complete characterization of the growth process in any particular country needs an understanding of the factors that lead to growth acceleration—that is, the transition from stagnation or crisis to stable growth or miracle growth—as well as the factors that lead to the avoidance of growth collapses and the maintenance of positive growth. It is not obvious that the factors that lead to growth acceleration will also lead to growth maintenance, as Rodrik (2005: 3) argues:

> igniting economic growth and sustaining it are somewhat different enterprises. The former generally requires a limited range of (often unconventional) reforms that need not overly tax the institutional capacity of the economy. The latter

challenge is in many ways harder, as it requires constructing a sound institutional underpinning to maintain productive dynamism and endow the economy with resilience to shocks over the longer term.

Once we view economic growth as transitions between the above growth phases, and in particular, the transitions from crisis/stagnant growth to stable/miracle growth, the key issues that need to be addressed are: What are the political and economic determinants of growth acceleration? And how are they different from the determinants of growth maintenance? Before we address these two questions, we propose three analytical tools that we will need in order to develop our theory of growth.

Our framework has two core variables, the political settlement and the rents space (market matrix), and one intermediary variable, the deals space. Our outcome variables are growth episodes (accelerations, stagnation, or decelerations) and structural transformation (represented by a move in the product space to more complex products).

1.4.1 *Core Variables*

Our first core variable is the type and nature of the *political settlement*, which refers to 'the balance or distribution of power between contending social groups and social classes, on which any state is based' (di John and Putzel, 2009: 4). The concept of the political settlement builds on NWW's insight that it is the nature of the elite bargain that structures the distribution of rents and

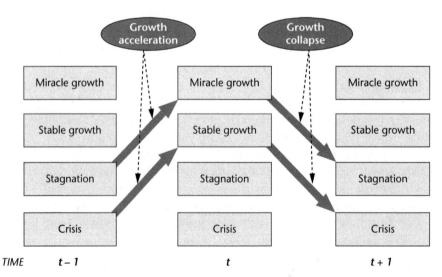

Figure 1.9. Transition paths between growth states
Source: Authors' illustration.

personalized institutional arrangements between members of the dominant coalition, and by doing so keeps the possibility of violence at bay. While NWW do not spell out how political power might be distributed within a dominant coalition, Khan (2010) provides clearer characterization of power relations within the ruling coalition and how this might affect the nature of the deals that political elites strike with economic actors, using the concept of the political settlement.

In Khan's notion of political settlements, institutions and the distribution of power have a circular and interdependent relationship. Khan defines power as holding power—that is, 'how long a particular organization can hold out in actual or potential conflicts against other organizations or the state'—and where holding power is

> a function of a number of characteristics of an organization, including its economic capability to sustain itself during conflicts, its capability to mobilize supporters to be able to absorb costs, and its ability to mobilize prevalent ideologies and symbols of legitimacy to consolidate its mobilization and keep its members committed.   (Khan, 2010: 20)

The relationship between holding power and institutions is two-way. The configuration of holding power at the level of society is supported by a range of formal and informal institutions that reproduce and sustain the specific configuration of relative power between organizations by enabling a consistent set of economic benefits to be created and allocated. In turn, relative power determines which institutions emerge, whether institutions are enforced, and what their effect is on economic performance. If the distribution of benefits by a particular institution is not accepted by groups who have high holding power, echoing AR's de facto political institutions, there would be opposition to the introduction of the institution or its enforcement would be contested, leading to a possible increase in political instability, even though the institution may be growth-enhancing.

Khan argues that two dimensions of power matter in characterizing the political settlement in a particular country. The first is the degree of distribution of horizontal power (Figure 1.10). Horizontal power refers to whether there is concentration of power in one dominant political group (who have the capability to resist any challenge to their control over political institutions), or whether power is dispersed across several political groups jockeying for political control. The second dimension of power that matters is vertical power, which refers to the distribution of power between elites and non-elites (or neo-elites, such as the middle class).

The weaker the concentration of horizontal power in the country, Khan argues, the more competitive is the settlement. In uncompetitive political settlements, power is concentrated in the hands of a dominant group or

Vertical/horizontal distribution of power		Horizontal distribution of power: power of excluded factions	
		Weak	Strong
Vertical distribution of power: power of lower level factions	Weak	Strong dominant party	Vulnerable authoritarian coalition
	Strong	Weak dominant party	Competitive clientelist

Figure 1.10. Distribution of horizontal and vertical power in dominant and competitive settlements

Source: Adapted from Khan (2010).

individual (which could be a dominant party or political leader), while in competitive political settlements, there are several political parties which compete for power and no single political party can be assured of power, as there is periodic turnover of the ruling party whenever elections occur. Whether the political settlement is uncompetitive or competitive has an impact on the leadership's time horizon, which can make a big difference to the effectiveness of development policy. Other things being equal (and of course they rarely are), the less competitive a political settlement, the longer the time horizon to which elites are oriented. In the case of the vertical distribution of power, weaker concentration of power implies greater strength of non-elites, such as the working class, peasants, or neo-elites, such as the middle class, to resist institutional arrangements that they see as corrupt or politically illegitimate. On the other hand, a stronger vertical concentration of power in the ruling coalition would allow it to enforce institutions more effectively than when lower-level factions are powerful and well organized.

The distribution of power in itself cannot explain why some political elites behave differently from others, even with the same distribution of power— e.g. in strong dominant settlements, such as in South Korea in the 1960s, why did political elites take long-term decisions for investment and growth, while in other strong dominant settlements, such as Zimbabwe under Mugabe, the ruling coalition used its considerable power for predatory purposes? As Hickey et al. (2015) argue, crucial in understanding the agential role that political elites can play in economic growth and structural transformation are the ideas and beliefs of such elites, which can be defined as the 'underlying interpretation (among elites) of how the world works, and the more specific question of the range of possibilities for action that an individual or group recognizes' (Mehta and Walton, 2014: 10). Ideas and beliefs shape how interests are structured, what policy actions may be seen as feasible, and what constitutes legitimate behaviour and positions. Thus, if elites are committed to laissez-faire economics, they may resist pressures to limit entry to certain industries. Alternatively, a shared pro-growth ideology among differing elite factions may lead to a continuity in institutional arrangements, even in the face of elite fragmentation and frequent cycling of power among political parties (Kelsall and Heng, 2014).

Our second core variable is the structure of economic opportunities in the economy, which we call the *rents space*. We divide the private sector along two dimensions, which capture the target market and the source of profitability, respectively. First, do firms cater to domestic demand, or rather use the country's factors of production to export to the rest of the world? Looking at major investments in developing countries (so-called emerging or frontier markets, see Musacchio and Werker, 2016), businesses generally have a value proposition to target just one or the other. Second, do they generate profits through discretionary rents under the control of politicians or bureaucrats, or through normal market competition, that is, by out-competing other firms? In many developing countries, perhaps due to the dynamic described by NWW of using rents to maintain stability, most of the larger firms' bottom line is disproportionately driven by these 'regulatory rents'. Dividing the private sector along these two dimensions generates a 'market matrix' or rents space, with four distinct groups of firms, as in Figure 1.11.

Regulatory rents are defined as those derived from some discretionary action of government, such as: offering licences for commercial use of a resource (e.g. mining); bestowing firm-specific (rather than industry-specific) tax advantages; market exclusivity; or application of applicable regulations. It could also be derived from deliberate government inaction, such as permitting monopolies to charge prices significantly above marginal cost, or not enforcing anti-trust law or pursuing competitive markets when it would be appropriate for consumer welfare.

Firms operating in competitive industries may still earn rents, but those come from competitive strategies undertaken for the firm to make a better

	Regulatory rents	Market competition
Export-oriented	Rentiers	Magicians
Domestic market	Powerbrokers	Workhorses

Figure 1.11. The rents space
Source: Pritchett and Werker (2012).

product at a higher margin, such as: brand differentiation, locational advantages, capital intensity, or increasing returns to scale generally. Rents in competitive industries can also be Schumpeterian—that is, rents deriving from innovation and information generation. Firms primarily compete against one another in product markets. When government offers industry-wide (e.g. car parts manufacturers) or special economic zone-wide tax advantages (e.g. tax holiday for ten years), for example, profitability may go up, but the nature of competition is unchanged.

Rentiers are the natural resource firms exporting to world commodity markets. Agricultural firms with concessions are usually here as well, since they get to use large tracts of land without going through formal property-purchasing channels. In general, rentier firms sign agreements with the state, which essentially give them the right to sell resources belonging to the state and its people—in exchange for a set of fees and taxes.

Magicians are the exporters that operate in competitive industries. They are labelled magicians since they make a market out of nothing (as opposed to firms serving the domestic population that can rely on a captive market). In a typical developing country, competitive-industry exports might include garments, manufactured goods, agricultural products, tourism, and processed items.

Powerbrokers are the firms catering to the domestic sector that operate in industries subject to regulatory rents. Most powerbrokers are in regulated industries (sometimes restricted to a single state-owned enterprise) that limit competition, such as power provision, port operation, and petroleum refining. Others, such as heavy construction companies, survive thanks to government contracts. In some countries that do a poor job of consumer protection or have local-level corruption, sectors like telecoms, banking, and real estate development have powerbroker characteristics. The key insight from economics about such monopolies or oligopolies is that they may wish to charge a price that far outweighs their costs. Governments know this and therefore regulate these markets more tightly. Since powerbrokers know that they will be regulated, they tend to form close relationships with government. In many developing countries, firms that would otherwise be in a competitive market may lobby to get their own monopoly, and in doing so earn excess profits.

Workhorses are those firms operating in competitive markets that serve the domestic economy. Among the workhorses in a developing country are its subsistence farmers, livestock raisers, builders, restaurant owners, petty traders, hairdressers, village lenders, and some of its importers. Much of the time, they provide the vast majority of goods and services in the market—particularly those goods and services consumed by ordinary citizens. Many of the workhorses operate in the informal sector, utilizing shadow markets and traditional dispute mechanisms in order to enforce contracts.

Table 1.1. Policy demands of firms, depending on their location in the rents space

	Transparent rules	Common infrastructure	Specialized infrastructure	Contract enforcement	Subsidies	Exclusivity
Magicians	x	x	x	x	x	
Workhorses	x	x		x		
Powerbrokers						x
Rentiers			x	x	x	x

This typology does not imply that rentiers and powerbrokers are bad, and that magicians and workhorses are good. Indeed, it may be the rentiers that provide the main engine of growth during growth accelerations. And it may be the power-brokers that provide the essential services that give citizens access to trade, water, sanitation, electricity, and communication. But firms in each of these quadrants have different demands of the state, even (in fact, especially) of those states that do not enforce all the rules. Understanding those divergent interests is important to understanding how the elites may or may not have an interest in growth.

Table 1.1 describes a number of policies with respect to the business envir-onment that might be unevenly pursued by different states, as well as whether those policies are likely to be demanded by the different categories of firms in the rents space.

All policy demands are not equal, of course. The subsidies or low taxes that rentiers want result simply in higher profits, whereas those pursued by magi-cians may result in greater competitiveness and a higher market share abroad. Magicians and workhorses crave improved infrastructure, with magicians and rentiers also lobbying for specialized infrastructure, like special economic zones and port facilities. Everyone except powerbrokers prefers good contract enforcement, while powerbrokers benefit from the murkiness of red tape and uneven enforcement, and prefer barriers to entry over regulated competition.

We are interested in the policy demands of the different firms in the rents space, since we see the overall business environment as being determined by the demands of different business actors. These demands lead to different capabilities (or institutional development) generated by the state, mediated through the political settlement.

Policy evolution in 'deals' environments is essentially the outcome of the interaction between the political settlement and the rents space. Powerbrokers are the classic force for red tape, where the impetus may come from strong politicians or bureaucrats creating rents for themselves or their cronies, or from strong businesspeople buying off politicians and bureaucrats to entrench their market position. The problem is that they advocate for policies that are detrimental to firms in the other quadrants.

When powerbrokers are strong and decisive, the economy trends towards bad rules that create the differential advantages of the powerbrokers through selective enforcement for 'friends'. When other economic actors are also strong, just not strong enough to set the rules, the situation trends not towards 'good rules', but rather towards 'poor enforcement', since strong enforcement would end up stifling the other sectors. Rentiers and workhorses end up not paying their taxes through an endless string of deals. In this environment, magicians are all but excluded, as the rent-seeking behaviour of powerbrokers in non-tradeable industries creates both bad rules and often high-cost infrastructure (e.g. by garnering rents from construction, monopolizing power or ports, etc.).

1.4.2 Intermediary Variable

Our intermediary variable is the *deals space*, where deals are defined to be a *specific* action between two (or more) entities (or individuals) that is not the result of the impersonal application of a rule, but rather of *characteristics* or *actions* of specific entities which do not spill over with any precedential value to any other future transaction between other entities. In our framework, the deals space captures the range of informal and personalized relationships that are observed between economic actors and political elites in developing countries. An earlier literature on the institutional determinants of economic growth has focused on rules, which are de jure policies or formal (parchment) institutions, such as courts and written contracts. However, the key feature that distinguishes 'developing' countries is the gap between the official, formal, legal, de jure laws and regulations and what actually happens. The stated 'rules of the game' have near-zero predictive power for what will actually happen. Let us start with a simple example to illustrate our point that deals, rather than rules, characterize the institutional arrangements observed in developing countries.

Bertrand et al. (2007) study the process of getting a driver's licence in Delhi. The official *rules* for getting a driver's licence looked a lot like everywhere else: (a) prove your age, residence, identity; and (b) demonstrate that you can operate a motor vehicle. The agent authorized by the state will then issue a legal document allowing you to drive. It is a simple mapping from 'states of the world' (meet the criteria) to 'policy implementation outcomes' (granting legal authorization to drive). In reality, what happens depends on whether the applicant hires a tout. Nearly all of those in the control group that did not hire a tout had to take the driver's examination. Of those who did hire a tout, only 12 per cent had to take the driving test. So, while the official rules predicted that 100 per cent of applicants would take a driver's examination, the reality was that this was entirely contingent upon whether the applicant hired a tout (and hence most did).

This is a *deal* that we later classify as 'open', since the ability to hire a tout was not restricted to any individual or group. While this example describes the gap between rules and deals in a bureaucratic setting, there is substantial evidence from the business environment as well. Pritchett and Sethi (1994) found only a weak correlation between the official tariff rate on products and the revenue collected in Pakistan, Kenya, and Jamaica. Stone et al. (1996) found that exporters in Brazil used facilitators to get around time-consuming permits, with these *deals* bringing down the *actual* time it took to get a permit to the same as in Chile, which had a more streamlined set of rules.

Of course, these specific examples just reveal what every in-depth study of nearly any governmental organization in a developing country reveals—that the gap between the official law and policies and actual practice is not a crack, but a chasm.

Further evidence relative to economic growth comes from recent papers comparing the Doing Business rankings—which include measures of the de jure regulation, such as days to get a construction permit—and the Enterprise Survey data, in which firms are asked about their actual experiences in regulatory compliance (Hallward-Driemeier and Pritchett, 2015). This allows comparison across an indicator such as days to get a construction permit between the de jure (rules) and the de facto (deals).

Figure 1.12 compares the Doing Business reported figure for the days it would take to get a construction permit for a typical construction such as a warehouse *in practice, if one were to follow the law,* and the average number of days that firms in the Enterprise Survey samples reported that it actually took them to get a construction permit, with various non-linear functional form regressions estimated between the two. We produce the figure for the 10th, 25th, 75th, and 90th percentiles in reported days, so as to be able also to compare the variation across firms. If the Doing Business measure were a good representation of the actual process, then the observations should line up on the 45-degree line. The three obvious facts (also true of the other two indicators that can be compared between Doing Business and Enterprise Survey: see Hallward-Driemeier and Pritchett, 2015) is that (a) for all but the 90th percentile figure, there is little or no correlation across countries between the Doing Business rankings and the Enterprise Survey results; (b) over most of the sample, the reported compliance times are much, much lower than the time that Doing Business surveys indicated is needed for compliance, particularly for firms in the 10th and 25th percentiles; and (c) only in the 90th percentile of unlucky, or 'sucker', firms does de jure start to resemble de facto. As Oscar Benavides, a former Peruvian president, was reported to have said: 'For my friends, anything. For my enemies, the law.'

The basic metaphor of 'rules' gets any discussion of development and 'institutions' off on the wrong foot. The rules of an actual game say which of

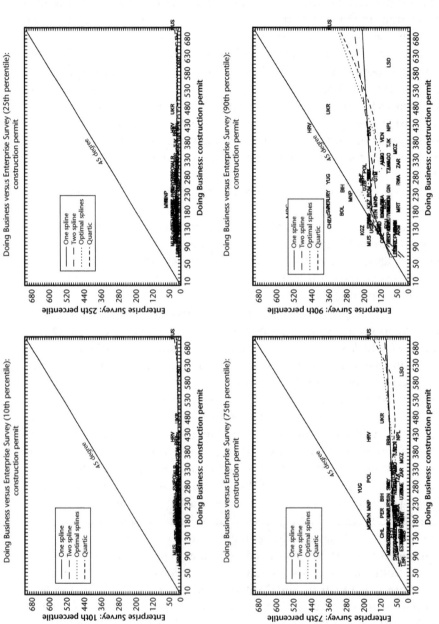

Figure 1.12. De jure and de facto, compliance with the law

Source: Adapted from Hallward-Driemeier and Pritchett (2015).

the players may do what in different situations. What defines the rules of a game is that they are *impersonal* and apply equally to everyone playing. The characteristics of a person outside of the game are irrelevant to their admissible actions inside the game. If the Queen of England plays chess, all that matters is whether she plays black or white. That she really is a queen outside the context of the game does not translate into what she can do with her chess queen.

While one can bend the definition of 'rule' to mean anything—including completely personalized and discretionary decision-making—we propose the term 'deal' to differentiate from rules.[7] For example, if I hire a tout to facilitate my driver's licence application, this is a deal because the outcome depends on states of the world that are specific to me. Or, if I pay a bribe to avoid customs duties on my imports, while people who do not pay a bribe are charged the full rate, this is a deal, as I have taken deliberate efforts to influence policy actors who have discretionary control over the outcome.

Figure 1.13 makes a basic distinction between deals and rules, and whether or not the official rules are conducive to inclusive growth. Since only highly mature and well-off nations have been able to create and enforce good rules, the challenges of development almost universally play out in countries with deal-based enforcement. As it turns out, not all deals systems are created equal. Figure 1.14 divides these environments along two dimensions: whether deals, once negotiated, are honoured (ordered vs. disordered); and whether deals are widely available or limited to an elite (open vs. closed). Ordered deals are deals that, once negotiated between investors and state officials, are honoured.

	Official laws/policies/regulatory climate for private sector growth	
	Bad (inhibits inclusive growth)	Good (conducive to inclusive growth)
Impersonally enforced (rules)	Strong enough institutions to inhibit economic growth through enforcement	Developed countries with good policies and strong institutions
Selectively enforced (deals)	Predominately deals-based economies	Deals and rules-based behaviour intermingle

Figure 1.13. Deals and rules, good and bad de jure policy
Source: Pritchett and Werker (2012).

---

[7] That is, one could always say the gap is between the 'official' rules of the game and 'informal' rules of the game—but if the informal rules of the game are that 'anything can happen', and if the actors themselves are uncertain what is possible and when actions are indexed by personal relationships, then this stretches the metaphor of 'rules of the game' to breaking point.

	Closed (deals are available only to specific individuals/ organizations)	Open (deals depend on actions of agents but not identities)
Ordered (once negotiated, deals will be honoured)	Only those with political connections get to make deals, but they can be confident that officials will deliver	Anyone can make a deal, and they can be certain that officials will deliver
Disordered (deals will be honoured so long as they are in the short-term interests of political elite)	Only those with political connections get to make deals, and even they cannot be certain that officials will deliver	Anyone can make a deal, but no one is certain that officials will deliver

Figure 1.14. Typology of 'deals' environments
Source: Pritchett and Werker (2012).

In this case, investors can be assured that the political elite can deliver on the deals they make with them. On the other hand, disordered deals are deals that investors make with the political elite, where there is no certainty that the deal will be delivered. Open deals are deals that are widely available to all investors, large or small, and not confined to an elite or a small group of favoured investors. On the other hand, closed deals are offered by the political elite to a small group of investors only.

1.4.3 *Towards a Theory of Boom and Bust Growth*

We now have the building blocks in place to develop a political economy theory of episodic growth. In our framework, economic growth and the degree to which that growth is characterized by structural transformation are an outcome of the nature of deals (the intermediary variable) offered to economic actors. This in turn is a function of the political settlement and the rents space (the core variables).

Exogenous transnational factors, such as commodity price shocks or disruptive technological change, a surge in foreign aid, global norms, or remittances, or donor-driven structural adjustment programmes, would influence the stability or nature of the political settlement, as well as the nature of the rents space, which will affect the deals space, and hence growth. Note that in our framework, transnational factors work their way through the political settlement and/or the rents space, so we are interested in capturing their *indirect effect* and not just their direct effect on growth outcomes. For example, in terms of the effects of transnational factors on the rents space, a commodity price boom may strengthen rentiers, a foreign aid surge may strengthen power-brokers, and improvements in global supply chain management, along with open trade, may strengthen magicians. In terms of the effects of transnational factors on the political settlement, a commodity price collapse or structural adjustment programme may make an existing political settlement unstable or lead to shifts in the distribution of power (e.g. a military takeover). Growth episodes then influence the political settlement and the rents space by positive or negative feedback loops, which in turn impact on the deals space, affecting future growth. We provide a schematic representation of the interrelationships in Figure 1.15.

According to our framework, economic growth is likely to accelerate when there is a movement in the deals space from disordered to ordered deals. Ordered deals mean that an investor's time horizon for realizing returns is lengthened, which makes a greater set of investments profitable in net present value. There may be an additional quid pro quo, in which ordered deals allow the state to ask investors to commit to the investment decision and engage in production, so that rents can be generated through the production process. This commitment to ordered deals needs to be seen as credible by investors: they must believe that the state or its agents will not renege on their implicit or explicit promise not to expropriate future rents, especially after investment

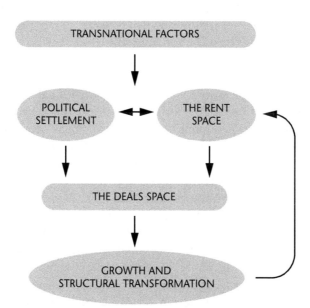

Figure 1.15. Interrelationships between political settlements, the rents space, and the deals space

Source: Authors' illustration.

decisions involving sunk costs in fixed capital have been taken. Investors also need to commit to share a part of their rents with the state (or its constituents, such as politicians), and when states raise revenues from taxes, to pay the state the necessary taxes (Sen, 2013).

A commitment to 'ordered deals' is more likely in at least two situations. One of them corresponds to the 'doorstep' conditions of NWW, when inter-actions among the elite begin to take place in a more impersonal manner; in our framework this would be most likely when the economy is further along in structural transformation, usually indicated by a larger share of workhorses and magicians, and supported by a political settlement whose legitimacy comes from economic growth and positive reforms. The other situation is orthogonal to these unambiguously positive outcomes. That is during dom-inant party political settlements, where a strong political leadership allows for the likelihood of deals, once negotiated, to be honoured (ordered deals) and for credible commitment by elites to economic growth. The growth acceler-ations that occur during such political settlements may just as likely arise in rentier and powerbroker quadrants, and support an ever-more exclusive pol-itical elite whose power comes from patronage or repression. To contrast with dominant party settlements, in competitive clientelism, due to cycling of factions in power, political time horizons are short, and credible commitment to ordered deals may not be present.

What now explains the ability of the economy to stay in a positive growth process and for growth not to slow down or collapse? Our hypothesis is that at least two potential drivers exist for the move from one episode of growth acceleration to the next episode maintaining growth. The first corresponds to the positive scenario above, in which open ordered deals drive growth. In this case, growth maintenance would depend on the continual movement in the deals space towards more open, more ordered deals. This is because openness in the deals space drives economic competition and facilitates new firm entry, which leads to structural transformation as countries produce more complex products and when resources shift from low-productivity sectors to high-productivity sectors. The second potential driver of a subsequent episode of growth after an acceleration corresponds to luck. Even if the first episode of ordered deals resulted in a closing of the deals space, the country could get hit by a shock that would drive at least another medium-term cycle of growth—for example, a positive movement in the commodity price or a new resource discovery, or a surge in aid or cheap finance to sustain a large fiscal deficit. Such shocks could keep driving consumption, even in the absence of structural transformation, but we hypothesize that such a game would eventually end.

We go beyond hypothesizing that ever-opening deals can lead to growth maintenance, and argue that closed ordered deals cannot continually drive structural transformation. The very nature of closed ordered deals precludes the development of strong organizations that implement policy in a neutral way. That is, suppose a political group gave a sweetheart deal with exclusive rights to telecom provision to a connected business owner and that this deal created profits by eliminating competition. The profitability of the deal is premised on the notion that no truly independent regulator exists that might regulate prices. Hence, even if such a regulator exists on paper, the elites who benefit from the deal have a vested interest in making sure that the regulator never actually acquires the capability to regulate prices or force competition. This implies that the persistence of closed ordered deals will not lead to the strengthening of state capacity around the regulatory functions of the government that may be necessary for structural transformation to occur. Without structural transformation, for all but a handful of petro states, there is a limit to the level of prosperity that can be generated.

There is nothing preordained in the evolution of institutions that suggests that the move from closed ordered or disordered deals to open ordered deals is linear. As economic growth originates in a country, there are two feedback loops that occur from the growth process to the deals space. These feedback loops can be both positive or negative—in other words, with a surge in economic growth the deals space may turn from being open ordered to being closed ordered or being disordered. The first of these feedback loops is economic in nature, and depends on the rents space. Since rentiers and powerbrokers benefit from closed deals, a growth episode that empowered them would be likely to lead to a closing of the deals space. In such an episode, we would expect to see closer personalized relationships with the political elite, to capture the process of licence allocation, or to create artificial barriers to entry. On the other hand, a growth episode that empowered magicians and workhorses would be likely to lead to an opening in the deals space. This is for two reasons. First, these are sectors that are most dynamic and where 'creative destruction' is most likely to occur, and where firms in these sectors would benefit the most from an open deals environment. Second, given the inherent contestability of these sectors and the presence of a large number of economic actors, a closed deals space that excludes many of these actors is not likely to find political traction. Finally, these two sectors depend on an efficient power-broker sector for cheap and high-quality inputs to their production process, such as well-functioning roads and reliable electricity provision, and would benefit from the competitive pressures that an open deals environment would bring to powerbroker firms, thereby further weakening the powerbrokers.

One implication of our framework is that the so-called 'natural resource curse' may be due more to weak institutions than to the natural resource endowments possessed by naturally resource-rich economies. Rentiers, in almost all less developed countries, work in deals environments. This means that they are usually happy to part with the minimal amount of taxes, so long as they are left free to extract and sell the resources. The influx of foreign exchange from the sale of the natural resources abroad strengthens the non-tradeable sector vis-à-vis the tradeables through an appreciation in the exchange rate. This allows the powerbrokers to organize themselves to appropriate the second and third rounds of rent from the natural resource sales as they echo through the economy. A utility or concrete producer cannot overcharge impoverished consumers: they need some money in the economy, an initial source of activity, to be able to have a market. When the natural resource sector is weak, there may still be other forms of unearned income that can lead to strong powerbrokers. Foreign aid and remittances also create domestic demand without a corresponding increase in business lobbying for good rules and good infrastructure. Isham et al. (2005) show that countries that are concentrated in 'point source' natural resources like petroleum have much worse indicators of *governance* than do either manufacturing exporters or, more weakly, non-point source natural resource (e.g. wheat, rice) exporters. This can therefore explain the whole cycle of natural resource exporters from boom to bust as not just the impact of terms of trade directly on volatility, but also as the reason: (a) why natural resource exporters do not develop effective institutions; (b) why it is difficult to translate point source natural resource wealth into structural transformation and higher capabilities outside the resource sectors; and (c) why, following Rodrik's 'Where did all the growth go?', the *interaction* of shocks and lack of institutional mechanisms to cope with shocks leads to growth declines.

The second of the feedback loops is mostly political in nature and depends on the nature of the political settlement and how it evolves over time. The evolution of the political settlement would depend in part on the relative holding power of the political interests attached to firms in the different quadrants of the rents space, since they will set the terms of government capabilities and the deals space going forward, subject to the political constraints of the settlement. In growth episodes where rentiers and powerbrokers gain influence, the political feedback effect from the growth process is likely to be negative for institutional quality. The one potential exception is during a dominant party political settlement with strong enforcement capabilities, in which the ruling coalition sees magicians and workhorses as politically salient for the purpose for maintaining growth (Khan, 2010).

Furthermore, the political feedback effect would depend on how influential groups—such as civil society, the judiciary, the middle class, and the media—view the growth process, as well as how non-elites mobilize themselves against elements of the growth process that they see as politically illegitimate. In countries with competitive political settlements, particularly in countries with strong civil society presence and electoral politics, the political feedback loop can be negative if the deals environment underpinning the growth episode is seen as exclusionary, or if the nature of economic growth is highly predatory. In dominant party political settlements, especially where the ruling coalition is vulnerable to challenges from excluded elites and from lower-level factions, the political feedback loop can itself lead to changes in the distribution of power and, consequently, in the political settlement, as groups such as civil society, the middle class, and elites excluded from the growth process begin to gain de facto political power, with greater political mobilization and pushback from accountability institutions such as the judiciary and the media. Therefore, while a shift from disordered to closed ordered deals is often necessary for growth to accelerate, the political feedback effect may turn negative if the deals space remains closed for too long.

If the positive growth episode is underpinned by closed ordered deals that do not become open over time, it is likely that both the economic and political feedback loops will turn negative and the closed ordered deals may become increasingly disordered, bringing the positive growth episode to an end. On the other hand, economic and political feedback loops can be positive if the deals space becomes increasingly open, and the magician and workhorse sectors become increasingly important in the growth process, leading to structural transformation, as the product space becomes more complex with the entry of new firms, products, and industries. In this case, the positive growth episode will carry on, and sustained economic growth will result. Structural transformation can thus be observed as an ever-larger share of the economy being generated by firms that desire a more open business environment, make more complex products and services, and are represented in the political settlement.

1.5 Case Study Countries

To test our framework, we have selected ten countries drawn from Africa and Asia that show significant variation across three dimensions: (a) the type of the political settlement (whether dominant or competitive); (b) where they are located in the deals–rules continuum; and (c) the nature of growth outcomes.[8] These countries are Bangladesh, Cambodia, India, Malaysia, and Thailand in Asia, and Ghana, Liberia, Malawi, Rwanda, and Uganda in sub-Saharan Africa.

Of these ten countries, Bangladesh, Ghana, India, Liberia, Malawi, and Thailand have had competitive political settlements for much of their recent

---

[8] This categorization follows North et al. (2009) and Levy (2014) in classifying developing countries depending on where they are in the personalized–impersonal institutions continuum.

Table 1.2. Case selection criteria

Type of political settlement	Personalized institutions and organizations	Hybrid—mix of deals and rules
Dominant	Cambodia Uganda Rwanda	Malaysia
Competitive	Bangladesh Ghana Liberia Malawi	India Thailand

growth experience.[9] In contrast, Cambodia, Uganda, Rwanda, and Malaysia have had dominant political settlements for much of their recent growth experience.[10]

We categorize the countries by the type of political settlement and their location in the deals–rules continuum in Table 1.2. While a specific developing country will be in one of the cells of Table 1.2 at any point in time, the evolution of the political settlement, along with its interaction with the rents space, means that a country might move around this matrix over time, as we will see in our case studies. From our framework we know that this may have different implications for economic growth.

In the deals–rules continuum, there are also marked differences across the ten countries. Bangladesh, Cambodia, Ghana, Liberia, Malawi, Rwanda, Uganda, and Rwanda have highly personalized deals, with weakly enforced rule of law (as captured by the low scores in measures of institutional quality such as Government Effectiveness and Rule of Law, see Table 1.3). In contrast, the institutional environment in India, Malaysia, and Thailand is more 'hybrid', with a mix of deals and rules (see Table 1.3).

We also observe from Table 1.3 that there is large variation in levels of per capita income and structural transformation in our ten case study countries. Liberia and Malawi are the poorest countries studied, with GDPPC of US$451 and US$515 (averaged over 2000–10). In contrast, Malaysia and Thailand have GDPPC of US$10,511 and US$6,875, respectively. Among other countries, Rwanda and Uganda have lower per capita income than Cambodia, Ghana, and India. We also see a wide variation in measures of structural transformation (as captured by the share of manufacturing value added in GDP and the Economic Complexity Index), with the highest levels of structural transformation observed in Malaysia and Thailand and the lowest in Ghana, Liberia, Malawi, Rwanda, and Uganda.

---

[9] For example, these countries having scores in the higher end of Polity's −10 to +10 range, suggesting more competitive polities.

[10] Table 1.3 shows that these countries have negative or low positive scores on Polity, suggesting authoritarian or semi-authoritarian polities.

Table 1.3. Selected indicators of democracy, economic development, and institutional quality in the case study countries, 2000–10 average

Case study countries	GDPPC (ppp, US$)	Democracy (Polity measure)	Manufacturing value added as a share of GDP (%)	Economic complexity	Control of corruption	Government effectiveness	Rule of law
Bangladesh	1,110	4	16.7	−0.9	−1.2	−0.8	−0.8
Cambodia	1,473	2	17.9	−0.9	−1.1	−0.8	−1.1
Ghana	1,698	7	9.1	−1.0	−0.2	−0.2	−0.1
India	2,558	9	15.2	0.2	−0.4	−0.1	0.1
Liberia	451	4	5.4	−0.6	−1.0	−1.5	−1.4
Malawi	515	6	11.4	−1.3	−0.7	−0.6	−0.4
Malaysia	10,511	4	27.6	0.9	0.3	1.0	0.5
Rwanda	822	−3	6.7	−0.4	−0.4	−0.6	−0.8
Thailand	6,895	5	34.5	0.6	−0.3	0.2	0.1
Uganda	972	−2	7.6	−1.1	−0.9	−0.5	−0.7

Source: The Quality of Government database, <http://qog.pol.gu.se/data>.

Note: Economic Complexity is the Hausmann et al. (2013) measure; Control of Corruption, Government Effectiveness, and Rule of Law measures are the World Bank's *World Governance Indicators* (and are from a range of −2 to +2, higher scores indicating better performance in the measures).

The unit of analysis in our case studies is an episode of growth (either an acceleration or deceleration in economic growth). Therefore, we need to periodize each country's growth and, in particular, establish when growth accelerations and decelerations occurred. We mainly follow the procedure set out in Kar et al. (2013b).[11] In Table 1.4, we set out the different growth episodes experienced by the ten sample countries in our study. We see that all countries have experienced two or more growth episodes in their post-independence history. All of our case study countries have experienced boom and bust growth, with accelerations (decelerations) followed by decelerations (accelerations). The longest acceleration episodes have been witnessed by Malaysia and Thailand from the late 1950s to the mid-1990s. The longest deceleration episode with negative GDPPC growth rates has been witnessed by Malawi from 1978 to 2002.[12]

---

[11] This procedure differs from previous approaches that have attempted to identify the timings of growth accelerations/decelerations which either have been ad hoc, in that they have simply eyeballed the data to establish the timing of the break, or have used a statistical method in a mechanistic way. The Kar et al. (2013b) approach combines the statistical approach with an economic filter to provide a more unified way of establishing breaks in GDPPC data.

[12] For all the case studies, we followed a similar methodology. We proceeded by reviewing the secondary literature on the history, politics, and economy of the country in question, with a view to understanding the political drivers of previous growth episodes. We also undertook an analysis of the secondary data on the country's economy, so as to describe the nature of growth and structural transformation in the country in its post-independence period. We then complemented the desk-based research with semi-structured in-depth interviews, which explored the relationship between politics, business, and growth with a number of government officials, industry experts, industry representatives, and the media in the country. We also conducted interviews with firms representing the magicians, workhorses, powerbrokers, and rentier sectors that we identified in the secondary data analysis, to gain an understanding of the deals environment.

Table 1.4. Growth episodes for case study countries

Country	How many growth episodes since the country's independence?	Growth acceleration episodes (dates; growth rates in GDPPC, ppa)	Growth deceleration episodes (dates; growth rates in GDPPC, ppa)
Bangladesh	3	1982–95; 1.6 1995–2010; 3.5	1972–82; −1.0
Cambodia	3	1982–98; 3.8 1998–2010; 6.5	1971–82; −6.2
Ghana	5	1966–74; 3.4 1983–2002; 1.1 2002–10; 4.0	1957–66; 1.1 1974–83; −2.7
India	3	1993–2002; 4.2 2002–10; 6.3	1950–93; 1.9
Liberia	5	1960–71; 2.5* 2005–10; 4.1	1971–80; −0.3 1980–90; −6.3 1990–2005; −4.7
Malawi	4	1964–78; 6.6 2002–10; 5.1	1954–64; 1.8 1978–2002; −2.2
Malaysia	2	1955–97; 4.9	1997–2010; 1.9
Rwanda	3	1962–81; 1.4 1994–2010; 8.6	1981–94; −5.7
Thailand	2	1955–96; 5.7	1996–2010; 2.0
Uganda	4	1962–70; 3.3 1980–8; −0.1 1988–2010; 3.5	1972–80; −3.8

Source: World Bank, *World Development Indicators*.

Note: All data from *Penn World Tables, Version 7.1* (Heston et al., 2012); GDPPC in ppp US dollars; last year in *Penn World Tables, Version 7.1* is 2010. * For Liberia, GDPPC data in 1960–70 is local currency unit, and in compound annual rate of growth.

1.5.1 *Outline of the Book*

Our first two case studies are Liberia and Malawi, the two poorest countries in our set of countries, with fragile growth experiences, where economic growth has been markedly boom and bust. We then present case studies of two Asian countries, Bangladesh and Cambodia, which have experienced growth accelerations in the recent past, following episodes of stagnant or collapsing growth. Next, we present three case studies of countries in sub-Saharan Africa where economic growth has been reasonably strong since the 1990s (at least until the end of the data) after periods of strong economic and political volatility: Ghana, Uganda, and Rwanda. We then examine the experiences of three countries with a 'mature' growth experience, and which have the highest levels of economic development among our case study countries: India, Malaysia, and Thailand. Finally, we present a brief synthesis of our main findings from the case studies and what our findings imply for development thinking and policy.

References

Acemoglu, D. and Robinson, J. 2008. 'The Role of Institutions in Growth and Development'. Working Paper No. 10. Washington, DC: Commission for Growth and Development.

Acemoglu, D. and Robinson, J. 2012. *Why Nations Fail: The Origins of Power, Prosperity, and Poverty*. London: Crown Business.

Ben-David, D. and Papell, D. H. 1998. 'Slowdowns and Meltdowns: Postwar Growth Evidence from 74 Countries'. *The Review of Economics and Statistics*, 80(4): 561–71.

Bertrand, M., Djankov, S., Hanna, R., and Mullainathan, S. 2007. 'Obtaining a Drivers License in India: An Experimental Approach to Studying Corruption'. *Quarterly Journal of Economics*, 122(4): 1639–76.

Bhagwati, J. N. 1982. 'Directly Unproductive, Profit Seeking (DUP) Activities'. *Journal of Political Economy*, 90: 998–1002.

Easterly, W., Kremer, M., Pritchett, L., and Summers, L. 1993. 'Good Policy or Good Luck? Country Growth Performance and Temporary Shocks'. *Journal of Monetary Economics*, 32: 459–83.

Hallward-Driemeier, M. and Pritchett, L. 2015. 'How Business is Done in the Developing World: Deals versus Rules'. *Journal of Economic Perspectives*, 29(3): 121–40.

Hausmann, R., Hidalgo, C. A., Bustos, S., Cosica, M., Simoes, A., and Yildirim, M. A. 2013. *The Atlas of Economic Complexity: Mapping Paths to Prosperity*. Centre for International Development, Harvard University.

Hausmann, R., Pritchett, L., and Rodrik, D. 2005. 'Growth Accelerations'. *Journal of Economic Growth*, 10: 303–29.

Heston, A., Summers, R., and Aten, B. 2012. *Penn World Table Version 7.1*. Center of Comparisons of Production, Income and Prices, University of Pennsylvania.

Hickey, S., Sen, K., and Bukenya, B. (eds). 2015. *The Politics of Inclusive Development: Interrogating the Evidence*. Oxford: Oxford University Press.

Isham, J., Woolcock, M., Pritchett, L., and Busby, G. 2005. 'The Varieties of Resource Experience: Natural Resource Export Structures and the Political Economy of Economic Growth'. *World Bank Economic Review*, 19(2): 141–74.

Jerzmanowski, M. 2006. 'Empirics of Hills, Plateaus, Mountains and Plains: A Markov-Switching Approach to Growth'. *Journal of Development Economics*, 81: 357–85.

di John, J. and Putzel, J. 2009. 'Political Settlements: Issues Paper'. GSDRC. Available online <https://core.ac.uk/download/pdf/103642.pdf>.

Jones, B. F. and Olken, B. A. 2008. 'The Anatomy of Start-Stop Growth'. *Review of Economics and Statistics*, 90(3): 582–7.

Jones, C. 1995. 'Time Series Tests of Endogenous Growth Models'. *Quarterly Journal of Economics*, 110(2): 495–525.

Jones, C. 1999. 'Growth: With or Without Scale Effects?' *American Economic Review*, 89(2): 139–44.

Jones, C. 2005. 'Growth and Ideas'. In *Handbook of Economic Growth*, Volume 1, Part B, pp. 1063–111. Edited by Aghion, P. and Durlauf, S. N. Amsterdam: Elsevier.

Kar, S., Pritchett, L., Raihan, S., and Sen, K. 2013a. *The Dynamics of Economic Growth: A Visual Handbook of Growth Rates, Regimes, Transitions and Volatility*. Manchester: University of Manchester Press.

Kar, S., Pritchett, L., Raihan, S., and Sen, K. 2013b. 'Looking for a Break: Identifying Transitions in Growth Regimes'. *Journal of Macroeconomics*, 38(B): 151–66.

Kelsall, T. and Heng, S. 2014. 'The Political Settlement and Economic Growth in Cambodia'. ESID Working Paper No. 37. Manchester: University of Manchester.

Khan, M. 2010. 'Political Settlements and the Governance of Growth-Enhancing Institutions. Draft Paper'. *Research Paper Series on 'Growth-Enhancing Governance'*, School of Oriental and African Studies, University of London.

Krueger, A. 1974. 'The Political Economy of the Rent-Seeking Society'. *American Economic Review*, 64(3): 291–303.

Levy, B. 2014. *Working with the Grain: Integrating Governance and Growth in Development Strategies*. New York: Oxford University Press.

Mehta, P. B. and Walton, M. 2014. 'Ideas, Interests and the Politics of Development Change in India: Capitalism, Inclusion and the State'. ESID Working Paper No. 36. Manchester: University of Manchester.

Musacchio, A. and Werker, E. 2016. 'Mapping Frontier Economies'. *Harvard Business Review*, 95(12): 40–7.

North, D. C. 1990. *Institutions, Institutional Change, and Economic Performance*. New York: Cambridge University Press.

North, D. C., Wallis, J. J., Webb, S. B., and Weingest, B. R. 2013. *In the Shadow of Violence: Politics, Economics, and the Problems of Development*. Cambridge, MA: Cambridge University Press.

North, D. C., Wallis, J. J., and Weingast, B. R. 2009. *Violence and Social Orders: A Conceptual Framework for Interpreting Recorded Human History*. New York: Cambridge University Press.

Pritchett, L. 1997. 'Divergence, Big Time.' *Journal of Economic Perspectives*, 11(3): 3–17.

Pritchett, L. 2000. 'Understanding Patterns of Economic Growth: Searching for Hills among Plateaus, Mountains and Plains'. *World Bank Economic Review*, 14(2): 221–50.

Pritchett, L., Sen, K., Kar, S., and Raihan, S. 2016. 'Trillions Gained and Lost: Estimating the Magnitude of Growth Episodes'. *Economic Modelling*, 55: 279–91.

Pritchett, L. and Sethi, G. 1994. 'Tariff Rates, Tariff Revenue and Tariff Reform: Some New Facts'. *World Bank Economic Review*, 8(1): 1–16.

Pritchett, L. and Werker, E. 2012. 'Developing the Guts of a Gut (Grand Unified Theory): Elite Commitment and Inclusive Growth'. ESID Working Paper No. 16. Manchester: University of Manchester.

Rodrik, D. 2005. 'Growth Strategies'. In *Handbook of Economic Growth*, Volume 1, pp. 967–1014. Edited by Aghion, P. and Durlauf, S. N. Amsterdam: Elsevier.

Sen, K. 2013. 'The Political Dynamics of Economic Growth'. *World Development*, 47: 71–86.

Sen, K., Pritchett, L., Kar, S., and Raihan, S. 2016. 'Democracy versus Dictatorship: The Political Determinants of Growth Episodes'. ESID Working Paper No. 70. Manchester: University of Manchester.

Stone, A., Levy, B., and Paredes, R. 1996. 'Public Institutions and Private Transactions: A Comparative Analysis of the Legal and Regulatory Environment for Business Transactions in Brazil and Chile'. In *Empirical Studies in Institutional Change*, pp. 95–128. Edited by Alston, L. J., Eggertsson, T., and North, D. C. Cambridge: Cambridge University Press.

2

Deals and Development in a Resource-Dependent, Fragile State

The Political Economy of Growth in Liberia, 1960–2014

Eric Werker and Lant Pritchett

2.1 Introduction

Liberia's growth collapse is the largest on the modern record. From its peak in 1972 to its nadir in 1995, Liberia's real income per capita fell by an astonishing 93 per cent. In 1972, on standard purchasing power comparisons,[1] Liberia was ranked just ahead of Thailand and Egypt, 107th of 163 countries—not rich, but by no means poor. Its GDP per capita was more than 80 per cent higher than that of China, Indonesia, Vietnam, and India. Among sub-Saharan countries it was thirteenth—ahead of Senegal and Botswana. By 2005, even after a substantial recovery from the nadir, Liberia's income was the second lowest in the world, ahead of only the Democratic Republic of the Congo and a small fraction of countries it had once led—its GDP per capita was only a tenth of Egypt's. Liberia is not a case of a 'poverty trap', but of a (lower) middle-income economy whose political and economic order disappeared into civil war and chaos.

There has been a recovery. Since 2006 the economy has been rebuilt by everyday Liberians, a massive injection of foreign aid, and new foreign investors. Most economic and governance metrics have improved, and by 2014 Liberia had recovered more than two-fifths of the peak-to-nadir gap in GDP

---

[1] *Penn World Tables 6.3* 'cgdp'.

per capita. Yet the new economy closely matches political and economic patterns that had characterized the heyday of the 1950s and 1960s. And the country remains only eleven places from the bottom of the Human Development Index ranking (UNDP, 2015), trailing, for instance, the Democratic Republic of the Congo, Afghanistan, and Haiti, which suggests the continued fragility of the recovery.

There is no unified narrative for Liberia's performance over this entire period. Its radically different economic fortunes attracted different groups and generations of scholars whose insights are rarely brought together. Moreover, even at the time, the simplicity of the narratives of each period was challenged. For instance, Liberia's world-beating economic growth in the 1960s was touted as a model for foreign investment-led growth, but even contemporary critics recognized the narrow distribution of privileges and described it as 'growth without development' (Clower et al., 1966). During the civil war, reporting on blood diamonds and Charles Taylor's accumulating fortune, not to mention the war's horrific and bizarre atrocities, suggested that war was lucrative. However, a comprehensive later analysis argues that the spoils of war were vastly overstated (Gerdes, 2013). Finally, the initial narrative of the post-war government of Ellen Johnson Sirleaf, culminating in her 2011 Nobel Peace Prize, was unbridled admiration as Liberia returned to economic growth and developmental policies. But those who actually visited Liberia and looked beneath the surface criticized the country's persistent poverty, political discontent, corruption, and nepotism.

This chapter presents a political economic history of Liberia since 1960, building on the framework of this book. We argue that, on the one hand, there has been a remarkable continuity in economic structures, but, on the other, changes in external circumstances and evolving social forces produced wildly different political settlements across (at least) five distinctive growth episodes. The divergence in the possible 'deals' made available by those who controlled (or did not) the state, catapulted Liberia from stable growth to stagnation and then to collapse, to wild fluctuation, and finally to rapid recovery and growth. Good and bad policies played a role, but more than anything they merely served to clarify the reality of the deals space. Recognizing the stability in economic structure is key to understanding why well-meaning reformers have so often been frustrated with its progress.

The arguments in this chapter are the result of applying several research methods. First, we reviewed scholarship and primary material from each of the growth episodes. Second, we conducted interviews with key informants who had occupied senior levels of government and business, beginning from the Tubman years through to today. Third, and perhaps most influentially, one of the authors (Werker) was unintentionally a 'participant observer' while working in Liberia from 2008 to the present. Werker worked as an advisor on environmental policy (funded by Conservation International), concession negotiations (pro bono, then later funded by the Open Society Foundation (OSF)), and then economic policy to the president (funded by OSF). Werker then founded and managed the Liberia programme of the International Growth Centre (funded by the UK Department for International Development (DFID) and managed by the London School of Economics (LSE)), which provided economic advice and funded economics research in the country. This chapter was inspired and informed by that lived experience— but we do not quote either directly or indirectly from government work or from social conversations and debates with senior members of Liberia's current government and business communities.

2.2 Growth Episodes and Political Settlements

The algorithm in the Effective States and Inclusive Development Research Centre's (ESID) handbook of economic growth (Kar et al., 2013) used to delineate growth episodes in the other chapters, in part due to a lack of data, did not generate meaningful breaks for Liberia. This chapter, unlike the others in the volume, uses World Bank data and identifies growth breaks based on a visual examination of the data and historical knowledge of the political settlements.

The growth episodes (see Figure 2.1) thus correspond to the political settlements that have characterized Liberia's history since the mid-twentieth century. Elite politics, domestic opposition—both representative and opportunistic—and foreign intervention have determined the settlements and the transitions. Each political settlement was associated with a growth episode defined by the set of deals available to different types of investors. We summarize the growth episodes in this section; Section 2.3 provides a more thorough investigation of the episodes through the lens of the framework described in Chapter 1.

During most of this period, the feedback loops from economic outcomes to politics and institutions have been negative: episodes of positive economic growth, stagnation, contraction, and collapse all produced weakened developmentalism of the state and of the regime(s) in power, which in turn produced worsening economic conditions. This negative feedback cycle was halted only by a foreign-brokered and -supervised peace settlement that ended fourteen years of civil war—and three decades of economic decline.

The first growth episode in Figure 2.1 is 1960–71, but begins in 1960 only because the data do—in reality the growth episode started in 1944, when William Tubman became president. Tubman consolidated power through a vast patronage network and is regarded as the father of modern Liberia and, compared with what followed, its 'benevolent' dictator (Sawyer, 2008). Tubman presided over nearly three decades of economic expansion driven

41

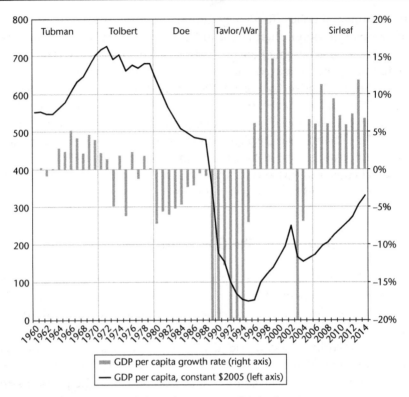

Figure 2.1. Liberia's growth performance and episodes

Source: World Bank, *World Development Indicators* data with authors' dating of episodes.

by foreign investment. The data show compound annual growth to be 2.5 per cent over 1960–71, but during the prior decade growth is asserted by early sources to have 'surpassed that of almost any other country in the world', with government receipts rising eightfold and even tribal incomes tripling (Clower et al., 1966: 23).

Stable rapid growth might be surprising, given the character of Tubman's political settlement. Tubman was the leader of the True Whig Party, a political party that efficiently represented 'Americo-Liberians', descendants of the freed slaves who were Liberia's colonizers in the middle of the nineteenth century (with the help of the American Colonization Society, a non-governmental organization). Despite constituting only a small minority of the population, the Americo-Liberians were able to establish control and extract rents from the land and the larger indigenous population through a mixture of violent force and, increasingly under Tubman, co-optation through patronage (Levitt, 2005).

In 1971, Tubman died and was replaced by his long-time vice president, William Tolbert. Tolbert attempted to continue Tubman's Americo-Liberian-centric policies, but while constructing a new political settlement. Tolbert tried to expand the patronage network, but Liberia suffered terms of trade shocks (Werker and Beganovic, 2011a). Per capita growth for the episode 1970–9 was −0.3 per cent annually, but this average hides annual volatility, with growth from −6.2 per cent to 2.3 per cent. Rising food prices, misguided government policy, and the increasing fragility of the political settlement led to Liberia's watershed moment. In April 1979, protests over increases in the government-controlled price of rice erupted into looting, which was suppressed by a violent police reaction. Within a year of the rice riots, Tolbert was killed in the executive mansion. A twenty-eight-year-old indigenous master sergeant of the Liberian army, Samuel Doe, led a coup to replace him.

The third growth episode coincided with Doe's decade in power, and full-blown collapse set in. Doe had excluded the Americo-Liberian elite from business and government opportunities and attempted to build a new settlement, where power was shared by co-ethnics and allied ethnicities (Ellis, 1999). Doe's even more fragile and hastily constructed political settlement led to a cumulative GDP per capita loss of nearly 50 per cent, or −6.3 per cent compounded annually, before Doe was murdered in 1990 and the country overrun by militias.

The fourth episode described in this chapter, from 1990 to 2005, in reality contains four sub-episodes, as two particularly brutal phases of civil war—which essentially shattered the economy and forced output levels to (less than) subsistence—were followed by relatively peaceful, but nonetheless disordered, recoveries. Even after the recovery from the nadir of 1995 to 2005, the compound annual growth rate from the episode was −4.7 per cent. Economic activity effectively stopped and started as militias fought over control of dwindling resources, using brutal and terrorizing tactics that ground even the most basic of economic activities to a halt. Nearly 10 per cent of the population was killed during this period (for comparison, the death rates of those *serving in the armed forces* of the United Kingdom and the United States during World War II were well below 5 per cent), with many more becoming refugees or internally displaced (Lyons, 1999).

Charles Taylor was the most powerful figure in Liberia's political settlements during this period and exercised control through warlord tactics of violence, looting, and highly targeted patronage. Yet most of the time there was no unified state control and power was shared with other militias, Nigerian peacekeepers, and Western-backed transitional governments. Ethnic militias aligned with the old Doe regime challenged Taylor, and in 2003 US and Nigerian intervention ended the war, forcing Taylor into exile (Kieh, 2010).

Following two years of a kleptocratic transitional government, long-time politician, activist, and technocrat, Ellen Johnson Sirleaf, was elected in 2005 and then re-elected in 2011. This fifth growth episode from 2005 to 2014 generated 7.9 per cent per year. Sirleaf's political party, and indeed that of her main challenger in the elections (which won more seats in the legislature), was multi-ethnic and included both the pre-coup elite as well as the once-excluded groups. With security guaranteed by United Nations peacekeepers, and foreign aid on top of a favourable commodity super-cycle fuelling economic recovery, Sirleaf was able to focus on rebuilding a modern state. Yet many patterns of political control and economic production remained. During this last growth episode, however, these patterns served to generate sustained rapid economic growth that would only slow when an Ebola outbreak struck Liberia in the second half of 2014 (Bowles et al., 2016), tragically coinciding with a global commodity price rout that threatened Liberia's export and foreign direct investment (FDI) prospects.

2.3 Deals, Rents, and Settlements During the Growth Episodes

2.3.1 *Tubman (Data Years 1960–70)*

The economic structure of the economy supported a complex and targeted patronage system that kept Tubman in power. Tubman's signature economic policy, dubbed the 'Open Door Policy', generated an extraordinary amount of rents for the state that could be redistributed through business opportunities, government expenditures, and government employment to buy acquiescence, if not loyalty.

The Open Door Policy specifically—although not explicitly—applied to the rentier quadrant in the market matrix. There was very nearly an open, ordered deals environment for foreign firms willing to bring their capital and expertise to Liberia to extract resources. The Open Door Policy 'heartily welcomes foreign investments into the country without any discrimination or hampering restrictions', claimed the Liberia Department of Information and Cultural Affairs in 1967, apparently without guile. 'It is no exaggeration to say that by 1960 Liberia offered private foreign capital one of the more attractive investment climates to be found in the underdeveloped world', acknowledged some of Liberia's most critical observers at the time (Clower et al., 1966: 118).

Firestone had long operated a rubber plantation from a massive concession that had allowed the US firm to break the British-Dutch rubber monopoly (Briggs, 1998). Rubber exports held steady through this period at around US$25 million per year. The growth industry was iron ore exports, which rose from US$20 million in 1957 to US$106 million a year in 1966, with some US$400 million invested by foreign capital in the decade (LICA, 1967: 41).

These mines sent substantial resources to government coffers, providing US$12.5 million in 1967, one-quarter of government revenue (LICA, 1967: 45). Yet, given the Tubman/True Whig Party political settlement, in which the Americo-Liberian families 'control the country and govern the tribes (about

95 per cent of the population) on a colonial pattern of indirect rule' (Clower et al., 1966: 6), the spoils were by no means widely shared. One later scholar described these families as a 'comprador class between the indigenes of the interior and the international market' (Outram, 1997: 357).

Through control over the law-making and concession-signing power for the rentier quadrant, Tubman fuelled a vast system of patronage. For instance, the National Iron Ore Company, in which the Republic of Liberia held 50 per cent of shares, sold 35 per cent of its shares to Liberians 'on an easy term plan under which purchasers were expected to pay 20 per cent of the price of the shares in three instalments, the remaining 80 per cent to be repaid by the purchasers out of future dividends'—in other words, a near-free equity. Which Liberians were offered this deal? '1,600 Liberians, including office employees, tribal people and Government officials, availed themselves of the opportunity' (LICA, 1967: 51–2). In other words, though the rentier industries may have been open and ordered, they were 'deals' that sustained the political settlement, right down to, presumably, the local chiefs who could maintain social order in the hinterland.

Tubman also controlled the powerbroker segment, and the Liberian elite occupied the plum positions in non-export industries. With foreign businesses operating in the rentier and even workhorse industries, well-connected Liberians preferred working in 'government, law, rubber farming, commercial transport, real estate, and as urban landlords of dwellings and commercial buildings' (Clower et al., 1966: 4). Besides, through their jobs, cushy by any developing-country standard, they had business opportunities and even quasi-feudal rights generated by the regime's economic policies:

> The highest echelons and their kin obtain the most lucrative material prerogatives: purchases of shares of stock in iron ore concessions at bargain rates; purchases of tribal land along new roads; sales of phantom services (public relations, advertising) to foreign concessions; sales of real economic services to concessions (e.g., trucking), but at a higher cost than the buyers would incur in providing their own services; acquiring compulsory labor for their rubber farms; the right to impose private levies in rice on tribal groups; the use of government vehicles and other equipment for private gain; extraordinarily large expense accounts; free housing and trips abroad; and government scholarships for training and education abroad regardless of merit. (Clower et al., 1966: 10)

For Liberia's powerbrokers, deals were closed and ordered—so long as Tubman remained in power.

Liberia's primary workhorses were the 'tribal' groups left out of the plum deals available to the better-connected. They engaged in agriculture and petty trading and other small businesses, usually in the informal sector. Despite being where the vast majority of Liberia's workers toiled, it was not where the money was. In 1960, domestic 'money' income was estimated at US$155 million,[2] with subsistence farming estimated to be a mere US$18 million (Clower et al., 1966: 42). Without the state paying much attention, except for sometimes arbitrary taxation, the deals in the main workhorse industries were open but disordered.

Somewhat ambiguously categorized were the foreign-invested non-tradeables, such as construction and banking, and other barely tradeables like beer, explosives, and window-making companies, which enjoyed market protection but at the pleasure of the Liberian hosts. In addition, a significant Lebanese and later Indian community was dominant in wholesale and retail. Some of these investors were attracted by the Open Door Policy—there was even an industrial park for light manufacturing, for example—and others, probably, by the riches it enabled. For these firms, deals were open and ordered for the most part, but required careful cultivation of political access to maintain powerbroker rents.

Not surprisingly, there were few magicians exporting in competitive industries. Transshipment by Liberia's traders and wholesalers from Liberia's Freeport to inland borders with neighbouring Guinea, Sierra Leone, and Ivory Coast was present, made competitive by the liberal economic environment in Liberia, as well as its relatively decent infrastructure and favourable geography. While smallholder rubber and oil palm farms might otherwise be categorized as magicians, during this growth episode they had rentier characteristics, as they were based on land acquisition through privilege and sometimes even compulsory labour. Cocoa was somewhat better.

Clower et al.'s (1966) indictment of Liberia experiencing 'growth without development' corresponds in our framework to a negative feedback loop between economic growth and societal institutions—that is, economic growth did not strengthen, but rather undermined institutions. For example, the government revenues and mining development led to the building of arterial roads throughout the countryside. Normally this would be a boon for upcountry populations, but in the case of Tubman's Liberia it actually displaced smallholder rice farming and moved it further into the bush. The elite commandeered the land beside the new roads and repurposed it for their rubber farms and, worse, could now reach the locals to hassle them with labour recruitment and unofficial tax collection (Clower et al., 1966: 33).

In addition, the economic boom ensured that the Americo-Liberian elite captured an emerging indigenous elite—who were 'reminded that they never had it so good and that loyalty to [Tubman] was the only assurance of steady socio-political progress', according to two liberal Liberian intellectuals (Dunn

---

[2] Current-day World Bank estimates for GDP in Liberia in 1960 are US$190 million, the same order of magnitude of the money income described in contemporary statistics.

and Tarr, 1988: 63)—and made sure that anyone with power and influence would be brought into the fold by 'jobs and money'. For example, 'students returning from abroad are embraced by the patronage system and their skins quickly thicken' (Clower et al., 1966: 12). Thus, the rising fortunes of the economy, buoyed by a rapid and significant increase in iron ore exports, led to the elite's hold on the economic environment through closed deals becoming even stronger.

Without sectoral national accounts data, we can construct only a stylized mapping of the rents space. We assume an economy two-fifths driven by rentiers (profits remitted abroad were nearly US$35 million in 1960, combined with the US$12.5 million in taxes from iron ore, as well as local wages and reinvested profits) (Clower et al., 1966: 42), with a 3 per cent share to magicians and the remainder split between powerbrokers and workhorses (see Figure 2.2).

The political settlement that Tubman created was, in Khan's typology, a classic 'potential developmental coalition' (2010: 65) settlement in which power was centred and there was limited dissent, either on the vertical dimension (between elites and non-elites) or the horizontal (among elites). The power gap between those benefiting from the settlement and those who were cut out was so large as to be insurmountable, since Tubman was especially effective at ensuring that there was no competition among elites. Any effective organization capable of mounting a challenge to Tubman's rule was

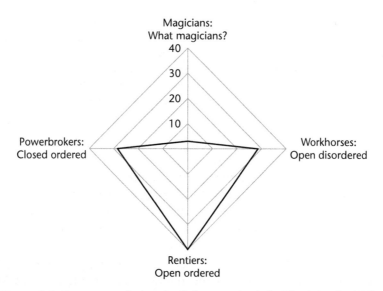

Figure 2.2. Rent spaces during the Tubman episode in Liberia in the 1960s
Source: Authors.

either run by, or derived its benefits from, the system that Tubman and his True Whig Party created.

2.3.2 Tolbert (Data Years 1971–9)

In *Political Order in Changing Societies,* Samuel Huntington argued that the cause of violence and instability in Asia, Africa, and Latin America was 'the product of rapid social change and the rapid mobilization of new groups into politics coupled with the slow development of political institutions' (1968: 4). When Tubman died in a London clinic in 1971 after twenty-seven years of power, his vice president of nearly two decades, William Tolbert, Jr, assumed the presidency. Tubman had begun the process of expanding the patronage network and extending it to the elites among the indigenous. But, as Huntington noted, the supply of limited inclusion whets rather than satiates demand and is further fuelled by economic modernization and raises, rather than lowers, pressures and potential instability. These tensions were exacerbated by Tolbert's relative weakness—as well as by international factors beyond his control that reduced the scope for patronage.

Tolbert attempted to construct a new patronage network, while retaining elite control over the political order and economic rents. Given Tubman's skill as well as tenure as a patronage boss, combined with the strength of the Americo-Liberian hegemony within the political settlement, this was no easy task. As Pham (2004: 74–5) describes:

> [Tolbert] set for himself the ambitious goal of rationalizing the national adminis-
> tration by taking on and eventually dismantling his predecessor's patronage
> network. His hope apparently was to carve for himself a base of support consisting
> of a broad coalition of the newly emergent groups in Liberian society who would
> most benefit from his 'de-Tubmanization' of the country, including educated
> young professionals and students, entrepreneurs, educated rural dwellers, and
> the professional military.

Yet, of course, Tolbert hailed from the old elite and still depended on it for maintaining order in the interregnum.

Schooling in Liberia had steadily expanded: primary enrolment went from 31 per cent in 1960 to 60 per cent in 1980, secondary enrolment climbed from 2 per cent to 20 per cent. A new liberal intellectual class was emerging, mostly drawn from indigenous Liberians, but also progressive Americo-Liberians. Two political organizations emerged in the 1970s, the Movement for Justice in Africa (MOJA) and the Progressive Alliance of Liberia (PAL), which began to influence politics and destabilize the political settlement. Whereas MOJA favoured a platform of 'labor rights, electoral and income distribution reforms', PAL emphasized 'immediate direct action in politicizing the urban

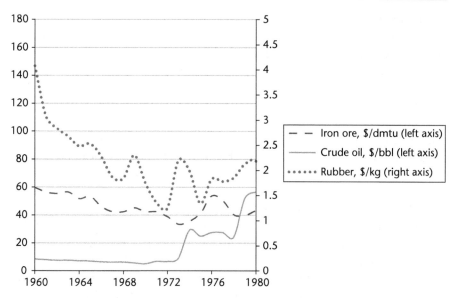

Figure 2.3. Commodity prices and Liberia's terms of trade
Source: World Bank <http://databank.worldbank.org/data/databases/commodity-price-data>.
Note: dmtu = dry metric tonne unit; bbl = barrel of oil.

masses and a confrontational attitude toward the government' (Dunn and Tarr, 1988: 87). In Khan's (2010: 65) terminology, this strengthening of the excluded factions within the horizontal distribution of power produced a shift to a 'vulnerable authoritarian coalition'.

Tolbert's government was responsive to these new voices. The country's development spending climbed from 9.5 per cent of the national budget in 1971 to 28.3 per cent in 1978: 'low-cost' housing estates were built, a rural development scheme was launched, and government salaries were raised. There was finally some high-level ethnic representation in the executive branch (Dunn and Tarr, 1988: 72, 76). But the 1970s oil shock hit Liberia's terms of trade hard. The prices of iron ore and rubber had been on a downward trend since the 1960s, with the revenue impact initially offset by rising volumes. Oil, Liberia's main import, became increasingly costly (Figure 2.3). The budget deficit rose from 1 per cent of GDP in 1975 to 15 per cent in 1979 and the national debt nearly quadrupled (Dunn and Tarr, 1988: 126). The economic foundation could not support the new political settlement that Tolbert was trying to build.

The rent and deals space reflected, and then magnified, this broader dynamic. In the rentier space there was rising resource nationalism. Liberians educated abroad were returning with new ideas about the appropriate deals the country should make with foreign investors. For example, during a renegotiation with one prominent foreign company in the 1970s, the company's lawyer was acting with the arrogance that had characterized their relationship with government officials for decades. A young Liberian replied, 'I'd like to remind you that we can nationalize you at any time we want'.[3] The tenor in the room immediately changed as the company realized that Liberia was not the same. The 'ordered deal' stability of Tubman showed risks of disorder, though not yet dramatically so—while deals were renegotiated, they were still honoured once signed.

Increasing disorder permeated the deals in the powerbroker space, which remained closed though less predictable as the shifting political settlement demanded greater sharing of the spoils. Some of this came from Tolbert's different style of honouring deals. A businessman quoted in the *Atlantic Monthly* said that 'When Tubman stole a dollar, he would give ninety cents back to the people in the form of food or minor amenities; as for Tolbert, he would return ten cents' (Unger, 1981, quoted in Pham, 2004: 76). But most of it came from the weaker grasp that Tolbert had on the country. In one example, a gambling bill was set to enable a profitable casino to be constructed at the fancy Ducor hotel in Monrovia. In the 'closed ordered deals' days, this specific benefit to a powerbroker would have sailed through the legislature. But citizen discontent emerged, channelled through the churches and MOJA. The bill passed anyway, but Tolbert vetoed it, attempting to side with the new social forces and show strength over the old elite. It ended up backfiring and revealing Tolbert's weakness to both sides (Dunn and Tarr, 1988: 73–5). For the powerbrokers it was clear: the predictability of the regime's honouring deals was now lower.

But disorder exploded dramatically in 1979, when a rise in the price of rice, purportedly to encourage local production (but perhaps cynically to generate windfall profits to the lucrative rice-importing business—which benefited 'relatives and friends of the president') resulted in massive public demonstrations, led by PAL (Dunn and Tarr, 1988: 76). This was the death knell for the Tolbert administration and the True Whig Party regime. Closed deals that depended on the regime, as well as open deals that depended on political stability more broadly, became more disordered.

During the decade 1971–80, the effect of these internal and external forces was to tug and pull, but not to break the political settlement, and the economy remained stagnant. Weak global economic conditions from the stagflation brought about by the oil crisis reined in the rentier quadrant. Exports from Liberia fell from 74 per cent of GDP in 1971 to 68 per cent of a smaller GDP in 1979.[4] In an effort to expand the patronage umbrella, Tolbert tried to enlarge the powerbroker quadrant. For example, Tubman only had one parastatal that

---

[3] Interview with key informant.
[4] World Bank *World Development Indicators*, accessed 5 August 2016.

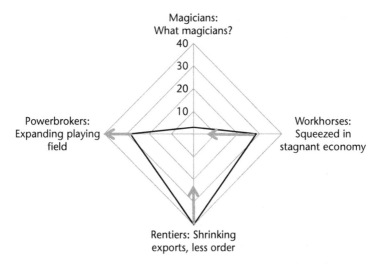

Figure 2.4. Changes to rents space during the Tolbert episode in Liberia in the 1970s
Source: Authors.

provided electricity, water, and communications services. Tolbert, however, established 'more than twenty public enterprises covering agriculture and forestry; manufacturing; transportation; communications; electricity; water and sanitation; trade; tourism; housing and land development; and finance' (Dunn and Tarr, 1988: 146). On top of that, and probably for purely venal motives, Tolbert—with the assistance of his brother, Stephen, whom he appointed as finance minister in 1972—co-founded and favoured a fishing venture that expanded into 'the first Liberian-owned multimillion-dollar conglomerate, the Mesurado Group of companies, that included fishing, frozen foods, detergent, feed, window manufacturing, household soap, agriculture, and other enterprises' (Pham, 2004: 47). With the rentier quadrant shrinking and the powerbroker quadrant being force-fed, it became clear that the workhorse quadrant would be squeezed (Figure 2.4).

We have a negative feedback loop between our political variables, the rents space, and the ability of the economy to generate innovation and structural transformation, let alone produce equitable outcomes. Combined with rising education and expectations and a new elite challenging the old regime, Liberia's political economy was delivering heaps of firewood to a growing pyre.

2.3.3 Doe (Data Years 1980–9)

In the months following the rice crisis, Tolbert's power was first threatened not by the army but by a political foe: Gabriel Baccus Mathews. Baccus was the co-founder and director of PAL, the more aggressive of the 1970s political movements in Liberia that organized the rice demonstration. Baccus had managed to form a political party against Tolbert's wishes, and was trying to get the president to resign, so Tolbert charged him with treason (Pham, 2004: 76–8). It was truly unexpected that the army, let alone a twenty-eight-year-old master sergeant, would successfully mount a coup d'état. But on 12 April 1980, Doe and his fellow junior officers killed Tolbert in the executive mansion and, ten days later, publicly executed thirteen senior leaders of the Tolbert government.

The likelihood of the demise of the Tolbert administration may have been predictable based on political economy logic, but the character of its replacement was not. The political settlement that Doe and his allies sought to create and maintain was challenged from the start.

After more than a century of True Whig rule, with the economic exclusion of the majority to benefit the minority America-Liberian population, there was a broad-seated desire to undertake redistribution. However, what resulted was implemented in a haphazard and often reckless (or wreckful) fashion. Doe and his junta raided government coffers of some US$300 million in public funds, arrested businessmen on trumped-up charges in order to extract bribes, and took over and crashed the government's fleet of Mercedes (Pham, 2004: 82). They seized the Tolberts' Mesurado Group and ran it into the ground, but not without assuming the liability for the wages of the employees because of 'preference for political over commercial considerations' (Dunn and Tarr, 1988: 46). Doe raised the wages of lower-income government workers and soldiers by 100–300 per cent. The public payroll increased from 18,000 in 1979 to an astounding 56,000 employees in 1983 (Dunn and Tarr, 1988: 38, 95–6).

Initially Doe tried to pull together, and maintain, a broad coalition as Liberia's first post-True Whig political settlement. His first cabinet drew from the military, former government, MOJA, and PAL's political party (Dunn and Tarr, 1988: 94). Representing the interests of the non-settler class broadly, the young and frustrated urban dwellers, and the army, he tried to please them all. But without 'the well-oiled America-Liberian government machinery to draw on, he recentralized power by allocating important government positions to his tribesmen, the Krahn' (Werker and Beganovic, 2011a). In the process of recentralizing power, including co-opting the Mandingo, another of Liberia's ethnicities that had traditionally been excluded from the levers of power even as they accounted for a large part of the trading sector (Ellis, 2007: 39, 61, 216), Doe set the ethnic fault lines for the later civil war.

This meant that in the early 1980s, despite Doe's promise not to 'bring back the same kind of government that we removed',[5] Liberia's closed deals

---

[5] Quoted in Dunn and Tarr (1988: 95).

would remain closed—but with new beneficiaries. At one point in that period, 31 per cent of cabinet positions were held by Krahn Liberians, despite their being just 5 per cent of the population (Dunn and Tarr, 1988: 199–200). The initial broad base of once-disaffected Liberians gave way to a narrow constituency. A popular Liberian slogan described Doe's Liberia as 'Same Taxi, New Driver' (Outram, 1997: 360).

Though most of the deals remained closed—delimited by the identifiable characteristics of the people they benefited—they grew increasingly disordered. Part of that disorder came from inept implementation and part from the belated realization that government actions were destroying the economic base on which the possibility of redistribution depended. Consider the following changes to taxes and fees (Dunn and Tarr, 1988: 130):

> Fiscal indiscipline and capricious government behaviour contributed to the economic problem. Between fiscal years 1980/81 and 1984/85, the government imposed a variable rate surcharge on luxury items and non-essential dutiable items each year, but repealed it the next year. The invoice entry fees on transshipment goods were levied in 1980/81, reduced in 1981/82, only to be raised again in 1983/84. The export tax on rubber was levied one year, withdrawn the next, but imposed in the following year.

The haphazard changes to the rules of business had the merchants running scared. One of our key informants recalled the chilling effect of one of Doe's first economic policies, to stop the transfer of funds abroad. It put the business community in a short-term, defensive position. The rising uncertainty from disordered deals had the effect of lowering investment.

Doe's administrators tried to keep the rentier deals ordered, but some of these attempts were undermined by economic mismanagement and political weakness, generating a self-reinforcing dynamic. For example, once external transfers were reopened, the confidence that payments would not be blocked in the future had already been lost. Business owners no longer kept money in the country; every time they booked profits, they transferred them abroad.[6]

In the rents space (Figure 2.5), one of the large iron ore mines had closed in 1977 and the other was scheduled to close in 1989. Oil refining, which had contributed 50 per cent of that industry's value added, stopped in 1982 (Dunn and Tarr, 1988: 134–5). To make up the loss in earnings and hard currency, Doe tried to reassure foreign investors.[7] He left the foreign investment deals intact, encouraged Firestone to continue producing during a crisis in its operations, and did not ask new investors in the mining sector for 'even a penny'—the government so desperately needed the new investment and employment.[8]

[6] Interview, key informant.   [7] Interview, key informant.
[8] Interview, key informant.

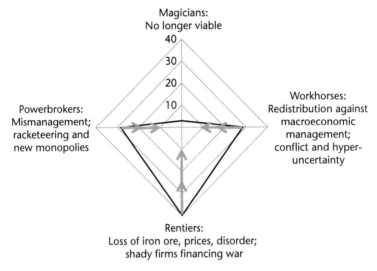

Magicians:
No longer viable

Powerbrokers:
Mismanagement;
racketeering and
new monopolies

Workhorses:
Redistribution against
macroeconomic
management;
conflict and hyper-
uncertainty

Rentiers:
Loss of iron ore, prices, disorder;
shady firms financing war

Figure 2.5. Changes to rents space during the Doe episode in Liberia in the 1980s and civil war episode in the 1990s and early 2000s

Source: Authors.

Note: Outside parts of arrows depict movement in rents space during Doe episode, inside parts of arrows depict movement in rents space during civil war; descriptions before semicolons describe movement during the Doe episode, descriptions after semicolons describe movement during the civil war.

For formal-sector businesses that had not already been expropriated, there was a fear of undertaking the closed deals arrangements of the previous period without proper protection, which extended to physical protection. The Doe administration generally left these businesses alone, so long as they stayed out of politics. 'If you didn't,' recalled one key informant, 'they could not only seize your business but kill you.' Another noted the importance of contacts: 'If you didn't have contacts, you were looted or killed. If you did, you could do anything.' The disorder from these policies was apparent, and Doe's men were especially impulsive. 'In Liberia, they say, if three days pass, everything is forgotten', noted a key informant.

Workhorse firms faced perhaps even greater disorder generated by the arbitrary and disorganized low-level corruption. One key informant told a tale laced with dark humour:

> The corruption went all the way down to the police on the street. They were really hunting for pay-outs. One day I was stopped in my car by a policeman who said I had run a red light. I said there was no working traffic light. He said, true, but if there was, it would have been red.

On top of the disorder generated by government actions was that from the overall macroeconomic mismanagement and political uncertainty. To solve the hard-currency shortage, the Liberian government minted its own coins (Liberia was on the US dollar), which became known as 'Doe dollars', and quickly traded at a discount (Ellis, 2007: 55). Real per capita incomes fell every year of Doe's government. Inflation was sometimes high, hitting 17 per cent in 1987.[9] External debt climbed from 74 per cent of gross national income (GNI) in 1980 to 320 per cent in 1989.[10] A 1985 coup attempt by Thomas Quiwonkpa, the other key leader of the coup in 1980, nearly succeeded in removing Doe, and in Doe's later years he would claim to have survived some thirty-eight assassination attempts (Ellis, 2007: 54–63). Making long-term investments in an environment of such economic and political uncertainty did not suit the risk appetite of most investors.

As the economy dried up, Doe relied on a last lifeline. The regime was propped up by US assistance intended to keep Liberia from Soviet and Libyan spheres of influence. Some US$500 million in American economic and military assistance between 1981 and 1985, more than all the US aid that the country had received prior to that time, bolstered the regime's survival (Pham, 2004: 89). The end of the Cold War changed the calculus, and aid dwindled from over US$50 million in 1986 to less than US$20 million in 1989, and in 1990 Liberia received no American aid except US$10 million in humanitarian assistance. The International Monetary Fund (IMF) and World Bank followed suit (Pham, 2004: 90).

Doe's fate was sealed as armed opposition to his government on several fronts gained control of Liberian territory. Holed up in the capital, Doe was eventually assassinated by warlord Prince Johnson in September 1990. But it was Charles Taylor who would play the larger role in defining Liberia's next political settlement, such as it was.

2.3.4 Civil War (Data Years 1990–2005)

Launched in December 1989 from the Ivory Coast, Taylor's insurgency swept through Liberia and arrived at the doorstep of Monrovia by July 1990. There Taylor and his forces would stay. One of Samuel Doe's few remaining external backers, Nigeria, set up a peacekeeping force, ECOMOG (the Economic Community of West African States' Monitoring Group), which helped retain control of the capital. After Doe was killed, ECOMOG protected Liberia's notional government, a transitional arrangement brokered by peace negotiators and led by civilian Amos Sawyer.

But geographical control and power still remained with Taylor, who refused to join power-sharing arrangements. Taylor continued to administer the vast

---

[9] World Bank data, GDP deflator, accessed 26 August 2016.
[10] World Bank data, external debt stocks (% GNI), accessed 26 August 2016.

majority of Liberia's physical area, which came to be known as 'Greater Liberia', complete with his own port in Buchanan, currency, and banking system (Pham, 2004: 104–10). Shut out of the 'legitimate' government, Taylor's 'only option was to acquire resources for his military operations by resorting to a "warlord political economy" of tapping the assets in areas under his control', according to Pham (2004: 124). Eventually he would win contested elections in 1997 (following a second transitional government) before being challenged again, and forced out to exile in Nigeria in 2003, after which another transitional government returned for two more years until 2005. As mentioned earlier, economic growth rates seesawed during this period, but income levels hovered at or below subsistence.

Taylor did not pursue economic strength through productive activities like agriculture, but rather sought to bring in foreign capital in order to exploit Greater Liberia's natural resources, as Outram (1997: 365) observed: 'To Taylor a functioning agricultural sector has been of only secondary importance. In these ways Taylor's practice has replicated the basic features of the pre-war political economy.' But the composition of the natural resources, the character of the foreign investors, and the resultant deals and rents space were markedly different. During the war years, foreign investment 'reinforced an informal, clandestine economy that thrived and took primacy after the collapse of Liberia's formal economy' (Johnston, 2004: 441) as we describe later in this section.

The mining, manufacturing, and even sometimes the agriculture sector were collapsing—declining not only in absolute terms, but even as a share of the rapidly contracting economy. Figure 2.6 shows a best guess of the composition of Liberian GDP from the earliest available year.[11] The unbroken line shows GDP relative to 1987 = 100 and the broken lines depict the share of the economy of different sectors. Mining fell from 10 per cent to 1 per cent of GDP as iron ore exports ceased. In fact, exports did not just cease, but the mines' heavy machinery was sold for scrap (Gerdes, 2013: 98). From 1991 to 1996, the manufacturing sector fell from 11 per cent to 1 per cent of GDP, as all but the most unsophisticated formal businesses could no longer operate. Subsistence agriculture and service traded off shares of the total economy as the population was forced to flee their farms for the cities and refugee camps, and then return.

This crowding out of the formal sector leaves 'citizens with few avenues through which to pursue political or economic objectives . . . since economic opportunities tend to be embedded in these informal networks, citizens must seek accommodations with them to survive', notes Johnston (2004: 445). This

[11] These data are from the Liberian IMF's analysts; they stress that the underlying data are weak and based on pre-war national income accounts, so these should be taken with a grain of salt.

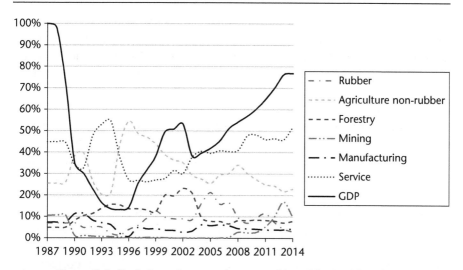

Figure 2.6. Evolution of economic composition, Liberia, 1987–2014
Source: IMF.

advantages young men through their participation in militias—the seemingly academic and metaphorical 'roving bandits' of Mancur Olson (2000) were real.

In the formal sector, some firms initially stuck it out, betting that Taylor would win the war and eventually become president of a sovereign state (Reno, 1997: 13). Among the rentiers (see Figures 2.5 and 2.6), the decline of iron ore mining was replaced, in relative terms, with a rise in forestry (reaching 16 per cent of GDP in 1994 and then 23 per cent of GDP in 2002) and rubber (13 per cent of GDP in 1999 and 21 per cent in 2005). Though 'blood diamonds' dominate the public conception of the Liberian war—personified by Naomi Campbell's appearance as a witness at Charles Taylor's trial (Bowcott, 2012)—forestry in fact was a more lucrative commodity in Liberia and just as susceptible to warlord control. Rubber firms, presumably because of their large sunk costs, also paid Taylor for the right to continue production (Reno, 1997: 13).

Despite this being a resource war (Le Billon, 2001), it was not an especially lucrative one, even for the handful of individuals connected to Taylor and other warlords. Gerdes (2013: 103) estimates that Taylor controlled an average of just US$14 million in annual profits before assuming the presidency, the bulk of which came from forestry and looting. For an economy that had previously topped US$1 billion,[12] this is not an impressive figure. Not surprisingly, the firms that could and would do business in Liberia in this time were shady, at best. Johnston (2004: 444–50) describes some of the players: a Dutch

---

[12] World Bank data, current dollars, <http://data.worldbank.org/country/Liberia>, accessed 23 August 2016.

gang trafficking drugs to Europe and America; Gus van Kouwenhoven of the Oriental Timber Corporation, with his 2,500-strong private militia, who helped finance the 1997 election; Leonin Minin of the Exotic Tropical Timber Enterprise, moving weapons from Ukraine to West Africa in his private jet.

In the powerbroker quadrant, the chief businesses were the extractive quasi-states themselves, as modern production was near impossible. Whereas the Tolbert brothers had built a sophisticated conglomerate that enjoyed special privileges, by the war years the leader's privilege was reduced to taxing the few businesses that remained, in an often arbitrary manner, as Gerdes (2013: 80) describes: 'there were checkpoints every few kilometres on Liberia's few roads...the checkpoints were sites of extortion that rendered any business unprofitable, lest the businessperson enjoyed special protection.'

When Taylor was finally elected president, he took the powerbroker opportunity seriously, pushing a kleptocratic deals environment that supported his patronage network. As the International Crisis Group (2002: 7) reported:

> In some cases, Taylor takes a personal ownership share, such as in Lonestar Communications, the country's cell phone firm. Mostly, however, he demands an up-front fee for the rights to an industry and then a cut of profits. Each of the inner circle makes money by grossly inflating prices.

One company was awarded a single licence for rice imports, another, the petroleum monopoly; two of Taylor's confidantes were at the top of an ownership scheme of the telecoms monopoly (Gerdes, 2013: 149–50). (The epilogue here is interesting: the telecoms company later sold a controlling block of its shares to South African mobile giant, MTN; one of the confidantes is now Liberia's richest man and a presidential aspirant to replace Johnson Sirleaf (Sieh, 2016).)

As for the workhorses, this was grim survival, especially during the periods of intense fighting: 'Large areas of faction territory in Liberia have become deserted or severely depopulated. Food production outside the ECOMOG zone has all but collapsed', reports Outram (1997: 364). By the end of 1994, over 80 per cent of the Liberian population had been displaced by fighting that engulfed 80 per cent of the national territory (Pham, 2004: 116).

The net effect on the business environment was to create hyper-disordered deals and this disorder ground the economy to a halt. Consider the different layers of uncertainty. Businesses saw multiple roving (not even a single stationary) banditry. At one point, for example, Taylor controlled 95 per cent of the country, but three years later it was down to half (Pham, 2004: 112). Factions sometimes split into two when leadership goals clashed (Pham, 2004: 114). International support encouraged a stalemate, with Ivorian and Burkinabe support for Taylor, and Nigerian support for Doe and subsequently the transitional governments (Waugh, 2011: 145), so it was hard for businesses to guess when the war might end. And different warlords had different styles. Prince Johnson, for example, 'collected taxes from marketers and businesspeople in his territory, though this appears to have taken the form of unsystematic extortions' (Gerdes, 2013: 116).

Compounding this top-down uncertainty, which loomed over the deals environment, was bottom-up predation and chaos. Besides the official army, none of the factions regularly 'paid or fed their fighters' (Outram, 1997: 362) so extraction was the norm. Even the Nigerian peacekeepers got a piece of the action, looting homes as the city changed hands (Pham, 2004: 111). And, despite Taylor's strongman tactics, as president he was less in control of both his ministers and legislators, who wanted a cut of deals and the power to approve them, than Tolbert and even Doe had been.[13]

In Khan's (2010: 65) political settlement typology, the horizontal (other warlords) and vertical (anarchic, local militias, and independent bureaucrats and lawmakers) challenges to power place this settlement firmly in the 'competitive clientelism' space, which Khan describes as having 'low enforcement capabilities' and 'short time horizons'.

The deals were also hyper-closed. As president, Taylor forced the Strategic Commodities Act through the Liberian Congress as evidence mounted against him for his role in Sierra Leone's diamond trade. It granted him 'the sole power to execute, negotiate, and conclude all Commercial contracts or agreements with any Foreign or Domestic investor for the exploitation of the Strategic Commodities of the Republic of Liberia' (*The Perspective*, 2001). Taylor appointed his brother head of the Forestry Development Authority (FDA), the government agency that assigns forestry concessions, which in normal times is a relatively backwater (if still corrupt) agency. With Robert Taylor in charge, the FDA 'did not hold [the Oriental Timber Company] responsible for any of the taxes that it agreed to pay when it signed a contract with the Liberian government' (Johnston, 2004: 451).

This personalization of power displacing even a patina of state-like behaviour reveals the negative feedback loop between the desperate economics of warlordism—and its accompanying macroeconomic collapse—and the development of political institutions. Far from creating a positive stressor that enlists extra effort and good intentions towards real reform, the economic misfortune of Liberia enabled and almost locked in the worst kind of politics.

The transitional 'governments' were little better. Describing the first such arrangement (1990–4), Gerdes notes that it 'gained a reputation for ineffectiveness, opportunism, corruption and, at best, patronage' (2013: 109); this label might have well described any of the three transitional

---

[13] Interviews with key informants.

governments that were attempts brokered by outside powers to establish order during the civil war (Morgan, 2006). That these governments had international recognition and jurisdiction over the capital allowed the bureaucrats to collect bribes while administering formal state functions like customs and duties, and collecting registration fees (Gerdes, 2013: 111). In the second iteration (1995–7), as an incentive to maintain the peace:

> Ministries, state-owned enterprises and government agencies were distributed among the warring parties...In essence, the situation was one in which the warring parties jointly enjoyed the material prerogatives of sovereign statehood, while able to simultaneously exploit the territories they controlled as non-sovereign armed entities. Yet violent competition between the parties continued.
>
> (Gerdes, 2013: 52)

Formalizing the political chaos did little to stabilize the deals environment.

The final iteration of transitional government, from 2003 to 2005, was successful (helped in no small part by an international peacekeeping force) in setting the stage for free and fair elections. But it could hardly be construed as legitimate. Control of ministries and agencies was doled out to the embattled government, as well as its two insurgent challengers, with a few 'neither financially lucrative nor politically powerful and often totally dysfunctional institutions' given to opposition parties and civil society (Gerdes, 2013: 174). The deals environment remained disordered, though modestly less so. Steel giant Arcelor Mittal bravely signed a concession deal for an old iron ore mine at the Guinean border in 2005. It, as well as the Firestone rubber concession, would be renegotiated by Sirleaf two years later.

2.3.5 *Ellen Johnson Sirleaf (Data Years 2006–14)*

Ellen Johnson Sirleaf was elected in November 2005 in what were the first elections in the history of the country that had not been under the influence of the dominant players in the political settlement (Sawyer, 2008). Startlingly for a post-conflict country, rebel forces—even in transformed guise—were basically absent from the political process (Harris, 2006). The two leading candidates and their parties represented broad coalitions, and had support from a variety of constituencies, geographies, and ethnicities. Sirleaf was able to turn an eight percentage point deficit in the first round of voting behind former football star George Weah into a commanding nineteen percentage point victory after the run-off. Her experience (both as an opposition figure to Liberia's repressive regimes and as an international technocrat) and education (a Master's degree from Harvard Kennedy School) were probably decisive over the talented and popular, but occasionally divisive and less educated, runner-up (Harris, 2006). However, Sirleaf's party did not win a majority, let alone the largest number of seats, in either the Senate or the House.

Sirleaf governed in a principled but pragmatic fashion. Francois et al. (2015) found that, across Africa, cabinet positions tend to be allocated to members of ethnicities more or less in proportion to their population shares, regardless of who is in power.[14] Sirleaf balanced her appointments between achieving such representation and rewarding those who had helped in her campaign, while still achieving 'the most qualified [government] Liberia ever had' (Gerdes, 2013: 218–19). Over time, her appointments and promotion patterns followed a mixture of competence, integrity, and loyalty. When faced with a political challenger, her inclination was to bring them into the tent, rather than face costly opposition from the outside.

The Sirleaf political settlement is developmentalist. Faced with a state that had suffered from nearly three decades of decline, mismanagement, and pillaging, Sirleaf and her administration had their work cut out (Radelet, 2007). Three-quarters of the population subsisted on less than a dollar a day. There were fewer than fifty physicians in a country of four million people. Half of Liberian children and youth were out of school. There was no grid electricity or piped water service. With mines out of production and the country facing sanctions on timber and diamonds, (formally reported) exports were only US$10 million. The national budget stood at US$85 million a year, around US$25 per capita. On top of all that, Liberia's debt stood at US$4.5 billion, equivalent to 800 per cent of GDP (and an astronomical 450 times exports).

Sirleaf enlisted the support of a variety of external actors, from official agencies like the World Bank and USAID (the US Agency for International Development) to philanthropists and social impact investors (Scharff, 2012). Under finance ministers Antoinette Sayeh, who would go on to become director of the African Department of the IMF, and Augustine Ngafuan, and international advisors, Liberia negotiated a 97 per cent haircut on its outstanding commercial debt, as well as a 100 per cent reduction of Paris Club debt (Werker and Beganovic, 2011b). A World Bank-supported four-pillar plan focused on peace and security, revitalizing economic activity, governance, and infrastructure.

The initial results on governance were dramatic, at least according to standard indicators. Figure 2.7 shows various measures of state capabilities, which jumped during the elections and at the beginning of the Sirleaf administration.

These indicators normally move at a glacial pace (Pritchett et al., 2013), and indeed after the jump to 2006 they have remained roughly constant and Sirleaf's re-election in 2011 did not register. Reality also improved, less

[14] Interestingly, Liberia is one of the few exceptions to this rule in their data, given the dominance of one or two ethnicities during the True Whig and Doe regimes.

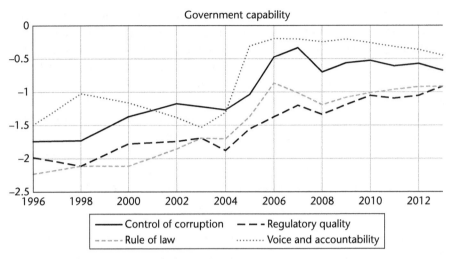

Figure 2.7. Evolution of state capabilities, Liberia, 1996–2013
Source: World Bank Worldwide Governance Indicators.

immediately but dramatically. By the beginning of 2011, Liberia had a professionalized army, a fire brigade, a budget of nearly US$400 million, newly paved roads, revitalized hospitals, 220 new schools, and the beginning of electricity, water, and wastewater services, all while enjoying greater civil liberties than at any point in its history (Sirleaf, 2011). Sirleaf even won the Nobel Peace Prize in 2011 for supporting women's rights and peace building.

Yet periodically this shining success story would meet with disenchantment. Reporters did not have to turn over many stones to realize that the comeback Liberian narrative was not without its faults. Concern usually focused on the persistent poverty, continuation of corruption, and signs of nepotism in the Sirleaf administration. The continued presence of corruption and nepotism indicated that the country still retained fragilities from its conflict period and the elite coalition was vulnerable, as the political settlement was far from institutionalized:

> Against the background of instability, the need to re-build governing capacity and enormous tasks ahead, the president needed a network of personally loyal officials. As the private use of office powers is deeply embedded in Liberian political culture, transgressions were to be expected and a 'zero tolerance' policy on corruption would have destabilized the government and eroded trust and support of the officials she needed. Johnson Sirleaf adopted a quiet approach to disciplining officials. (Gerdes, 2013: 219)

In turning to non-institutionalized mechanisms for government administration, Sirleaf joined more than a century-and-a-half of Liberian leaders.

Alarmingly, Liberia's traditional economic model—which in prior political settlements had funded patronage, led to a destructive coup, and funded a brutal civil war—re-emerged in the new post-war environment. Between 2006 and 2011, Liberia signed new agreements for the astounding sum of more than US$16 billion in foreign investment (Sirleaf, 2011), the majority for natural resource extraction. The logic was the same as in previous settlements, though this time it was more developmentalist: raise revenue for the state, so as to invest in the country's poverty reduction strategy and create local economic activity. The economic logic of natural resources as the attraction for foreign investors was inevitable: given the small population and low income level, the domestic workhorse sector offered little upside, and the supporting conditions for magicians exporting manufactures or services would take time to build.

The net result of the economic recovery on the rents space was therefore a four-pronged approach. The rentier quadrant expanded, due to targeted recruiting of foreign investment. Here, the Sirleaf administration sought a range of nationalities for the foreign investors and strived to attract high-calibre international firms (Werker and Beganovic, 2011a). As in previous regimes, deals were signed by the Liberian government with broad ministerial representation on the negotiating team, and the concession agreements for the most part were made public. These were basically open, basically ordered deals; even the renegotiations were seen as legitimate. Naturally, some of the agreements got better marks than others (Global Witness, 2009; Kaul et al., 2009).

Yet closed, disordered deals prevailed in the forestry sector, where ambitious donor-funded reforms had put in place world-class regulations, but where the economics and some behind-the-scenes rigging of regulations and bids failed to attract top investors. In one outlandish loophole, some 40 per cent of the country's forests were granted logging permits by the FDA in just two years, on the grounds that they were 'private use'. Sirleaf issued a moratorium on logging under such conditions, but the activity continued (Global Witness, 2013).

In the powerbroker space, some (relatively) open, ordered deals funded by foreign aid attracted foreign investment. International port operator, APM Terminals, signed on to a deal to renovate and run Monrovia's container terminal. Two Chinese-owned construction companies 'bid' against one another in donor-funded road projects. But mostly it was the previous players, whether Liberian (including state-owned enterprises) or foreign nationals but locally based, who emerged to dominate key import markets, petroleum distribution, cement, beverages, and flour mills. Local organizations like the Liberian Business Association lobbied for special breaks that would prevent non-Liberians from operating in certain sectors—effectively trying to create powerbrokers out of workhorses. These closed deals were reasonably ordered, but involved extensive and costly jockeying to maintain the anti-competitive position.

Liberia's workhorses were still the vast majority of the population and initially contributed the lion's share of the economy. Yet many operated in the informal economy, whether growing and trading local agricultural products or selling and reselling imported goods. The large formal-sector workhorses in Liberia tend to be dominated by the foreign or ethnic-minority business owners (including Lebanese, Indians, and Fulani), whose internal sources of capital, networks, and contract enforcement probably offered them competitive advantages in a climate of weak institutions, including the occasional powerbroker privilege.[15] For the most part, deals in this quadrant were disordered, although the return to political stability and government efforts to develop new policies around small and medium-sized businesses heralded a greater degree of order than in decades.

Finally, there was a small but brave return of magicians, who traded on the few domestic sources of differentiation to sell products abroad. One example was garment manufacturer Liberty and Justice, which leveraged the Liberia story and social financing to export T-shirts to the United States. They faced the same untested business environment as the workhorses, navigating petty corruption and the inconsistent application of regulations. Efforts to restart smallholder tree crop production, like palm oil and cocoa, held some promise.

Our best efforts to measure the rents space in 2010 (Figure 2.8) reveals a very stable share of magicians (very low) and powerbrokers (about a quarter of the economy) relative to the Tubman years. Rentiers were still low, at around 10 per cent of the economy, with workhorses at 61 per cent of GDP. During the Tubman years, rentiers were estimated at 40 per cent, so this represents a substantial reversal, permitted by the vast amounts of foreign aid flowing into Liberia on top of the debt relief and peacekeeping expenditures. Jonathan Said, author of the Malawi chapter in this book (Chapter 3), estimated that by 2014 the rentier share of the economy had climbed to 25 per cent, as iron ore output increased; this gain largely came at the expense of the workhorse sector, whose growth rate, though positive, was much slower. As can be seen in Figure 2.8, despite the democratic governance and improving institutions, the rents space transmogrifies back towards that during the Tubman period.

According to Khan's typology (2010: 65), the political settlement in this period remains 'competitive clientelistic'. The vertical distribution of power definitely leaves strong lower-level factions, such as the bureaucrats who continue to engage in corruption despite top-down reform. According to

---

[15] The powerbroker privileges available to well-connected Lebanese and Indian business owners did not extend to citizenship, even for those whose families had been living in the region for multiple generations (Ludwig, 2016).

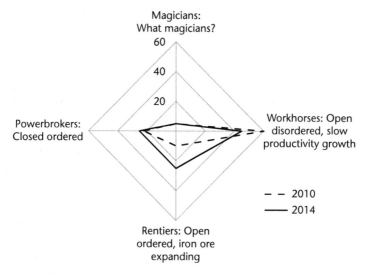

Figure 2.8. Evolution of rents space during Sirleaf episode in Liberia
Source: Authors.
Note: Dotted line depicts 2010; solid line depicts 2014.

Transparency International, in 2015 Liberia was the worst country in Africa for the percentage of responders who came into contact with public servants and paid a bribe, despite being one of the better-ranked African countries in the overall corruption perception index, suggesting a gap between top-level and on-the-ground government performance.[16]

The horizontal distribution of power also leaves strong operators outside the administration. Sirleaf's party does not have a legislative majority and there are regular challenges to the administration's work from well-known individuals. Fellow Nobel Prize winner, Leymah Gbowee, accused Sirleaf of nepotism (Allison, 2012). George Weah beat Robert Sirleaf, son of the president, in a 2014 senate race. Yet Liberia still retains a strong executive, and Sirleaf's efforts to be inclusive of potential challengers, while at the same time undertaking regular cabinet reshuffles, has made her administration assertive, if not dominant. The 2011 election is a case in point. Footballer George Weah ran again, this time as vice-presidential candidate to Harvard-educated lawyer, Winston Tubman (and nephew of the former president). When it was apparent that the Tubman/Weah ticket would lose the run-off, they boycotted the vote—claiming vote rigging—in a possible ploy to get a negotiated power-sharing arrangement (Ford, 2011). It backfired, as regional organizations and

---

[16] Respectively, <http://www.transparency.org/news/feature/corruption_in_africa_75_million_people_pay_bribes> and <http://www.transparency.org/cpi2015#results-table>, accessed 25 August 2016.

Nigerian President Goodluck Jonathan lent their support to the electoral process (*Guardian*, 2011). The next year, Sirleaf appointed Weah as Liberia's first 'Peace Ambassador', and he accepted.

The feedback loops during the Sirleaf settlement have been both positive and negative. On the positive side, the return to political stability and a legitimately elected civilian government thoroughly enabled a period of rapid economic growth. Revenue from natural resources, aid, and concessional lending has been reinvested in the state as well as public goods like infrastructure. On the negative side, the need to maintain political stability amid a period of plenty (at least through the Ebola crisis of mid-2014) has brought about new closed deals, relationship-based politics, and a return to an economic model that facilitates patronage politics over policies to serve the public interest. Liberia is thus on a knife edge in terms of whether it can engage in responsible, resource-led development and facilitate ever-opening deals, or whether the temptations of office in a rentier-driven economy lead to a continued cycle of closed deals unfavourable to broad growth, in the chokepoints of the economy.

2.4 Conclusion

Liberia went to hell and back, in a process that few foresaw, but that with hindsight seems inevitable and driven by the factors of the framework proposed by this book. Liberia's political settlement into the 1960s was that natural resources could be exploited by foreign investors in enclaves, and that the rents accruing to the state could be the basis for a political settlement, with closed ordered deals accruing to an elite large enough to maintain political order. However, ever-expanding expectations required an ever-widening patronage net; but, without any source of productive economic growth other than the resource economy, this could not be either stable (due to predictable shocks to resources) or sustained, as the growth in demands for patronage exceeded the growth of supply of sources. When the in-group tried to shift the political settlement in the 1970s and terms of trade deteriorated, the scheme exploded, opening up the regime to a coup. The challenger could build a political settlement only through exclusionary tactics that threatened the viability of the economy during the 1980s, further reducing the economic base, and was finally ousted by an insurgent. Brutal, anarchic civil war supported the 'unsettlement' of warlordism in the 1990s and early 2000s, during which power was maintained through violence, and deals were hyper-disordered. Thus we see four continuous, powerful negative feedback loops that traced Liberia's downfall, producing Olson's (2000) trajectory of state formation almost in reverse.

This experience illustrates the potentially non-linear impacts of shocks to a fragile economic and political order. Many countries experienced terms of trade shocks in the 1970s (or financing shocks in the 1980s) and did not suffer catastrophic collapse. Therefore any adequate characterization of the impact of shocks on growth has to allow for potentially amplifying negative feedback loops that set off downward spirals of near unlimited damage—whereas other countries with more robust political, economic, and social mechanisms for coping can weather equally large shocks, but with the damage limited in time and magnitude.

Outside intervention, and a lot of it, enabled a new political settlement from the mid-2000s, but old patterns were quick to reappear. They were, however, at least accompanied by rapid economic growth and pockets of political development.

Liberia's political settlement appears to have almost come full circle (Figure 2.9), from Tubman's developmental coalition to Tolbert and Doe's vulnerable authoritarian coalitions, to the competitive clientelism of the civil war and Sirleaf years.

The core hypothesis of the framework—that ordered deals drive positive economic growth episodes—is found to be true in this case study. Our historical analysis points to the reflexivity between expectations and (dis)order, further driving the relationship. When investors expected that the deals they made might not be honoured during the Doe settlement, for example, they cut back, forcing further policy changes that created further disorder.

The hypothesis that rentier- and powerbroker-based economic elites will not bring about a movement towards rule-based commerce is also found to be true. Outside the framework's predictions, we were struck by the stickiness of Liberia's rents space and therefore underlying economic interest. This does not bode well for the prospect of structural transformation. Should real structural transformation occur, we think—as with the resetting of the political settlement following the peacekeeping intervention in Liberia's civil war— that it will likely be driven by outside factors, such as wage pressures in Asia or technological changes. The one path available to policymakers is conscientiously to develop productive sectors in the magician and workhorse quadrants that could gradually alter the domestic political economy.

This chapter attempts to bring together the many insights gathered by scholars and observers of each of Liberia's growth regimes in a parsimonious framework. Despite its rapid growth, Tubman's Liberia indeed was 'without development' because of the fundamental structure of the economy and of the political settlement. Despite its reliance on resources, Liberia's civil war was not wealth-creating, but wealth-destroying, through the disorder of deals created. And despite the tremendous accomplishments of the Sirleaf regime, its continued corruption, combined with a reliance on Liberia's historical

		Horizontal excluded factions	
		Weak	*Strong*
Vertical excluded factions	*Weak*	Potential developmental coalition Tubman 1960s	Vulnerable authoritarian coalition Tolbert 1970s Doe 1980s
	Strong	Weak dominant party	Competitive clientelism Civil war 1990–2005 Sirleaf 2006–

Figure 2.9. Structure of the ruling coalition and Liberia's political settlements

Note: Table reconstructed from Khan (2010: 65), populated for Liberia based on analysis from this chapter by authors.

economic model, reveals a more powerful threat to structural transformation than poverty or low capacity alone: that the elite's fundamental interest in either political transformation or economic diversification is minimal, however noble the leader.

References

Allison, S. 2012. 'Fellow Nobel Peace Prize Winner Criticizes Ellen Johnson Sirleaf'. *Guardian*, 10 October.

Bowcott, O. 2012. 'Charles Taylor and the "Dirty-Looking Stones" Given to Naomi Campbell'. *Guardian*, 26 April.

Bowles, J., Hjort, J., Melvin, T., and Werker, E. 2016. 'Ebola, Jobs and Economic Activity in Liberia'. *Journal of Epidemiology and Community Health*, 70: 271–7.

Briggs, E. 1998. *Proud Servant: The Memoirs of a Career Ambassador*. Kent, OH: Kent State University Press.

Clower, R., Dalton, G., Harwitz, M., and Walters, A. 1966. 'Growth Without Development: An Economic Survey of Liberia'. St Evanston, IL: Northwestern University Press.

Dunn, D. E., and Tarr, S. B. 1988. *Liberia: A National Polity in Transition*. Metuchen, NJ: The Scarecrow Press.

Ellis, S. 1999. *The Mask of Anarchy: The Destruction of Liberia and the Religious Dimension of an African Civil War*. London: Hurst.

Ellis, S. 2007. *The Mask of Anarchy: The Destruction of Liberia and the Religious Dimension of an African Civil War*, 2nd edition. New York: New York University Press.

Ford, T. 2011. 'Sirleaf Victory in Liberia Marred by Boycott and Violence'. *Guardian*, 11 November.

Francois, P., Rainer, I., and Trebbi, F. 2015. 'How Is Power Shared in Africa?' *Econometrica*, 83(2): 465–503.

Gerdes, F. 2013. *Civil War and State Formation: The Political Economy of War and Peace in Liberia*. New York: Campus Verlag.

Global Witness. 2009. 'Recommendations for Future Concession Contract Negotiations and for the Consideration of the China Union Contract by the Liberian Legislature'. 13 February.

Global Witness. 2013. 'Logging in the Shadows.' 10 April.

Guardian. 2011. 'Liberia's Presidential Runoff Takes Place Amid Confusion Over Call for Boycott'. 8 November.

Harris, D. 2006. 'Liberia 2005: An Unusual African Post-Conflict Election'. *Journal of Modern African Studies*, 44(3): 375–95.

Huntington, S. 1968. *Political Order in Changing Societies*. New Haven, CT: Yale University Press.

International Crisis Group. 2002. 'Liberia: The Key to Ending Regional Instability'. Freetown: Africa Report No 43, 24 April.

Johnston, P. 2004. 'Timber Booms, State Busts: The Political Economy of Liberian Timber'. *Review of African Political Economy*, 31(101): 441–56.

Kar, S., Pritchett, L., Raihan, S., and Sen, K. 2013. *The Dynamics of Economic Growth: A Visual Handbook of Growth Rates, Regimes, Transitions and Volatility*. Manchester: University of Manchester.

Kaul, R., Heuty, A., and Norman, A. 2009. 'Getting a Better Deal from the Extractive Sector: Concession Negotiation in Liberia, 2006–2008'. New York: Revenue Watch Institute.

Khan, M. 2010. *Political Settlements and the Governance of Growth-Enhancing Institutions*. London: School of Oriental and African Studies.

Kieh, G. K. 2010. 'United States Foreign Policy and the Second Liberian Civil War'. *African Journal of International Affairs*, 13(1–3): 121–44.

Le Billon, P. 2001. 'The Political Ecology of War: Natural Resources and Armed Conflicts'. *Political Geography*, 20(5): 561–84.

Levitt, J. I. 2005. *The Evolution of Deadly Conflict in Liberia*. Durham, NC: Carolina Academic Press.

LICA. 1967. *Liberia: Open Door to Travel and Investment*. Monrovia: Liberian Department of Information and Cultural Affairs.

Ludwig, B. 2016. 'A Black Republic: Citizenship and Naturalisation Requirements in Liberia'. *Migration Letters*, 13(1): 84–99.

Lyons, T. 1999. *Voting for Peace: Postconflict Elections in Liberia*. Washington, DC: Brookings Institution Press.

Morgan, E. P. 2006. 'Liberia and the Fate of Interim Government in the Regional Vortex of West Africa'. *Strategic Insights*, 5(1).

Olson, M. 2000. *Power and Prosperity: Outgrowing Communist and Capitalist Dictatorships*. New York: Basic Books.

Outram, Q. 1997. ' "It's Terminal Either Way": An Analysis of Armed Conflict in Liberia 1989–1996'. *Review of African Political Economy*, 24(73): 355–71.

The Perspective. 2001. 'Taylor Moves to Own Minerals'. 18 January.

Pham, J. 2004. *Liberia: Portrait of a Failed State.* New York: Reed Press.

Pritchett, L., Woolcock, M., and Andrews, M. 2013. 'Looking Like a State: Techniques of Persistent Failure in State Capability for Implementation'. *Journal of Development Studies*, 49(1): 1–18.

Radelet, S. 2007. 'Reviving Economic Growth in Liberia'. Center for Global Development Working Paper 133. Washington, DC: Center for Global Development.

Reno, W. 1997. *Humanitarian Emergencies and Warlord Economies in Liberia and Sierra Leone*, No. 140. Helsinki: UNU World Institute for Development Economics Research (UNU/WIDER).

Sawyer, A. 2008. 'Emerging Patterns in Liberia's Post-Conflict Politics: Observations from the 2005 Elections'. *African Affairs*, 107(427): 177–99.

Scharff, M. 2012. 'Matching Goodwill with National Priorities: Liberia's Philanthropy Secretariat, 2008–2012'. Princeton, NJ: Innovations for Successful Societies.

Sieh, R. 2016. 'Liberia: Urey Outlines His Plans for Liberia, if Elected President'. *Front Page Africa*, 31 January.

Sirleaf, E. J. 2011. 'Annual Message to the Sixth Session of the 52nd National Legislature of the Republic of Liberia'. Delivered 24 January, Monrovia, Liberia.

UNDP (United Nations Development Programme). 2015. *Human Development Report.* <http://hdr.undp.org/sites/default/files/2015_human_development_report.pdf>.

Unger, S. J. 1981. 'Liberia: A Revolution, or Just Another Coup?' *Atlantic Monthly*, June.

Waugh, C. M. 2011. *Charles Taylor and Liberia: Ambition and Atrocity in Africa's Lone Star State.* London: Zed Books.

Werker, E. and Beganovic, J. 2011a. 'Liberia: A Case Study'. Paper presented at the International Growth Centre Workshop on Growth in Fragile States, Oxford, UK.

Werker, E. and Beganovic, J. 2011b. 'Liberia'. Harvard Business School case 712011.

3

Powerbrokers and Patronage

Why Malawi Has Failed to Structurally Transform and Deliver Inclusive Growth

Jonathan Said and Khwima Singini

3.1 Introduction

Between 1954 and 2012 Malawi experienced four growth regimes: stagnation prior to independence in 1964; then a long episode of growth acceleration; and then a longer episode of sharp deceleration; with a weak growth acceleration episode currently playing itself out since 2003. During this entire period, Malawi failed to structurally transform its economy and deliver broad-based inclusive growth. We explain the reasons for this through an analysis of the relationship between the political settlement, the deals space, and the rents space, and how these interplayed and evolved.

The literature so far has largely focused either on Malawi's political settlement (Harrigan, 2001; Booth et al., 2006; Cammack et al., 2010) or on economic drivers of growth (Stambuli, 2002; Lea and Hanmer, 2009; Ngwira, 2012). This chapter adds the deals and rents spaces, thus allowing for a combined analysis of the political settlement, informal institutions, and the sources of economic rents. This is helpful to deepen our understanding of the underlying drivers at play and to provide more insight as to why the democratization of Malawi in 1994 has so far failed to deliver structural transformation and inclusive growth.

We conclude that Malawi's lack of structural transformation is the result of two unfavourable combinations. First, between 1964 and 1994 Malawi had a dominant party political settlement with a flawed long-term developmental vision. This vision led to a growth acceleration up to the late 1970s, but then unravelled itself due to the patronage system introduced by Hastings Banda that stood at its heart. This system focused on rentiers and powerbrokers in the rents space, while actively undermining workhorses and magicians. Second, from 1994 to date, the combination of a competitive clientelist political system—which took hold with the introduction of a multiparty democratic system—and a rents space in which rentiers and powerbrokers continued to entrench Malawi's patronage system, prevented a new long-term developmental vision from taking hold and prevented the lessons from Banda's time from being learnt. In turn, this has prevented the structural reforms necessary to allow both workhorses and magicians to achieve growth at scale and to drive structural transformation and inclusive growth.

These combinations of the political settlement and the rents space have prevented structural transformation in three ways. First, rentiers, though exporting, are low in economic complexity, with minimal economic incentive for innovation and diversification (tobacco and tea). Second, powerbrokers are largely importation or captive market businesses that combine with government services to provide rents for political elites (maize input supply, construction, transport, poultry, and finance). The combination of a rentier- and powerbroker-based patronage system has kept the deals space largely closed, despite varying phases of orderliness and disorderliness in deal-making between political and business elites. So, third, political elites have had limited incentives since the 1980s to develop state capacity, because rentiers and powerbrokers do not require it to accumulate rents. In asking for tax breaks and preferential licences rather than the removal of binding constraints for value addition or the improved quality of government services, the demands of the political elite require a closed orderly deals space that can be provided without much state capacity.

Malawi remains stuck with an unfavourable combination of a competitive clientelist system and a patronage system dependent on powerbrokers and rentiers. The near-constant politics of re-election, succession, and patronage-seeking continue to take the upper hand over a long-term developmental vision. More complex government services and programmes that are needed to address the structural challenges faced by workhorses, which includes the vast majority of Malawians, and by magicians, where higher economic complexity lies, remain largely unaddressed.

Nonetheless, while still in their infancy relative to the welfare needs of the country, state capability, workhorses, and magicians are gradually developing. This is driven by three factors: technology improvement (for example agricultural yield improvements or access to mobile phones); regional integration (new entrants into magician sectors); and predictable aid (better infrastructure). Positive, though short-lived, feedback loops in the deals space—for example Bingu wa Mutharika's response to constant drought and crop failure under Bakili Muluzi; and an increased emphasis on magicians since 2013 following the 2012 foreign exchange crisis—help to a certain degree, but are too short to have a large-scale impact on structural transformation.

3.2 Overview of Growth and Structural Transformation

Malawi's economic growth since 1954 is characterized by four regimes: (a) stagnation between 1954 and 1964; (b) growth acceleration between 1965 and 1978; (c) GDP per capita decline between 1979 and 2002; and (d) growth acceleration between 2003 and 2012. The growth of real GDP per capita from 1954 to 2010 is shown in Figure 3.1. There were three structural breaks in Malawi's growth path between 1954 and 2012 (Kar et al., 2013). These are indicated in Figure 3.1 and occurred in 1964, 1978, and 2002.

In the period of economic stagnation prior to 1964, Malawi was adjoined to modern-day Zimbabwe and Zambia, forming the Federation of Rhodesia and Nyasaland. Its economy was largely dependent on limited external colonial support. The primary British focus was on modern-day Zimbabwe, followed by modern-day Zambia and its copper. Nyasaland was the backwater.

The British pound was used as currency during this period (Pauw et al., 2013). The pound was extensively overvalued, given Malawi's trading position and its

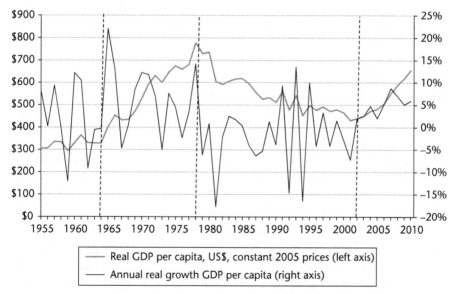

Figure 3.1. History of Malawi's GDP per capita (1955–2010) with growth breaks filtered from four possible Bai–Perron breaks

Source: Penn World Tables 7.1—PPP converted GDP per capita (chain series), at 2005 constant prices.

limited capacity to export. Fiscal policy was also ill-suited, with most expenditure concentrated in modern-day Zimbabwe. Infrastructure investment had
stalled by the 1950s—the main item of infrastructure was the railways built in
the early 1900s for the extraction of raw crops, largely tobacco, tea, and coffee.

In 1964, Malawi entered a growth acceleration regime that lasted until 1978.
Malawi attained independence that year under the leadership of Banda, who
assumed a dualistic development policy that balanced active government
interventions with targeted private-sector leaders in strategic sectors. He
selectively identified strategic partners to enforce growth in rentier sectors to
be sectoral pace-setters in technology, innovation, and quality control. These
pace-setters also had the capacity to attract investment. Such companies
included Lonhro (formerly owned by the Tiny Roland family) in sugar, the
Conforzi family in tea, David Whitehead in textiles, and Limbe Leaf in
tobacco. This came at a time when the production of commodities such as
tobacco became more cost-effective in developing, rather than developed,
countries. Investment in tobacco was well-coordinated, with constraints on
land, extension services, market linkages, research, and transport all being
addressed through public and private players in the sector.

The government promoted agricultural development through estate farming models. Its policies supported large-scale agriculture, awarding preferential
access to land, investment, and credit. It established a monopoly state marketing board—the Agricultural Development and Marketing Corporation
(ADMARC)—that channelled profits into the estate sector and subsidized
investments in industry. During this period the production of estates grew at
an average annual rate of 17 per cent, while smallholder production grew at
3 per cent (Ngwira, 2012). The government supported this development
policy through a fixed exchange rate regime that undervalued the Malawi
Kwacha. This supported higher rates of savings (Simwaka et al., 2012).

The government also created a major, dominant powerbroker firm. Press
Corporation dominated a number of domestic sectors: retail, wholesale, oil
distribution, property, banking, insurance, ranching, pharmaceuticals, and
transport. It also invested in tobacco. At its peak it accounted for one-third
of Malawi's GDP and employed 10 per cent of the wage-earning workforce
(Meredith, 2006). Banda's plan included a symbiotic relationship between
Press Corporation and ADMARC, the former in agriculture and production,
and the latter in marketing. Smallholder farmers were largely excluded.

The government's centralized approach to development policy allowed
Malawi to exploit its existing support structures, such as its rail and road
network. Malawi exported 95 per cent of its products through the Mozambican
ports of Nacala and Beira (Lea and Hanmer, 2009). From 1964 to the late
1970s, the increase in rentier-based exports corresponded to the growth in
GDP per capita (see Figure 3.2). During this period, annual average real growth

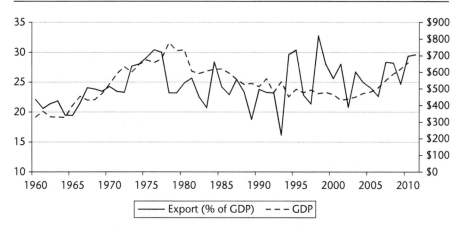

Figure 3.2. Percentage of exports (left axis) and GDP per capita in Malawi in US dollar prices (right axis)

Source: *Penn World Tables*—PPP converted GDP per capita (chain series), at 2005 constant prices and World Bank, *World Development Indicators*.

exceeded 5 per cent, and over the whole period GDP per capita more than doubled (Booth et al., 2006). Real GDP per capita peaked in 1977 at US$778.

Malawi's third growth regime ran from 1978 to 2002, and is one of sharp deceleration that saw a decline in Malawi's Economic Complexity Index to −1.72 in 1982 and to an all-time low of −1.88 in 2000.[1] Real GDP per capita slumped to US$431 in 2001 after twenty-three years of decline.

Following the 1973 oil price shock, commodity prices fell in the late 1970s and Malawi's terms of trade declined by 43 per cent from 1980 to 2002. As world demand declined, credit became more expensive internationally. This hit Malawi's rentier sectors hard and estate bankruptcies followed, which induced a domestic banking liquidity crisis (Cammack et al., 2010). Similarly, South African demand for migrant labour declined, reducing Malawian remittance incomes. In 1977, civil war broke out in neighbouring Mozambique and lasted until 1992. Access to the ports of Beira and Nacala was blocked. Transport costs shot up as exports were diverted to Tanzania and South Africa, via Zambia and Zimbabwe. The Mozambican civil war resulted in an influx of over one million refugees into Malawi, equivalent to 10 per cent of Malawi's population, placing a large strain on public expenditure.

The start of structural adjustment (e.g. through the partial decontrol of prices of some commodities in 1983), a severe drought in 1979–80, bad

---

[1] The decline in the index in the late 1970s and 1980s was also a result of a decline in the global score for a number of products which Malawi exported, such as tobacco and legumes, as the rise in commodity prices shifted the production of such crops from developed economies to less-developed economies. *The Atlas of Economic Complexity*, MIT media lab, Country Profile Malawi. <http://atlas.media.mit.edu/en/profile/country/mwi/>.

weather conditions in 1981, food shortages, and the closure of the most cost-effective rail routes also contributed to this growth regime. The government maintained a fixed exchange rate regime, but resorted to constant devaluations and fiscal deficits on the back of its efforts to fund welfare expenditure. The cumulative effect of all these factors manifested themselves in an inflation rate of 83 per cent in 1995 after it had been maintained at around 10 per cent in the 1960s and 1970s (Naferankhande and Ndhlovu, 2006).

This growth regime is ultimately characterized by four underlying structural constraints that had developed gradually over time since the 1960s, but emerged on the back of these external shocks, on the gradual liberalization of the economy, and on ageing Banda's loss of interest in economic policy in the 1980s (Cammack et al., 2010).[2] These were: weak and deteriorating state capacity; the exclusion of the majority of the population from the productive economy due to the estate-based nature of agriculture; the dependency on rentiers for exports; and the closed nature of the deals space. These exposed the fundamental weakness in Banda's development strategy in the 1960s and 1970s.

In the 1990s, the government continued the gradual liberalization of the agricultural sector. In 1996, the Special Crops Act was repealed, allowing smallholder farmers to export crops (Diagne and Zeller, 2001). This led to a large shift in smallholder production, from nearly nothing in 1990 to around 70 per cent of total production of export crops in 2009 (Lea and Hanmer, 2009), reflecting a surge in the workhorse share of GDP.

When multiparty democracy commenced and Muluzi became president in 1994, the already weak and demoralized civil service continued to weaken, due to less centralized corruption, political appointments, and poor wages (Cammack, 2010). This made it difficult for the state to implement development and poverty-alleviation policies. The spread of HIV/AIDS and fiscal ill-discipline reduced capacity even further. Debt undermined spending on services (Cammack, 2010). Public services and infrastructure deteriorated, the inability to deal with poor rains and drought increased, corruption with impunity increased, and anti-corruption institutions were handicapped by the regime. Private investment slowed in the late 1990s as the lending rate increased from 17 per cent in 1980 to 56 per cent in 2001 (see Figure 3.3). Donors recognized these weaknesses, but did not cut aid between 1994 and 2001 in their support of a new democracy in Africa, and in order to avoid a collapse of the economy[3] (Cammack, 2010).

---

[2] Some observers and visitors claimed in the 1980s that he did not appear astute enough to his government all of the time and that he seemed uninterested in the details of development policy (Pryor, 1990).

[3] When asked why donors gave money to Muluzi, the head of the IMF in 2005 said that this was because there was going to be economic meltdown and the government was doing nothing about it.

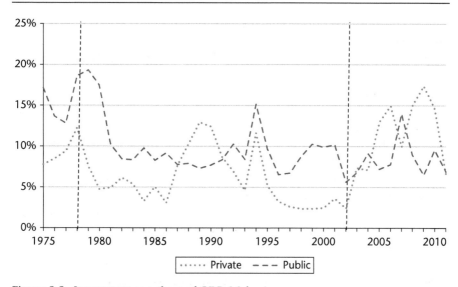

Figure 3.3. Investment as a share of GDP, Malawi

Source: World Bank, *World Development Indicators*, and Reserve Bank of Malawi. Measured as the ratio of gross fixed capital formation to GDP.

Malawi entered a growth acceleration regime from 2003 to 2012. This period benefited from a move to more orderly deals with the election of Mutharika in 2004. He brought in a former IMF economist as the minister of finance, who set sound macroeconomic policies and opened up to the private sector by strengthening public–private dialogue.

The change in government served as an encouraging basis for a number of growth factors to kick in from 2004. First was the return of development partners, following aid being cut in 2002 until the ousting of Muluzi. If debt relief is added to official development assistance, total aid inflows equalled 93 per cent of GDP in 2006 and 50 per cent in 2007, according to the OECD's aid database (OECD, 2013).

Second, the introduction of a large fertilizer and seed subsidy programme and the gains made in the health sector, particularly in HIV/AIDS, supported the acceleration. The introduction of the Farm Inputs Subsidy Programme proved successful in preventing droughts and famines that had plagued Malawi right up to 2005, and allowed Malawi to create a maize surplus for the first time in almost two decades (Chinsinga, 2012).

Third, good rains in Mutharika's first term, something Muluzi did not enjoy in his two terms, and a boom in the tobacco sector and other cash crops, also contributed to the growth acceleration.

Fourth, a key factor behind the growth acceleration from 2006 onward was the fixing of the exchange rate above market equilibrium, resulting in a sharp decrease in inflation and a boom in consumption—mostly of imported goods—as evidenced by the rapid increase in Malawi's trade deficit, which rose from 7 per cent in 2001 to 21 per cent in 2010.

Things changed in Mutharika's second term. The combination of an over-valued fixed exchange rate, a structural trade deficit, in which Malawi imported double what it exported in 2010, and the cutting of aid following a reversal of Mutharika's development stance to one aimed at electing his brother in 2014, led to a foreign exchange crisis in 2011. This brought about a deceleration in growth to 1.8 per cent that year from 9 per cent in 2008. Growth recovered in 2013.

In summary, Malawi has failed to structurally transform its economy over the past fifty years. It remains highly dependent on the export of tobacco. In 1995, tobacco accounted for 68 per cent of all goods exports, rising from 41 per cent in 1965. Its share of goods exports remained at 58 per cent in 2010. The dependence on tobacco and tea contributed to Malawi's lack of structural transformation over the past five decades, because companies invested in these rentier sectors had little incentive to innovate and expand into new sectors, due to the relatively high cost of developing new products compared with their existing business model (Government of Malawi, 2012).

3.3 Evolution of Malawi's Deals Space, Rents Space, and Political Settlement

This section analyses the evolution of Malawi's political settlement, its deals space, and its rents space, in order to bring out feedback loops between the three and the role they played in the growth story presented in Section 3.2. Figure 3.4 sets out Malawi's growth regimes relative to its political leaders.

3.3.1 *Economic Stagnation: 1954–64*

The period of stagnation at this time came about because of a lack of infra-structure investment—which by the 1950s had all but dried up—a lack of fiscal expenditure, and ill-suited monetary policy. Despite a strong dominant party regime, with colonialism in its dying years, deals were closed and disorderly, and this led to stagnation of GDP per capita at a very low base.

3.3.2 *Growth Acceleration: 1964–78*

In 1964, Malawi achieved independence and assumed a strong dominant party system that lasted until 1978. Political elites rallied behind its new leader, Hastings Banda, in a newly independent African country.

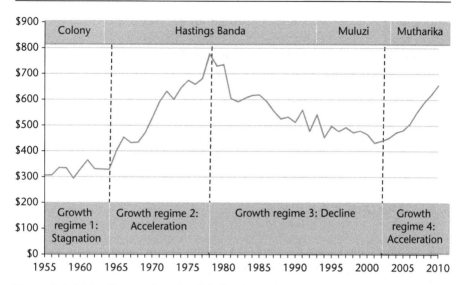

Figure 3.4. Malawi's growth and political regimes
Source: *Penn World Tables 7.1*—PPP converted GDP per capita (chain series), at 2005 constant prices.

Banda promoted a long-term developmental vision based on attracting rentiers in each major export sector of the economy, while setting up a large dominating powerbroker. This entrenched Malawi's economic structure that has lasted to the present day. Selected investors in tobacco, tea, sugar, textiles, and other rentier industries enjoyed privileged access to the president, who, guided by their expertise, used the public sector to deliver the factors necessary for investment and growth. His closest ally was apartheid South Africa, which invested in Malawi's infrastructure, including the construction of the new capital, Lilongwe.

To survive as president, Banda also built a patronage system that promoted loyalty and made clients dependent on his largesse (Harrigan, 2001). His form of clientelism fitted with his conservative, capitalist, support-the-strong development policy, in that he provided benefits such as land, credit, and training to favourites, based on his unfulfilled expectation that this would create a middle class that would develop the nation (Cammack, 2010). The main thrust of Banda's development policy was to generate capital for reinvestment through the agricultural and manufacturing sectors, such that access to these rent-earning opportunities provided Banda with a useful fund of political patronage (Frankenberger et al., 2003). At independence, agriculture was divided into a small 'estate' sector and a much larger smallholder sector. Banda converted customary land to leasehold farms for commercially oriented smallholders, which were subsequently classified as 'estates' and licensed to grow tobacco. In this way, a few privileged Malawians were granted customary land and so joined the largely expatriate estate (tea, tobacco, and coffee) sector, then responsible for most of the country's exports (Stambuli, 2002). According to Cammack et al. (2010: 10), 'Building on colonial development thinking, Banda thus fostered the creation of an elite class of Malawians that he thought would spearhead agricultural development and national growth while excluding those individuals deemed to be less productive.'

Therefore this period is characterized by a strong dominant party that provided a closed but orderly deals space for rentiers and powerbrokers, but left the space disorderly for workhorses and magicians.

3.3.3 *Sharp Deceleration: 1978–2003*

1978–94

The lack of openness and the nature of Banda's patronage system meant that growth in the first part of Banda's rule prevented inclusive, broad-based growth, which in turn created a negative feedback loop on the rents space and on the political settlement. The majority of the population (80 per cent) was unable to participate in the productive economy and benefit from the wealth it generated, such that their demands for food security, healthcare, education, and public services could not be satisfied by the nature of the growth Banda provided. This strengthened the push for liberalization and structural adjustment by civil society and development partners, which in turn placed Banda's patronage and rent-capturing structure under threat. The lack of sustainability in the nature of growth achieved before 1979—which failed to deliver a middle class—and the succession politics that it led to, contributed to deteriorating institutions that prevented Malawi from addressing a number of structural constraints, leading to a decline in GDP per capita in the 1980s (Cammack et al., 2010):

> Economic restructuring under the tutelage of the IMF and World Bank disrupted in significant ways the system for channelling rents that had worked, with limitations, under Banda [in 1964 to 1978]. The policy of reforming the estate sector to reduce subsidies and make it more competitive, together with the shift against import-substitution industrialization, heralded a major change in the types of rent-creation and distribution that could be encouraged. (Cammack et al., 2010: 20)

Therefore the lack of sustainability in Banda's developmental vision, due to its marginalization of workhorses and magicians, provided a window for development partners to temporarily undo Banda's rent system, turning the political settlement into a weak authoritarian dominant party system. This negative feedback loop came about because, as the economy and markets opened up, the position of elites came under threat, and succession politics emerged for the first time. Banda's deputy, John Tembo, dominated through the 1980s—but was later undone, first by the Church, who turned against the regime due to weak government services, famine, and drought, and then by Muluzi's camp within Banda's party—the Malawi Congress Party (MCP). Muluzi represented those who had been sidelined by Tembo in the 1980s.

Succession politics led to a deterioration of institutional capacity, a lack of development policy, and a return to disordered deals in the second half of Banda's thirty-year term as president. Since the private productive sector lacked the capacity to compete in sectors beyond tobacco, tea, sugar, and coffee, fiscal revenues and public sector wages declined, while debt increased. The civil service lost its ability to address market and coordination failures and to supply welfare services to the burgeoning population. Disorder increased for rentiers as state capacity to support them dwindled, such that they failed to expand. While suffering on the back of weaker macroeconomic indicators, order largely remained for powerbrokers, epitomized by Press Corporation and its sustained control of various captive markets.

1994–2002

In 1994, Malawi transitioned to a competitive clientelist political settlement, following the launch of a multiparty democracy. Muluzi won the elections of 1994 and then again those of 1999. The deals space opened up, particularly for medium- and large-scale private traders, but also for smallholder farmers, who became eligible to trade in cash crops following the repealing of the Special Crops Act, though their rents were negligible.

However, the deals space also became more disorderly than prior to multi-party democracy, for two reasons. First was the combination of Muluzi's economic and political approach. His economic approach was free-for-all trade without any effort to account for market failures. Muluzi was a trading businessman who emerged from the Malawi Confederation of Chambers of Commerce and Industry (MCCCI). The business elite who supported Muluzi were essentially traders who made their rents by importing consumables such as fertilizers, fuel, and various consumer goods previously not available in Malawi. Muluzi's politics favoured his religion, ethnic background, and region, in order to build the patronage structure he deemed necessary to win multiparty elections in a competitive clientelist political settlement.

This combination led to a surge in corruption surrounding government contracts and an increase in the mismanagement of state resources. Politically connected business elites, such as Kalaria, benefited from insider knowledge and illegal deals. Although initially Muluzi followed donor advice and relied on advisors who prioritized development, within a few years he had surrounded himself with politicians who had an interest in short-term gains and aimed to use state resources, aid, and the development process to stay in power and get rich (Cammack, 2011). Many government contracts were given to powerbroker companies, who did not fulfil the requirements to deliver on those deals. Similarly, Muluzi was accused of exporting Malawi's maize reserves in 2001 for personal gain, shortly before the onset of a drought which resulted in a famine.

The second reason for the increase in disorderliness was the illegal dismantling of Press Corporation, which was divested for political reasons because it was the basis of support for John Tembo. Development partners liked this, as they saw Press Corporation as dominating sectors and preventing other firms from growing. However, in doing this they missed the fact that the indigenous class lacked the capacity to fill the Press Corporation gap, thus increasing the disorderly nature of deals. Powerbrokers therefore suffered in the mid-1990s, although Muluzi's own band of powerbrokers—such as Kalaria—would soon emerge to take up captive markets lost by Press Corporation.

These two factors combined to further weaken macroeconomic management and to sustain a lack of government strategic direction and coordination, which in turn led to economic instability and continued indebtedness. The disorderly nature of the rents space meant that there was minimal new investment. In the later Muluzi years, order returned for powerbrokers, but these had little interest in investing, given the trade-based nature of their rents. Traditional rent-generating sectors (tobacco, tea, and sugar) were not complemented by new growth sectors, leading to stagnation in the export-oriented side of the rents space and thus for workhorses too.

However, this outcome led to a positive feedback loop. When Muluzi tried to alter the constitution in 2002, so that he could stand for a third term, donors cut aid, despite the risk of economic meltdown and persistent famine. Muluzi then relied on Muslim funding and his main business associates to support his election campaigns. But a block by the national assembly and public demonstrations against Muluzi—which epitomized Muluzi's inability to keep the patronage system under control, due to disorderly deals—prevented constitutional change and forced Muluzi to appoint a successor as his party's presidential candidate in the 2004 elections.

3.3.4 *Weak Growth Acceleration: 2003 Onwards*

2003–9

In 2004, Mutharika defeated John Tembo, although Mutharika did not win a majority of seats in parliament. The party undertook extensive political manoeuvring to form a government of national unity that included several opposition parties. In 2005, Mutharika left Muluzi's party, citing his anti-corruption campaign, and formed a new party called the Democratic Progressive Party (DPP). A number of ministers and politicians transitioned to the new party, epitomizing the ongoing strength of clientelism in Malawi's political system.

This period of growth acceleration was kick-started by the birth of the uranium mining sector, which expanded by 23 per cent in 2003. The return of aid following Muluzi-free elections, debt relief, and good rains also helped.

Yet the acceleration phase was primarily driven by the more orderly, and to a certain extent more open, deals space under Mutharika. This allowed the economy to start benefiting from the structural adjustment policies that had commenced in the 1980s, but had so far yielded no returns. The lack of growth and the disorderly nature of deals during Muluzi's time gave Mutharika a platform to distance himself from Muluzi. It gave him the capacity to strengthen his patronage base by delivering growth, while at the same time expanding his personal wealth, in a similar vein as Hastings Banda in the 1960s and 1970s.

Mutharika was able to consolidate corruption at the centre of government. He centralized rent-seeking activities at the top of government, such that contracts, though given out through corrupt practices, were better supervised and controlled. Rampant corruption and the creation of rents for patronage purposes were reduced (Cammack et al., 2010), thus benefiting powerbrokers and rentiers. Companies were expected to perform against a contract, unlike in Muluzi's time, in return for a long-term relationship with the president, whom they would bankroll.

Mutharika also followed Banda's lead in identifying strategic partners to support him for his re-election campaigns. These were primarily Chinese mining and infrastructure investors, Paladin Mining, Mully Brothers, and Mota-Engil—who won most road construction and rehabilitation projects, and who are also building a new railway line, funded by mining company Vale, joining Tete in Mozambique to the Nacala railway. Powerbrokers Mully Brothers benefited from the distribution of fertilizers under Mutharika's national patronage system—the Farm Input Subsidy Programme for the country's staple crop, maize. This programme also represented an improvement in the orderliness of the rents space for workhorses for the first time.

This equation allowed political elites at the top of government to be committed to economic growth and hence led to ordered deals, which spurred investment and growth. Growth peaked at 9 per cent in 2009.

2009–12

In time, the rents space started to close, entrenching itself more and more around Mutharika's strategic business partners, as he tried to assume Hastings Banda's developmental vision. Mutharika won the 2009 election by a landslide against a newly formed Muluzi–Tembo alliance, on the back of his Farm Input Subsidy Programme, which allowed him to capture both powerbrokers and workhorses. Mutharika's objective shifted away from growth towards personal wealth and succession. He had no reason to fear parliament and the opposition, as he had in his first term, and his own policies emerged more clearly (Cammack et al., 2010). He did not need to balance growth with the efforts to develop his patronage base. Autocratic tendencies that surfaced in a muted fashion between 2004 and 2009, controlled by a desire to outperform Muluzi, emerged more forcefully, having secured growth and a positive response by the electorate.

As in the first half of Banda's presidency, growth secured in the first phase led to a negative feedback loop: economic growth and food security between 2004 and 2009 led to an easy election victory, which gave Mutharika the comfort he needed to be able to focus on succession—required by the competitive clientelist settlement—and on building his patronage and wealth. In 2013, it emerged that Mutharika's private assets increased from approximately US$1 million on his election in 2004 to approximately US$150 million at his death in 2012 (*Nyasa Times*, 2013a).

Mutharika also maintained an overvalued fixed exchange rate to finance his Farm Input Subsidy Programme and to support import-based powerbrokers and workhorses. This, and the ongoing neglect of magicians, resulted in a foreign exchange crisis in 2010 and 2011, which led to a disorderly rents space. Together with Mutharika's efforts to move to closed deals, this caused real annual economic growth to decline from a peak of 9 per cent in 2009 to 1.9 per cent in 2012. Malawi experienced chronic shortages of fuel, fertilizer, medicine, and other imported inputs and consumables. Mutharika also entered into conflict with the tobacco sector, still the country's main foreign exchange earner, arriving at a point where he expelled two managing directors of major tobacco companies. Some tobacco companies left, deeming Malawi too risky and reflecting disorder in the rents space for certain rentiers (order remained in the mining and cotton rentier sectors). Increasingly autocratic tendencies in the management of governance and of development assistance led to the British high commissioner being expelled in 2011, which in turn prompted donors to cut aid that year.

2012 ONWARD

While grooming his brother Peter to take over from him, Mutharika died in April 2012. His vice president, Joyce Banda, who had been forced out of the party after falling out with Mutharika, assumed the presidency on the back of positive feedback loops from the disorder of Mutharika's second term. Economic strife drove the army and the minister of justice to intervene to put an end to an attempted coup d'état by Peter Mutharika. A large number of party members abandoned the DPP and joined Joyce Banda's Peoples' Party, reflecting the persistent strength of Malawi's clientelist patronage system.

The initial days of Joyce Banda's presidency, which started in 2012, saw a return to an orderly deals space for all categories of the rents space, with the reversal of distortionary policies, such as the freeing up of the exchange rate, and the return of budget support aid, which was cut in 2011. This was driven by a reaction to the acute foreign exchange crisis Malawi had experienced in 2010 and 2011. Joyce Banda adopted an Economic Recovery Plan to give the perception of economic direction and reinstated an IMF-extended credit facility.

Yet, with elections looming in 2014, her focus soon switched to securing her patronage base, which was necessary for her to survive in a competitive clientelist political settlement. Once again, this led to disorderly deals. While she attempted to open up dialogue with the private sector and institute some reforms, her electoral strategy followed the patronage approach of her predecessors, but without sufficient control mechanisms. This consisted of handouts of maize, seed, fertilizer, goats, and cows to poor communities across the country, but also of state pilfering. By November 2013, the total value of the pilfering and false contracting was estimated at US$155 million, or 4 per cent of GDP (*Telegraph*, 2013). Aid was cut again and budget support, which accounted for 41 per cent of the national budget in 2013–14, was frozen indefinitely in November 2013.

Joyce Banda lost the 2014 elections to Mutharika's brother, Peter, who became Malawi's fifth president. Her electoral strategy failed largely because of a corruption scandal in 2013 that implicated her (*Nyasa Times*, 2013b) and went public (for which the Internet and media were critical), the rise in maize prices in 2013, the continued allegiance of workhorse smallholder farmers to Mutharika due to the Farm Input Subsidy Programme, and the fact that the bureaucracy and patronage system remained allied to Peter Mutharika, which gave him a strong handle on the electoral process. The Electoral Commission became convinced of the need for a recount of votes, following anomalies in the first official count. But, while the law allowed the commission to recount, it did not provide for a time extension for the publication of results. The court announced this with one hour and thirty minutes left before results had to be published, leaving no room for a recount and an official victory for Peter Mutharika. Mutharika won, with 36 per cent of the vote, ahead of the MCP candidate, with 27 per cent. Joyce Banda got 20 per cent. Mutharika won in the south, MCP in the central region, and Joyce Banda in the north, reflecting the regional nature of the patronage system.

3.4 The Nature of Deals in the Rents Space

We estimate Malawi's rents space in 2013 to be distributed as follows: 41 per cent of GDP is captured by powerbroker sectors; 34 per cent by workhorses; 21 per cent by rentiers; and 4 per cent by magicians (see Figure 3.5). This has

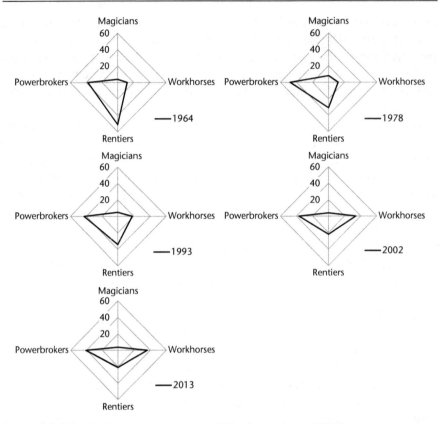

Figure 3.5. Distribution of rents space in Malawi, as a share of GDP

Source: Author estimations.

Notes: *Magicians* have fluctuated between 4 per cent and 8 per cent, reflecting lack of importance in the patronage system, both under dominant party and competitive clientist political settlements. *Workhorses* started at 12 per cent of economy in 1964, despite including vast majority of population. Gradual increase as deals space has slowly opened and become more orderly, though orderliness has only started improving since 2004. *Powerbrokers* stable throughout all regimes, around 40 per cent of economy. They survived on back of patronage system, which guarantees a degree of orderly deals, with some turbulence in the 1990s. *Rentiers* started at 52 per cent at independence. Gradual decline to 20 percent of economy today, reflects limited scope for growth and closed deals space.

deteriorated slightly when compared with 2002, when powerbrokers accounted for 37 per cent of GDP, workhorses 36 per cent, rentiers 22 per cent, and magicians 4 per cent. In 1978, powerbrokers accounted for 48 per cent of the economy and workhorses only 12 per cent. Rentiers accounted for 31 per cent and magicians 8 per cent. We estimate that in 1964 rentiers accounted for 52 per cent of the economy, reflecting the colonial legacy, while powerbrokers accounted for 38 per cent, with workhorses at 12 per cent, and magicians at 4 per cent. Magicians, who have relatively high economic complexity and are key for structural transformation, have remained weak throughout this period.

Following the advent of multiparty democracy, workhorses have come to occupy a larger share of the economy, largely at the expense of rentiers, who have limited scope for growth, while powerbrokers continue their domination on the back of Malawi's entrenched patronage system. We now discuss evolution of the nature of the deals in the rents space.

3.4.1 *Magicians: Competitive and Export-Oriented*

Magicians persist in small numbers in the agricultural, light manufacturing, and accommodation and travel sectors. Most of these players are small- and medium-sized businesses that have a more formal relationship with government and limited access to the deals space. Some deals are made on matters of business and export licensing, access to seeds, extension services, tax, electricity connection, water access, etc.

Agro-processing and other forms of manufacturing are generally dominated by the Malawian-Indian community who were evicted from rural areas in the 1970s—thus causing their deals space to become disorderly. It remained so through the 1990s. It has gradually become more orderly, but these firms largely try to keep government and politicians at arm's length. Such companies have limited relations to the political elite and rely on the MCCCI to represent them on issues such as tax, energy, and water supply, though many feel they cannot rely on the MCCCI to represent their interests.

Many companies of this type are based in sectors that have relatively higher economic complexity in the product space, such as manufacturers of food and dairy products, beverages, plastics, packaging, and welding. Such companies are less reliant on government contracts or natural resources than they are on foreign exchange availability, an efficient tax system, the cost of transport to markets, the cost of finance, and access to energy. Although gradually improving, as epitomized by an increased focus on exports following the foreign exchange crisis of 2011, the government continues to struggle to enforce formal and informal agreements here, unless the implementation of the agreement is solely dependent on the actions of senior politicians. This suggests a gradual improvement in orderliness and openness of the deals space for magicians, while remaining, on balance, largely disorderly and closed, mainly because Malawi's competitive clientelist political system is impeding the emergence of a long-term development vision.

While possibly being held back by democratization, the slow gradual growth of magicians is driven by external factors, such as technological, infrastructure, and human capital improvements and regional integration. However, many binding constraints and coordination failures remain. This is due to their exclusion from the patronage system and the generally disorderly and closed nature of their deals space.

3.4.2 Workhorses: Competitive and Domestic-Oriented

This category includes the vast majority of Malawians who participate in the economy as subsistence and smallholder farmers, retailers, and providers of small-scale services such as hairdressing, cooking, and tailoring. Deals are largely characterized by maize and legume fertilizer subsidies, the maize market itself, various domestic crop markets accessing transportation services and extension services, accessing seed, securing business permits, and evading tax.

Their deals space was largely closed and disorderly in the time of Hastings Banda. In his first fifteen years in power, he favoured estate-based agriculture and state-based trading. The Special Crops Act, which was repealed in 1996, marginalized workhorses, and in his last fifteen years in power structural reforms and the decline in economic growth meant that it became much harder to access basic government services and support programmes. Similarly, numerous droughts, crop failures, and famines set in. Most workhorses lacked access to deal makers, thus making the deals space both closed and disorderly.

With the advent of multiparty democracy, the deals space became much more open, following the liberalization of numerous markets, including the primary cash crop, tobacco, and agricultural trading. However, deals remain disorderly because of the continued limited state capability to provide government services, to provide land titling, and to deliver support programmes.

In 2003, the deals space continued to open up, with some 1.6 million farmers becoming eligible for support under the Farm Input Subsidy Programme. This programme suggested an improvement in the orderliness of the deals space for workhorses and was a key benefit of a competitive clientelist system. It complements gradually improving access to government services through slight improvements in state capability. Similarly, while formal land titling and property rights remain weak, there has been increased recognition and protection of smallholder land rights through the strengthening of civil society. The deals space for workhorses returned to disorderliness in 2011 on the back of the foreign exchange crisis that drove up the cost of essential imported items.

3.4.3 Rentiers: High Rent and Export-Oriented

The deals space for rentiers was closed but orderly under Hastings Banda as he favoured few strategic partners—one per major sector—in the form of agriculture and forestry estate concessions, and manufacturing companies. The deals space for rentiers became more disorderly in Hastings' latter years as the state became incapacitated on the back of structural adjustment and political upheaval. This disorderliness continued in Muluzi's first term, as corruption became more rampant and the government's capacity to follow up on deals weakened further.

However, mining concessions signed since 1999 suggest that a degree of orderliness returned in this particular sector. Deals have been informal since then, due to a weak institutional framework for the sector, which the government is gradually trying to fix. From 2003 onward, the orderliness of mining deals has increased, with better capacity of the government to follow through on its side of deals made. Similarly, the governments of Mutharika and Joyce Banda maintained a very close working relationship with mining concessions, including Chinese explorers, as a key source of rents.

Similarly, the cotton rentier sector has been able to increase the orderliness of its deals with government by securing ever-more government support in Mutharika and Joyce Banda's presidencies, while keeping the sector fairly closed and oligopolistic. While mining scores low on economic complexity, cotton scores better, but Malawi lacks the cost competitiveness to be able to compete externally.

Yet, despite the opening up of mining and support for cotton, no new agricultural and forestry concessions have been signed, suggesting a continuously closed deals space and limited scope for growth. This has remained true to the present day, largely because multiparty democracy brought about an increased awareness and protection of subsistence and smallholder farmer rights to access land.

The tobacco and tea sectors have seen a gradual increase in disorderliness as other rentiers (mining) have become more central to the patronage system of the political elite in recent years. Yet companies in sectors such as tobacco and tea still remain large enough to have direct ministerial and presidential access on an informal basis when issues arise with government bureaucrats that threaten their business, such as fraudulent labour cases or delayed licences. Political interest in such sectors is generally not based on personal patronage, but on national priorities, such as foreign exchange generation, donor conditions, or minimum prices.

3.4.4 *Powerbrokers: High Rent, Weak Competition, and Domestic-Oriented*

Powerbroker sectors in Malawi are those that capture the largest rents. They mostly comprise construction, fertilizer imports, fuel imports, financial services, government services, telecommunications, transport services, and some agriculture (e.g. Illovo and Carlsberg) and manufacturing sectors. Deals are centred on securing government contracts (e.g. construction, fertilizer imports, and finance through government bonds), on limiting competition and new entrants (e.g. transport, dairy, and finance), securing preferential access to inputs (e.g. poultry), securing preferential licences (e.g. forestry), and extracting income from government (e.g. civil service and politicians via allowances). Deals are much more informal than formal. Rents are gained primarily from taxpayers and aid (fertilizers, construction, financial services) and secondly from the domestic market (e.g. telecommunications, poultry, sugar).

While under Hastings Banda rents were largely extracted from rentier and powerbroker sectors, in Malawi's multiparty democracy since 1994 most political rents have come to be extracted from powerbrokers. Powerbrokers have largely managed to maintain a closed and orderly deals space through most of Malawi's independence period, with close, strategic relationships with the political elite throughout. This relationship has formed the corner-stone of the Malawian patronage system established by Hastings Banda, and was further entrenched by multiparty democracy in 1994. While orderliness suffered in times of economic crisis, such as in the 1980s and the 1990s, proximity to the political elite has meant a degree of continuity in orderli-ness. Players changed, such as Group 5 (construction) and Kalaria (retail, fertilizers, etc.) in Muluzi's time being replaced by Mota-Engil and Mully Brothers, respectively, in Mutharika's time, but the space has generally remained orderly and closed.

An example of how the political elite benefit from powerbrokers in maize production is through using their access to government-donor information to support their business interests. A company interviewed for this research cited an example in 2013, where a donor published a large tender to buy maize the next day, which drove up the price. Politicians and bureaucrats with access to this information prior to publication informed their business interests and friends to buy maize the day before the tender, knowing that the next day the price of maize was to rise. The interviewee claims that many business decisions in agricultural commodity trading are based on such information.

Personal interactions with politicians are more important for companies reliant on natural resources, such as land, water, or minerals, or on gov-ernment contracts, such as farm input suppliers, medicine suppliers, and construction companies. Typically such companies are located in the lower-complexity sections of the product space, because they are either in enabling sectors with captured markets or they produce final goods but enjoy monopolistic or oligopolistic market power with an ability to limit external competition.

In conclusion, the political elite's rents space is mostly linked to sectors within the product space that are generally less conducive to long-term growth. This is because they have a lower level of economic complexity and source their rents from government expenditure, which depends on taxes, aid, and natural resource extraction, which in turn has limited scope for growth and import trading, and which is ultimately constrained by lack of exports and a cap on aid.

Magician sectors, which are key for the development of the product space and long-term growth, have largely been disconnected from the political elite since independence, because they have never formed part of the political patronage and clientelist system, and because competitive clientelism has prevented a long-term developmental vision from taking hold. As such, the bottlenecks faced by these sectors are typically not political priorities. This may explain why, as emerged from the interviews for this research, the structural constraints faced in the 1990s have largely gone unaddressed since multiparty democracy.

3.5 Conclusion and Policy Insights

Following a pre-independence period of economic stagnation, Malawi has experienced three growth episodes: a strong acceleration between 1964 and 1978; a strong deceleration between 1978 and 2003; and a period of weak acceleration since 2003. During these growth regimes, Malawi has failed to structurally transform its economy, remaining largely dependent on the same export and domestic sectors as in 1964.

This chapter has analysed the evolution in the dynamics of Malawi's political settlement, its deals space, and its rents space to try to explain the failure to achieve structural transformation, adding depth to the conventional narrative that is based either solely on a political settlement analysis or on a purely economic analysis. It has also brought out dynamics and feedback loops between these three elements.

At independence, Malawi inherited an economy largely dependent on rentier sectors in the form of tobacco, tea, and coffee. Malawi's first president, Banda, declared a one-party state, which set Malawi on a strong dominant party political settlement until 1978. This enabled him to build on the rentier system he inherited. Through a closed, orderly deals space he selected strategic partners, one per major sector, and supported their investment. In turn, he used this and a network of powerbroker businesses that fed off the rentier model to develop a patronage system necessary to guarantee his survival.

The lack of openness and the nature of Banda's patronage system meant that growth in the first fifteen years of Banda's rule created a negative feedback loop on the rents space, and hence on the political settlement in the last fifteen years of his rule. Succession politics also contributed to deteriorating state capacity that, in turn, prevented Malawi from addressing a number of structural constraints, leading to a decline in GDP per capita in the 1980s. As the deals space for workhorses, rentiers, and magicians became more disorderly and the political settlement turned into a weak authoritarian regime, a positive feedback loop set in, that allowed development partners, the Church, and civil society to secure multiparty democracy in 1994.

Despite being partly eroded in the 1980s on the back of structural adjustment, the patronage system that Banda had built ultimately survived, leading to an unhelpful combination of unaddressed market failures and competitive clientelism in a multiparty democracy. This is delivering two types of feedback loop between growth and the deals space. On the one hand are negative feedback loops, in which positive growth leads to a worsening of the rents space through more disorderly deals—such as Mutharika's second term relative to his first term and Joyce Banda's second year relative to her first year. On the other hand, periods of negative growth (or significant slowdowns in growth) register positive feedback loops on the deals space. Negative growth leads to a reaction in the electorate, because it manifests itself in drought or shortages of key supplies, and similarly the powerbroker patronage base. This has driven new governments to deliver growth—such as Mutharika in 2004, following the failures of Muluzi, and Joyce Banda in 2012, following the foreign exchange crisis and decline in growth in Mutharika's second term.

Yet positive feedback loops from negative or weak growth are too small and short-lived to deliver permanent gains in the orderliness and openness of the rents space, particularly for magicians. Positive feedback loops are focused on restoring patronage and hence are too short-lived to bring about the reform needed for magicians to grow at scale. As a result, the only underlying change was an increased share of the rents space by workhorses. The near-constant re-election and succession politics brought about by competitive clientelism, and the dependency of the patronage system on import and captive market powerbrokers, have kept magicians disconnected, thus preventing structural transformation and capping the potential growth of workhorses. This is epitomized by the foreign exchange crisis, the trade deficit, and the aid crisis of the 2010s, which is undermining the sustainability of the Farm Input Subsidy Programme.

As a result, while minimal economic transformation took place in the 1960s—such as through new investments in sugar and brewing—on the back of Hastings Banda's strategic partner policy and his strong dominant party political system, this unravelled in the 1980s, as it failed to empower workhorses and magicians. From 1994 the combination of a competitive clientelist political system and a rents space dependent on powerbrokers and rentiers—which are both low in economic complexity—have combined to further prevent the structural transformation of Malawi. Although there is a slight positive trend in the product space, with more complex sectors and markets developing on the back of technological improvements, regional integration, and infrastructure gains, such as plastics, packaging, dairy, food processing, and oil seeds, these sectors remain in their infancy compared with mining, tobacco, tea, and raw sugar. The structural transformation required to support burgeoning welfare requirements needed by a rapidly growing population with expectations of improved living standards remains elusive.

3.5.1 *Policy Insights*

Dominant party systems and longer-term limits in competitive clientelist settlements deserve increased consideration. The strong dominant party political system of 1964 to 1978 was the only period in which a long-term developmental vision took hold. Multiparty democracy has further entrenched the patronage system set up by Hastings Banda, in which power-brokers and rentiers provide political elites with rents. Election time frames and succession politics have continually superseded long-term planning.

At the same time, multiparty democracy efforts to empower workhorses need to be complemented with explicit efforts to develop magicians, for example through export-oriented industrial policy. Multiparty democracy facilitated an improved deals space for workhorses in 2004, though mainly as a system for re-enforcing the powerbroker patronage system, rather than building up magicians and exports. As a result, the deals space worsened in 2011 on the back of the foreign exchange crisis that benefited import-based powerbrokers. A permanent increase in orderliness and openness for workhorses thus probably requires a permanent increase in orderliness and openness for magicians.

In Malawi's competitive clientelist political settlement, there is merit in progressives in government and development partners exploring a more explicit partnership with the political elite that can find and demonstrate a way to deliver a long-term developmental approach based on state and magician capability, while at the same time helping elites maintain to a degree a client and patronage base. This could allow Malawi to grab on more rapidly to the tailwinds being created by regional integration and by technological, human capacity, and infrastructure improvements.

References

Booth, D., Harrigan, J., Cammack, D., Kanyongolo, E., Mataure, M., and Ngwira, N. 2006. 'Drivers of Change and Development in Malawi'. ODI Working Paper No. 261. London: ODI.

Cammack, D. 2010. 'The Politics of Chameleons Revisited: The Burden of Malawi's Political Culture'. In *Democracy in Progress: Malawi's 2009 Parliamentary and Presidential Elections*. Edited by Ott, M. and Kanyongolo, F. Zomba. Malawi: Kachere Press.

Cammack, D. 2011. 'Malawi's Political Settlement in Crisis'. Africa Power and Politics, Background Paper No. 4. London: ODI.

Cammack, D., Kelsall, T., and Booth, D. 2010. 'Development Patrimonialism: The Case of Malawi'. Africa Power and Politics Working Paper No. 16. London: ODI.

Chinsinga, B. 2012. 'The Future of the Farm Input Subsidy Programme (FISP): A Political Economy Investigation'. Civil Society Network of Agriculture, Malawi. <http://www.cisanetmw.org/downloads/cisanet_paper_future_of_fisp(1).pdf>.

Diagne, A. and Zeller, M. 2001. *Access to Credit and Its Impact on Welfare in Malawi*. IFPRI Research Report 116. Washington, DC: IFPRI.

Frankenberger, T., Luther, K., Fox, K., and Mazzeo, J. 2003. *Livelihood Erosion through Time: Macro and Micro Factors that Influenced Livelihood Trends in Malawi Over the Last 30 Years*. Lilongwe, Malawi: CARE.

Government of Malawi. 2012. *Malawi National Export Strategy 2013–2018*. Lilongwe, Malawi: Ministry of Industry and Trade.

Harrigan, J. 2001. *From Dictatorship to Democracy: Economic Policy in Malawi 1964–2000*. Farnham: Ashgate.

Kar, S., Pritchett, L., Raihan, S., and Sen, K. 2013. *The Dynamics of Economic Growth: A Visual Handbook of Growth Rates, Regimes, Transitions and Volatility*. Manchester: The University of Manchester.

Lea, N. and Hanmer, L. 2009. 'Constraints to Growth in Malawi'. Policy Research Working Paper 5097. Washington, DC: World Bank, Southern Africa Poverty Reduction and Economic Management Unit.

Meredith, M. 2006. *'The State of Africa: A History of Fifty Years of Independence'*. London: The Free Press.

Naferankhande, M. D. and Ndhlovu, T. M. 2006. 'Inflationary Experiences in Malawi: An Investigation of the Underlying Determinants'. Final Research Report. Nairobi: African Economic Research Consortium.

Ngwira, N. 2012. 'Drivers of Economic Growth in Malawi'. Paper presented at the ECAMA Conference November 2012.

Nyasa Times. 2013a. 'Malawi Ex-Pres. Bingu wa Mutharika's K61bn "Wrongful Self-Enrichment" Exposed'. <http://www.nyasatimes.com/malawi-ex-pres-bingu-wa-mutharikas-k61bn-wrongful-self-enrichment-exposed/>.

Nyasa Times. 2013b. 'Malawi President Banda Implicated in Cash-Gate, CCJP tells PAC'. <http://www.nyasatimes.com/malawi-president-banda-implicated-in-cash-gate-ccjp-tells-pac>.

OECD. 2013. *Query Wizard for International Development Statistics*. Online resource <https://stats.oecd.org/qwids/>.

Pauw, K., Dorosh, P., and Mazunda, J. 2013. 'Exchange Rate Policy and Devaluation in Malawi'. IFPRI Discussion Paper 01253. Washington, DC: IFPRI.

Pryor, F. 1990. *Malawi and Madagascar: The Political Economy of Poverty, Equity and Growth*. New York: Oxford University Press.

Simwaka, K., Ligoya, P., Kabango, G., and Chikonda, M. 2012. 'Money Supply and Inflation in Malawi: An Econometric Investigation'. *Journal of Economics and International Finance*, 4(2): 36–48.

Stambuli, P. 2002. 'Political Change, Economic Transition and Catalysis of IMF/World Bank Economic Models: The Case of Malawi'. Paper presented at Conference on Malawi after Banda: Perspectives in a Regional African Context.

Telegraph. 2013. 'Britain Suspends Aid to Malawi over Corruption Claims and Attempted Murder of Whistleblower'. 18 November. <http://www.telegraph.co.uk/news/worldnews/africaandindianocean/malawi/10457574/Britain-suspends-aid-to-Malawi-over-corruption-claims-and-attempted-murder-of-whistleblower.html>.

4

Navigating the Deals World

The Politics of Economic Growth in Bangladesh

Mirza Hassan and Selim Raihan

4.1 Introduction

Over the past forty years since independence, notwithstanding many external and internal shocks, Bangladesh has increased its per capita income fourfold, cut poverty by more than half, and achieved many of the Millennium Development Goals. Bangladesh's economic growth rates in recent years have been higher than most South Asian countries and many sub-Saharan African countries. These positive development experiences provide the basis for optimism that, despite many policy and institutional constraints, and global uncertainties, Bangladesh will perhaps be able to continue with the current rate of economic growth. Bangladesh's reasonably high and steady growth performance (and also remarkable progress in some social development indicators) has been perceived as a 'paradox' or 'development surprise' by the World Bank (on both growth- and social development-related achievements) as well as by other observers of Bangladesh's development (World Bank, 2007a; World Bank 2007b; World Bank 2010; Mahmud et al., 2008; IGS, 2009; Asadullah et al., 2014).

The conventional narrative on economic growth in Bangladesh tends to ignore the role of deep determinants of growth—political institutions and processes, rent management strategies, and the deals environment—and mainly emphasizes the proximate determinants, such as appropriate industrial policy, trade policy, and savings. The conventional narrative sees Bangladesh as a paradox, since a steady and reasonably high rate of growth took place in the context of 'bad' or 'weak' governance. The fundamental assumption here is that standard 'good governance' institutions (as unequivocally advocated by Islam

(2016), and in a more nuanced way argued by Khan (2015)) or 'market enhancing governance institutions' (Khan, 2008) are preconditions for a high and sustained growth rate in the economy.

In contrast, this chapter provides an alternative explanation of the 'Bangladesh paradox'. It argues that strong economic growth has been possible in Bangladesh (despite a lack of, or weaknesses in, many of the market-enhancing institutions) because a reasonably robust form of 'growth-enhancing governance' exists in the country. Such growth-enhancing governance is characterized by de facto rent-sharing (across political divides), the political elites' ability to separate economic and political rents (based on contingent needs), and, more critically, a largely ordered deals environment (irrespective of being open, closed, or semi-closed in various sectors of the economy). This has created enabling conditions—de facto credible commitment of the state and transactional certainty—which are critically important to the private sector for economic growth to take place. The support of political elites for such growth-enhancing governance has been a defining feature of the political settlement in Bangladesh for the past few decades, and is the key explanatory factor for the maintenance of strong growth in the country.

The rest of the chapter is organized as follows: Section 4.2 describes the growth episodes and patterns of structural change, noting that there have been three growth episodes in the post-independence period. Section 4.3 discusses the political context of each of the three growth episodes. Section 4.4 describes the deals environment in Bangladesh's key growth sector, the ready-made garments (RMG) sector. Section 4.5 discusses the future trajectory of Bangladesh's economy, in light of current developments in its political economy. Section 4.6 concludes.

4.2 Growth Episodes and Structural Change

4.2.1 *Growth Episodes*

We use the methodology outlined in Chapter 1 for identifying the growth breaks in Bangladesh between 1972 and 2010. There are two growth breaks in Bangladesh: one occurred in 1982, and another in 1996. These two growth breaks make three growth episodes: (i) between 1972 and 1982; (ii) between 1983 and 1996; and (iii) between 1997 and 2010. Figure 4.1 plots the trend in per capita GDP, the trend in growth rate of the per capita GDP, and the growth episodes.

The first growth episode had a negative average growth rate, which turned into a small positive number (1.6 per cent) during the second episode. However, during the third episode the average increased to a considerably higher number, around 4 per cent. This suggests that during the second growth

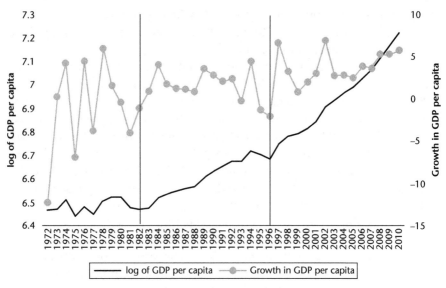

Figure 4.1. Growth episodes in Bangladesh
Source: Kar et al. (2013).

episode in Bangladesh, the economy was transformed from a negative growth phase into a positive growth phase, and the major acceleration in economic growth took place during the third episode.

4.2.2 *Pattern of Structural Change*

The overall structure of the Bangladesh economy has undergone a significant transformation over the past four decades, whereby the share of agriculture in GDP has declined, and the shares of the industrial and services sectors have risen gradually (Figure 4.2). During the first growth episode, the average share of agriculture in GDP was as high as 46.5 per cent, which came down to 36.5 per cent during the second growth episode, and further to 23.2 per cent during the third growth episode. The share of industry increased from only 10.7 per cent in the first episode to 11.7 per cent in the second, and further to 27.6 per cent in the third. Finally, the share of services increased to 59.2 per cent in the third episode from around 43 per cent in the first episode.

Liberalization of trade during the 1980s and 1990s, and associated economic reforms, led to large growth in import penetration and export orientation in Bangladesh. The import penetration ratio (the ratio of import to GDP) was only about 12 per cent during the early 1970s, and has increased to more than 30 per cent in recent years. Extensive export promotion measures and favourable market access in the European Union and USA have helped Bangladesh's

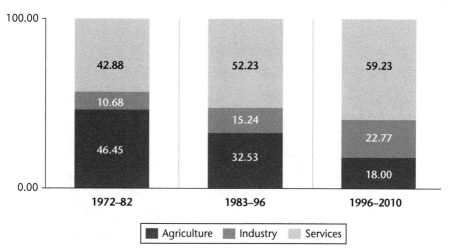

Figure 4.2. Composition of GDP (% share in GDP) in Bangladesh
Source: Authors' calculation from *Statistical Yearbook of Bangladesh* (various sources).

exports rise remarkably during the past forty years. The export orientation ratio (the ratio of exports to GDP) rose significantly, from only 6.5 per cent in the early 1970s to more than 23 per cent in recent years.

Figure 4.3 shows the movement of the composition of exports across the growth episodes. During the first growth episode, export composition was heavily dominated by raw jute and jute goods. During the second growth episode, the RMG emerged as the leading export sector, and during the third growth episode, more than three-quarters of total export earnings were due to RMG products, with the relative significance of all other sectors declining. The growth of Bangladesh's RMG exports had largely been attributable to the international trade regime in textiles and clothing, which, until 2004, was governed by the Multi-Fibre Arrangement (MFA) quotas. The duty-free access for Bangladesh's RMG products in the European Union has also greatly supported the growth of the sector. However, apart from RMG, export performances of all other major commodities, such as raw jute, jute goods, tea, leather and leather products, and frozen food and shrimps, have been rather weak.

The high concentration of the export basket in Bangladesh has been associated with exports of low-level complex products. Figure 4.4 shows the trend in the Economic Complexity Index (ECI) for Bangladesh, which is constructed using export data during the three growth episodes. The ECI for Bangladesh has always been negative, suggesting a very low level of economic complexity. The ECI had a declining trend during the first growth episode, which intensified further during the second growth episode. During the third episode, there was an increasing trend in the early stages, but in later stages the ECI again showed a declining trend.

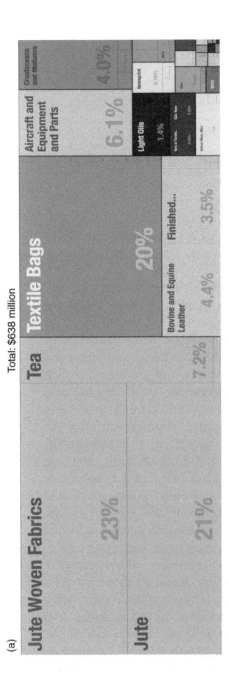

Total: $638 million

(a)

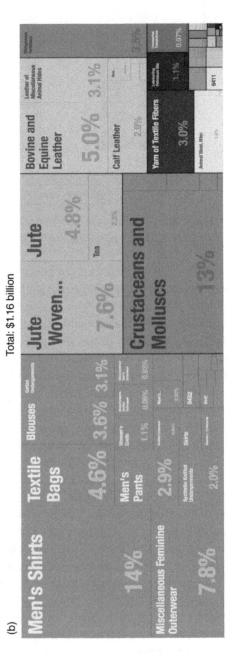

Total: $1.16 billion

(b)

Figure 4.3. Movement of the composition of Bangladeshi exports. (a) Product space during the 1972–82 growth episode: composition of exports in 1978. (b) Product space during the 1973–96 growth episode: composition of exports in 1988. (c) Product space during the 1997–2010 growth episode: composition of exports in 2004

Source: Atlas of Economic Complexity, http://atlas.cid.harvard.edu/

Total: $9.01 billion

(c)

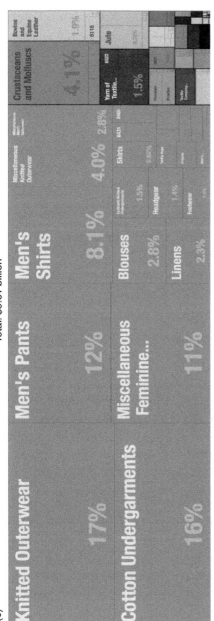

Figure 4.3. Continued

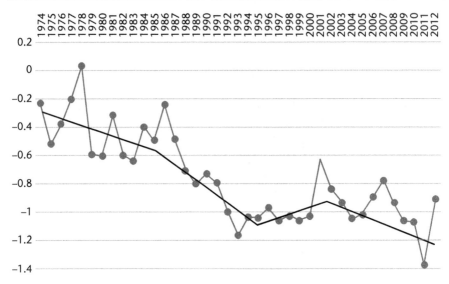

Figure 4.4. Economic Complexity Index for Bangladesh
Source: Hidalgo and Hausmann (2009).

4.3 Political Context of Growth Episodes in Bangladesh

4.3.1 *First Growth Episode (1972 to 1982)*

POLITICAL SETTLEMENT

The political economy context of the first growth episode (1972–82) can be broadly divided into two phases: a dominant party regime, characterized by economic populism and illiberal rule that ended up being a one-party state (1972 to late 1975, the first phase of Awami League (AL) rule); and a populist military dictatorship that later transformed into a dominant party regime (late 1975 to early 1982, the first phase of Bangladesh Nationalist Party (BNP) rule). Both phases can be subsumed under the category of basic stage of limited access order (LAO) (see North et al., 2009).[1]

During the first phase, the AL regime followed a public sector-dominated economic strategy (nationalization, drastically reducing the scope of the market economy) due to economically contingent reasons (dearth of local entrepreneurs) and political economy imperatives (patronage dispensation to the core constituencies of an 'intermediate regime'[2] and the regime's inability to

---

[1] For a very useful discussion of this period from a LAO perspective, see Khan (2013).
[2] The term indicates a state controlled by a coalition of the middle class and rich farmers. The term was used by a prominent member of the first Planning Commission to describe the nature of the first AL regime (Sobhan and Ahmed, 1980).

prevent outright plunder by political cadres). Other reasons included the prevailing ideology (preference for adopting 'socialist' economic policy by some of the top leaders of the AL, including Sheikh Mujibur Rahman, the first prime minister, then first president, and founding father of Bangladesh) among the militant young leadership of the regime as well as some of the left-leaning economists, who were part of the hugely influential first Planning Commission (Kochanek, 1993; Maniruzzaman, 1980; Maniruzzaman, 1982; Sobhan and Ahmad, 1980; Islam, 1979; Islam, 2013; Karim, 2005; Islam, 2016). Also, since the private business sector was very small and politically weak as a collective force, the decision to nationalize industries could be made without any serious resistance (Islam, 2013; and see Kochanek (1993) for the weakness of the collective forums of business). Globally influential and popular left economic discourses (such as 'dependency' theory, and the neo-Marxist critique of capitalism) and practices (social democracy in Europe, actually existing socialisms of Soviet Union, China, and Cuba) also played some role in shaping the Bangladeshi regime's 'socialistic' economic policies.

In 1972, the nationalized units accounted for the overwhelming proportion of the total fixed assets of the manufacturing sector in Bangladesh, and private-sector participation was severely restricted to the medium, small, and cottage industries. During the later phase of the regime, there were some indications of the ruler's intention to move away from the basic stage of LAO, at least in the economic domain. For instance, in 1974, significant revisions were made to the industrial policy by relaxing the limits on private investment from 2.5 million taka to 30 million taka, and also by providing scope for domestic and foreign private investments. In contrast, politics went in the reverse direction that essentially reinforced the basic form of LAO. By the earlier part of 1975, the regime abandoned a pluralist form of democracy altogether, and became a near totalitarian state.[3] This was a short-lived regime, which soon experienced a violent overthrow by a military coup d'état in August 1975.

The second phase (late 1975 to early 1982) of the growth episode was politically governed by General Ziaur Rahman (popularly known as General Zia), a populist military dictator, later the founding father of the BNP. Under him, the country experienced a dramatic shift in economic strategy, by abandoning the public sector-led 'socialist' policy and embracing private-sector-led development. Such a reversal in policy and ideology received the enthusiastic backing of conservative politicians, pro-market senior bureaucrats, and most importantly, Western nations, which set the stage for the pro-market economic reforms under the guidance of the World Bank and the IMF. For

---

[3] Formation of the one-party state by creating the Bangladesh Krishak Sramik Awami League.

instance, the new Industrial Investment Policy, declared in December 1975, increased the private investment ceiling to 100 million taka, withdrew restrictions on private-sector participation in large-scale manufacturing, allowed direct foreign investment in the private sector, and reactivated the Dhaka stock exchange, among many other policy changes. This radical departure in economic ideology and strategy further eroded the economic basis of the basic stage of LAO, and perhaps planted the seed for the transition of LAO towards its semi-maturity stage in the economic domain. Ironically, military dictator General Zia's initiation of a constrained form of pluralist politics[4] (between 1976 and 1978) replaced the totalitarian mode of rule of the former regime, and the later years of his rule (1979 to early 1982) also saw the evolution of a dominant party state. In this sense, General Zia also presided over the incipient process of the erosion of basic LAO in the political sphere.

In terms of political trajectory, the above discussion indicates that this growth phase experienced a high degree of volatility in political settlements—a dominant party regime morphing into a near totalitarian state that was violently overthrown by a coup d'état resulting in a military dictatorship (vulnerable authoritarian rule), followed by a short-lived dominant party regime.

RENTS SPACE

Figure 4.5 presents the rents space under the first growth episode. This episode did not have any rentiers. The textile sector was given a high degree of protection from foreign competition, thus enjoying high rent, and may be categorized as powerbrokers. Sectors such as electricity generation and distribution; gas, water, and sanitary services; construction; trade services; transport, storage, and communication; real estate, housing, and business and banks; mining and quarrying; and petroleum and petroleum products producers were also powerbrokers during this episode. Sectors in the magicians' category, such as raw jute, jute textile, and raw leather, were partially export-oriented. Towards the end of this growth episode, the RMG sector started emerging, which also falls into the magicians category. In the workhorses category the sectors were crops and horticulture; livestock; forest and related services; fishing; chemical and rubber; metal and mineral products; machineries; electrical machinery and apparatus; transport equipment; other manufacturing industries; wood and furniture; paper and printing; and other services. Figure 4.6 shows that the workhorses had the largest share (58 per cent), followed by powerbrokers (33 per cent) and magicians (9 per cent).

---

[4] For a detailed empirical account of this phase, see Ali (2010) and Ullah (2016).

	High rent	Competitive
Export-oriented or imports-competing	RENTIERS	MAGICIANS Raw jute, jute textiles Raw leather Beginning of RMG
Domestic market	POWERBROKERS Textile Electricity generation and distribution Gas, water, and sanitary services Construction Trade services Transport, storage, and communication Real estate, housing, renting, and business services Banks Mining and quarrying Petroleum and petroleum products	WORKHORSES Crops and horticulture Livestock Foresty and related services Fishing Chemical and rubber Metal and mineral products Machinery Electrical machinery and apparatus Transport equipment Other manufacturing industries Wood and furniture Paper and printing Other services

Figure 4.5. Rents space in Bangladesh during the 1972–82 growth episode
Source: Authors' illustration.

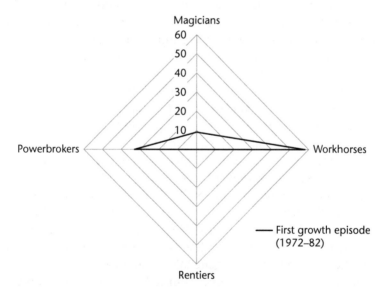

Figure 4.6. Share of actors in GDP in Bangladesh in the first growth episode
Source: Authors' calculation from the national accounts data.

DEALS ENVIRONMENT

Barring a few years (1972–5), the Bangladeshi state has been staunchly pro-business. But it manifested major syndromes of a 'soft state', dithering in its implementation of pro-business reforms, especially related to privatization and relaxing bureaucratic control over business through regulatory reforms. Bangladesh was also the first country in South Asia to liberalize its economy.

A combination of external pressure (by the World Bank and IMF) and domestic politics (marginalization of 'socialistic' and left 'populist' ideologies with the demise of the first regime of the AL, post-1975 politics being dominated by pro-market elites—both politicians and technocrats (Kochanek, 1993), absence of any effective far left politics, and trade unionism stifled by laws), created an enabling space for the state to formulate and adopt business-friendly regulatory and economic policies during the later phase of the growth episode. Such meta-/macro-level features of the elite political settlement largely shaped the meso-level deals world, and structured state–business relations during this growth episode.

A clearly discernible shift in the deals environment occurred after 1975—from a largely closed and disordered environment (governing the processes of nationalization of industries, allocations of permits and licences, uncertainty with land reform, adjudication of property rights, etc.) to an increasingly open and ordered one. The post-1975 regime, in its drive to create new entrepreneurs and to bolster private-sector-led industrial growth, followed a de facto extremely lax form of regulatory governance in sanctioning industrial loans from specialized publicly owned banks, that led to massive defaulting (see various articles in Sobhan, 1991). This 'primitive accumulation' strategy was based on cronyism to a limited extent (for a few politically connected and partisan business actors), but mainly on open deals (for the multitude of business individuals with no political identity). The latter category generated a proactive form of market-led corruption (unsolicited bribing of officials by entrepreneurs), as well as massive rent-seeking, mainly by bank officials (Islam and Siddique, 2010), but also by staff of the relevant ministries, and the process was largely governed by an ordered form of deals (transactional certainty). The Zia regime's liberal bank loan dispensation policy was also a patronage policy to shore up loyal political constituencies and to develop and consolidate the newly formed political party,[5] first Jatiyatabadi Gonotantrik Dal (JAGODOL), which later became BNP (presently one of the two most important political parties in Bangladesh)—perhaps a fitting example of politically productive 'political rent' generation and allocations. This means of rent management also proved to be economically productive, as manifested in the emergence of the RMG sector at the end of this growth episode, as well as the creation of indigenous entrepreneurs, especially in the RMG sector (Rashid, 2008)—a critical element that was in acutely short supply during the first decade of independence, as indicated earlier in this section. Such entrepreneurs, in very limited numbers, were also created through the disinvestment of publicly owned industries. Retrospectively, one could argue,

---

[5] Sobhan (1993) and Islam and Siddique (2010).

it would be a stretch of the truth to claim that the regime's loan disbursement and patronage policies constituted full-blown crony capitalism, since the specific nature of the deals (more open than closed) tends not to indicate so. A form of crony capitalism eventually developed during the regime of General Ershad's (1982–90) kleptocratic rule. The crony capitalism of this period, however, affected mostly trade and service sectors, rather than manufacturing, which probably enabled the relatively robust nature of industrial development that took place during the later decades.

4.3.2 Second (1983–96) and Third (1997–2010) Growth Episodes

POLITICAL SETTLEMENT

These growth episodes need to be politically divided into two broader phases: the dictatorial/quasi-dictatorial rule of General Ershad (1983–90); and the vulnerable democratic transition period (1991–2010), characterized by illiberalism and zero-sum elite conflicts, consequently showing little signs of the democratic process being consolidated. The first phase again can be divided into two distinct political stages: military dictatorship/vulnerable authoritarianism (1983–6); and dominant party rule (1986–90). The first stage undid the relative democratic progress that citizens enjoyed under the later stage of the BNP regime, but this form of political governance (constrained pluralism under dominant party rule) was largely restored in the second political stage. This means that similar political dynamics (a limited form of citizen rights regressing and then progressing) were manifested in the basic stage of LAO during the growth phase (1983–90). General Ershad was head of state throughout this period, having taken over power through a bloodless coup in 1982 (from the BNP) after the assassination of General Zia in 1981. He was ousted from power (in 1990) due to a political movement led by both the AL and the BNP and also, at the end of his rule, the military junta declined to back him any further (see Ali (2010) for an empirically rich account of this period).

On the economic front, General Ershad essentially deepened the pro-market economic reform initiated by the previous regime, particularly privatization of large public enterprises and publicly owned banks, which led to serious resistance from the industrial workers and public sector employees trades unions (for a useful account on this, see Monem (2014)). The regime enacted restrictive laws to contain trade union movements that saw a reversal of rights gained by the workers during the last phase of the Zia regime (Faruque, 2009). Strategies to contain union movements were not only limited to denying associational rights and the use of extra-legal coercions—Ershad also utilized his patronage network to co-opt powerful union leaders and influential left leaders with deep connections to the labour movement, by accommodating them in the cabinet, among other strategies.

A hallmark of economic governance of this period is the evolution of a full-blown crony capitalism, characterized by General Ershad's personalistic, kleptocratic, and centralized control over the patronage distribution process. This process has been vividly described by Kochanek (2003: 68–9):

> The assassination of Zia and the military coup of General H. M. Ershad in March 1982 took the culture of patronage to new heights. Unable to secure the legitimacy of his regime, Ershad used state power and patronage to retain control. It was Ershad who created the culture of private gain as patronage came to dominate the political and economic system. Under Ershad, state power was used to accumulate private wealth, including his own. Ershad centralized power in his own hands, personally reviewed a large number of files, and Ershad's Presidential Secretariat in the words of one observer 'sounded like a brokerage house with calls requesting the status of a contract, an import license, or a bank loan'. Like a traditional patrimonial leader, Ershad attempted to build support by providing important social groups with patronage and benefits. These groups included the military, trade union leaders, business, and other key social groups. Even development projects were affected. The decision on whether or not to proceed with a project was determined by the number and size of contracts and commissions made possible by the project, favouritism, nepotism, personal gain, and rent-seeking took precedence over routine procedures, equitable queuing, or public interest. A complex web of interlocking exchanges between the political elite and civil society, based on personal interests, motivations, and obligations, came to dominate over public responsibility.

The second political phase (1991–2010)[6] saw internal progress within the LAO, a 'paradigmatic' shift from the previous *basic* stage to *semi-maturity* and also the emergence of competitive clientelism (Khan, 2013). We are categorizing the LAO in Bangladesh as semi-mature, due to the low level of *political development* that occurred during this period. Following Fukuyama (2011), political development is understood here as a process of maintaining a stable balance between state-building,[7] rule-of-law consolidation, and democratization. This period also witnessed the rise and consolidation of the politico-institutional form called *partyarchy*: a democratic political system in which 'political parties monopolize the formal political process and politicize society along party lines' (Coppedge,1994: 18). Partyarchy[8] took two distinctly

---

[6] It would be empirically more appropriate to extend this political phase up to 2013. We are limiting this to 2010 to keep it compatible with the end limit of the period of growth episodes (i.e. 2010) analysed in this volume.

[7] State building indicates the development of impersonal organizations within the state and consolidation of legitimate state violence capability. See Hassan (2013) for a detailed discussion of the low level of political development, covering the three domains of Fukuyama, in Bangladesh during this period.

[8] For empirical discussions on partyarchy, in the context of Bangladesh's elite political settlement effecting democratization, private sector governance, and social provisioning, see Hassan (2013); in the context of Bangladesh's local governance and rule of law, see Hassan et al.

different forms during this political phase—monopolistic and duopolistic—impacting political and economic domains, respectively. This means, in the political domain, the ruling party tends to monopolize 'political rents' (near monopolistic control over power-bestowing institutions), but in the economic domain it follows a duopolistic strategy in sharing economic rents with the opposition political actors, contingent on the nature of economic domains (see later in this section). The effects of the monopolistic partyarchy on the political sphere led to non-consolidation of electoral democracy and recurring political instability, mainly related to regime succession. This implies eventual non-evolution of a self-enforcing and robust elite political settlement, with regard to regime succession, despite numerous attempts by the contending political elites[9] to reach such a settlement. The establishment of an interim neutral caretaker government to oversee the elections was the optimum solution that the political elites managed to devise, but this 'credible commitment' device later proved useless, due to machinations by successive incumbents to manipulate the system in their own favour.[10]

More relevant for our current analysis is the examination of the effects of duopolistic partyarchy on the economic domain (especially in relation to the generation and allocation of rents), since it has deeply affected the deals environment. Before we delve into this aspect, it would be helpful to discuss briefly the 'political' role of business in the broader polity and economy as it evolved during this competitive clientelistic phase. Such macro-contextual analysis of the role, as well as the political capacity, of business will help us to understand its ability to shape the deals environment and also to navigate within it.

One of the major features of this political phase is that it witnessed the growing influences of business actors in the political and economic governance of the country (Kochanek, 1993; Kochanek, 2000; Hassan, 2001; CGS and BRAC RED, 2006; Majumdar, 2012; Jahan and Amundsen, 2012; Rashid, 2008; Taslim, 2008; Hassan and Pritchard, 2013; Hassan and Pritchard, 2016). Such influences were manifested in the domination (increasing presence of business actors and control through resources) over formal political institutions (parliament, political parties), electoral politics (money politics), and the

---

(2014); and for the concept's application to analyse donor-supported police sector reform in Bangladesh, see Biswas (2016).

[9] Pressures for a settlement also came from prominent civil society actors, the UN, the USA, and European Union governments, and the elite bargaining process was also mediated by high-profile international dignitaries, such as former US President Carter, among others.

[10] See Hassan (2013) for the analysis (from political settlement and LAO approaches) of the complex processes of elite conflicts surrounding succession (1994–5), evolution of a related elite settlement (1996), breakdown of such a settlement (2006), re-establishment of the settlement by a military-backed technocratic regime (2007–8), and its final breakdown (2012). See also Hassan and Nazneen (2017) for the post-2012 status of elite settlement in politics in Bangladesh.

political process in general—at both national and sub-national levels. Such domination ensured that business had disproportionate influence in the relevant institutions and policy processes, which effectively shaped policy outcomes since these actors were increasingly present (in some cases substituted by loyal surrogates to work on their behest) in relevant parliamentary committees, governing boards of public banks, and other regulatory bodies. Informal influences were also at work and these were manifested in the increasing level of policy capture by market actors in relation to tax, regulations, and loan rescheduling. The sectors that particularly benefited were garments, real estate, banks, and transport. Although state power tends to be heavily concentrated in the hands of the prime minister (both in a de jure and de facto sense), and a culture of personalized rule essentially characterizes political governance of the country (CGS and BRAC RED, 2006; BIGD, 2014; Blair, 2010), even then elite business groups/individuals have been able to exert de facto veto power over the prime minister or finance minister's policy decisions. Three recent examples in this regard are: reversing the commitment to implement value-added tax laws, notwithstanding huge pressures from the IMF; allowing more private-sector banks, despite the central bank's objection on the grounds of demand saturation; and compromising the Dhaka urban plan (due to lobbying by the powerful real estate companies), which was prepared (laying out environmental safeguards) to maintain the liveability of the capital city.

The prominent status of the business actors, which further increased over this political phase, can also be gauged from the fact that it was even possible for them to alter, albeit only to a certain extent, the prevailing de facto rules of the game defining competitive politics and the nature of politicized law enforcement. Two illustrations will suffice.

First, as discussed earlier in this section, a durable elite consensus on regime succession failed to emerge during this political phase, which led to political instability (mainly *hartals* or shutdowns), following each electoral cycle that affected large and medium-sized businesses in the short term (mainly transporting goods on time). This generated uncertainties related to business transactions and investments. As a result of hard bargaining, owners of manufacturing firms, by early 2000, began to enjoy de facto exemption from *hartals* and there was hardly any evidence of factories being targeted by the opposition political activists during such protests.[11]

---

[11] As a caveat, two other reasons (from the supply side) need to be mentioned. First, political elites have strong incentives to maximize revenue, and therefore readily agreed to ring-fencing business from political instability. Second, by the earlier decade of 2000, a large number of political elites became businesspersons themselves, and thus business-friendly policies became easy to formulate and implement, even in critical and sensitive political domains.

Second, responding to business demands, political elites took initiatives (in the early 2000s) to contain the powerful criminal gangs, politically linked or otherwise, involved in extortions (which were chaotic and unpredictable, besetting the business community for the most part of the 1990s), by conducting special law and order drives.[12] A special security force (Rapid Action Battalion) was also created to address the extortion-related crisis, among other remits. As a consequence, over time extortions became routine and predictable in nature, mainly conducted by local-level political leaders of the ruling party ('stationary bandits'). Such local party leaders were also able to protect businesses from harassment by myriad forms of 'roving bandits'[13] (for instance, non-local thugs with no partisan identity, and also politically affiliated but non-local extortionists). The state/party thus ensured a modicum of 'rule of law' (the term 'rule by law' would be more appropriate here), thereby reducing any transactional/investment uncertainty emanating from the prevailing de facto political property rights governing state–business relations and also from increasingly criminalized politics. These two illustrations also indicate positive movements within LAO, implying some degree of consolidation of its semi-mature state, at least in the economic domain, during the relevant political phase.

The above analysis should not give the impression that the business elites lacked constraints. Reasonably free and highly aggressive media and citizen activism have managed to ensure a certain degree of business accountability. Bangladesh's existing democracy, which evolved over this political phase, provided space to societal actors to exert some degree of institutional constraint on the behaviour of business. Such actors included civil society watchdogs, chiefly environmental, human rights, and pro-labour groups, and, more critically, the media—the latter mainly used investigative reports to expose financial scandals and illegal practices of businesses (plunder of financial institutions, land grabbing by real estate firms, and non-payment of workers' wages and the deplorable state of safety conditions in the RMG sector are a few of the relevant examples of media *exposés* observed during this period and beyond[14]).

As noted earlier in this section, partyarchy operated in a duopolistic manner in the economic domain, particularly in relation to the generation and allocation of economic rents. This observation needs further elaboration.[15]

---

[12] Such interventions saw a manifold increase in extrajudicial killings by the security forces.

[13] The notion of stationary and roving bandits is from Olson (1993).

[14] In the case of RMG, monitoring by myriad forms of transnational actors also became important during the later part of the relevant political phase and beyond. Such global influences will be discussed in Section 4.4.

[15] The section borrows heavily from Hassan (2013).

Although the economic domain is subject to duopolistic partyarchy, a certain degree of monopolistic control still exists in this domain: for instance, when the ruling party politicizes the key decision-making positions in the institutions which deal with economic policies and rents/resource allocations (nationalized banks, National Board of Revenue, procurement agencies, regulatory bodies, etc.). Economic actors with the 'wrong' political identity still tend to get access to these institutions and a share in the rents and patronages, albeit asymmetrically.

The specific modalities of rent-sharing across the political divide vary. One of the most important determinants of such variations is the significance to national development[16] of any particular economic domain. The ruling party tends to monopolize the distribution of rents and patronage in relatively non-critical domains, such as small-/medium-scale government procurements, granting of trade/import licences, medium- and small-scale construction contracts, leases of water bodies, government-owned lands, or ferry stations. Notwithstanding this monopolization, ruling political elites also share these rents with rival political elites and business actors with no political identity. But businesses not affiliated with the ruling party can only access such rents by paying informal commissions to the relevant authorities. In contrast, in the domain of critical economic activities, such as large-scale infrastructure building or power generation, efficiency criteria tend to prevail, to a reasonable extent, over patronage distribution that is largely based on narrow political considerations.

Long-term contracts and licences for banks, telecommunications, or financial institutions (leasing companies, merchant banks) are much less vulnerable to monopoly partyarchal control. A prominent reason for this is that relevant market actors adopt politically strategic measures to circumvent such partisan control. Businesses owned by opposition politicians typically co-opt ruling political elites as shareholders and front persons to secure contracts or licences; in such cases, ruling party individuals act as 'front persons' for the contract-/licence-seeking business groups. Firms owned by non-partisan individuals, which are critically dependent on state contracts, similarly co-opt politically connected businesspersons or prominent political actors from both the AL and the BNP as major shareholders/directors (particularly in privately owned banks).

The dynamics of rent generation and sharing in other large economic sectors, like power generation and infrastructure, are more complex, and aspects of predation and productive rent allocations are both manifested in these sectors.

---

[16] For the ruling coalition, economic growth/development is crucial for enhancing and preserving developmental legitimacy.

RENTS SPACE

Figure 4.7 presents the rents space during the second growth episode. A significant change in the rents space during this episode was that the RMG sector eventually became the leading export sector. As mentioned earlier in this section, this sector grew in an international environment of a protected market through the quota system. This sector also received support from the government in the form of subsidies, tax exemption, and other incentives.

According to Figure 4.8, the share of rentiers in GDP during the second growth episode remained at 0 per cent. The workhorses continue to have the largest share (54 per cent), although reduced by four percentage points compared with the first growth episode, followed by powerbrokers (38 per cent) and magicians (8 per cent).

During the third growth episode (Figure 4.9), the RMG sector became the dominant export sector. After 2004, with the phasing out of the MFA, the rent in the international market for the RMG shrunk. During this growth episode, export-oriented sectors, such as footwear, pharmaceuticals, and frozen fish and shrimp, experienced expansion.

During the third growth episode, the share of rentiers in GDP also remained at zero (Figure 4.10). The share of powerbrokers increased further to 44 per cent. The share of magicians also increased to 12 per cent, while the share of workhorses reduced to 44 per cent.

	High rent	Competitive
Export-oriented or imports-competing	RENTIERS	MAGICIANS RMG becoming the leading exports Raw jute export Raw leather export Leather goods
Domestic market	POWERBROKERS Textiles Electricity generation and distribution Gas, water, and sanitary services Construction Trade services Transport, storage, and communication Real estate, housing, renting, and business services Banks Mining and quarrying Petroleum and petroleum products	WORKHORSES Crops and horticulture Livestock, forest, and related services Fishing Chemical and rubber Metal and mineral products Machinery Electrical machinery and apparatus Transport equipment Other manufacturing industries Wood and furniture Paper and printing Other services

Figure 4.7. Rents space during the 1983–96 growth episode in Bangladesh

Source: Authors' illustration.

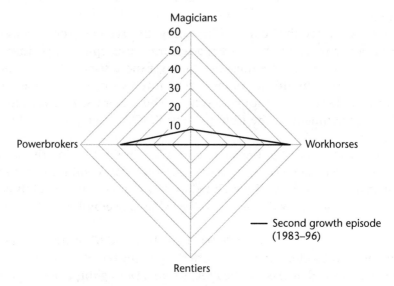

Figure 4.8. Share of actors in GDP in the second growth episode in Bangladesh
Source: Authors' calculation from the national accounts data.

	High rent	Competitive
Export-oriented or imports-competing	**RENTIERS**	**MAGICIANS** RMG are the dominant exports Leather and leather goods Frozen fish and shrimp Pharmaceuticals Jute and jute goods
Domestic market	**POWERBROKERS** Electricity generation and distribution Gas, water, and sanitary services Construction Trade services Transport, storage, and communication Real estate, housing, renting, and business services Banks Mining and quarrying Petroleum and petroleum products	**WORKHORSES** Crops and horticulture Livestock, forest, and related services Fishing Chemical and rubber Metal and mineral products Machinery Electrical machinery and apparatus Transport equipment Other manufacturing industries Wood and furniture Paper and printing Other services

Figure 4.9. Rents space during the post-1996 growth episode in Bangladesh
Source: Authors' illustration.

DEALS ENVIRONMENT

During the regime of Ershad, which largely overlapped with the second growth phase (1983–96), closed but ordered deals can be observed to cover a diverse set of economic activities—granting of licences and permits for export and import, and large construction projects, but not necessarily setting up of

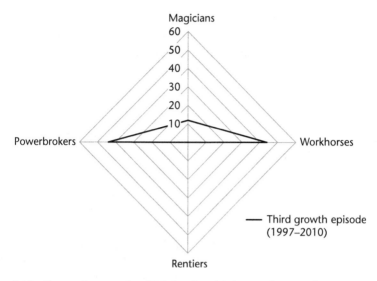

Figure 4.10. Share of actors in GDP in the third growth episode (1997–2010) in Bangladesh

industries.[17] A milestone initiative in the modernization of the economy—the establishment of the first telecommunications (mobile phone) business in the private sector—was done through a closed deal, owned by a senior member of Ershad's cabinet, which continued to function as a monopolist under his rule. Similar to the previous BNP regime, the governance of industrial loan sanctioning and the privatization of nationalized industries continued to be largely characterized by a mix of cronyism (in greater form) and open ordered deals. Such a mode of state–business relations resulted in the creation of significant numbers of local entrepreneurs (with especially rapid increases in the number of RMG factory owners)[18] and capital formation in the private sector, which perhaps, to some extent, explains the growth acceleration, albeit weak in nature, noticeable during Ershad's rule.

The competitive clientelistic phase saw the complex evolution of the deals environment, possibly due to the relatively newer forms of rent management in the economy—a complex mix of monopolistic but predominantly duopolistic rent allocations (sharing rents across the political divide)—as discussed earlier in this section. Following such de facto rent management practice, direct access to state resources/privileges (permits, licences, leases, etc.) tended to be closed and ordered in nature, and an individual's political identity mattered critically here. But even in these closed domains of businesses,

---

[17] Ershad's crony capitalism, it appears, marginally affected the manufacturing sector, RMG included.
[18] See Rashid (2008).

market actors with the wrong political identity (or no political affiliation, as in the case of the majority of businesses) were also able to partner with political insiders to access state resources. Such strategic practices of the firms, in effect, transformed closed deals into an open deal. Syndication of business firms (alliance of firms owned by ruling and opposition party actors along with non-partisan businesses) was another popular strategy used by business, particularly at the sub-national level (district and small towns), to access state resources (construction of public buildings, roads, etc.). This considerably opened up an otherwise politically important[19] closed deal space.

Domains of the economy considered critical (such as large power projects and large infrastructure projects) were mainly subject to open deals (which usually went to technically competent firms, both domestic and foreign), although individuals connected to the highest level of political authority were usually needed as interlocutors/agents to negotiate and seal the deals. Investors, both domestic and foreign, were able to navigate the labyrinth of closed and open deals with the help of readily available and easily identified influential agents (a few well-known political leaders close to the Prime Minister's Office or to the influential ministers in charge of the relevant ministries, as well as well-connected lobbyists).

The business environment, during the relevant phase, was also predominantly characterized by de facto ordered deals, irrespective of being closed or open. The case of the development of the privately owned Korean Export Processing Zone was a major exception to the rule, where for decades deal-making was subject to the capricious behaviour of the political elites, across regimes. This created serious uncertainty for a high-profile Korean investor and sent the wrong signal to global investors in general. But such incidents are very rare in Bangladesh. Also rent allocations, during the competitive clientelistic phase, became more centralized (primarily within the Prime Minister's Office), particularly in relation to the critical domains of the economy (the power sector mainly, but also large infrastructure, to some extent). Such movement towards centralization was observed less during the BNP regime and more during the AL regime. Centralization of rent allocations, in the Bangladesh case, implied closed, but not necessarily disordered, deals. Decentralized rent allocations, hardly seen in the critical domains of the economy, tended to be largely governed by a stable and predictable network of actors, and consequently ordered. It should be noted that an ordered deals environment provides predictability and reduces uncertainty only for players who are

---

[19] We are referring to the political imperatives of national political elites to maintain and nurture political party and associated party fronts by doling out patronage at the sub-national levels. The target beneficiaries here are the 'core constituencies' (Geddes, 1994) meaning the rank and file or foot soldiers of the party.

willing to play by the rules of game. Foreign investors who cannot make recourse to informalities (due to legal restrictions imposed by the countries of origin), or domestic businesses who would like to play only by the formal rules, might not be able to navigate through the system or might find it largely closed and disordered. As observed by our business informants, there were a few instances of business firms quitting certain sectors as they found themselves becoming less competitive by following formal and transparent procedures.

4.4 Deals Environment in the RMG Sector

The RMG sector, as we have already noted, has contributed substantially to the growth of the economy, and is Bangladesh's key magician sector. In this section, we briefly discuss the deals environment in the RMG sector. As we will see, the nature of the deals environment is atypical of what one might expect in a magician sector, and might be related to the specific character of state–business relations in Bangladesh.

In the export-oriented RMG sector, individual firms experienced open deals, at least in the initial stage of the development of the industry. Gradually the nature of the deals environment, as experienced by the individual firms in recent decades, seems to have changed towards being closed. Such evolution in the deals environment has been noted by the *New York Times* (Yardley, 2013):

> Even after the quota system expired in 2005, the trade group [Bangladesh Garments Manufacturing and Exporters' Association, or BGMEA] steadily expanded its regulatory responsibilities. Today, it enjoys a near stranglehold on exports: only factories that are among its members are allowed to export woven garments, with some exceptions. The group regulates the importation of fabric and issues certificates of origin, the required proof that a garment is made in Bangladesh. It has arbitration committees to settle disputes and administers the often-complex practice of subcontracting.

From the perspective of an individual RMG entrepreneur, subsuming oneself in the BGMEA-led closed deal-based structure, is a rational strategy, since operating in an open deal environment,[20] i.e. through bypassing BGMEA and maintaining bilateral interfaces with the state's regulatory authority, in relation to duty-free import processes, would be prohibitively costly, in terms of the informal transaction costs it would incur and an excessive amount of

---

[20] The option, in theory, exists.

time. Therefore the evolution of earlier open deals towards closed deals has been based on the voluntary compliance of individual firms.

As implied above, the sector as a whole enjoys closed deals. Parts of the closed deals actually have legal and quasi-legal bases (bonded warehouse schemes, cash incentives, statutory regulatory ordinances, etc.), but these tend to be highly exclusive in nature. At the same time, the sector enjoys privileges that are quite extraordinary. For instance, the state has delegated authority for rule enactments, and enforcement of these, to its collective forum, BGMEA, as well as to BKMEA (Bangladesh Knitwear Manufacturing and Exporters Associations). The most prominent of these is the power to issue customs certificates—utilization declarations and utilization permits governing duty-free importing process. Such an act of the state tends to blur the distinctions between legality and illegality.[21] In this sense, one can legitimately categorize such privileges as deals-based, rather than strictly rule-based, since these were exclusive to this sector and indicate the RMG sector's ability to generate and preserve a closed deal environment that allowed it to accrue substantial rent for decades and also achieve spectacular economic performance.

The individual firms also saw quite a rapid shift from a relatively disordered (during the late 1970s and early 1980s)[22] to an ordered deals environment in the subsequent decades. The transition occurred, not because of government prodding (through statist policy inducement or coercive rule enforcement by a strong state),[23] but largely due to market actors' strong incentive to ensure its survival and expand in a globally competitive market. This is not to ignore the Bangladeshi state's 'developmental vision' (across regimes, authoritarian or democratic, since 1975), one of the core components of which has been facilitating high export growth for macroeconomic stability and employment generation in a country lacking natural resources. We only want to emphasize the fact that the enactment of various beneficial rules, and myriad forms of deals that the RMG sector has enjoyed, was mainly the outcome of effective demands and skilful negotiations by a sector characterized by strong collective action capability, thanks to the economic and political clout it gradually acquired.

Retrospectively, one could argue that the existing deals environment, which this sector enjoyed, was essentially incentive-compatible with the

---

[21] As one prominent Bangladeshi lawyer observed: 'BGMEA has no regulatory authority under the laws of the country. It's a clubhouse of the garment industry' (Yardley, 2013).

[22] See Rashid (2008) for the effects of the chaotic policy regime and bureaucratic constraints that RMG firms had to face in the earlier stage of the development of the sector, and how initiatives taken by politically, socially, and administratively well-connected entrepreneurs gradually reduced this chaotic environment that led to a more ordered deals environment.

[23] As Ahmed et al. (2014: 262) correctly pointed out, in the context of RMG: 'in contrast to other developing countries, [in Bangladesh]...the approach of each party's [AL, BNP, JP] industrial policies has been relatively hands-off.'

participating actors and thus remained a self-enforcing equilibrium.[24] That the ordered deals environment could evolve and be maintained was mainly due to three factors: (a) de facto policy capture (regulatory agencies, Prime Minister's Office, parliamentary committees),[25] due to its enhanced political power over time; (b) the creation of BGMEA (1985) and later BKMEA (1996), which efficiently solved the myriad forms of collective action problems experienced by the sectors, particularly during the earlier phase; and (c) the development of an optimal degree of integration of BGMEA and BKMEA with the most relevant agencies of the state, the National Board of Revenue and the Ministry of Commerce.

Over the decades, RMG owners became one of the most powerful and best organized business groups in Bangladesh. Their political power derived from the sector's significant contribution to economic growth, its close political integration with the state, including parliamentary representation (Rashid, 2008), and the class of the owners—former military personnel, bureaucratic officials, and members of the white collar managerial class were pioneers of the RMG sector (Rashid, 2008; Kabeer and Mahmud, 2004). The political power of this sector is manifested in the extraordinary tax privileges and subsidies that it has been enjoying for the last three decades. Pointing to the tax privileges of the RMG sector, the finance minister observed: 'In recent years we have seen the birth of a new rich class, but government cannot collect adequate tax from this class' (Ahmed and Shah, 2013). Since the minister's observation, the sector's tax deduction at source went down from 1.2 per cent to 0.8 per cent (in 2013), from 0.8 per cent to 0.4 per cent (in 2014), and from 0.4 per cent to 0.3 per cent (in 2015). Similarly, the cash incentive it receives, on export value, increased from 0.25 per cent (in 2014) to 1 per cent (in 2015) (Transparency International Bangladesh, 2015). According to the *New York Times* (Yardley, 2013), the subsidies and tax breaks that this sector received exceeded tax revenues from the industry by roughly US$17 million. Such exemptions and financial incentives have not changed over the decades, although the profitability of the sector has been rising and the sector has witnessed substantive expansion over time.

The embeddedness of the RMG sector with the state enabled the former to ring-fence the potential deleterious effects of the state's weak capacity and bureaucratic malfeasance.[26] The success of such embedded policymaking also

---

[24] The open deal was particularly needed to ensure a large number of firms to meet the growing global demand and to maintain a reputation as a reliable and timely supplier of garments. Retrospectively, Bangladesh proved to be reasonably successful on both counts over the last four decades.

[25] See Rashid (2008); Hossain (2011).

[26] Such ring-fencing has allowed the RMG sector to reduce transaction costs (thus generating a form of de facto rent), which many other sectors, deprived of such closed deal arrangements, failed to earn.

indicated that the RMG sector had been able to capture, to a large degree, the relevant policy process of the state.[27] Such embedded relations between the RMG sector and the state in Bangladesh is in sharp contrast to the reality of 'embedded autonomy' as experienced in the fast-growing East Asian countries (in the 1970s and 1980s) documented and theorized by Peter Evans (1995). His idea of 'embedded autonomy' depicts state–business relations, which are characterized by the autonomy and capacity of the 'developmental' state to discipline business, if required (for suboptimal performance, for instance). In the Bangladesh case, the RMG sector largely dictated policy process, as manifested in the state's inability to reform the tax and privileges that the sector continues to enjoy and to discipline the industry for its gross violations of rules relating to factory standards and safety compliance.

4.5. Future Trajectory

As we noted in Section 4.3, since 1991 the reasonable level of stability (albeit experiencing a few hiccups, which were non-fatal) of the electoral political governance in Bangladesh was underpinned by a pact among the major political parties that provided legitimacy to regime succession. The agreement enabled a constitutional reform that created a neutral caretaker government (CTG) system to oversee the election. Due to complex political reasons (International Crisis Group, 2015) the CTG system was abolished 'unilaterally' by the incumbent AL government in 2011, and the subsequent election in 2014 was held under a partisan government (under the AL). The major opposition parties (the BNP and Jamaat-e-Islami) boycotted the election, as it was not being managed by a neutral CTG. The AL-led alliance came back to power with half of the parliamentary seats uncontested. The integrity, credibility, and legitimacy of the 2014 election were questioned by the major opposition parties, local civil society, media, and the international community.

As a consequence, the competitive clientelistic phase (as embedded in a competitive political settlement) ended in Bangladesh in 2014. What emerged after that, in the political domain, may be called a dominant party settlement.[28] Such a political development has been a major setback in the

---

[27] Saxena observes: 'The two groups [BGMEA and BKMEA] have been effective advocates of favorable policies and have been criticized for being too close to state officials' (2014: 106).

[28] Levy (2014: 26) has provided a very useful definition of dominant party settlement from an LAO perspective: 'A dominant political settlement can be characterized as [a] . . . combination [whereby] . . . the disparity between the violence potential of the rulers and the opponents is very large. The rulers' grasp on power is strong in the sense that it would take an extraordinary level of commitment by the opponents . . . to mount a credible challenge to the status quo. There is thus an "equilibrium" in which the political leadership can govern as a "principal" and engage others in the country as "agents" (or subjects).'

movement of LAO towards maturity, especially in the political domain. Although it is too early to comprehend fully the implications of this shift in the political settlement on the nature of rent management and the deals environment, it would be useful to reflect on some of the discernible indications, on a provisional basis, pertinent to state–business relations and their impacts on future economic growth. The first thing to note is that one of the features of rent management, the practice of rent-sharing across the political divide, seems to have altered to a certain extent. Our business informants observed that, in the post-2014 dominant party settlement context, partisan considerations have been increasingly influencing the nature of political elites' dealings with the market actors. This is especially true for high-value projects. Such changes in political elites' behaviour will perhaps alter the nature of the rules of the game governing the rent-sharing process as observed before 2014. This means that certain changes in the dynamics of the deals environment will perhaps occur.

Second, as many of our business informants have noted, there has been a steep rise in crony capitalistic practices with the advent of the dominant party settlement, although a steady increase of this was also observed during the later years of the competitive period.[29] Print media have exposed numerous cases of 'plunders' in the banking sector, by politically connected businesses. Licensing of private banks has also been subjected to a blatant form of crony capitalism. Such elite behaviour has, willy-nilly, led to a 'vision' of the dominant party state, which is apparently guiding its current developmental strategy. This seems to have two components: political stability, maintained through authoritarian politics; and crony capitalism. A sophisticated ideologue of the current regime (who happens to be a prominent technocratic advisor to the prime minister) candidly observed: 'If the country has good leadership and peace, economic growth will definitely occur. Democratic deficit is not a major problem. Singapore and South Korea [the latter during the 1960s, 1970s, and part of 1980s] are excellent examples in this regard—countries which have managed to develop' (*Prothom Alo*, 2016). Note that the advisor mentioned two countries that are well known for their statist-authoritarian mode of development, but at the same time which managed, successfully, to discipline the business class (Davis (2004), for South Korea; Rodan (2004), for Singapore). The other interpretation of the vision came from an influential cabinet minister, who is also a prominent national leader of the ruling party. He remarked: 'We believe in democracy, but not over-democracy. Sheikh Hasina [the prime minister] is going on the path that

---

[29] A prominent national daily observed: 'Unfortunately, a regime of impunity has hindered effectiveness of the rule of law and corruption has multiplied with crony capitalism' (*Daily Star*, 2013).

Mahathir Mohamad followed in Malaysia. We will follow that model of democracy' (*Prothom Alo*, 2015). It is clear that the strategic developmental vision of the political elites[30] is a mix of cronyism and fast economic growth of the perceived Malaysian type, rather than the 'developmental state' of the Singapore/South Korea variant—the one articulated in the vision of the technocrat advisor. Evidence, so far, tends to indicate that the regime has been very keen to follow the current Malaysian developmental pathway, which has lately shown increasing trends of cronyism (see Rodan (2004); and Sen and Tyce, Chapter 10, this volume).

Third, the mode of rent-seeking has also changed from the previous relatively centralized form to an increasingly decentralized one (again critical domains of the economy—large power plants or infrastructure are still mostly subject to a centralized rent allocation process). This has been an inevitable consequence of increases in the number of rent-seekers. Business now has to engage with rent-seekers with veto powers at various points down the bureaucratic hierarchies. Some of our business informants have observed that this increasing decentralization of the rent-seeking process may weaken the hitherto robust, incentive-compatible and self-enforcing ordered (irrespective of closed or open types) deals environment that they have enjoyed over the last two decades.

Fourth, politico-ideological changes have taken place which appear to have influenced the organizational dynamics of collective action for market actors. The current regime (AL), being sensitive to the reality of the weak electoral legitimacy it enjoys, has further tightened its political and ideological grip over civil society groups, including various business associations. This has somewhat muted the critical voices of business leadership, and the hitherto informal strategy of business forums, to maintain a bipartisan posture in their leadership composition (a hedging strategy to cope with the regime change), seems to have started losing its strategic relevance. The potential impacts of such politico-ideological changes on the business community's negotiating capacity to survive and prosper in the existing deals world will surely vary, contingent on the political strength of the various business sectors' collective forums.

Although there is anxiety among business actors regarding the current political settlement and its possible negative implications for ordered dealmaking, still this settlement has provided, since 2014, increasing political stability (no country-wide shutdowns or blockades of highways—thanks to the regime's repressive political management) that has contributed, among other factors, to the reasonably high and stable growth rates in recent years.

---

[30] It is strategic in the sense that the 'vision' is also an outcome of domestic political imperatives, as discussed later in this section.

The future trend in growth performance can be assessed in the light of these positive and mostly negative feedback loops, as discussed earlier in this section. Despite experiencing massive political and reputational crises (e.g. the Rana Plaza disaster), labour movements for higher wages, and intense global pressures for ensuring factory standards and social compliance, and workers' associational rights, the RMG sector—one of the most important sectors contributing to Bangladesh's growth performance—has managed to perform reasonably well. During previous decades, its high performance, notwithstanding the many domestic challenges the industry faced, was possible due to the combination of closed/semi-closed/ordered (collectively) and de facto closed/ordered (enjoyed by individual firms embedded in their collective forums) deals that it enjoyed in the economic domain. In the political domain, a robust and resilient anti-labour elite political settlement between RMG owners and political elites—across political divides—has enabled it to cope with the sustained movements and critiques that it faced from the labour, media, and human rights actors, both local and global. Such a settlement has lately become increasingly vulnerable to both domestic and international pressures.

In the economic domain, the decades-long closed and semi-closed deals are now being questioned by the state and local and global stakeholders. BGMEA has vigorously protested against any such policy reform initiatives. Its political capacity to thwart successfully similar policy initiatives many times in the past has proved the robustness of the hitherto elite political settlement. With the crises the sector is now facing, its continuing high performance and its vision to attain an annual export volume of US$50 billion by 2021 will largely depend on the nature of the evolving political settlement and the deals that it will be able to renegotiate with the political elites, and also how and to what extent it will be able to neutralize its national/global reputation as 'greedy' entrepreneur, promoter of 'economic injustice', and 'violator of labour/human rights'.

The negative trend in the ECI, as experienced throughout the three growth episodes, indicates the serious challenges that the country faces in effecting structural transformation in the economy. To achieve such transformation, Bangladesh will have to move beyond relying on one or two sectors and must start producing complex products with higher added-value. Some sectors (for instance, transport and power) will also need modernization and governance reform to provide support to the growth of diversified manufacturing sectors. Potential sectors, in the area of manufacturing, are leather and footwear, agro-processing, electronics, pharmaceuticals, information and communications technology (ICT), light engineering, and ship building. Unlike the RMG sector, these sectors tend to have weak collective action capacity, which is a liability (for a sector as a whole) while operating in a predominantly deals-based world.

Their weakness in collective action capacity is perhaps due to the small numbers of firms involved in these sectors. Unlike the RMG sector, no 'accidental rent' (in the form of the MFA) enabled any of these sectors to take off in a robust manner, except for the pharmaceutical sector, which has been enjoying similar rent for the last few decades (e.g. exemption from patent rights, which will continue until 2033). This sector took advantage of the rent, which contributed to a substantive modernization of the industries, remarkable economic performance (the sector managed to produce almost its entire product [97 per cent] as demanded in the domestic market), and also did reasonably well as an exporting sector, compared with other developing countries.

4.6 Conclusion

During the growth episodes considered in this chapter, Bangladesh's social order has seen shifts back and forth in the political domain—regressing and progressing in the maturation process of an LAO. In contrast, in the economic domain, there has been the survival of an ordered deal environment—reaching a perpetual state of self-enforced equilibrium—underpinned by an elite political settlement, despite the shifts in politics. We have argued in this chapter that such a resilience of the ordered deals environment (irrespective of being open or closed) substantially contributed to the positive trend in growth during the period under study.

Our findings have two implications for the overall framework of this book, as set out in Chapter 1. First, we have shown that the robust and resilient forms of ordered deals evolved in Bangladesh, *not* in a context of a matured LAO, in which intra-elite relations take place in an impersonal manner, but against the backdrop of a semi-matured LAO, whereby elite interactions continue to be conducted in a personalistic and discretionary mode (i.e. elites have yet to develop the rule of law, even for themselves). This may be in part due to the existence of military dictatorships and dominant party settlements (exhibiting mostly centralized rent management), at various points in Bangladesh's relevant growth episodes. However, the ordered deals environment continued to exist, even during the competitive clientelistic settlement phase, when one might have expected that the high intensity of competition in Bangladesh's polity would have led to a shortening of the time horizons of political elites in the deals that they offered to economic actors.

Why has an ordered deals environment persisted, even when the political settlement moved decisively to competitive clientelism? There are two reasons. First, there is a strong ideological preference for market-led growth among political elites. Given their fragile democratic legitimacy, political elites felt that they needed to prioritize the simultaneous building of developmental legitimacy, hence the incentives to nurture and promote the private sector (by supplying a reasonable degree of predictability and stability in the economic domain), in a country largely deprived of natural resources. Second, the business community has become politically stronger, as manifested in policy/regulatory capture, increasing dominance over party, parliament, and electoral political processes, and leading to the establishment of vertical political integration (VPI): 'the blurring of the lines between the asset holders and the government' (Haber et al., 2003: 31),[31] which can be observed in a more robust and quasi-institutionalized form in some sectors (as in RMG) and in an ad hoc or fluid forms in others (real estate, pharmaceuticals, textiles). An ordered deals environment has consequently been an outcome of such integration.

A second implication of our findings for the overall framework is the *atypical* nature of the deals environment in the key magician sector, the RMG sector, which, though ordered, has been closed (when typically magicians prefer open deals to a closed deals environment, as argued in Chapter 1). This sector enjoyed various rents, which are extra-legal in nature, and has shown little interest in open deals. While the ordered nature of the deals has been instrumental in the RMG sector's growth, both domestic and international stakeholders have increasingly challenged the closed nature of the deal-making between the BGMEA and the state. With the shift of the political settlement to a dominant party settlement since 2013, it is likely that the political equilibrium that underpinned the closed ordered deals environment in Bangladesh's key magician sector may become unstable over time, possibly calling into question the sustenance of 'the Bangladesh paradox'.

References

Ahmed, F., Greenleaf, A., and Sacks, A. 2014. 'The Paradox of Export Growth in Areas of Weak Governance: The Case of the Ready Made Garment Sector in Bangladesh'. *World Development*, 56: 258–71.

Ahmed, M., and Shah, J. 2013. 'Everything Is for the Garments Factory Owners'. *Prothom Alo*, 18 May.

Ali, S. 2010. *Understanding Bangladesh*. London: C. Hurst & Co.

Asadullah, N., Savoia, A., and Mahmud, W. 2014. 'Paths to Development: Is There a Bangladesh Surprise?' *World Development*, 62: 138–54.

BIGD. 2014. *The State of Governance Bangladesh 2013: Democracy, Party, Politics*. Dhaka, Bangladesh: BRAC Institute of Governance and Development, BRAC University.

[31] Haber et al. (2003) developed and elaborated the concept of VPI in the empirical context of Mexico.

Biswas, N. 2016. 'The Limits of Reform: Elites, Politics and the Police in Contemporary Bangladesh'. Unpublished doctoral thesis, City, University of London.

Blair, H. 2010. 'Party Overinstitutionalisation, Contestation, and Democratic Degradation in Bangladesh'. In *Handbook of South Asian Politics: India, Pakistan, Bangladesh, Sri Lanka, Nepal*. Edited by Bass, P. R. London: Routledge.

CGS and BRAC RED. 2006. 'The State of Governance in Bangladesh'. Dhaka, Bangladesh: BRAC University.

Coppedge, M. 1994. *Strong Parties and Lame Ducks: Presidential Partyarchy and Factionalism in Venezuela*. Stanford, CA: Stanford University Press.

Daily Star. 2013. 'The Day to Remember'. Editorial, 26 March.

Davis, D. 2004. *Discipline and Development: Middle Classes and Prosperity in East Asia and Latin America*. Cambridge: Cambridge University Press.

Evans, P. 1995. *Embedded Autonomy: States and Industrial Transformation*. Berkeley, CA: University of California Press.

Faruque, A. 2009. *Current Status and Evolution of Industrial Relations System in Bangladesh*. ILR School, Cornell University.

Fukuyama, F. 2011. *The Origins of Political Order: From Prehuman Times to the French Revolution*. London: Profile Books.

Geddes, B. 1994. *Politician's Dilemma: Building State Capacity in Latin America*. Berkeley, CA: University of California Press.

Haber, S., Razo, A., and Maurer, N. 2003. *The Politics of Property Rights: Political Instability, Credible Commitments and Economic Growth in Mexico, 1876–1929*. Cambridge: Cambridge University Press.

Hassan, M. 2001. 'Demand for Second Generation Reform: The Case of Bangladesh'. PhD thesis, ICS, University of London.

Hassan, M. 2013. 'Political Settlement Dynamics in a Limited-Access Order: The Case of Bangladesh'. ESID Working Paper No. 23. Manchester: University of Manchester.

Hassan, M., and Nazneen, S. 2017. 'Violence and Breakdown of the Political Settlement: An Uncertain Future for Bangladesh?' *Conflict, Security and Development*.

Hassan, M., and Pritchard, W. 2013. 'The Political Economy of Tax Reform in Bangladesh: Political Settlements, Informal Institutions and the Negotiation of Reform', ICTD Working Paper No. 14. Brighton: IDS.

Hassan, M., and Pritchard, W. 2016. 'The Political Economy of Domestic Tax Reform in Bangladesh: Political Settlements, Informal Institutions and the Negotiation of Reform'. *Journal of Development Studies*, 52(12): 1704–21.

Hassan, M., Islam, M., and Zakaria, S. 2014. 'Partyarchy and Political Underdevelopment'. In *The State of Governance Bangladesh 2013: Democracy, Party, Politics*. Dhaka, Bangladesh: BRAC Institute of Governance and Development, BRAC University.

Hidalgo, C., and Hausmann, R. 2009. 'The Building Blocks of Economic Complexity'. *Proceedings of the National Academy of Sciences*, 106(26): 10570–5.

Hossain, N. 2011. 'Exports, Equity and Empowerment: The Effects of Readymade Garments Manufacturing Employment on Gender Equality in Bangladesh'. Background paper for World Development Report.

IGS (Institute of Governance Studies). 2009. 'The State of Governance in Bangladesh'. BRAC University, Dhaka, Bangladesh.

International Crisis Group (2015). 'Mapping Bangladesh's Political Crisis', Asia Report No. 264. International Crisis Group, Brussels.

Islam, M., and Siddique, M. 2010. *A Profile of Bank Loan Default in the Private Sector in Bangladesh*. Dhaka, Bangladesh: University of Chittagong.

Islam, N. 1979. *Development Planning in Bangladesh: A Study in Political Economy*. Dhaka, Bangladesh: University Press Limited.

Islam, N. 2013. *Making of a Nation, Bangladesh: An Economist's Tale*. Dhaka, Bangladesh: University Press Limited.

Islam, S. 2016. *Governance for Development: Political and Administrative in Bangladesh*. New York: Palgrave Macmillan.

Jahan, R., and Amundsen, I. 2012. 'The Parliament of Bangladesh: Representation and Accountability'. CPD-CMI Working Paper 2012:2. Center for Policy Dialogue and Chr. Dhaka and Bergen: Michelsen Institute.

Kabeer, N., and Mahmud, S. 2004. 'Globalisation, Gender and Poverty: Bangladeshi Women Workers in Export and Local Markets'. *Journal of International Development*, 16(1): 93–109.

Karim, S. 2005. *Sheikh Mujib: Triumph and Tragedy*. Dhaka, Bangladesh: University Press Limited.

Khan, A. 2015. *The Economy of Bangladesh: A Quarter Century of Development*. London: Palgrave Macmillan.

Khan, M. 2008. 'Governance and Development'. In *A Ship Adrift: Governance and Development in Bangladesh*. Edited by Islam, N., and Asaduzzaman, M. Dhaka, Bangladesh: Bangladesh Institute of Development Studies.

Khan, M. 2013. 'Bangladesh: Economic Growth in a Vulnerable Limited Access Order'. In *In the Shadow of Violence: The Problem of Development for Limited Access Order Societies*. Edited by North, D., Wallis, J., Webb, S., and Weingast, B. Cambridge: Cambridge University Press.

Kochanek, S. 1993. *Patron-Client Politics and Business in Bangladesh*. Dhaka, Bangladesh: University Press Limited.

Kochanek, S. 2000. 'The Growing Commercialization of Power'. In *Bangladesh: Promise and Performance*. Edited by Jahan, R. Dhaka, Bangladesh: University Press Limited.

Kochanek, S. 2003. 'The Informal Political Process in Bangladesh'. Report prepared for the Department of International Development, UK High Commission, Dhaka, Bangladesh.

Levy, B. 2014. *Working With the Grain: Integrating Governance and Growth in Development Strategies*. Oxford: Oxford University Press.

Mahmud, W., Ahmed, S., and Mahajan, S. 2008. 'Economic Reform, Growth, and Governance: The Political Economy of Aspects of Bangladesh's Development Surprise'. Washington, DC: World Bank.

Majumdar, B. (ed.) 2012. 'Ninth National Parliament Election 2008: Information on Participating Candidates'. *Prothom Alo* and Shujan (in Bangla).

Maniruzzaman, T. 1980. *The Bangladesh Revolution and Its Aftermath*. Dhaka, Bangladesh: Bangladesh Books International.

Maniruzzaman, T. 1982. *Group Interests and Political Changes: Studies of Pakistan and Bangladesh*. New Delhi, India: South Asian Publishers.

Monem, M. 2014. *The Politics of Privatisation in Bangladesh*. Dhaka, Bangladesh: OSDER.

North, D., Wallis, J., and Weingast, B. 2009. *Violence and Social Orders: A Conceptual Framework for Interpreting Recorded Human History*. Cambridge: Cambridge University Press.

Olson, M. 1993.'Dictatorship, Democracy and Development'. *American Political Science Review*, 87(3): 567–76.

Prothom Alo. 2015. 'Government Placing Development Against Democracy'. 18 May.

Prothom Alo. 2016. 'Democratic Deficit Is Not a Big Problem'. 22 June.

Rashid, M. 2008. 'Bad Governance and Good Success'. In *A Ship Adrift: Governance and Development in Bangladesh*. Edited by Islam, N. and Asaduzzaman, M. Dhaka, Bangladesh: Bangladesh Institute of Development Studies.

Rodan, G. 2004. *Transparency and Authoritarian Rule in South East Asia: Singapore and Malaysia*. London and New York: Routledge Curzon.

Saxena, S. 2014. *Made in Bangladesh, Cambodia, and Sri Lanka: The Labor Behind the Global Garments and Textiles Industries*. Amherst, NY: Cambria Press.

Sobhan, R. (Ed.) 1991. *Debt Default to the Development Finance Institutions: The Crisis of State Sponsored Entrepreneurship in Bangladesh*. Dhaka, Bangladesh: University Press Limited.

Sobhan, R. 1993. *Bangladesh: Problems of Governance*. New Delhi, India: Konark Publishers Private, Limited.

Sobhan, R., and Ahmad, M. 1980. *Public Enterprise in an Intermediate Regime: A Study in the Political Economy of Bangladesh*. Dhaka, Bangladesh: Bangladesh Institute of Development Studies.

Taslim, M. 2008.'Governance, Policies, and Economic Growth in Bangladesh'. In *A Ship Adrift: Governance and Development in Bangladesh*. Edited by Islam, N. and Asaduzzaman, M. Dhaka, Bangladesh: Bangladesh Institute of Development Studies.

Transparency International Bangladesh (TIB) 2015. 'Programs Taken to Establish Good Governance in the RMG Sector'. (In Bengali.)

Ullah, M. 2016. *President Zia of Bangladesh: A Political Biography*. Dhaka, Bangladesh: Adorn Books.

World Bank. 2007a. 'Bangladesh Strategy for Sustained Growth'. Bangladesh Development Series, Paper No. 18. The World Bank Office, Dhaka, Bangladesh.

World Bank. 2007b. 'Governance and Growth: The Bangladesh Conundrum'. In 'Bangladesh Strategy for Sustained Growth'. Bangladesh Development Series, Paper No. 18. The World Bank Office, Dhaka, Bangladesh.

World Bank. 2010. 'Bangladesh Country Assistance Strategy 2011–2014'. The World Bank Office, Dhaka, Bangladesh.

Yardley, J. 2013. 'Garment Trade Wields Power in Bangladesh'. *New York Times*, 26 July.

5

Not Minding the Gap

Unbalanced Growth and the Hybrid Political Settlement in Cambodia

Tim Kelsall and Seiha Heng

5.1 Introduction

Since 1960, many countries have experienced growth accelerations, but only a few have maintained growth. An adequate theory of growth must thus explain both how some countries kick-start growth, and how some maintain it over decades. For us, the key is to be found in the relationship between what we call the 'political settlement' (ongoing, formal and informal bargains between elites about how power should be organized and exercised) and the environment for business (the 'deals environment'). Put simply, some political settlements create the possibility of a transition from disorder to order in the deals environment, and this creates a potential for accelerated growth. Of these, a smaller subset manages to maintain order while also permitting an increased openness of the deals environment, so that new firms can enter, innovate, compete, and structurally transform the economy (Pritchett and Werker, 2012; Sen, 2012).

Over the past forty years, Cambodia has had one of the world's most volatile growth experiences. A prolonged economic collapse between 1970 and 1982 was followed by a gradual but unstable recovery up until 1998, while post-1998 saw another period of growth acceleration and sustained high growth. Policy observers such as the World Bank attribute Cambodia's success to a combination of good geographical fortune, early demographic transition, a peace dividend spurred by opportune policy, and 'hand-in-hand' government–investor relations in key sectors, notably garments (Guimbert, 2010b). This chapter subsumes these insights within a broader theory of political settlements, economic deals, and feedback loops, providing additional analytical leverage over the prospects for sustained growth.

We argue that while growth collapse can be traced to the failure of Prince Sihanouk's post-independence political settlement, war, and the disastrous Khmer Rouge regime, growth acceleration and maintenance have been based on a political settlement which has created a balance between technocrats and rent-seekers within Hun Sen's dominant coalition. Technocrats are given just enough latitude to support growth industries like garments, tourism, electronics, and rice, while rent-seekers are given the political backing to generate profits, a proportion of which are funnelled to the masses through ruling party patronage projects.

Through interviews conducted with government officials, industry experts, and firms in four economic sectors, we show that there has been a positive feedback loop between support for competitive export industries, state capacity, and structural transformation. However, there has also been a negative feedback loop from overreliance on high-rent industries, to insufficiently inclusive growth and political instability. At the time of writing, the political settlement that has underpinned growth and stability for the past fifteen years is facing a severe challenge.

5.2 Growth and Structural Transformation

Between 1970 and 2010, Cambodia averaged growth of 2.3 per cent per year (a figure which is almost exactly the same as for the United Kingdom) (see Figure 5.1). But while the UK's growth has been steady and virtually uninterrupted, Cambodia's has had a high degree of volatility. GDP per capita shrank at 6.2 per cent per year in the 1970s, falling from US$1,041 in 1970 to US$504 in 1982. In 1982, there was a period of growth acceleration, with per capita income growing at 3.8 per cent a year for the next sixteen years. Then in 1998 there was another acceleration, with per capita income growing at 6.5 per cent a year, taking it to US$1,892 in 2010 (Kar et al., 2013).

Growth has been accompanied by structural change. Between 1995 and 2010 there was a shift from agriculture to the industrial sector (NIS, 2011) (see Figure 5.2). In 1995, agriculture accounted for 44.7 per cent of total GDP and 81.4 per cent of the labour force, while in 2010 its share had fallen to 27.4 per cent of GDP and 57.5 per cent of the labour force. Industry meanwhile had risen from 15.1 per cent of GDP and 16.3 per cent of the labour force, to 26.4 per cent and 27.4 per cent, respectively.

Within industry, manufacturing has led the way, rising from 8.9 per cent to 20.5 per cent of GDP during 1995–2010, with construction the next most

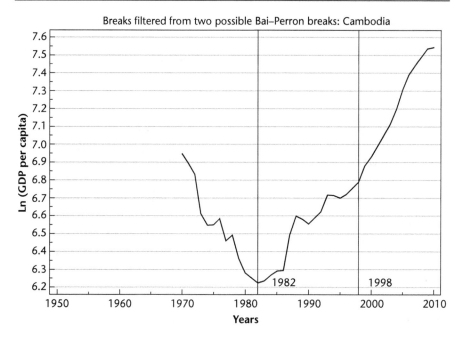

Figure 5.1. Growth episodes in Cambodia

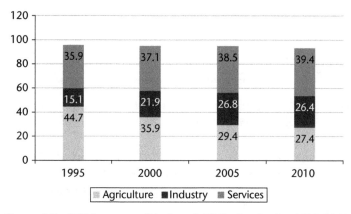

Figure 5.2. GDP by sectors (% of total GDP), Cambodia, 1995–2010
Source: National Institute of Statistics (2011).

important sector (see Figure 5.3). Textiles, wearing apparel, and footwear have been the most important categories, rising from 15 per cent of manufacturing in 1995 to 76 per cent in 2010. Services have also increased in importance, rising from 35.9 per cent of GDP and 2.3 per cent of the labour force in 1995, to 39.4 per cent of GDP and 15.1 per cent of the labour force in 2010 (NIS, 2011; and Figure 5.4). Much of this service sector growth has been driven

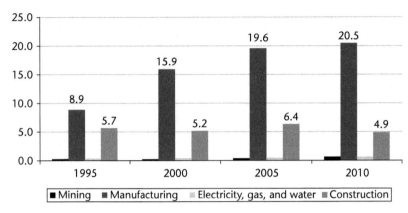

Figure 5.3. Share of industry in GDP in Cambodia, 1995–2010 (% of GDP)
Source: Asian Development Bank (2012a).

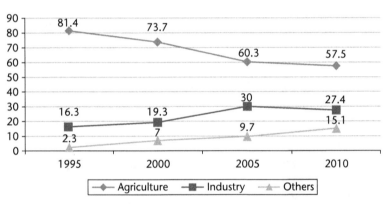

Figure 5.4. Employment shares by sectors in Cambodia, 1995–2010 (%)
Source: Asian Development Bank (2012a).

by tourism. Tourist arrivals were just 0.22 million in 1995, but by 2010 they were 2.5 million, with gross receipts totalling almost US$1.8 billion (Ministry of Tourism, 2012). There has been growth in telecommunications and banking too.

Despite the decline in its share in GDP, Cambodia's agricultural output has also grown substantially. As Table 5.1 shows, paddy is by far the largest crop sub-sector, but cassava has also grown dramatically. Rubber is expected to increase more significantly in coming years as new investments reach maturity. There is also a growing amount of palm oil and sugar production.

Structural continuity and change is also reflected in the composition of Cambodia's exports. In 1968, tropical agricultural products (mainly rubber), cereal, vegetable oils, cotton, rice, soy, and other products, accounted for around 75 per cent of exports. Twenty years later, these three categories still

Table 5.1. Crop production in Cambodia, 1995–2010 (1,000 tonnes)

Kind of crop	1995	2000	2005	2010
Food crops	3,624	4,359	6,809	11,650
Paddy	3,448	4,026	5,986	6,549
Maize	55	157	248	773
Cassava	82	148	536	4,249
Sweet potato	39	28	39	79
Vegetables	193	196	172	377
Mung bean	20	15	45	72
Rubber	35,427	42,007	29,464	42,466

Source: Asian Development Bank (2012a); Ministry of Agriculture (2011).
Note: Food crops consist of paddy, maize, cassava, and sweet potato.

accounted for 80 per cent of exports, although their absolute value had plummeted—from US$71 million, or 0.03 per cent of world trade in 1968, to just US$8.46 million, or 0.0003 per cent of world trade in 1988 (Figures 5.5 and 5.6; Hausmann et al., n.d.: 129).[1] By 1995, however, the first signs of transformation were visible, with a shift to forestry products and manufactures. By this stage, more than a third of Cambodia's exports were accounted for by wood in the rough, another 20 per cent by sawn wood or wood chips, and another 14 per cent by natural rubber, but now with garments, a new category, comprising around 20 per cent of total exports. Since 1995 the garment sector has continued to grow. The value of all exports, meanwhile, increased from US$8.46 million in 1988 to US$4.38 billion in 2008 (Hausmann et al., n.d.: 129).

As of 2008, Cambodia was the ninety-eighth most complex economy in the world, thirty places from the bottom (Hausmann et al., n.d.: 66). Overall, it showed the forty-seventh biggest increase in economic complexity of the ninety-nine countries for which (1964–2008) data are available. The increase in complexity between 1998 and 2008 was particularly impressive, however, besting 80 per cent of the field (Hausmann et al., n.d.: 83).

At the time of writing, Cambodia is experiencing another wave of structural transformation, with the arrival in the country of electronics and light engineering firms, transferring the most labour-intensive aspects of their production from higher-wage China and Thailand (Figure 5.7). Table 5.2 summarizes the main economic trends, in addition to anticipating the main points of the political discussion below.

---

[1] *The Atlas of Economic Complexity* records trade in goods, but not services.

Total: $19.6 million

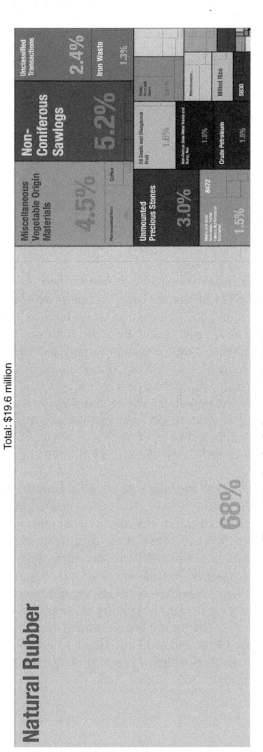

Figure 5.5. Cambodia's exports in 1974

Source: Atlas of Economic Complexity <http://atlas.cid.harvard.edu/>.

Total: $14.7 million

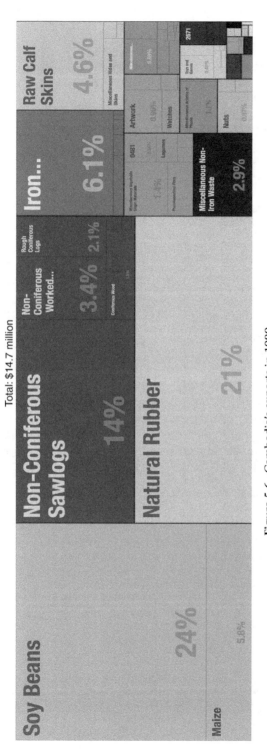

Figure 5.6. Cambodia's exports in 1989

Source: Atlas of Economic Complexity <http://atlas.cid.harvard.edu/>.

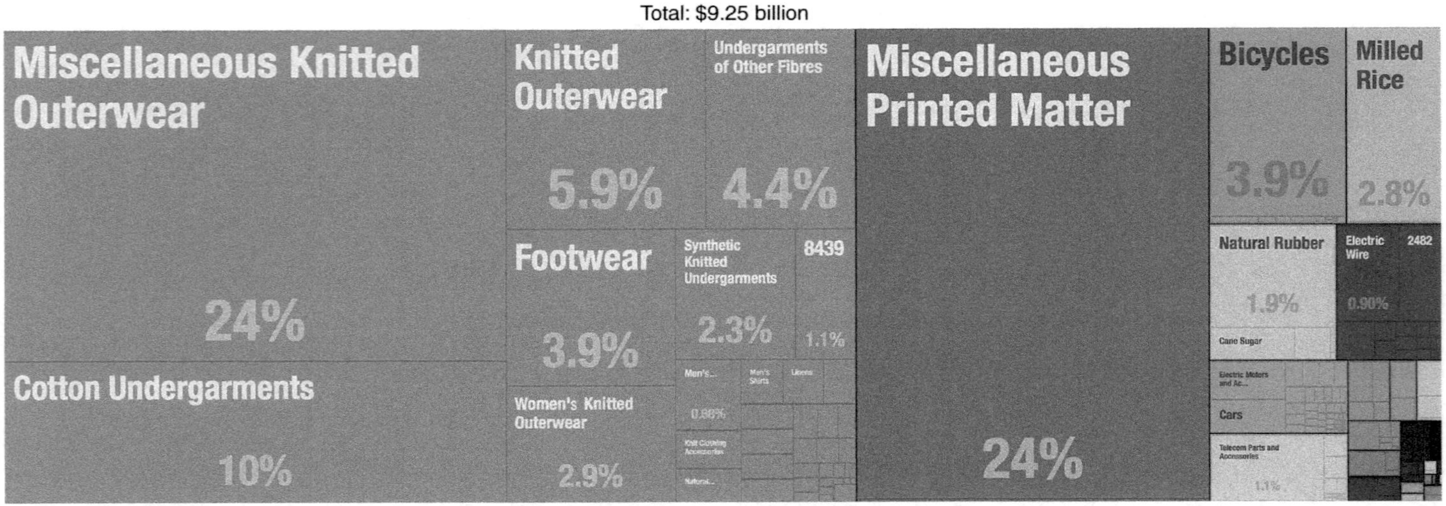

Total: $9.25 billion

Figure 5.7. Cambodia's exports in 2013
Source: *Atlas of Economic Complexity* <http://atlas.cid.harvard.edu/>.

Table 5.2. Growth episodes and regime features in Cambodia: main characteristics

Growth	Regime and political settlement		Rents and product space		Deals environment
Growth episode	Political regime	Political settlement type	Main economic actors	Main exports	Nature of deals
Collapse (1970–82)	Lon Nol Republic	Competitive clientelism	State firms, concessionaires, importers	Rubber, logs	Semi-open, disordered
	Khmer Rouge	Weak dominant party	State industry and agriculture	Cement, rubber	Centrally planned economy
Acceleration (1982–98)	Kampuchean People's Revolutionary Party	Vulnerable authoritarian coalition	Agricultural cooperatives, small farmers, foresters, smugglers	Soy, rubber, logs	Closed, semi-ordered
	CPP/FUNCINPEC coalition	Competitive clientelism	Timber producers, garment manufacturers	Logs, garments, rubber	Semi-open, disordered
Miracle growth (1998–2013)	CPP dominated	Dominant party with moderately strong internal and external factions	Timber producers, garment manufacturers, tourist operators, agribusiness, infrastructure	Garments, misc. printed matter, bicycles	Dependent on sector, but tending towards semi-open, semi-ordered

5.3 Politics of Economic Growth in Cambodia

To understand this pattern of bust and boom, we need to understand Cambodia's politics. Cambodia has experienced five political settlements since 1970. The first two were characterized by economic collapse, the third by economic recovery, the fourth by continued but uneven recovery, and the fifth by exceptionally strong levels of growth. Each of these political settlements involved distinctive ways of doing business, or developments in the deals environment.

Our story starts in 1970, when Cambodia's independence leader, Prince Norodom Sihanouk, was overthrown in a coup and replaced by General Lon Nol. For the previous five years Cambodia had been rocked by insurgency and economic decline, as Sihanouk's political settlement unravelled under the pressure of the war in neighbouring Vietnam and a local insurgency, spearheaded by the Maoist Khmer Rouge. The coup was supported by Cambodia's business community and the USA, and paved the way for a resumption of American aid, which Sihanouk had voluntarily renounced in 1963. The environment for business deals did not improve, however. The political settlement took the form of a game of musical chairs, in which Lon Nol presided over a rapid succession of governments in which politicians and their military allies took turns to feed at the trough of aid money. Meanwhile, insurgents occupied much of the countryside and productive assets were destroyed by bombing. Many investors left the country (Chandler, 1991; Slocomb, 2010).

Lon Nol's regime surrendered in 1975, overrun by the Khmer Rouge. The political settlement in what was now called 'Democratic Kampuchea' took the form of a clique of intellectuals who used a mixture of ideology, coercion, and terror to maintain control over their party cadres and the wider population. This clique set about implementing an extreme leftist ideology inspired in part by China's 'Cultural Revolution', the aim being to rid Cambodia of capitalist and imperialist influences and return it to 'Year Zero'. They planned a structural revolution in agriculture, evacuating the capital, Phnom Penh, and sending its inhabitants to toil night and day on communal irrigation works and collective farms in the countryside. The market economy and even money were banned, replaced by central planning. To all intents and purposes, the deals environment ceased to exist. The effect was disastrous: although the irrigated acreage expanded considerably, rice yields, rather than tripling, halved (Chandler, 1991; Slocomb, 2010). Industry apparently fared slightly better, as after the initial evacuation, a limited number of workers and technicians were sent back to Phnom Penh to man basic industries (Slocomb, 2010). Indeed, figures show the Khmer Rouge period to be the apogee of Cambodia's structural transformation (Figure 5.8). Given the generalized economic breakdown, however, these statistics are grossly misleading.

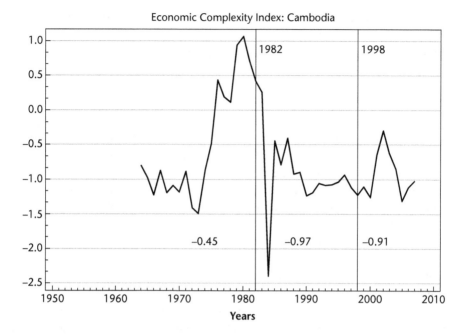

Figure 5.8. Economic complexity, Cambodia

Source: Atlas of Economic Complexity <http://atlas.cid.harvard.edu/>.

Note: The values are from Hausmann et al.'s (n.d.). Measure of Economic Complexity averaged over the period 1964–82, 1983–98, and 1999–2007, respectively.

The Khmer Rouge was overthrown in January 1979 by the Kampuchean People's Revolutionary Party (KPRP), a group of Khmer Rouge defectors and old-school socialists backed by Vietnamese troops. Heavily dependent on Vietnamese support, and opposed by the Khmer Rouge and certain former royalists, the first months were chaotic (Slocomb, 2010). Our data show the nadir of the economic crisis to be 1982. Thereafter, as the regime tightened its grip on power, the country entered a new economic phase, growing slightly for the first few years and then strongly for the next sixteen.

Characterizing the political settlement during this period is not straightforward. Evidence points, however, to the grafting of Vietnamese-inspired democratic centralism on to local power-sharing arrangements, often by means of force, at other times by means of turning a blind eye to local rent-generating practices.

Although officially a planned economy, this was never strong enough to extinguish the market, and would have perished were it not for the operations of private smugglers and the Chinese business community. At an early stage, certain members of the regime, young Foreign Minister Hun Sen included, recognized that by granting protection and privileges to such businessmen,

139

vital economic functions could be fulfilled and political advantage gained. Under this closed, semi-ordered deals environment, a modicum of political stability and economic growth was attained. By the late 1980s, Hun Sen was prime minister, the market economy had been legitimized, and key business-men had become influential allies of the regime (Gottesman, 2004: 90; Slocomb, 2010).

Insurgency continued in pockets of the country, however, and the regime continued to feel vulnerable. After the fall of the Berlin Wall, an international solution became available. In 1990, Vietnamese troops withdrew and the warring factions in Cambodia signed a peace agreement, which, although short-lived, led to a ceasefire, a United Nations peacekeeping force, and a resumption of Western aid. The People's Republic of Kampuchea (PRK) was renamed the State of Cambodia and then, after a return to constitutional monarchy in 1993, the Kingdom of Cambodia (Slocomb, 2010); the KPRP was renamed the Cambodian People's Party (CPP).

Elections were held in 1993, pitting Hun Sen's ruling CPP against FUNCINPEC (*Front Uni National pour un Cambodge Indépendant, Neutre, Pacifique et Coopératif*), a royalist party led by Norodom Ranariddh, Sihanouk's son. FUNCINPEC won a majority in the election, but the CPP refused to relinquish power. The solution was a power-sharing government, with Ranariddh and Hun Sen first and second prime ministers, respectively. This structure was replicated throughout the government, with a FUNCINPEC minister and CPP deputy-minister, or vice versa, in every ministry. A party-centric competition for spoils was thus brought into the heart of the regime, a battle in which the CPP progressively gained the upper hand (Roberts, 2001).[2]

The environment for business changed post-1990, with renewed inter-national recognition, foreign aid, and openness to the outside world. For the first time, the government made serious attempts to attract international capital and some foreign investment followed. Growth was patchy, however, not least because investors were confronted by a deals environment that had become unpredictable and disordered, thanks to a political settlement in which two political parties competed for ascendancy under the UN-brokered power-sharing deal.

The case of Ariston provides a good example. In what could have been Cambodia's biggest investment deal of the 1990s, Ariston, a Malaysian

---

[2] Citing Ashley, 'rather than depoliticizing a one-party state (controlled by the CPP), power sharing…created two separate and competing party states operating within every ministry, province, military command and police commissariat. Instead of working with their counterparts from the other party, officials from the prime ministers' level down conducted business with their party clients and colleagues. [This has] served to weaken the state by building and reinforcing parallel structures of personal and party authority, operating both within and outside the state' Roberts (2001: 129).

company, was scheduled to spend US$1.3 billion developing the Sihanoukville port, airport, and a power station. In return, it was to receive a monopoly over the casino sector, which it would use to help repay its investment. However, even after the company had begun making contractual payments to the government, the Casino Control Law failed to materialize. Apparently, the reason was that although the company had the strong backing of the first prime minister (FUNCINPEC's Norodom Ranariddh), the CPP already controlled several existing casinos and so opposed the law. Ariston complained about 'bureaucratic chaos', the government failing 'to honour its commitments', and a 'disorganized environment' (Fitzgerald, 1996; Vittachi, 1996). Its criticisms echoed those of Finance Minister Sam Rainsy, who in 1993 had complained that economic administration was 'confusing and irrational'. Cambodia was a 'jungle economy', in which foreign investors were subjected to 'endless arbitrary contributions to people and institutions not legally entitled' to collect (Burslem, 1993; Dodd, 1994; Hayes, 1993).

Further evidence comes from the forestry sector. As Slocomb notes: 'From very early on its history, the PRK recognized the development of export industries as a life and death matter for the regime' (Slocomb, 2010: 219), and by the late 1980s Cambodia's forests were being heavily exploited (Gottesman, 2004; Le Billon, 2000; Slocomb, 2010). Powerful informal networks linking politicians, businessmen, and the armed forces grew up around timber exports to Thailand. This continued under the post-1993 power-sharing system, with both prime ministers linked to informal forestry networks. A plethora of other actors also struggled to get its cut, employing 'red-taping, illegal logging, intimidation, kidnapping, and murder'. Foreign loggers paid bribes, bought illegal logs, or created 'joint ventures' with local leaders and businessmen (Le Billon 2000: 800).

Power sharing came to an end in 1997, when, following an attempt by Ranariddh to mount a Khmer Rouge-backed coup, the CPP won an armed confrontation with FUNCINPEC on the streets of Phnom Penh (Gottesman, 2004; Roberts, 2001). A year later the Khmer Rouge disintegrated and the CPP consolidated its power by winning the 1998 general election. Foreign investors appear to have welcomed this. Although the government lacked an overall majority and still governed in a coalition with FUNCINPEC, the latter was indisputably the junior partner. One investor expressed high hopes that Hun Sen would bring security, 'the number one factor for foreign investment', to the country, while for another, 'In terms of business, not of politics, one prime minister is better than two' (Eckardt, 1998).

Power consolidation paved the way for the increased foreign investment that Sam Rainsy had called for back in 1993. Rainsy himself had been sacked as finance minister in 1994; however, with the technical assistance of international donors, in particular the World Bank, at least some of the strengthening in state capacity he advocated was continued. The principal effect was the 1994 Law on Investment, which created the Council for the Development of Cambodia, a sole and one-stop service organization 'responsible for the rehabilitation, development, and the oversight of investment activity'. Foreign investors were provided guarantees against nationalization and price regulation, and permitted to own 100 per cent of their businesses. They were also provided with a variety of incentives, including a corporate tax rate of 9 per cent, tax exemption for up to eight years, non-taxation of remitted profits, import duty exemption for several types of industry, and permission to bring in foreign management, technical personnel, skilled workers, and spouses (Slocomb, 2010).

In the forestry sector, the centre imposed an increased degree of order over local anarchy (Slocomb, 2010). This involved granting timber concessions to large foreign investors and conducting a violent crackdown on illegal operators, including many thousands of rural poor who had eked out a living in the interstices of the previously anarchic system. The legalization process, which saw an increased proportion of forestry revenues flowing through the Treasury, 'enabled Phnom Penh not only to further its own personal interests but also to consolidate its power at the local level by undermining "unruly clients"' (Le Billon, 2000: 801).

In sum, 1998 marks the inauguration of a new political settlement, dominated by a CPP-centred coalition that has changed little over the subsequent fifteen years (see Figure 5.9). The settlement involves a balance between rent-seekers and technocrats within the inner circle of power. As we shall see, technocrats are given just enough latitude to support growth industries such as garments, tourism, electronics, and rice, leveraging a system of formal and informal investor channels that provide a positive feedback loop between growth and investments in state capacity. Rent-seekers (*oknha*) are given the political backing to generate profits, a proportion of which are funnelled back to the political elite, and thence to the masses in the form of CPP-backed patronage projects.[3]

The main beneficiaries of this patronage are CPP leaders, village development committees, pagoda committees, policemen, and, arguably, the Vietnamese community. Some also reaches farmers, workers, lower-level civil servants, monks, students, and soldiers. These latter groups are swing constituencies,

---

[3] According to Ear (2011), 'The title of "*oknha*" comes from Cambodia's peerage system and is bestowed by His Majesty the King. It is designated for individuals whose "Contributions [to national reconstruction] values in excess of $100,000". The title of *oknha* is the preserve of businessmen interested in formalizing their relationship with the state (and by extension the CPP). As of April 2008 there were officially 220 *oknha* of whom less than ten were women.' See also Hughes and Conway (2003); Pak (2007); Un (2005: 203–30); and Hughes and Un (2011: 1–26).

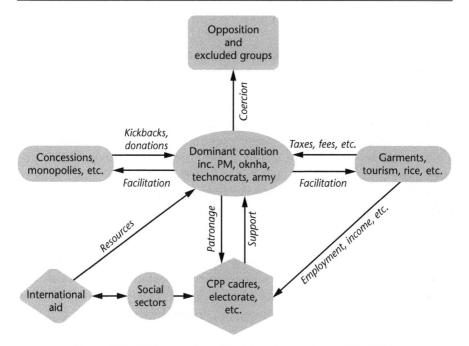

Figure 5.9. CPP's growth and legitimation strategy, 1998–2013
Source: Author's illustration.

however. In 1998, 2003, and 2008, enough of them supported the ruling party to deliver CPP election victories—although not without a tough challenge on the first two occasions (Cock, 2011; Heder, 2005). In the 2013 general election, the opposition, led by the newly created Cambodia National Rescue Party (CNRP), was much stronger. CNRP was part of a larger challenger coalition comprising pro-opposition trades unions, media, the Teachers' Association, and diaspora groups, with growing links to formerly excluded groups, such as the jobless and landless, some of whom had lost land to government-sponsored Economic Land Concessions (discussed in Section 5.4.2).[4] CNRP even claimed that in the absence of widespread irregularities it would have won the poll, and subsequently organized a string of mass demonstrations, refused to join the parliament, and threatened economic strikes and boycotts (Ponniah and Chanrasmey, 2013). At the time of writing (early 2014), the standoff, which has potentially damaging consequences for Cambodia's continued growth, had not been resolved.

---

[4] See among others Roberts (2001: 32–4, 116–17) for the significance of patronage in Cambodian socio-political relations.

5.4 Evolution of the Deals Environment in Cambodia

We have seen, then, that Cambodia's economic collapse in the 1970s was associated with a disordered or non-existent deals environment, first under Lon Nol and then the Khmer Rouge. In the 1980s, a degree of order returned under the PRK, and the economy began to recover. After 1990, however, UN-brokered power-sharing disrupted that order, so that even though the economy became increasingly open, economic growth was unstable. After 1998, with the consolidation of CPP power, the deals environment became both more open and ordered, and strong growth has been sustained. Important social groups have been excluded from that growth, however, and the political settlement of the past fifteen years is facing a stiff challenge.

This section draws on interviews with government officials, industry experts, and firms in four economic sectors, to provide more insight into these processes. We show that there has been a positive feedback loop between support for competitive export industries, state capacity, and structural transformation. However, there has also been a negative feedback loop from overreliance on high-rent industries, to insufficiently inclusive growth and political instability.

5.4.1 *Magicians*

The main driver of Cambodia's growth and structural transformation in the post-1990 period has been the garment industry. Investors have been lured to Cambodia by the combination of political stability, cheap labour, an open investment regime, and preferential trade agreements with purchaser nations. A mixture of formal and informal institutions, meanwhile, has helped to resolve industry problems and injected increasing amounts of order into the deals environment.

For example, soon after the first investors arrived in Cambodia in 1994, they created the Garment Manufacturers' Association of Cambodia (GMAC), which the government later instructed every firm in the industry to join. Then, in 1999, apparently at the initiative of the prime minister and with the assistance of the International Finance Corporation, the government established the Government-Private Sector Forum (G-PSF). This has been supported by a system of industry-specific and cross-cutting working groups, bringing together private-sector representatives and ministerial officials to solve industry problems.

Working together, this growth coalition has progressively simplified, streamlined, and made export procedures more transparent. The garment industry now has its own single-window export processing facility, where firms know the informal fees that need to be paid, and how much to pay to expedite processing. The level of informal fees has also been reduced. As one informant said to us: 'What we have in the garment industry currently is extremely efficient, transparent, predictable corruption', a sentiment that was agreed to by all of our informants.[5] At customs, previously under-the-table fees have even been formalized and publicized.

In addition to formal lobbying through the G-PSF, GMAC's secretary-general will often intercede with government officials at different levels of the administration to resolve problems facing individual firms. GMAC also curries favour with the government in other ways, for example contributing rice or cash to provincial government ceremonies. Firms themselves also do quite a bit of this, as well as conducting other forms of informal lobbying, such as entertaining or playing golf with relevant ministers, especially when a political decision that might affect the industry is looming.

Not all is perfect, however. The main problem currently facing the garment industry is industrial relations. Cambodia has over 2,000 unions, and in most garment factories multiple unions are operating. As one informant said to us, 'The government can't control the unions', while others complained that the government tended to pressure employers, but not unions, to comply with the Labour Law. This was particularly evident in 2013, an election year, when unions saw an opportunity to press home their advantage, and there was a large number of strikes (Aun and Dene-Hern, 2013). Nevertheless, foreign investment has continued to flow into Cambodia's garmenting sector. It seems the level of industrial action is not sufficient to upset the country's relative cost advantages, when wages in nearby Thailand and China are spiking.

State capacity-building around garments has had positive feedback effects for other export industries. According to one well-placed source:

> We opened the road for many other exporting industries, we cleared the path really, clarifying certain issues ... [the government] look[s] to us and says, 'ok, this is being done for [the garment] industry and it should apply to other industries'. So we are really spearheading a lot of the trade facilitation that is being seen.

---

[5] To quote an industry representative at length: 'for businesses we are in a very good position ... we've moved from real corruption per se [in 2002], where you don't know how much to pay, you don't know who to pay to, or what service you're going to get in return, it's murky ... and over the years we've worked on clarifying that, and lowering the amount of money to the extent that today we have a very highly transparent but corrupt system in that the payments are informal ... they don't go through the government ... but it's highly transparent. To the private sector we don't really care if it's formal, well, we would like it to be formal because then we get receipts for it, but what we really want is service ... as long as we get the service we were promised. ... [Now] we can always pay for express, whereas in a really rigid system that might not be available ... we are undergoing the process of having the system formalized, and it's a natural, painful process, and we may go backwards before we go forwards, but I think it's necessary, it will take two, three, four, five years.'

For example, in the past few years, electronics firms such as Minebea, Sumitomo, and Hana have begun transferring the most labour-intensive aspects of their South East Asian operations to Cambodia. The pioneers have received strong encouragement from the Council for the Development of Cambodia (CDC), and benefit from a government-Japanese investor forum held at the CDC several times a year. The prime minister has also taken a personal interest in the industry, opening at least one electronics plant. The manufacturer we spoke to claimed to have good personal relations with ministers, with whom he could meet face to face, informally, to discuss industry problems. For example, he was lobbying on all fronts to try and secure a reduction in the electricity tariff for large users, to accelerate processing times for importing components through customs, and to reduce the number of signatures required to process exports.

Another industry in the garmenting slipstream is milled rice. With the release of the prime minister's 'Policy Paper on the Promotion of Paddy Production and Rice Exports' in 2010, expanding exports of processed rice has been identified as a major goal in Cambodia's ongoing structural transformation (Guimbert, 2010a; Royal Government of Cambodia, 2010).[6] The policy aims to put Cambodia among the world's top rice exporters, setting a target of one million tonnes by 2015. In 2011, the first Cambodian Rice Forum was staged and, following the G-PSF that year, a new technical working group for rice was created. Spurred on by the policy, many existing rice millers have upgraded their plants and some new investors have entered the industry (Rann, 2013). Since then, a number of measures have been taken to assist rice exports, for example, concessions on the importation of machinery, new certificate of origin and phytosanitary documents, and a single window for export facilitation at the CDC. The government has also had some success in concluding deals for Cambodian rice with foreign governments.

Exports have risen exponentially as a result, but further dramatic expansions will be required to meet the 2015 target. This will involve overcoming additional challenges of quality, marketing, costs, and finance. Focusing only on the last two, Cambodian millers currently lack sufficient finance to purchase what rice there is available, meaning that much still flows out of the country in unprocessed form. Costs are another issue. Currently, Cambodian rice is competitive in price when it leaves the farm gate, but high transport and electricity prices mean that by the time it leaves the country it is more expensive than rice from neighbouring Vietnam.

The combination of formal and informal lobbying that is characteristic of the garment sector also applies to rice, but the government has arguably been

---

[6] For an earlier account of the rice industry, see Ear (2011).

slower in responding to industry demands than it has in the case of garments. There are a number of factors behind this. To begin with, the coordination problems affecting rice are arguably more challenging than for garments. Personalities are also important. As one rice industry representative said: 'Some ministries are good, some are not. Much depends on the minister. If the minister is pushing, it is ok; if not, nothing happens. It is not always easy to get a ministry to reform or streamline its procedures.'[7] Third, while the garment sector is dominated by expatriates, the majority of rice millers are Cambodian. As a result, their entwinement in local politics is probably greater. Recently, the prime minister has encouraged some of the country's biggest tycoons to enter the sector. Indeed, there have recently been moves to integrate Cambodia's various rice industry associations into a single body, chaired by the son of a deputy prime minister. Whether the increasing closeness of the CPP and the rice industry will enhance the growth coalition behind it, or make it more prone to predation, remains to be seen.

5.4.2 Rentiers

As we saw in Section 5.2, one of the first industries promoted by the regime after the fall of the Khmer Rouge was forestry, and today the large-scale exploitation of forest resources and tropical agricultural products continues. Most large-scale agro-forestry takes place on what are called Economic Land Concessions (ELCs). According to some non-governmental organizations (NGOs), since 2000 Cambodia has granted more than two million hectares in ELCs to more than 200 firms. Around 28 per cent of that area is held by CPP senators Lao Meng Khin, Mong Reththy, and Ly Yong Phat, together with An Marady, another tycoon (Vrieze and Kuch, 2012).[8]

The deals environment in which this takes place is best described as semi-open and semi-ordered, but without a level playing field. To grasp this, one needs to understand that ELCs are granted by the Ministry of Agriculture, Forestry, and Fisheries (MAFF), and must also be approved by the Ministry of the Environment. Although the ministry is supposed to allocate ELCs according to the principle of spatial planning—identifying suitable blocs of land for development, advertising them, and then awarding the concession to the best or highest bidder—in practice, it responds to requests from investors who have already identified blocs of land. There appear to be two main routes to acquiring land from MAFF. One is to approach the ministry directly or

---

[7] Another senior technocrat explained to us that he was battling vested interests in the government every day to try and push through reforms.

[8] The government, meanwhile, puts the figure at 1.2 million hectares granted to 118 agro-industrial firms, including twenty-eight Chinese and twenty-seven Vietnamese companies.

through an agent, following its procedures, and paying its informal fees, so as to acquire the land desired. Another is to induce political connections in the Council of Ministers (Cambodia's cabinet), to put pressure on MAFF. Investors who pursue the first route are at some risk of having their concession grabbed by someone pursuing the other. We spoke to one investor who had lost money because ultimately his agent could not deliver, a fact he attributed to insufficiently strong political connections. Another investor, however, claimed that as long as one was careful and exercised due diligence, political connections were not necessary.

Once acquired, investments appear to be semi-secure. Cambodia's land law currently lacks clarity, and much land has multiple claimants. Investors often find themselves embroiled in conflicts with local communities, NGOs, or other investors, and have to be able to play the game of local politics: 'You have to work both ends simultaneously and you have to be on the land, developing it, otherwise someone else will occupy it. You can't be an absentee landlord here.' The same source had suffered encroachments by a powerful local tycoon, whom he claimed had falsified land documents.[9]

Perhaps the biggest constraints on success are operational, rather than political. Given prevailing human resource constraints in Cambodia, managing a large agribusiness venture is risky. Agriculture and agro-industry has its own technical working group in the G-PSF, chaired by land magnate Mong Reththy, and one of our sources credited the latter with doing a great deal to smooth the way for agribusiness in Cambodia. Yet, aside from making land available and opening up the countryside with road-building projects, it is not clear that the government is actually providing much support.

Although the government claims that the agro-export sector will create employment and reduce poverty, currently the reverse appears to be true, with claims that over 400,000 people have been displaced or involved in land conflicts since 2000 (Vrieze and Kuch, 2012). In fact, it is possible to identify a negative feedback loop between agro-exports and the entire possibility of growth maintenance. Not only does the land sector provide a source of easy rents for the political class, obviating the need to focus on more dynamic growth industries, it has created a political backlash that endangers political stability. The government has belatedly recognized this fact, and in May 2012, shortly before commune council elections, the prime minister announced a moratorium on ELCs (Zsombor and Aun, 2012).[10] Consequently, the deals

---

[9] Hughes and Un (2011: 9) note that both productive and speculative investment in land 'reflect a certain level of confidence in Cambodian institutions, either formal or neo-patrimonial'.

[10] The government has also granted numerous concessions for mineral exploration and is developing a small oil industry. Although data on these industries are scarce, analysts have predicted that they are likely to cement inequality, elite self-enrichment, and truncated democracy (Un and So, 2009).

environment in the large-scale agro-export sector is now closed. Whether it will open again, and whether when it does so it will be any more ordered or open to all-comers than hitherto, is difficult to know at this stage.

5.4.3 *Workhorses*

Competitive domestic industry in Cambodia is dominated by small and medium enterprises (SMEs).[11] The deals environment here is best described as semi-ordered and relatively open. We spoke to a number of successful SME operators in the retail, tourism, construction, and Internet businesses. Most of our informants were quite young, and had been given a start in business by their parents, especially through education. The main constraints on their businesses included taxes, the high cost of credit, electricity, and human resources. Some also complained of unfair competition, either from foreign or unlicensed businesses, but political interference was not regarded as a major problem. The regulatory environment and the corruption that accompanied it was described as 'a bit confusing', with most SMEs facing a less transparent and predictable set of arrangements than, for example, the garment industry. However, this was regarded as a nuisance, rather than unmanageable.

Currently SMEs are registered with a variety of government ministries, with no overall body coordinating them. At the Ministry of Industry, Minerals, and Energy, there has been for several years a Small Industry Department, with about thirty employees, but we were told that it lacked political clout. It had had some success setting boundaries and coordinating inspection regimes between ministries, but more ambitious attempts to reduce small business registration costs by introducing a single window have lacked buy-in from other ministries. One informant argued that the problem is that SMEs lack connections to the top political leadership, who prefer to push for large-scale agro-industrial development. Although some small businesses are represented by bodies such as the Young Entrepreneurs' Association, or the Federation of Small and Medium Enterprises (FASMEC), which co-chairs the SME subcommittee of the manufacturing and SME working group at the G-PSF, vast swathes of the sector are unrepresented. Partly in consequence, SMEs face serious problems accessing finance, building capacity, and upgrading production.

---

[11] According to the preliminary results of the 2011 economic census, there are about 505,000 firms employing between one and one hundred workers each (NIS, 2011). SMEs involved in 'wholesale and retail trade, repair of motor vehicles, and motorcycles sector' comprised the largest proportion of establishments (58 per cent), followed by those dealing in the 'manufacturing sector' (14 per cent), and 'accommodation and food service activities sector' (14 per cent) (NIS, 2011). There are also estimated to be around nine million peasant farmers (Ear, 2011).

We also conducted interviews with small-scale rubber planters, of which there are around 20,000 in Cambodia. The planters receive some technical support from the government's General Directorate of Rubber, and the Agence Française de Développement is supporting farmers' associations. Nevertheless, the farmers complained about their relations with processors and traders, some of the technical advice they received, and the difficulties they experienced upgrading their production. Although small rubber remains profitable and a potential source of poverty alleviation, the growth coalition behind it appears weak.

5.4.4 *Powerbrokers*

Monopolistic or semi-monopolistic areas of the domestic economy include: electricity and water supply; concessions to manage and operate heritage sites, tourist attractions, and casinos; and rail transport and domestic air transport. In addition, government sometimes awards contracts to private companies for major infrastructure projects, such as power, roads, airports, ports, and special economic zones. There are also a number of large urban development projects either recently completed or underway in Phnom Penh. Other large domestic industries include banking, telecoms, brewing, and petrol supply, all of which are dominated by a few large players, with a smattering of smaller operators. Prominent in most are the biggest Cambodian tycoons or *oknha*, large East Asian foreign companies, or both. The business environment in this sector appears to be semi-ordered and semi-open, although there are some interesting sub-trends.

Probably the most important sector is urban real estate, with Phnom Penh in particular home to several developments worth many hundreds of millions of dollars. Although most of these lack transparency, NGOs claim that land has been acquired at a fraction of its market value, providing an opportunity for large rents to be made. The kinds of legal ambiguity we saw for the ELC sector also apply in urban areas, but, as is the case there, this has done little to deter investment projects. For those with political connections, land and project approval appears relatively easy to obtain. It is also probably the case that those without political connections can easily acquire them as long as they have money (Sahmakum Teang Tnaut, 2012).

Because most land in the city is already occupied, projects have sometimes been delayed by conflicts, but developers do seem to enjoy the consistent support of state authorities. The most obvious case is Boeung Kak Lake, where more than 4,000 families have lost their homes to the Chinese-backed Shukaku company. Shukaku is associated with the wife of the CPP senator, Lao Meng Khin, said to be personally close to the prime minister's family, as well as being one of the biggest financial contributors to the CPP (So, 2010).

Boeung Kak, however, is just the tip of the iceberg. NGOs estimate that more than 10 per cent of the capital's population has been evicted over the past two decades, with most moved to woefully inadequate relocation sites on the outskirts of the city (Sahmakum Teang Tnaut, 2012).

Another important area of the domestic high-rent economy is infrastructure projects, many of which suffer from a lack of regulatory oversight and transparency. A case in point are public–private partnerships, of which a great number, some quite large, are being implemented. According to the Asian Development Bank, public–private partnerships 'are not standardized, and they tend to be issued on a reactive, unsolicited, and negotiated basis, rather than through proactive government preparation and competitive tendering' (Asian Development Bank and Agence Française de Développement, 2012: xi). In this context, there are fears that some of the larger hydropower projects, undertaken by partnerships between Chinese companies and local tycoons, have saddled the government with excessive contingent liabilities. Specialists suspect that procurement practices generally suffer from rigged specifications, limited publicity, collusion, kickbacks, and falsification of key information (Asian Development Bank, 2012b).

The sector we looked at most closely, telecommunications, appears by contrast to have transitioned from a fairly ordered but closed environment, to a much more open but disordered environment. The mobile industry dates from the early 1990s, with Mfone starting in 1993, Hello in 1996, and Mobitel in 1997 (Kierans, 2010). These three players, described by a rival operator as 'a kind of cartel, with poor service and high charges', dominated the market until 2006. After Cambodia's accession to the World Trade Organization (WTO), however, the Ministry of Posts and Telecommunications came under pressure to open the industry, and responded by issuing at least eight new licences. By 2009, there were nine mobile operators, making Cambodia one of the most crowded markets in the world (Kierans, 2010).[12] A price war ensued, accompanied by suspicions of price dumping, threats of legal action, and blocking of interconnects (Finch and Nguon, 2009).[13]

Shortly thereafter, the government decided to intervene by setting a floor price. However, new entrants argued that price-floor regulation was contrary to Cambodia's Investment Law and Constitution, as well as regional norms, and the regulation was not enforced.[14] Fierce competition continued and market consolidation ensued (Renzenbrink, 2013). The government again

---

[12] Our informants presumed that greed and corruption were at least partly responsible for the issuing of so many licences.

[13] There were disputes among our informants about whether or not these prices were regionally out of line.

[14] The truth of the matter is complex, since a couple of months after issuing *Prakas* 232 the Royal Government issued Notice 145, which permitted ministries to set a floor price.

attempted to impose a price floor in April 2013, but again backed down (Kunmakara, 2013; Reuy and Renzenbrink, 2013). Since the biggest operators are said to have links to the inner circle of power, allegations of improper political influence were traded back and forth, with the truth of the matter somewhat difficult to discern. What is clear is that all operators dislike the uncertainty surrounding the rules of the game, and are investing less than they otherwise would. According to one operator, 'You can't invest if it's impossible to make money', while for another the price-floor decision led to 'an immediate revision of our investment strategy'.

Despite what one investor described as the 'Wild West' environment for business, the bigger operators have continued to make investments in infrastructure and innovative products, and the industry has grown.[15] However, the disordered nature of competition has doubtless constrained the nature and level of investment, meaning that the expansion of an industry with many positive externalities has been far from ideal. All our informants consequently expressed a desire for better and more transparent regulation, claiming that the current regulator—the Telecommunication Regulator of Cambodia— lacked technical capacity and was neither neutral nor independent.

The telecommunications industry thus provides a curious twist to our deals environment tale. Closed and relatively ordered in the 1990s, as we would expect such a sector to be, WTO accession had thrown the sector open. The precise form of this openness, however, has been conditioned by a mixture of rent-seeking in the Ministry of Telecommunications, personal links between industry owners and the inner circle of power, and the desire of CEOs for a more predictable and transparent deals environment.

5.5 Political Dynamics of Growth Maintenance

We have seen that the consolidation of Hun Sen's political settlement post-1998 has helped maintain high growth for the past fifteen years. But can this growth be sustained? The deals and development framework hypothesizes that maintaining growth requires that the deals environment, as well as remaining relatively ordered, must become progressively more open, and be buttressed by increasingly sophisticated state capabilities. It also predicts that growth in competitive sectors creates positive feedback loops for the deals environment generally, while growth in less competitive sectors can create negative feedback loops.

---

[15] Interviews, October 2013.

We have found some evidence of positive feedback loops from growth in garments, to increased state capacity, to investment in new industries such as electronics. Hun Sen has long been a champion of the free market, and this fact, combined with WTO membership, means that just about every economic sector in Cambodia remains at least semi-open. Although well-connected rent-seekers tend to be given the first and best pieces of the economic pie, it is relatively easy for newcomers with money to acquire political connections, and in some cases it is not always necessary to have political connections at all. New entrants create competition and in some cases fuel growth, meaning that, from a purely technical point of view, the prospects for sustained growth appear good.

Negative feedback loops do exist, however. First is a negative loop from unsolicited tendering and inadequate regulation, to inefficient energy and infrastructure, which acts as a constraint on other industries. Second, there is also arguably a negative loop caused by the steady flow of easy rents to the political class in areas such as land and urban real estate, which generates a certain amount of complacency when it comes to building capacity in more dynamic industries. As we have seen, the coalition behind garments has been quite effective, but even it suffers from inadequate regulation of industrial relations.[16] The coalition behind milled rice has also achieved some success, but is not strong enough to loosen all the binding constraints on growth. SMEs, meanwhile, receive little support from government and are more or less left to fend for themselves in a confusing, if not completely hostile, business environment.

Third, there is a negative feedback loop from the character of Cambodia's growth to its political stability. As we have seen, ELCs and large-scale urban developments have generated large economic rents for the political class and connected businessmen, a significant proportion of which have been ploughed back into rural communities in the form of patronage spending.

For a long time, it could have been argued that this less palatable side of Cambodia's growth was actually a key pillar of the political settlement and hence the whole system's stability. But this is no longer the case. Land acquisitions have hurt the livelihoods of a significant number, and also appear to have damaged the image of the government in the eyes of an increasingly youthful and politically motivated electorate. In the 2013 election, the opposition ran on a populist platform that included a US$150 per month minimum wage, pay increases for teachers and civil servants, a review of economic land concessions, and pensions for the elderly. The election outcome suggests that

---

[16] Ear (2011) argues persuasively that international actors, in particular the International Labour Office, have been instrumental in solving collective action problems and cementing the growth coalition behind garments, with no equivalent body playing that role in rice.

a significant proportion of the population prefer this to the government's patronage policies. Indeed, a high-ranking technocrat confided in us that: 'We knew there was a gap developing, but we didn't think we would need to address it until 2018—we thought we could get another five years of growth first.'[17]

If Cambodian growth were entirely determined by domestic political forces, then, we would say at this point that it hangs in the balance, and is possibly even tipping towards deceleration. In reality, however, Cambodian growth is also shaped by powerful neighbourhood effects. Despite continuing frailties of state capacity, industrial relations problems, and political unrest in 2013, investors continued to flock to the country, driven by price changes in Thailand and China. In 2014 and 2015, GDP growth remained at 7 per cent or more. There is no room for complacency, however. So long as the conditions that led to political crisis remain unresolved, the re-emergence of unrest seems likely at some point. Were that to coincide with a less favourable set of external conditions, Cambodia's growth could rapidly come off the rails.

5.6 Conclusion

Cambodia's growth experience is somewhat remarkable internationally, being characterized by an extreme collapse, followed by a lengthy and accelerating recovery. The details of this recovery provide general support for our hypothesis that growth accelerations are facilitated by political settlements that can oversee a shift from disorder to order in the deals environment, and are maintained via a progressive opening of the deals environment, with a positive feedback loop between competitive export industry, ideology, and state capacity.

However, Cambodia's growth experience has had two faces, and its less progressive side also provides support for the idea that a political elite which depends for its survival on high-rent industries is likely to prove complacent when it comes to building state capacity in more dynamic areas, bringing us to the crossroads at which we presently find ourselves.

The Cambodia case also points to a number of refinements of our theory. To begin with, as a small country, Cambodia's growth has been heavily influenced by external factors. For example, despite continuing frailties of state capacity and recent industrial relations problems in the garment industry, investors continue to flock to the country, driven by price changes in Thailand

---

[17] Another senior technocrat, however, rejected the idea that economic performance was responsible for the election result, claiming that the living standards of '98 per cent' of the population had improved under the last government. (Interview, August 2013.)

and China. Were Cambodia located in landlocked Africa rather than coastal South East Asia, the story would be rather different, we suspect. Consequently, the external environment or 'neighbourhood effects' should probably acquire the status of a variable in our model.

Second, Cambodia highlights the importance of electoral feedback loops. While the state is arguably doing just enough in terms of state–business relations to keep high growth on track, inattention to the character of growth, in particular perceptions of a widening gap between rich and poor, together with an increasingly youthful and educated electorate, has sparked a political backlash. This has come even in the face of quite impressive progress, according to official statistics, on poverty reduction and the Millennium Development Goals.

This electoral feedback could have either positive or negative implications for growth. On the one hand, it creates pressure for reforms, for example a more transparent and competent bureaucracy and a more open regulatory environment, which our model predicts will be necessary to keep growth on track in the medium and long term. On the other hand, very serious political instability would probably deter investment and growth. In mid-2016, the strikes and mass demonstrations of late 2013 and early 2014 have cooled, with the CPP engaged in a game of cat and mouse with the opposition. Investment remains fairly robust. Nevertheless, there is a sense that the threat of major political instability has merely been deferred rather than satisfactorily addressed. Whatever the eventual outcome, it seems that electoral feedback and popular action should play an elevated role in our model.

Another potential refinement stems from the fact that our model is currently based on there being a clear difference between rent-seekers in the natural resource sector and magicians in competitive export sectors such as garments. However, it is not obvious to us that a garment manufacturer relocating their operation from China to Cambodia in search of cheap labour and preferential trade arrangements (which function somewhat like rents) is doing anything more miraculous than an investor trying to make an honest buck in the sustainable teak or palm oil industry (in fact the latter may be more difficult to make profits in and thus require greater experimentation and innovation in the production process). Thus the model may benefit from a rather more nuanced appreciation of the relationship between economic sectors and the nature of investors therein.

Fine-grained analysis of sectors also suggests that making generalizations about the deals environment for the entire country is difficult. It is different for different sectors, and for different subgroups of investors within sectors, at any point in time. Without clear metrics for identifying and measuring the nature of the deals environment, assessing the overall direction of change is challenging.

155

Finally, it is worth noting some of the anomalies generated by the way in which economic complexity is calculated. As we saw in Section 5.2, our analysis currently depicts Democratic Kampuchea as the acme of economic complexity in Cambodia, when any sensible reading of the data suggests the opposite is in fact the case.

References

Asian Development Bank. 2012a. 'Key Indicators for Asia and Pacific 2012: Cambodia'. Accessed 10 August 2013.

Asian Development Bank. 2012b. *Cambodia: Country Governance Risk Assessment and Risk Management Plan*. Mandaluyong City: Asian Development Bank.

Asian Development Bank and Agence Française de Développement. 2012. *Assessment of Public–Private Partnerships in Cambodia: Constraints and Opportunities*. Manila: Asian Development Bank.

Aun, P., and Dene-Hern, C. 2013. 'Government to Meet over January Minimum Wage Increase'. *Cambodia Daily*, 26 November.

Burslem, C. 1993. 'Rainsy to Hike Taxes, Review Concessions'. *Phnom Penh Post*, 16 July.

Chandler, D. 1991. *The Tragedy of Cambodian History: Politics, War, and Revolution since 1945*. Bangkok: Yale University Press and Silkworm Books.

Cock, A. 2011. 'The Rise of Provincial Business in Cambodia'. In *Cambodia's Economic Transformation*. Edited by Hughes, C., and Un, K. Copenhagen: Nordic Institute of Asian Studies Press.

Dodd, M. 1994. 'Rainsy Rails at Mafia Money Laundering'. *Phnom Penh Post*, 11 March.

Ear, S. 2011. 'Growth in the Rice and Garments Sectors'. In *Cambodia's Economic Transformation*. Edited by Hughes, C., and Un, K. Copenhagen: Nordic Institute of Asian Studies Press.

Eckardt, J. 1998. 'Investors Bullish on Hun Sen-led Gov't'. *Phnom Penh Post*, 21 August.

Finch, S., and Nguon, S. 2009. 'Mobitel Files Lawsuit in Row with Beeline'. *Phnom Penh Post*, 24 September.

Fitzgerald, T. 1996. 'Ariston: "We can no longer be polite" '. *Phnom Penh Post*, 31 May.

Gottesman, E. 2004. *Cambodia after the Khmer Rouge: Inside the Politics of Nation Building*. Chiang Mai: Silkworm Books.

Guimbert, S. 2010a.'Cambodia Moves to Increase Exports of its "White Gold" (Rice)'. East Asia and Pacific on the Rise blog. The World Bank. <http://blogs.worldbank.org/eastasiapacific/cambodia-moves-to-increase-exports-of-its-white-gold-rice> (accessed 15 September 2016).

Guimbert, S. 2010b. 'Cambodia 1998–2008: An Episode of Rapid Growth'. Policy Research Working Paper 5271. The World Bank East Asia and Pacific Region. <http://documents.worldbank.org/curated/en/957361468016740248/Cambodia-1998-2008-an-episode-of-rapid-growth> (accessed 12 January 2017).

Hausmann, R., Hidalgo, C. A., Bustos, S., Coscia, M., Chung, S., Jimenez, J., Simoes, A., and Yildirim, M. A. (n.d.). *The Atlas of Economic Complexity: Mapping Paths to Prosperity*. Center for International Development, Harvard University.

Hayes, K. 1993. 'Rainsy Appeals for Foreign Investment'. *Phnom Penh Post*, 30 July.

Heder, S. 2005. 'Hun Sen's Consolidation: Death or Beginning of Reform?' In *South East Asian Affairs 2005*. Singapore: Institute of Southeast Asian Studies Publishing.

Hughes, C., and Conway, T. 2003. *Understanding Pro-Poor Political Change: The Policy Process—Cambodia. Second Draft, August 2003*. London: Overseas Development Institute.

Hughes, C., and Un, K. 2011. 'Cambodia's Economic Transformation: Historical and Theoretical Frameworks'. In *Cambodia's Economic Transformation*. Edited by Hughes, C., and Un, K. Copenhagen: Nordic Institute of Asian Studies Press.

Kar, S., Pritchett, L., Raihan, S., and Sen, K. 2013. *The Dynamics of Economic Growth: A Visual Handbook of Growth Rates, Regimes, Transitions and Volatility*. Manchester: University of Manchester.

Kierans, K. 2010. 'Cambodia: A Land of Opportunity'. *Asia's Media Innovators Vol 2.0*. Singapore: Konrad-Adenauer-Stiftung Media Programme Asia. <http://www.kas.de/medien-asien/en/publications/20526/>.

Kunmakara, M. 2013. 'Government Tells Telcos Off'. *Phnom Penh Post*, 8 April.

Le Billon, P. 2000. 'The Political Ecology of Transition in Cambodia 1989–1999: War, Peace, and Forest Exploitation'. *Development and Change*, 31: 785–805.

Ministry of Agriculture, Forestry and Fisheries. 2011. *Annual Report for Agriculture, Forestry and Fisheries 2010–2011*. Phnom Penh: MAFF.

Ministry of Tourism. 2012. *Tourism Statistics: Annual Report on 2012*. Phnom Penh: Statistics and Information Department.

NIS (National Institute of Statistics). 2011. *Statistical Yearbook of Cambodia 2011*. Phnom Penh: Ministry of Planning.

Pak, K. 2007. *Accountability and Neo-Patrimonialism in Cambodia: A Critical Literature Review*. Phnom Penh: Cambodia Development Resource Institute.

Ponniah, K., and Chanrasmey, K. 2013. 'Rainsy Threatens General Strike'. *Phnom Penh Post*, 25 September.

Pritchett, L., and Werker, E. 2012. 'Developing the Guts of a GUT (Grand Unified Theory): Elite Commitment and Inclusive Growth'. ESID Working Paper No. 16. Effective States and Inclusive Development Research Centre. Manchester: University of Manchester.

Rann, R. 2013. 'Getting into the Milled Rice Game'. *Phnom Penh Post*, 26 July.

Renzenbrink, A. 2013. 'Resuregent Mobile Deals Could Hurt Margins, Analysts Say'. *Phnom Penh Post*, 2 September.

Reuy, R., and Renzenbrink, A. 2013. 'Ministry Cancels Telco Limits'. *Phnom Penh Post*, 7 May.

Roberts, D. W. 2001. *Political Transition in Cambodia 1991–99: Power, Elitism and Democracy*. Richmond: Curzon Press.

Royal Government of Cambodia. 2010. 'Policy Paper on the Promotion of Paddy Production and Rice Exports'. Phnom Penh.

Sahmakum Teang Tnaut. 2012. *A Tale of Two Cities: Review of the Development Paradigm in Phnom Penh*. Phnom Penh: STT.

Sen, K. 2012. 'The Political Dynamics of Economic Growth'. ESID Working Paper No. 5. Manchester: University of Manchester.

Slocomb, M. 2010. *An Economic History of Cambodia in the Twentieth Century*. Singapore: NUS Press.

So, S. 2010. 'Land Rights in Cambodia: An Unfinished Reform'. *Asia Pacific Issues*, 97: 1–8.

Un, K. 2005. 'Patronage Politics and Hybrid Democracy: Political Change in Cambodia, 1993–2003'. *Asian Perspective*, 29(2): 203–30.

Un, K., and So, S. 2009. 'Politics of Natural Resource Use in Cambodia'. *Asian Affairs*, 36(3): 123–38.

Vittachi, I. 1996. 'Ariston Balks on $2m Payment till Law Passed'. *Phnom Penh Post*, 22 March.

Vrieze, P., and Kuch, N. 2012. 'Carving up Cambodia: One Concession at a Time'. *Cambodia Daily Weekend*, 10–11 March.

Zsombor, P., and Aun, P. 2012. '32 Land Concessions Approved since Moratorium'. *Cambodia Daily*, 18 November.

6

Political Settlements and Structural Change

Why Growth Has Not Been Transformational in Ghana

Robert Darko Osei, Charles Ackah, George Domfe,
and Michael Danquah

6.1 Introduction

The typical economic growth story of Ghana starts with how, for the first two-and-a-half decades after independence, growth experienced significant fluctuations. The era of structural adjustment and Ghana embracing multiparty democracy followed these growth fluctuations. This latter period has seen more stable and improved growth (Killick, 2010). Writing on the growth performance of Ghana, authors such as Bogetic et al. (2007) argue that the factors which explain Ghana's growth include high commodity prices, increased investments, an improved policy environment, and improved aid effectiveness. They subsequently argue that the country could sustain its medium-term growth prospects if it invested more in infrastructure, improved the investment climate as well as public sector efficiency, and maintained macroeconomic stability. This view is pervasive in the wider economics literature on Ghana (see, inter alia, Aryeetey and Harrigan, 2000; Osei and Quartey, 2014; Osei, 2012).

In Fosu's (2012) characterization of the responsiveness of the country to economic reforms in the 1980s, he argues that positive macroeconomic changes occurred because of the reforms. He makes a further point about the political economy–growth nexus, arguing that the country had reached 'the growth-enhancing democratization regime' (Fosu, 2012: 496). This political economy–growth connection tends to be implicit in many of the writings on

Ghana's economic growth. An oft-cited argument is that political stability will encourage investment and therefore growth (see, for instance, Darko, 2010). Taken to its logical extension, this argument would suggest that growth maintenance occurs with political stability, and consequently a politically stable country will allow structural transformation of the economy to take place in a way that makes it less fragile. Unfortunately, this has not been the case for Ghana, and growth has not translated into significant changes in the structure of the economy (Osei, 2012; Killick, 2010). Indeed, despite macro-economic instability during periods closely aligned with electoral cycles, Ghana has remained a politically stable country. However, the progress that was anticipated in the late 1980s and early 1990s has not materialized. This suggests that a greater investigation into the political economy–growth nexus is needed, to understand better how the country can more effectively consolidate the initial gains made through economic growth.

In this chapter, the deals and development framework conceptualized in Chapter 1 is used to theorize that the nature of political settlements in a country has a bearing on the environment for business (deals environment), and that in turn affects the very factors that are critical for growth to be accelerated and maintained. In other words, this chapter explores the extent to which the nature of the political settlement, interacting with the rents space, has influenced the nature of the deals environment and contributed to Ghana's growth and transformation story.

The chapter is organized as follows. Section 6.2 discusses Ghana's growth episodes over the post-independence period to date. As part of that discussion, recent trends in growth as well as structural transformation will be examined. In Section 6.3, the framework discussed in Chapter 1 is used to explain the growth episodes. This is done under five main themes, namely: the nature of the deals environment over the identified growth episodes; the rents space in Ghana; the evolution of politics and political settlements in Ghana; how political settlements and the rents space have contrived to affect the nature of deals environment; and the nature of feedback loops for all these variables. Section 6.4 presents a summary of the main findings and some concluding comments.

6.2 Ghana's Growth Episodes

As discussed in Chapter 1, Kar et al. (2013) combine a statistical and an economic-based filter to identify major trend shifts in economic growth in 125 countries over the period 1950–2010. For Ghana they find five growth episodes over the period covering the immediate post-independence period to date. More specifically, they identify transitions between breaks in growth

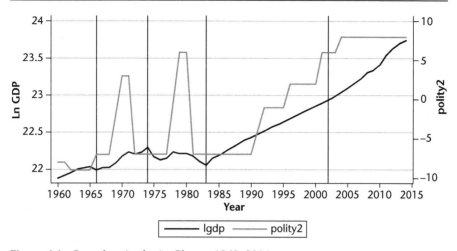

Figure 6.1. Growth episodes in Ghana, 1960–2014

Source: World Bank, *World Development Indicators*, 2015 and Polity IV data.

Notes: The vertical lines reflect the periods when the breaks in growth are identified in Kar et al. (2013); lgdp is log of GDP, and polity2 is the Polity 2 measure from Polity IV data.

over the years 1966, 1974, 1983, and 2002. Apart from the 1974 break, all the identified breaks have been associated with an increase in economic growth (see Figure 6.1). Indeed, these breaks are consistent with those that have been implicitly identified, albeit in an ad hoc way, in research on Ghana (see, inter alia, Jedwab and Osei, 2012; Killick, 2010). As can be noted from Figure 6.1, three of these breaks are related to the period when there was high volatility in the Polity index (which is extensively used in the literature as a measure of democracy) and therefore political instability was high in Ghana. This is not to suggest any causation, but rather to highlight the correlation between the Polity index and growth over the years. However, the level of democracy alone is not adequate in explaining these identified growth episodes. Therefore, this chapter seeks to analyse Ghana's growth story using the conceptual framework discussed in Chapter 1 and situate the discussions within these identified growth phases.

6.2.1 *Growth Without Structural Transformation*

TRENDS IN ECONOMIC GROWTH

We note that between 1960 and the early part of the 1980s real GDP growth fluctuated around zero. Indeed, real GDP growth over this period averaged about 1.1 per cent, which translated into a negative per capita growth of −1.3 per cent. From 1983 onwards, the trend did change positively, with a marked reduction in the fluctuations in real GDP growth and a positive per capita

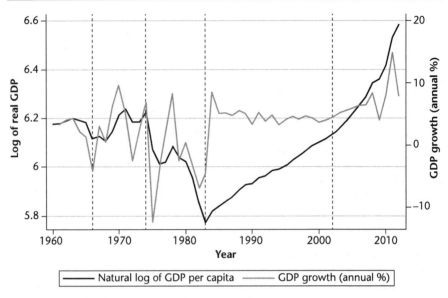

Figure 6.2. Evolution of real GDP for Ghana, 1960–2014

Source: World Bank, *World Development Indicators*, 2015.

Note: The vertical lines reflect the periods when the breaks between growth episodes are identified.

GDP—real GDP averaged about 4.3 per cent over the period 1983–99. This change in the economic fortunes of Ghana during the early 1980s has been widely investigated within the literature (see, inter alia, Killick, 2010; Kraev, 2004; Jedwab and Osei, 2012). This literature concludes that a combination of policy measures alongside increased foreign aid flows were the catalysts for changing the fortunes of the country. This continued right through to the late 1990s. The growth situation has improved further since 2001. The period from 2000 to 2012 saw an increased acceleration in the growth rate—it increased from the 1983–99 annual average of about 4.4 per cent to about 6.5 per cent. The very tail end of the sample has, however, seen a slowdown in this growth, reaching under 5 per cent in 2014.

It is shown in Figure 6.2 that economic growth in Ghana picked up from the mid-1980s and showed some features of growth maintenance. Unfortunately, this has not been associated with a marked transformation of the economy.

Figure 6.3 highlights the contribution of GDP shares for Ghana over the period 1960 to 2014. The importance of agriculture was reduced over this period, overtaken by the services sector from the early 1980s. Importantly, two features of the trends in GDP shares are worth pointing out. First, the services sector has become more important relative to agriculture over the years (this is especially apparent after GDP revisions undertaken by the government in

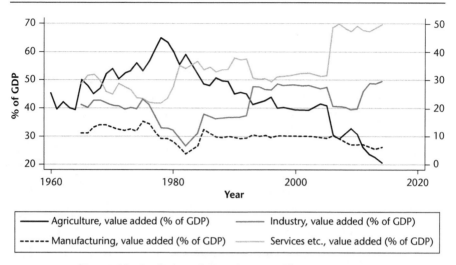

Figure 6.3. Evolution of GDP shares in Ghana, 1960–2012
Source: World Bank, *World Development Indicators*, 2015.

2010). Second, manufacturing shares have actually declined over the years. Do these trends in GDP share reflect the changing structure of the economy?

The literature on economic development (for example, Herrendorf et al., 2013) suggests that when a country is developing, there is initially a manufacturing sector boom, with the contribution of agriculture to national income declining, while that of other sectors, especially manufacturing, rises. In the case of Ghana, we observe a declining agriculture sector that is associated with an increasing share of the services sector, while the manufacturing sector, at best, has been stagnant. (The rise in industry shown in Figure 6.3 captures the petroleum boom; manufacturing is a subset of industry.) This suggests that Ghana might have leapfrogged the manufacturing sector boom stage, which is typically associated with an increased supply of jobs for the many that are leaving the agriculture sector. According to McMillan and Rodrik (2011), structural transformation is growth-enhancing if it is associated with a shift of resources from low-productivity sectors to high-productivity sectors. Jedwab and Osei (2012) have argued that labour from the declining agriculture sector has not necessarily moved to highly productive wage employment sectors in services and manufacturing. Rather, they have moved to the equally low-productivity areas of the services sector. In essence, Ghana has urbanized without industrialization (Gollin et al., 2013).

TRENDS IN THE STRUCTURE OF GHANA'S EXPORTS
As highlighted in Figure 6.4, even though the dominance of cocoa has decreased, primary products continue to dominate Ghana's exports. The

(a)

Total: $281 million

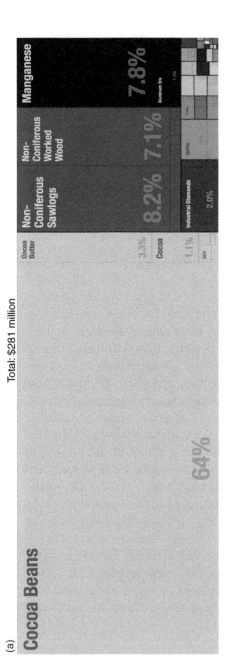

(b)

Total: $440 million

Figure 6.4. Trends in the composition of exports from Ghana, 1962–2013
Source: Atlas of Economic Complexity <http://atlas.cid.harvard.edu/>.

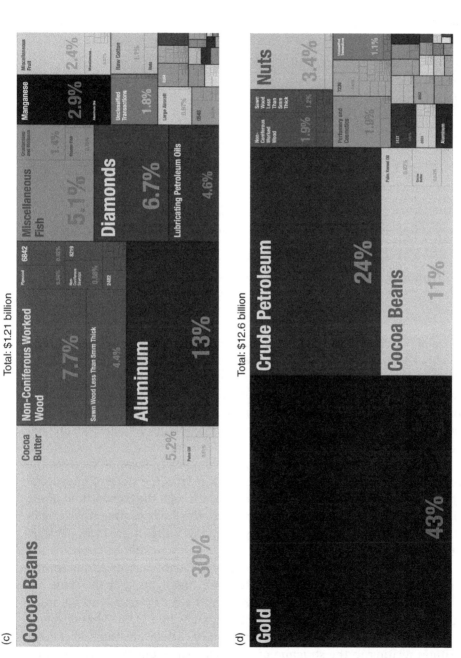

Figure 6.4. Continued

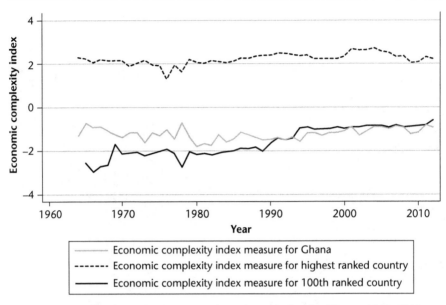

Figure 6.5. Trends in the Economic Complexity Index for Ghana, 1960–2012
Source: Atlas of Economic Complexity <http://atlas.cid.harvard.edu/>.

share of raw cocoa beans decreased from about 65 per cent in the early 1960s to about 11 per cent in 2013. The start of oil production, which was about 24 per cent of exports in 2013, means that all other items have had their shares reduced. In the early 1960s, over 80 per cent of all exports came from primary produce—cocoa, crude minerals, and timber. By 2013 this list had expanded, but it was still dominated by primary exports, notably gold, petroleum, and cocoa beans, butter, and paste.

The Hausmann et al. (2013) economic complexity measure captures the productive structure of a given economy. It reflects the stock of knowledge that the country possesses and measures this through the composition of the output of any given country. In other words, the index captures the capabilities of the country by using the array of products that it produces (Hidalgo and Hausmann, 2009).

Figure 6.5 plots the economic complexity of Ghana, as well as that for the 1st and 100th ranked countries. This graph highlights that the trend for Ghana over the years supports the argument made with respect to the structure of the Ghanaian economy—that the composition of GDP has changed, but the structure remains largely unchanged. There are three important features relating to the structure of the Ghanaian economy since the early post-independence period that this graph shows. First, the economic complexity measure for Ghana in 2012 is not considerably different from what it was in 1960. Second, the measure for the 100th ranked country (based on the 2010 economic complexity data) has caught up with Ghana in terms of productive capacity over the period. Finally, there seems to have been little convergence between Ghana and the highest ranked country over the years. These trends suggest that, in spite of the changes in the composition of output in Ghana, true structural transformation, of the kind suggested by McMillan and Rodrik (2011), has yet to occur.

6.3 Explanation of the Growth Episodes

6.3.1 *The Deals Environment in Ghana*

Using the conceptual framework developed in Chapter 1, we provide an assessment of the nature of the deals environment in Ghana. As noted in the framework, the deals environment remains central to firms' decisions about investment, production, innovation, and, consequently, sustained growth. Generally, openness in the deals space facilitates new firm entry and drives competition. The result is that there is an increase in the production of more complex products and a shift of resources from low-productivity sectors to high-productivity sectors. In other words, the movements within the deals space may explain the growth path for countries. The evolution of the deals space is not linear and so it is not automatic that institutions will evolve, independently, from one state to the other over time. The following section examines the evolution of the deals environment in Ghana in relation to the previously identified growth episodes.

DEALS ENVIRONMENT (1957–66)

Following on from Ghana's independence from the United Kingdom in 1957, the regime led by Kwame Nkrumah subscribed to a central planning approach for the economy. While Ghana did experience a significant and sharp growth increase at the end of this period, this success was short-lived. As part of the central planning process, legislative controls were imposed on imports, capital transfers, licensing of industry, minimum wages, the rights and powers of trade unions, prices, rents, and interest rates (Killick, 2010: 56–60). Unfortunately, the capacity of the state to regulate, negotiate, and enforce these legislative controls was low. This lack of transparency, coupled with weak institutions, meant that you needed to 'know someone' to be able to get the government contracts. Therefore, for businesses that dealt with government agencies, connections really did matter. This unfortunately encouraged and entrenched a deals space that was closed but somewhat ordered for the formal sector. For the informal sector the deals space was largely open but disordered and was therefore limited in scope in terms of opportunities to expand. It is not surprising that this period experienced a growth decline in 1966.

DEALS ENVIRONMENT (1966–83)

Following the military overthrow of Nkrumah's civilian government in 1966, the ideological stance changed to one that was more pro-private business. The new government, led by Kofi Abrefa Busia, introduced reforms to liberalize exporting sectors of the economy, among other policies (see Frimpong-Ansah, 1992). It is fair to say that the government at the time sought to make the deals space more open by liberalizing not just trade, but also devaluing the exchange rate to reflect the market fundamentals. This liberal stance led to the overthrow of the government in January 1972. The reforms during this period, however, did not significantly affect relations among economic agents. It is therefore reasonable to assert that, even though the intent to make the deals space more open was there, it never materialized in practice over this period. Indeed, as Killick (2010: 64) notes:

> There remained much continuity after 1966; attempts to move towards greater use of the market mechanism were half-hearted and partial; and the soldiers who overthrew Busia in 1972 rapidly demonstrated a faith in a command economy similar to Nkrumah's, even though they displayed little interest in his socialism.

The 1972–83 epoch was one of sustained deterioration in the economy under five different governments. The policies of the period emphasized import substitution, underpinned by a restrictive foreign exchange regime, quantitative restrictions on imports, and price controls, with the state playing a major role as producer. Very few business leaders had the political connections necessary to make deals. However, even for the connected, they could not be certain that officials would deliver. Indeed, this problem was exacerbated by the capricious nature of the changes in government, coupled with the haphazard way in which policies were implemented. It is little wonder that Killick (2010: 398) describes this period as the 'black years'. The deals space was largely disordered and closed in this period, which was reflected in highly variable growth.

DEALS ENVIRONMENT (1983–2001)

The beginning of this period was characterized by Ghana undertaking a World Bank-sponsored structural adjustment programme (SAP). Under the SAP, exchange rate policy, fiscal and monetary policies, and trade policies all saw dramatic changes. There was a renewed push for market-friendly interventions, and the policy prescription of 'stabilize, privatize, and liberalize' (Rodrik, 2006: 973) was applied within Ghana to numerous infrastructure projects in telecommunications, roads, and power. Generally, and for the formal sector, the deals environment become more ordered over this period, yet remained closed. However, the formal economy's dependence on the state lessened somewhat during this time. One of the immediate benefits of the SAP was a turnaround in growth. This was made possible due to the injection of foreign aid, as well as the deals space becoming partially opened (through de-controlling prices and relaxing some of the import restrictions) to allow some level of economic activity to begin.

DEALS ENVIRONMENT (2001–12)

The period from 2001 to 2012 saw a strengthening of the judicial and legislative arms of government. Additionally, laws to guide and promote business decisions improved, with the aim of reducing reliance on personal connections to secure government contracts. One such example was the introduction of the procurement law in 2003. The act enshrined the public procurement authority that changed the bidding process for public contracts in Ghana. The more formal and transparent process meant that deals became more open. While challenges remain (see Ameyaw et al., 2012), this act was a significant leap forward from the disordered, closed nature of the deals space before.

This period saw the biggest attempted shift towards a more open and ordered deals space. Although there might be some closed deals for natural resource exporters, particularly in the mining and petroleum sector, as well as firms in energy production, deals partially opened for many firms in the local market. For instance, among businesses interviewed as part of this study, differences in opinion were evident over whether the business playing field was level, with rentiers and powerbrokers supporting the view that it was. Their focus and examples were in relation to gaining contracts from the public sector. In their view, it is important always to have good relationships with key actors in society. This, they claim, is necessary for their business growth. One of the points all interviewees agreed on was that good relationships with actors such as politicians, technocrats, and union leaders are important for business growth. They further argued that, while the relationship with low-ranking bureaucrats and union leaders is predictable and ordered, the relationship with high-ranking civil servants and politicians is less so.

6.3.2 Nature of the Rents Space in Ghana

In the framework in Chapter 1, the rents space combines with the nature of political settlements to engender the type of deals environment that prevails in a given country. In order to understand how this framework applies to the Ghana case, this section discusses the rents space using sectoral GDP contributions for 2014.

Figure 6.6 shows that workhorses (32.3 per cent) lead Ghana's rents space, followed by powerbrokers (30.2 per cent), rentiers (28.9 per cent), and

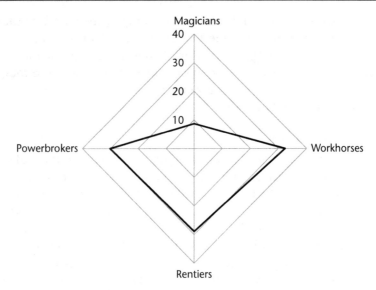

Figure 6.6. Contribution of Ghanaian firms to GDP
Source: Author's estimation based on 2014 budget statement.

magicians (8.7 per cent). This classification is very much consistent with Sutton and Kpentey's (2012) enterprise map of Ghana. It is argued that the nature of Ghana's rents space is influenced by two key factors: first, it is a resource-rich country; and second, in the last twenty-five years it has been a highly aid-dependent country. Ghana is rich in point source resources (see Auty, 2001) such as gold, diamonds, and, more recently, oil. State-owned enterprises and a few multinational companies have dominated these sectors. Additionally, Ghana has a diffuse resource in cocoa, which many smallholder farmers are involved in cultivating. However, due to the use of the state-owned cocoa marketing board, cocoa has features of a point-sourced resource, i.e. a single identifiable source of cocoa, which has meant that the rents of this sector have been captured by the state.

This resource-rich nature of Ghana has been important for the development of both the rentiers and powerbrokers. However, in the case of powerbrokers, its importance has been reinforced by the large inflow of foreign aid to Ghana. The large aid inflow has supported many social programmes, mainly channelled through the government (Osei et al., 2005). This in turn has supported domestic contractors as well as service providers, and reinforced the importance of powerbrokers in Ghana. Interviews with businesses point to the fact that connections with political elites will get a firm a contract to supply goods and services. We therefore have a situation where rentiers and powerbrokers, who control approximately 60 per cent of the economy, have strong links with officials within government and, as a result, will typically favour a closed deals environment.

Workhorses appear to be important in Ghana, based on their contribution to GDP. However, their true influence is exaggerated by this statistic. This is due to the fact that sectors in which a majority of workhorses operate (wholesale retail traders, food crop farmers) contain a large number of small enterprises that are not well organized. Therefore, as they have no collective voice, this lack of organization, plus the high levels of competition within these sectors, means that the economic rents gained within them are almost zero. Due to these factors, firms in this sector, which are characterized by the ease of entry into these markets, favour a more open deals environment.

Magicians have remained the least important component of the Ghanaian economy and they have continued to struggle throughout the country's economic history. This sector of the economy consists of manufacturing, services, and other non-traditional exporters. The magicians in Ghana are typically dynamic, but operate in a competitive market. They typically benefit from, and therefore prefer, an open deals environment.

In summary, firms that operate in a less competitive market setting therefore dominate Ghana's rents space. These firms typically favour a closed deals space. Firms that would prefer a more open deals space, due to operating in a more competitive environment, constitute around 40 per cent of the economy but lack sufficient organization to influence the deals space. Consequently, the deals spaces in Ghana are skewed in favour of a closed deals environment.

6.3.3 *Political Settlements and How They Have Evolved in Ghana*

Political settlements, as noted in Chapter 1, refer to the balance of power between social groups and/or classes. Where the balance of power favours only a few elite members, then the economic and social choices made are likely to reflect the preferences of this group and therefore benefit them disproportionately. In other words, the ideas and beliefs of the political elite will shape the policy actions that are undertaken in any given country. The extent to which the ideas of the political elite influence policy actions will be a function of the horizontal and vertical distribution of power, as well as their own beliefs. In terms of the horizontal distribution of power, where excluded factions are weak, there will tend to be a dominant party (see Chapter 1 and or Khan (2010) for more discussion on political settlements). The nature of the political settlements will have a bearing on the policy choices that are made and consequently on the deals environment that evolves.

In the case of Ghana, this chapter seeks to understand how political settlements and the nature of the rents space have contributed to the deals environment that exists and therefore to growth. Section 6.3.4 discusses the evolution of Ghanaian politics, and how this has in turn affected the nature of the political settlement.

NATURE OF POLITICS AND POLITICAL SETTLEMENTS (1957–66)

After a few years of political agitation, the British government granted the Gold Coast independence on 6 March 1957. Prior to the declaration of independence, general elections were held on 17 July 1956. The Convention People's Party (CPP) of Kwame Nkrumah won 57 per cent of the total votes cast and was thus granted the mandate by the British to form a government (Nohlen et al., 1999). While the CPP described itself as socialist, the main opposition, the United Party (UP), was pro-capitalist. The pre-independence agitation therefore gave way to an internal ideological wrangling between the CPP and the UP (McLaughlin and Owusu-Ansah, 1994). The country became a republic on 1 July 1960, with Nkrumah emerging victorious in the presidential elections. Shortly after this, Nkrumah nearly gained absolute political power and proclaimed himself life president. He amended the constitution in 1964 to allow him to dismiss any judge from the bench. He succeeded in controlling the judiciary, the media, the clergy, and the traditional chiefs (Boafo-Arthur, 2000). Within Ghana, he was the fulcrum around which everything happened. Most of his political opponents had to flee the country, and the few who stayed and challenged him were prosecuted under the Preventive Detention Act. Therefore, the political settlements in Ghana over this period gradually moved from being competitive around the period of independence to being dominated by the time Nkrumah was deposed in 1966 by the National Liberation Council (NLC), led by Emmanuel Kwasi Kotoka.

NATURE OF POLITICS AND POLITICAL SETTLEMENTS (1966–83)

The NLC assumed the executive powers of Ghana after toppling the CPP administration in 1966. The leadership of the coup justified their takeover by claiming that the CPP administration was abusive and corrupt (McLaughlin and Owusu-Ansah, 1994). Their main preoccupation, therefore, was to restore order to the inherited political settlements. Political parties were sanctioned to operate by the end of 1968. In 1969, the first competitive nationwide political contest since 1956 was held (Miller et al., 2009).

The pro-capitalist Progress Party led by Busia won the elections and took over from the NLC. This government initiated two policy measures soon after assuming office: the expulsion of large numbers of non-citizens from the country, and an accompanying measure to limit foreign involvement in small businesses. While the government became popular among local business entrepreneurs for the introduction of these two policy measures,[1] the decision to devalue the national currency in 1971 was seen as the catalyst for the instability that engulfed Ghana and Busia (Asamoah, 2014; Manboah-Rockson, 2016).

Also during this period, upon recommendation from the IMF, Busia introduced austerity measures, including a wage freeze and tax increases. These measures severely affected the middle class and the salaried workforce, and eventually precipitated protests from the Trade Union Congress. On 13 January 1972, the army staged a coup to end the Second Republic (Miller et al., 2009). Once again, the elements that favoured a dominant political settlement had prevailed.

The government's intention of utilizing local capacity to build an independent economy was overridden by oil price hikes in 1974, a decline in cocoa output, drought, and the lack of foreign exchange. Disillusionment with the government developed and allegations of corruption, favouritism, and incompetence in the management of the economy were levelled against the new military head of state, Ignatius Kutu Acheampong, and his associates. The government's response to the discontent was to issue a decree to forbid propagation of rumours. Additionally, a number of independent newspapers were banned, and some of their journalists detained. Disaffection with the government deepened, and in July 1978 some officers of the Supreme Military Council forced Acheampong to resign and replaced him with his second-in-command, Lieutenant General Frederick W. K. Akuffo.

Akuffo's tenure as president was also short-lived, as Flight Lieutenant Jerry Rawlings toppled this government on 4 June 1979. Interestingly, the new military government, which called itself the Armed Forces Revolutionary Council, made sure that the planned elections took place, and Ghana returned to constitutional rule by the end of September 1979. However, after twenty-seven months in office the civilian government of the People's National Party, led by Dr Hilla Limann, fell, once again brought down by Rawlings and his colleagues, who argued that the civilian government could not perform to expectations.

Upon assumption of executive powers on the eve of 31 December 1981, Rawlings established the Provisional National Defence Council (PNDC) and suspended the 1979 constitution, which effectively banned the existence of political parties within Ghana. This period therefore saw continued contestation of the nature of political settlements with 'vampire' elements (Frimpong-Ansah, 1992)—elites who maintained control over key elements of the Ghanaian economy regardless of the political administration, and managed to keep the political

---

[1] The policies forced foreigners out of the retail sector of the economy, especially Lebanese, Asians, and Nigerians, who were perceived as unfairly monopolizing trade, to the disadvantage of Ghanaians.

settlement as a strong dominant party, as such a settlement best served their interests. The few attempts over this period to move political settlements towards a competitive one were short-lived.

NATURE OF POLITICS AND POLITICAL SETTLEMENTS (1983–2001)

In an attempt to solve the mounting economic problems confronting the country, the PNDC government proclaimed an SAP package, popularly known as the Economic Recovery Programme (ERP), in 1983 (Kraev, 2004). While aid immediately started flowing to Ghana with the start of the ERP, donors applied pressure on the government to open up the political process (Whitfield, 2011). In response to this, the government planned a process to return to democratic rule by 1992. Overall, Ghana enjoyed remarkable political stability throughout the period, with occasional protests, but no civil unrest, and no effective opposition to the SAPs imposed on Ghana (Kraev, 2004).

Not only did Rawlings' National Democratic Congress (NDC) win the November 1992 presidential elections, but also a subsequent boycott of the December parliamentary elections by the New Patriotic Party (NPP) and the other opposition political parties gave way to the NDC-dominated first Parliament of the Fourth Republic. Rawlings held on to power, successfully serving two terms, which ended in 2000. The process of change in the nature of the political settlement had begun. Even though competitive elections started, the biggest change in political settlement during this period was in the ideas of the elites towards stronger faith in markets as a means of allocating resources. This in turn was somewhat driven by donors using foreign aid to shape ideas around development.

NATURE OF POLITICS AND POLITICAL SETTLEMENTS (2001–14)

The current economic and political climate has its roots in 1992, when the country adopted constitutional rule. After the demise of Rawlings from the political scene, John Agyekum Kufuor, who stood on the ticket of the opposition party, the NPP, won the election, and became president on 7 January 2001. He was re-elected in 2004. After eight years of absence, the NDC won the 2008 general elections. The new president, Professor Evans John Atta Mills, died in July 2012, before the end of his first term. His vice president, John Dramani Mahama, took over and won the 2012 general election to become the president of Ghana.

Many years after Rawlings left power, and even though elections have become highly competitive, the degree of political patronage remains high. Ghana's current political system is multiparty, but the results of the various presidential elections since 1992 indicate a de facto two-party system. While the executive wields excessive powers, the country still displays a number of features of an institutionalized democracy, which makes it a success story of democratic development in Africa (Oduro et al., 2014). There is a winner-takes-all approach to governance, which is implicitly engendered by the constitution. Even worse was the institutionalization of political patronage at the technocratic level. There have been changes in technocratic heads when there is a change in the ruling party. This compromises continuity within ministries, government departments, and agencies; and it makes technocrats less apolitical.

6.3.4 *Political Settlements, Rents Space, and the Deals Environment in Ghana*

It is important to recall the argument made earlier in the chapter that Ghana has experienced growth with limited structural transformation. Implicit in that discussion is the fact that the deals environment has not favoured sustained private investments for the maintenance of growth and employment creation. This chapter has argued that generally the deals environment in Ghana has been closed—being ordered in some years and disordered in others. In this section, we provide an assessment of the extent to which this environment has been produced by the interaction between the nature of the political settlement and the rents space.

In large part, the discussion of the evolution of politics in Ghana shows that political settlements have been largely dominant from the early years after independence to the 1990s. More recently, however, this has changed to one that is more competitive clientelist, albeit dominated by two political parties. Vertically also, one notes an increasing degree of power for lower-level factions. This increasing degree of power is, however, not uniform across the board and relates more to 'party foot soldiers'. Additionally, groups such as trade unions have slowly begun to increase their influence, which in turn has led to some degree of power over policies, even during the phase when political settlements were largely dominant. Other lower-level factions, such as disability groups, have had limited influence on policy.

The uneven distribution of power at the lower levels has not favoured groups that are biased towards a more open deals environment. These lower-level factions typically seek to benefit disproportionately, and directly, from rents within the economy. Typically, party foot soldiers will push for one of their own to be appointed to a position of power. They therefore use their power to achieve this critical objective of patronage. For these foot soldiers, it is an avenue by which they can access the deals space and benefit from the limited jobs available, largely in the public sector. It is common knowledge in Ghana these days that recruitment to the public services is linked to political cronyism. For these lower-level factions, it is one of the few avenues available to extract some part of the rents. According to an entrepreneur interviewed as part of this study, the reason why people make use of government-initiated credit facilities and yet fail to pay back their loan is because 'we view it as payback for voting for them'.

Trade unions are no different in this regard. They will typically use their collective bargaining position to extract as much of these rents (in the form of wages) as possible for their members. Trade union members constitute a small proportion of the labour force and yet absorb a significant part of the government budget. It is no wonder that the strongest members of the trade unions have been civil servants and (private-sector) mineworkers. Most trade union agitation and negotiations are centred around wage increases, and are not always focused on ideas. Even in cases such as the economic partnership agreements (and trade generally), where they have had a position on the policy, it has been in support of an outcome that is not competitive. It is fair to say that the trade unions have not been forceful in driving some of the basic tenets of an open deals environment. This position is consistent with Asem et al. (2013), who argue that regulatory change in Ghana has been driven by external donors using foreign aid as both carrot and stick.

Business associations, such as the Private Enterprise Foundation and the Association of Ghanaian Industries, have not made great strides in pushing for change generally. Their degree of importance in the rents space is low and this limits their influence in driving change. This may be partly due to the fact that most members of these private-sector groups operate as magicians or work-horses, with limited rents and therefore limited influence on the political establishment.

To a very large extent, the type of deals environment that has dominated the Ghanaian landscape has been a result of the interplay between the rents space and the nature of political settlements in Ghana. Over the 1957–66 period, the government subscribed to a central planning approach. This meant that legislative controls were imposed on imports, capital transfers, licensing of industry, minimum wages, the rights and powers of trade unions, prices, rents, and interests rates (Killick, 2010: 56–60). This encouraged and entrenched a deals space that was closed but ordered within the formal sector. Not much changed in the period that followed until 1983, with half-hearted attempts in market-based reform. As a result, the political settlement remained uncompetitive and highly personalized. Indeed, the unpredictable nature of the changes in government, coupled with the haphazard way in which policies were implemented, meant that not only did the deals space remain closed, but it had become quite disordered by the end of this period.

In the initial years of structural adjustment up to the start of multiparty democracy, political settlements in Ghana remained dominant. However, some of the sources of rents and political patronage, particularly those that emanated from import and exchange controls, were diminished with the SAP. The consequence was that the deals environment became more ordered, even though it remained closed, especially for the dominant and high-rent-seeking sectors like mining. All the firms interviewed as part of this study (apart from the workhorses) argued that having connections is necessary for business growth. One entrepreneur asserted: 'That is the order of the day in Ghana. If you can't pay your way through by giving bribes, you can't succeed in anything.' The period from 2002 to date has probably seen the biggest attempted shift towards a more open and ordered deals space. Donors have contributed to these changes, particularly in the regulatory environment, with limited private-sector influence on these changes. The discovery and production of oil, coupled with the change in the country's status to middle income, has meant that the influence of donors is waning.

6.3.5 Feedback Loops

We have noted that interactions between the political settlements and the rents space have been important in shaping the deals environment, which consequently affects growth. Furthermore, and as noted in Chapter 1, the nature of growth can also have feedback effects on the rents space and political settlements interaction and therefore affect future growth. We discuss the importance of this feedback effect on the growth story of Ghana.

There are some key features of Ghana's growth episodes that one can tease out from the story so far. First, in the period up to 1983, growth maintenance was absent for Ghana. Generally, over this period, the dominant political settlement, fuelled by the presence of strong rentiers and powerbrokers, meant that the deals environment remained largely closed. In the first and second growth episodes, growth was driven by natural resource sectors. Over much of this period, resource rents acted as a cushion for the political elite, who therefore could afford to leave the deals space closed. However, once the resource rents shrank, the ruling elites became less dogmatic and more willing to embrace new ideas. This explains why a government with socialist leanings went to the IMF/World Bank and began the implementation of an SAP. However, the economy over this period remained vulnerable and, consequently, adverse external shocks, such as that experienced in the 1970s due to oil price increases, had negative implications for growth.

Second, over the post-1983 period, some degree of growth maintenance became apparent. Here the political settlement moved from being a strong dominant party towards a competitive clientelist one. Furthermore, under the SAP, some of the key avenues for rent extraction, and therefore political patronage, were dismantled. This had the effect of opening up the deals space, while encouraging growth among workhorses and magicians. The effect on the political settlement in Ghana was to change the ideas and beliefs of political elites. This had a positive effect on the regulatory environment and consequently the deals space. Here the feedback has been reinforcing. Ideas have mattered for Ghana. From 2001 onward, the ruling elites recognized that they needed a vibrant economy of workhorses and magicians as the basis for growth and therefore prioritized this. They pushed for regulatory changes that favoured a more open deals space. For some sectors the deals space remained closed. The important idea here is that the opening up of the deals space did help to maintain growth for a period in the 2000s. This in turn has helped create a growing middle class that owes its prosperity to the growth of the private sector, and which is increasingly becoming a strong political faction. There is no doubt that this will help maintain the momentum for a more open deals space. This view is reflected in the optimism of businesses interviewed for this chapter. They were generally positive about the business environment, and some stated that the source of their optimism for future business growth in Ghana is the growing middle class. However, exporting firms further argue that their growth will have to be supported by strategic government policies, citing the example of interest rates.

6.4 Conclusion

This chapter provides an assessment of how the nature of political settlements, interacting with the rents space, has affected the nature of the deals space and consequently economic growth in Ghana. It centres the discussions on four growth episodes. The first growth transition was in 1966 (a significant increase in the growth) and coincided with Nkrumah's 'big push' for industrialization within Ghana (Meng, 2004). The second, in 1974, was negative (i.e. a significant decrease in the growth rate) and coincides with an external oil price shock. The third, in 1983, was positive and coincides with the start of the SAP. Finally, the fourth, beginning in 2002, was positive and was concomitant with improved state–business relations. Our discussions were also enhanced by interviews with twenty-one enterprises and key informants on the nature of the deals space as experienced by them, as well as their prospects for growth. The main findings of this study can be summarized as follows.

First, we note that Ghana has seen sustained economic growth since the mid-1980s. We note further that this growth has been associated with the changing contributions of different sectors. In particular, we note that the services sector has become more important relative to agriculture over the years, with the manufacturing sector remaining the same as it was at the start of independence. Also, labour from the declining agriculture sector has not necessarily moved to higher productivity wage employment in the services and manufacturing sectors. Rather, it has largely moved to equally low-productivity activities in the services sector. We note that the country's exports have continued to be dominated by a small number of products: mainly timber, gold, cocoa, and, more recently, oil—all resource-based. We therefore argue that true structural transformation has yet to occur in Ghana.

Second, our discussion of the deals environment over the different growth episodes suggests that it has largely been closed. There is no doubt that the closed nature of the deals space has influenced the fact that economic growth in Ghana over the years has not been of the transformative type. But, there seems to have been a change in the deals space from around 2000. Here we have also argued that the nature of the deals space varies according to different types of firms. For firms in sectors that contribute the most to GDP, the deals space remains closed. Firms interviewed affirmed this, by noting that knowing top politicians or bureaucrats is critical to securing government contracts.

Third, the chapter argues that political settlements in Ghana have generally been characterized by dominant party settlements, even though there has been a shift towards a more competitive type in recent times. One of the main changes in political settlements has been in the ideas of political elites, driven in part by donors and in part by less dogmatic views on economic policy. We also see increasing power for lower-level and mid-level factions. We argue that there is still some way to go for Ghana, in spite of the strides it has made democratically. In particular, we argue that political patronage is exploited, even at the expense of strengthening institutions.

Fourth, we argue that the interplay of political settlements and the rents space has been important in shaping the nature of the deals space. In the first two growth episodes, the dominant political settlements were made possible by the nature of the rents space. The government subscribed to a central planning approach, as it saw itself largely as a redistributor of wealth. After the near growth collapse, brought about by the disordered deals environment, resource rents became minimal and so the elite began to embrace new ideas around market-based reforms. Added to this were other forces—increasing power to lower-level factions and donors using foreign aid as leverage to encourage political leadership to consider new ideas. These factors combined to make the deals space more ordered and increasingly more open.

We conclude by noting that Ghana has exhibited two interesting features of the feedback loop between political settlements, rents space, the deals environment, and growth. In the first and second growth episodes, where growth was largely driven by natural resource sectors, the feedback effect was negative. In other words, natural resource-driven growth resulted in a political settlement that was characterized by a dominant party settlement and favoured a closed deals space. This in turn resulted in lower growth and further pressure for a dominant political settlement. Within the 1960–83 period, therefore, growth maintenance was difficult. On the other hand, during the phase where growth increasingly emanated from workhorses and magicians (from 1983 onwards), it conferred positive feedback on the political settlement and the deals space. There were two sources of this positive feedback for Ghana. The first was the change in the ideas and beliefs of political elites in favour of less control of the markets. The second source was a growing middle class, which has increasingly become a strong faction pushing for political settlements that favour a more open deals space.

References

Ameyaw, C., Mensah, S., and Osei-Tutu, E. 2012. 'Public Procurement in Ghana: The Implementation Challenges to the Public Procurement Law 2003 (Act 663)'. *International Journal of Construction Supply Chain Management*, 2(2): 55–65.

Aryeetey, E., and Harrigan, J. 2000. 'Macroeconomic and Structural Developments Since 1970'. In *Economic Reforms in Ghana: The Miracle and the Mirage*. Edited by Aryeetey, E., Harrigan, J., and Nissanke, M. Oxford: James Curry Ltd.

Asamoah, O. 2014. *The Political History of Ghana (1950–2013): The Experience of a Nonconformist*. Bloomington, IN: Author House.

Asem, F., Busse, M., Osei, R., and Silberberger, M. 2013. 'Private Sector Development and Governance in Ghana'. Working Paper. London: The International Growth Centre.

Auty, R. 2001. 'Why Resource Endowments Can Undermine Economic Development: Concepts and Case Studies'. Paper prepared for the BP-Amoco Seminar, Lincoln College, Oxford.

Boafo-Arthur, K. 2000. 'The Political Economy of Ghana Foreign Policy: Past, Present and the Future'. *Ghana Social Science Journal*, 1(1).

Bogetic, Y., Bussolo, M., Ye, X., Medvedev, D., Wodon, Q., and Boakye, D. 2007. 'Ghana's Growth Story: How to Accelerate Growth and Achieve MDGs?' Background paper for Ghana Country Economic Memorandum. Washington, DC: World Bank.

Darko, K. O. 2010. *The Politics of Government Business Relations in Ghana, 1982–2008*. New York, USA: Palgrave Macmillan.

Fosu, A. 2012. 'Growth of African Economies: Productivity, Policy Syndromes and the Importance of Institutions'. CSAE Working Paper No. WPS 2012/11. Oxford: University of Oxford.

Frimpong-Ansah, J. H. 1992. *The Vampire State in Africa: The Political Economy of Decline in Ghana*. London: James Curry Ltd.

Gollin, D., Jedwab, R., and Vollrath, D. 2013. 'Urbanization With and Without Structural Transformation'. Mimeo. George Washington University, Washington, DC.

Hausmann, R., Hidalgo, C. A., Bustos, S., Cosica, M., Simoes, A., and Yildirim, M. A. 2013. *The Atlas of Economic Complexity: Mapping the Paths to Prosperity*. Centre for International Development, Harvard University.

Herrendorf, B., Rogerson, R., and Valentinyi, A. 2013. 'Growth and Structural Transformation'. NBER Working Paper 18996. Cambridge, MA: National Bureau of Economic Research.

Hidalgo, C. A., and Hausmann, R. 2009. 'The Building Blocks of Economic Complexity'. *Proceedings of the National Academy of Sciences*, 106(26): 10570–5.

Jedwab, R., and Osei, R. D. 2012. 'Structural Change in Ghana, 1960–2010'. IIEP Working Paper No 2012–12. Institute for International Economic Policy. Washington, DC: George Washington University.

Kar, S., Pritchett, L., Raihan, S., and Sen, K. 2013. *The Dynamics of Economic Growth: A Visual Handbook of Growth Rates, Regimes, Transitions and Volatility*. Manchester: The University of Manchester.

Khan, M. H. 2010. 'Political Settlements and the Governance of Growth-Enhancing Institutions'. *DFID Research Paper Series on Governance for Growth*. London: School of Oriental and African Studies, University of London. <https://eprints.soas.ac.uk/9968/1/Political_Settlements_internet.pdf>.

Killick, T. 2010. *Development Economics in Action: A Study of Economic Policies in Ghana*, 2nd edition. London: Routledge.

Kraev, E. 2004. 'Structural Adjustment Policies in Ghana in the 1990s: An Empirical Analysis and Policy Recommendations'. UN Development Programme commissioned paper.

Manboah-Rockson, J. 2016. *Politics and Struggle for Democracy in Ghana: An Introduction to Political Science*. Johannesburg: Partridge Publishing.

McLaughlin, J., and Owusu-Ansah, D. 1994. 'Historical Setting'. In *Ghana: A Country Study*. Edited by Berry, L. V. Washington, DC: Federal Research Division, Library of Congress.

McMillan, M. S., and Rodrik, D. 2011. 'Globalization, Structural Change and Productivity Growth'. NBER Working Paper No. 17143. Cambridge, MA: National Bureau of Economic Research.

Meng, J. 2004. 'Ghana's Development: Miracle or Mirage?' *History*, 107(6).

Miller, F. P., Vandome, A. F., and McBrewster, J. (eds) 2009. *History of Ghana*. Mauritius: Alphascript Publishing.

Nohlen, D., Thibaut, B., and Krenn, M. 1999. *Elections in Africa: A Data Handbook*. Oxford: Oxford University Press.

Oduro, F., Mohammed, A., and Ashon, M. A. 2014. 'A Dynamic Mapping of the Political Settlement in Ghana'. Centre for Democratic Development Working Paper Series. Accra: CDD-Ghana.

Osei, R. D. 2012. 'Aid, Growth and Private Capital Flows to Ghana'. WIDER Working Paper No. 2012/22. Helsinki, Finland: UNU-WIDER.

Osei, R. D., Morrissey, O., and Lloyd, T. 2005. 'The Fiscal Effects of Aid in Ghana'. *Journal of International Development*, 17(8): 1037–53.

Osei, R. D., and Quartey, P. 2014. 'Economic Growth, Poverty and Structural Transformation in Ghana'. In *Readings in Key Economic Issues in Ghana*. Edited by Twerefou D., Quartey P., Boakye-Yiadom L., and Baah-Boateng W. Tema, Ghana: University of Ghana Readers, Digibooks Publishers.

Rodrik, D. 2006. 'Goodbye Washington Consensus, Hello Washington Confusion: A Review of the World Bank's "Economic Growth in the 1990s: Learning from a Decade of Reform"'. *Journal of Economic Literature*, 44(4): 973–87.

Sutton, J., and Kpentey, B. 2012. *An Enterprise Map of Ghana*. London: International Growth Centre.

Whitfield, L. 2011. 'Growth Without Economic Transformation: Economic Impacts of Ghana's Political Settlement'. DIIS Working Paper No. 2011:28. Copenhagen: Danish Institute for International Studies.

7

Dominance and Deals in Africa

How Politics Shapes Uganda's Transition from Growth to Transformation

Badru Bukenya and Sam Hickey

7.1 Introduction

Uganda is generally seen as one of Africa's leading success stories when it comes to economic growth. Since emerging from a prolonged period of instability in 1986, Uganda's economic growth has been impressive, averaging 7.7 per cent between 1997 and 2007 (Ssewanyana et al., 2011). Moreover, much of this growth has been pro-poor, with the country's poverty headcount falling dramatically during the 1990s from 56 per cent to 35 per cent, and now to 19.7 per cent (Republic of Uganda, 2014). However, serious questions remain concerning the extent to which Uganda is positioned to achieve the structural transformation of its economy that is required to sustain this growth trajectory into the future. This is in part because the country remains dependent on a limited range of agricultural commodities, while the advent of oil also raises concerns regarding the possibility of incurring Dutch Disease.[1] This chapter argues that both the roots of this challenge and the means of addressing it are closely shaped by deeper forms of politics and power relations within the country, which we refer to as the 'political settlement' (Khan, 2010). New theoretical work (see Chapter 1) has shown how the political settlement directly shapes the capacity and commitment of government and political elites to invest in the kinds of institution-building and relationships that can

---

[1] For more discussions on this, see Bategeka and Matovu (2011).

underpin shifts towards growth and structural transformation, particularly in terms of whether states generate the capacity to maintain macroeconomic stability, regulate and discipline capital, and build relationships with productive capitalists that are based on performance rather than collusion (Evans, 1995; Gore, 2000; Khan, 2005). Going further, Sen (2012) shows that the politics of achieving and then sustaining growth are likely to involve different drivers. He hypothesizes that what matters is the character of the 'deals space' within which political and economic elites and regulatory institutions interact to produce deals that are either relatively ordered or disordered (i.e. whether deals will be honoured), and open or closed (i.e. whether economic opportunities are open to all investors or restricted to those with political connections). The nature of this space is in turn shaped by the type of capitalists present within a given economy, their relative economic and organizational power vis-à-vis the ruling coalition, and the types of demands this leads them to make on public institutions (Pritchett and Werker, 2012).

Building on other recent research into the politics of growth and development in Uganda (Hickey et al., 2015; Kjær, 2014), we argue that the country's record of economic growth and prospects for achieving structural transformation both have been and are being closely shaped by the dynamics of the political settlement and the deals space. Moving forward with the policy directions identified by Hausmann et al. (2014) as being critical for structural transformation in Uganda, including support for agricultural processing and manufacturing, we draw attention to the politics and political economy of enacting and implementing such policy solutions. We argue that this is likely to include closer attention to state capacity, particularly through protecting the economic and regulatory technocracy from patronage politics; shifting the balance of power between different types of capitalists (including by building the associational power of what we term the 'magicians' and 'workhorses' vis-à-vis more monopolistic and rentier forms of capital); and supporting high-level dialogical spaces within which more productive forms of state–business relations can be nurtured.

The substantive part of this chapter (Section 7.2) is structured in accordance with the four main growth episodes that characterize Uganda's growth story since independence (Kar et al., 2013), each of which reflects the outworkings of the country's shifting political settlement dynamics in general and of the deals space involving state–business relations in particular. Section 7.3 uses primary research to set out the nature of the 'deals environment' in contemporary Uganda. This helps establish the basis for a discussion of the country's prospects for achieving structural transformation (Section 7.4) and of the policy, political, and political economy shifts this is likely to require (Section 7.5).

7.2 Shifting Political Settlement in Uganda: From Colonial Origins to the Present

Uganda's contemporary political economy, and the nature and level of its economic development, have been closely shaped by both its colonial legacy and the shifting nature of its political settlement in the post-independence period. The main economic legacy of colonial rule in Uganda flowed from Britain's divide-and-rule approach to governing its then trusteeship (Kabwegyere, 1974; Kiwanuka, 1970). This politicized several important dimensions of difference, including ethnicity, region, and religion, in ways that created structural challenges for the country to form a united approach to state-building and development. In economic and social terms, the treatment of northern Uganda as a labour reserve in relation to the plantation economy of the southern areas left a legacy of uneven development and regional inequalities, which would also undermine the possibility of stable governance and inclusive development.

A further legacy of relevance here was that of weak bureaucratic capacity, exacerbated by the belated incorporation of natives into the country's top administrative ranks. By 1961, just a year before independence, the bureaucratic apex of Uganda was still exclusively occupied by the departing colonial officers, with mid-level management also under their control. It was only in the lower ranks that Africans and Asians had some presence, with a combined composition of 50 per cent vis-à-vis Europeans (Kabwegyere, 1974). This imbalance was also reflected in the economy. By the late 1940s, all banks were British- or Indian-based and Africans were largely excluded from wholesale trade (Brett, 2006). This failure to build a productive indigenous capitalist class, which Whitfield et al. (2015) argue has been the critical failure of postcolonial political settlements in Africa, would have both economic and political implications with regards to the developmental nature of the political settlement that emerged in Uganda over the postcolonial period. The remainder of this section discusses the four main periods that Uganda has experienced since independence, as defined both in terms of its growth trajectory and the closely related character of its changing political settlement over this period.

The first episode stretches from independence in 1962 until 1970, whereby an initially stable and inclusive political settlement helped enable a steady growth in GDP per capita of around 3.3 per cent per annum. The second episode, from 1972 to 1980, coincided with the high degree of political and economic instability heralded by the rule of President Amin, during which time the growth rate per capita averaged −3.8 per cent. Between 1971 and 1979, Uganda experienced a loss in growth cumulatively estimated at 38 per cent (Bigsten and Kayizzi-Mugerwa, 2001: 18). In the third period, there was an initial but also uneven recovery from 1980 to 1988 (the growth rate per capita in this period was −0.1 per cent), during which time the second regime of President Obote initially involved the return of more stable governance, before becoming mired in disorder through guerrilla warfare and revenge attacks, which in turn undermined the settlement. The final growth period started within two years of the National Resistance Movement (NRM) coming into power and establishing both stability and an inclusive ruling coalition in 1986: from 1988, economic growth accelerated, to an average rate of 3.5 per cent per annum for the period 1988–2001, and of over 7 per cent on average between 2001 and 2010. As discussed below, the key factors that shaped this highly uneven pattern of growth from a political settlements perspective concerned the ability of successive political leaders to maintain stability and credibility through building ruling coalitions that were 'inclusive' enough.

When Uganda became independent on 9 October 1962, Milton Obote's Uganda People's Congress (UPC) depended on an opportunistic alliance with the Buganda monarchy's Kabaka Yekka party (Kabwegyere, 1974). Obote initially sought to build a fairly inclusive coalition, which comprised members from a cross-section of ethnic groups (Lindemann, 2010). However, a power struggle between the prime minister and the ceremonial president, the traditional ruler of Buganda, meant that the alliance ended bitterly in 1966. Obote's government became exclusive, oppressed its political opponents, and constructed patronage networks within the military and bureaucracy (Nabuguzi, 1995; Gukiina, 1972; ICG, 2012). Uganda's effective transition to a one-party state involved damaging strategies, which greatly extended the administrative budget of the state, while also undermining its operational capacity.

On the economic front, the independence government initially aimed to enhance the equitable distribution of wealth and access to opportunities, to address inequities from the colonial era, with government playing a significant role in the economy, largely through state controls and engagement in production activities. This strategy largely delivered: between 1961 and 1970, growth averaged 5.6 per cent, and 1963 and 1969 both witnessed spikes of 11.7 per cent (Figure 7.1). In addition, GDP per capita increased by 9 per cent during the same period.

The environment for business during this period can only be discussed in general terms, given the lack of literature on the topic. At the time of independence, a substantial portion of the economy comprised non-monetary subsistence agriculture. The monetary economy, which consisted of industrial goods manufacturing (powerbrokers), wholesaling and retailing (workhorses), and the import and export trade of both commodity and industrial products (magicians), was largely in private hands (Alibaruho, 1974; Leliveld, 2008).[2]

---

[2] Rentiers are the natural resource firms exporting to world commodity markets; magicians are the exporters that operate in competitive industries; powerbrokers are the firms catering to the

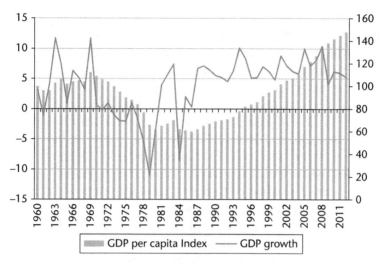

Figure 7.1. GDP growth and GDP per capita for Uganda

Source: Bigsten and Kayizzi-Mugerwa (2001) for 1960–98 data, and UBOS (2014) for later years.

The only sectors with strong government control were mining (rentiers), and copper and cement production (Ryan, 1973). Between 1961–2 and 1966–7, the government's participation was limited to measures to promote domestic savings and private investment. These were most visible in the agricultural sector, with subsidies on essential agricultural equipment and fertilizers, the expansion of extension services and research, and export marketing of crops through the formation of statutory boards, such as the Coffee Marketing Board and the Lint Marketing Board (Leliveld, 2008). This policy remained in force until the 1966 crisis that shifted the incentives for the Obote administration from national development to political survival. By abrogating the independence constitution and harassing the opposition, the 1966 crisis dismantled the democratic political system upon which the free market enterprise economic development processes were premised. Deals became disordered as investors lost confidence in constitutionalism and the rule of law. Indeed, 1967 witnessed the first episode of capital flight in Uganda's post-independence history (Ryan, 1973). Paradoxically, instead of looking critically at its own policies, the government blamed the business community for the capital flight, and low savings and investment rates (Leliveld, 2008).

In 1968, the business environment further shifted from open to a semi-open state, when Obote's government instigated policies to regulate licensing provisions for traders, which were 'intended slowly to squeeze Indians out of the

domestic sector that operate in high-rent industries; workhorses are those firms operating in competitive markets that serve the domestic economy. See Chapter 1 of for a fuller elaboration of these types, and Section 7.4 for a discussion of each type within Uganda.

commercial sector, but [also] for punishing political enemies of the government' (Kasfir, 1983: 89). The business environment was further stifled in 1969, when, in a bid to accelerate African control of the economy, Obote decreed, without prior consultation, that the government was to take a 60 per cent stake in over eighty leading firms, including private banks (Ryan, 1973). The government's change from capitalist to socialist ideology, as seen in three Marxian-oriented policy documents (*The Move to the Left* (Obote, 1969); *The Common Man's Charter* (Obote, 1970); and the Nakivubo Pronouncements of 1970), caused the second wave of capital flight from 1968 to 1970 (Hundle, 2013: 8). Because the criteria for nationalization were not made clear, there was great uncertainty as to whether the nationalization exercise was complete (with the eighty firms initially targeted), or whether more firms would subsequently be added to the list (Ryan, 1973). In 1970, Obote's last year in office, private capital outflow exceeded the inflow by a multiple of sixteen (Ryan, 1973). Unsurprisingly, a 'mini-exodus' of Indians from Uganda was underway as early as 1969 (Hundle, 2013). While the behaviour of the state discouraged both local and foreign entrepreneurs from expanding their investment portfolios, new entrepreneurs, mainly UPC stalwarts (cabinet ministers and soldiers), grabbed the opportunity to participate in the joint ventures, thus deepening the role of public institutions and actors in the economy. Political connections became significant in making business deals—suggesting an uneven playing field, even for African entrepreneurs.

After the military coup in 1971, Idi Amin's government embarked on an 'economic war' ostensibly aimed at empowering local Ugandans vis-à-vis non-indigenes. In 1972, approximately 80,000 Asians were expelled and their assets divided among the president's loyalists, the majority of whom lacked business acumen. This expulsion of Uganda's most autonomous and productive economic interest group helped further to collapse the boundaries between politics and the political economy, in ways that deepened the clientelist nature of the political settlement (ICG, 2012; Golooba-Mutebi and Hickey, 2013).[3] Between 1970 and 1980, Uganda's economy contracted at an annual rate of 5.5 per cent (Bigsten and Kayizzi-Mugerwa, 2001: 18). As shown in Figure 7.2, the level of investment declined by up to 10 per cent of GDP, and the country registered negative domestic savings.

As with the later years of Obote's independence government, Amin's ruling coalition was underpinned by a high degree of exclusion, with the civil service and military exhibiting a 'striking ethno-religious bias in favour of a Nubian-Kakwa core group and Muslims in general' (Lindemann, 2010: 21). As economic

---

[3] As Khan (2010) explains, the developmental character of political settlements is closely shaped by the productive nature of capitalists and the relationships that they have with the ruling coalition.

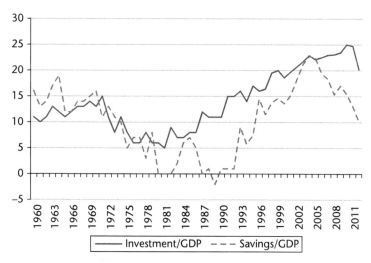

Figure 7.2. Investment and savings (% of GDP) for Uganda

Source: Bigsten and Kayizzi-Mugerwa (2001) for 1960–98 data, and UBOS (2014) for later years.

decline reduced the resources available for patronage, Amin's government presided over a predatory state, where military and government officials looted citizens with impunity. Against this background—what Khan refers to as a high level of horizontal power, which tends to undermine the stability of a ruling coalition—there were many disgruntled groups, some of which eventually took up arms to overthrow him.

During Amin's time, the environment for business was both closed and disordered. The cabinet played little role in making decisions on policy. Arbitrary decrees were frequently issued without consultation. Often these would be ignored by civil servants when they could be safely forgotten. As noted by one observer, during Amin's time:

> It became increasingly difficult to know what the rules were, whether to comply with them, and whether compliance would ensure personal safety. The predictability the state is expected to provide in a capitalist order, whether peripheral or not, was severely eroded. (Kasfir, 1983: 90)

The disappearance of goods from the shelves that accompanied the destruction of Asians' trading networks opened new possibilities for the underground economy locally known as *magendo*. By 1975, entrepreneurs bought consumer goods at retail prices from Uganda's neighbours, smuggled them into the country, and sold them at exorbitant prices. Smuggling accelerated with the 1976 coffee boom, which greatly increased producer prices everywhere in East Africa except Uganda (Kasfir, 1983). Smuggling coffee out of Uganda became a source of foreign exchange that supported the return flow of

189

consumer imports. The operation of *magendo* in Uganda was significantly dependent on, and continued to be related to, the state—officials provided protection and capital. Bigger operators, assisted by the breakdown in state law and order, developed private 'enforcement' systems to organize this trade, but this was too fragile to constitute the order needed for long-term private investment. Therefore, as in the later years of the Obote regime, business profitability depended greatly on connections with state agencies.

The partial economic recovery that occurred during the period 1979–86 reflects the fact that Obote's second regime was able to achieve at least a degree of political stability and also inclusivity within the ruling coalition, even if this did not arrive swiftly (Lindemann, 2010; Golooba-Mutebi, 2008). Obote then embarked on an Economic Recovery Programme (ERP) with the support of the IMF and World Bank, which yielded some positive results: growth resumed during the first three years of implementing the programme at an average of 5.7 per cent, albeit within an unstable macroeconomic environment, where inflation was 45 per cent on average per annum. However, the economic programme was undermined by the political failures of the government. Obote's promise of a government of national unity was never fully realized: all ministries were allocated to UPC members, who were predominantly from Obote's own Langi ethnic group and the neighbouring Acholi (Lindemann, 2010; Golooba-Mutebi, 2008). Those from Buganda, Ankole, and the 'West Nile' in particular perceived Obote II as ethnically partial with regard to sharing the national cake. Around five different rebel groups formed to fight against this perceived exclusion, including the National Resistance Army (NRA), which waged a guerrilla campaign within the Luwero Triangle area (Lindemann, 2010). The intensification of conflict in 1984 rendered the ERP untenable, as the bulk of spending was being allocated to defence. Increasingly unpopular and unstable, Obote's government was deposed in the July 1985 coup d'état.

Within a few years of taking power in 1986, the NRA/NRM had established a set of power relations and policy ideas which would provide the basis for one of Africa's most successful episodes of economic recovery and sustained growth. This involved not only a period of what we have termed 'stable growth', with the initial recovery rate between 0 and 5 per cent on average in the first part of this period, but also of 'miracle growth' (Kar et al., 2013), at an average of over 7 per cent between 2001 and 2010. The main underlying conditions for this impressive period of growth were the inclusive nature of the ruling coalition, and within this a more specific, and transnational, 'pro-growth' policy coalition, but also a shift of development ideology, and a related strategy of encouraging the Asian business community to return and restart their enterprises.

President Museveni moved quickly to form a broad-based ruling coalition. Most significant groups were represented at the higher levels of government, with the notable exception of those from the north (Lindemann, 2010; Tripp, 2010). The general level of political stability helped create a more ordered deals environment capable of turning around the economy. Growth resumed to an average of around 5 per cent between 1986 and 1990 (Belshaw et al., 1999: 681). The president was also persuaded to allow the development of a highly capable economic technocracy, with clear and autonomous responsibility for setting and implementing policies for macroeconomic stability and growth, and with whom donors felt they could do business (Mosley, 2012; Mutebile, 2010). The Bank of Uganda and the Ministry of Finance were developed as bureaucratic 'islands of excellence', with high levels of donor funding, and given strong powers to enforce fiscal discipline across spending ministries.

Under pressure from the IMF and World Bank, the government embarked on an ERP in May 1987, which, after a slow start, was embraced enthusiastic-ally by the government. This was partly as a means to secure international financial support, but there was a strong political logic to this policy turn, in that it offered the means required to distribute resources to the different groups or factions on whom the ruling coalition relied for support. For example, the liberalization of coffee markets helped to secure the 'vertical' support of the smallholders who formed the bedrock of the NRM's rural support base, and who were now able to gain market prices at the farm gate (Dijkstra and Van Donge, 2001). In terms of securing elite buy-in (or what Khan terms 'managing horizontal power relations'), the process of privatiza-tion that was unrolled aggressively in the mid-1990s was directly used to bind in powerful elites through the distribution of rents in the form of ownership of newly privatized entities (Mwenda and Tangri, 2005). Even the policy of encouraging Asian businesspeople to return to Uganda—and of returning their property to them, along with other incentives to help them get the economy moving again—had a political dimension: such concessions came with expectations of political loyalty and financial support for the NRM, thus further bolstering the capacity of the ruling coalition to remain in power. Importantly, and as eloquently described by Roger Tangri (2015: 17), President Museveni has sought to avoid 'the rise of wealthy, autonomous, and assertive black entrepreneurs who emerge outside his ambit and who could challenge his authority. He has viewed them as a potential political threat.'

7.3 From Sustained Growth to Structural Transformation?

Uganda's strong economic growth since 1992 has been driven mainly by the services, manufacturing, and construction sectors (Figure 7.3). In 2010, the share of value added contributed by the services sector was almost half of total GDP, from about 32 per cent in 1990, and that of agriculture diminished

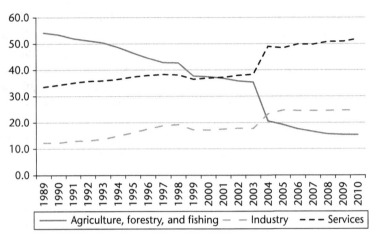

Figure 7.3. Sector composition of GDP (%) for Uganda
Source: UBOS, *Statistical Appendix 2012*.

steadily from 50.3 per cent to about 15.2 per cent in the same period. The recent decline in agriculture partly reflected the fall in productivity of the sector, a deterioration in farming methods synonymous with poor technologies, and the fact that resources, especially in form of labour, were being reallocated to services. The use of inferior inputs and the lack of value addition to raw materials have also limited the productivity and profitability of the sector. Recent numbers suggest that this trend has not changed.

With respect to exports, there has been a gradual diversification away from coffee to other agricultural exports, such as tea and raw tobacco, and also refined petroleum, fish fillets, and cement (Figure 7.4). Uganda has also witnessed some degree of structural transformation, improving from 1995, where its economic complexity measure was −1.14 and ranked 107th out of 125 countries, to an economic complexity measure of −0.48 and a rank of eighty-third out of 125 countries in 2012. Moreover, Hausmann et al. (2014) find that Uganda's economic complexity was higher than might have been predicted by its level of income, suggesting a high potential for future growth. In contrast, research by the IMF, World Bank, and Bank of Uganda suggests that progress has been limited, with the pace of structural transformation actually slowing during the 2000s (Brownbridge and Bwire, 2016; Selassie, 2008). Alongside some arguably regressive shifts within Uganda's political settlement over the 2000s, this has led some to question whether the country will be able to generate the capacity and commitment required to achieve the shift from sustained growth to structural transformation.

That the president is ideologically committed to structural transformation is not in doubt. The new political economy of development that emerged in the

Total: $750 million

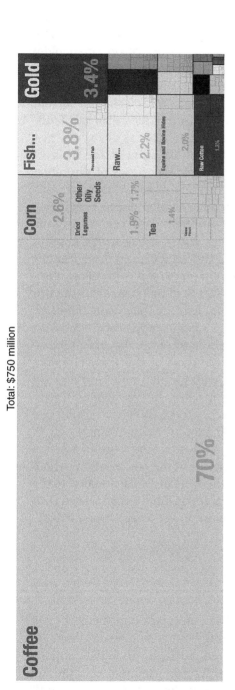

Total: $2.68 billion

Figure 7.4. Changing structure of Uganda's exports, 1995 and 2012
Source: Atlas of Economic Complexity <http://atlas.cid.harvard.edu/>.

mid-2000s has led to a resurgent focus on this vision, with Uganda graduating from debt and reducing its reliance on aid as new financial flows became available from the discovery of commercial quantities of oil and rapidly increasing levels of investment from China (Hickey, 2013). However, the shifting dynamics of the political settlement since the early 2000s, and particularly since the return of multiparty politics in 2005 (Golooba-Mutebi and Hickey, 2013), suggest a deepening of clientelistic, rather than capitalist, tendencies. Three main tendencies are particularly relevant here. The first concerns the shifting patterns of inclusion and exclusion at the heart of power, which in turn shapes the stability and time horizons of the ruling elite. At its pinnacle, the ruling coalition has become more exclusionary, with the president's ethnic group and the Baganda benefiting disproportionately compared with the ethnic groups from northern and eastern Uganda (Lindemann, 2010; Tripp, 2010; Tumushabe, 2009). Along with the president's reluctance to appoint a successor, this also helps explain the defections of several high-level elites, some of whom went on to form political organizations that raised a credible threat to the NRM's hold on power. This intensification of political competition has also led the president to adopt increasingly populist measures to secure the support of his rural base, with the 2011 elections a hugely expensive affair because of this dynamic. Importantly, the same election saw a marked relaxation of the normally strict approach to fiscal and monetary discipline, with the autonomy and capacity of the economic technocracy to maintain macroeconomic stability undermined by this political imperative (Mwenda, 2014). Growth levels dipped for two to three consecutive years, further exacerbated by rising levels of inflation requiring a strong monetary response from the Bank of Uganda once it regained control of the economic policy in the post-election period. Such dynamics within Uganda's political settlement are largely inimical to the prospects of developing the kinds of relations and institutions associated with delivering either structural transformation or improved levels of service delivery (Golooba-Mutebi and Hickey, 2013; Kjær, 2014).

7.3.1 *Evolution of Uganda's Rents Space*

As Figures 7.5–7.8 make clear, there has been an increase in the economic importance of powerbrokers over time, along with a decrease in the workhorses' share in GDP. Magicians have not seen much growth in their importance in Uganda, even during the strong growth phase witnessed since the late 1980s. Rentiers have had almost no presence in Uganda's rents space until recently, though this may change with the expected production of oil from 2019 onwards (see Section 7.4.3 on rentiers).

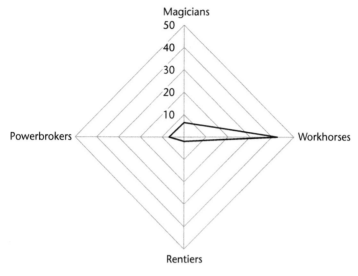

Figure 7.5. Uganda's rents space, 1969
Source: Based on Rujumba (1999).
Note: Sector contribution to GDP in %.

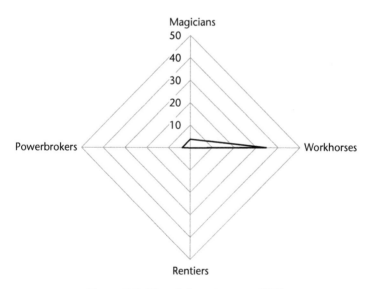

Figure 7.6. Uganda's rents space, 1979
Source: Based on Rujumba (1999).
Note: Sector contribution to GDP in %.

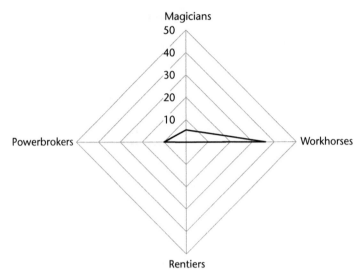

Figure 7.7. Uganda's rents space, 1988

Source: Based on Rujumba (1999).

Note: Sector contribution to GDP in %.

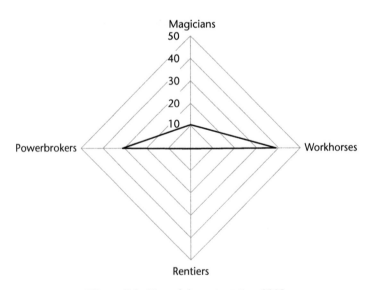

Figure 7.8. Uganda's rents space, 2013

Source: Authors' calculations, from UBOS.

Note: Sector contribution to GDP in %.

7.4 Deals Environment in Uganda Today

This chapter so far has shown that the different growth episodes that Uganda has experienced since independence have been closely related to the changing nature of the political settlement, particularly in terms of the level of stability allowed by intra-elite conflicts and bargaining, and the extent to which political leaders were able to secure the buy-in of enough powerful groups to maintain and allow a longer-term vision to emerge. However, it is important to go further in identifying the more specific causal mechanisms through which these underlying sets of power relations and ideas shape the nature of growth within Uganda's political economy, and what this means for the country's prospects going forward. As noted at the outset, the more specific ways in which the political settlement interacts with the economy in developing countries is refracted through the 'deals' environment. Within clientelist political settlements, deals that involve largely informal institutions and arrangements tend to prevail over rules-based approaches. Deals can be relatively ordered or disordered, in terms of the likelihood of their being honoured and lasting, and also relatively open or closed, with reference to whether deals are widely available to all investors, large or small, as opposed to being captured by a smaller number of investors with strong political connections (Pritchett and Werker, 2012). Initial analysis suggests that as long as deals are ordered, they can be relatively closed and still enable growth to take off. However, to sustain growth over the long run and enable a shift towards structural transformation, it seems likely to require a shift from an ordered-closed deals environment to a deals space which maintains order, but also becomes more open to entry of new firms in ways that drive up competition (Pritchett and Werker, 2012).

Importantly, different kinds of deals environments may prevail within different economic domains. Pritchett and Werker (2012) divide domestic political economies into four different domains, according to the level of rent-seeking versus competition along one axis, and whether the sector is import- or export-oriented along the other axis. As indicated in Figure 7.9, this generates four groupings, each containing capitalists which are likely to make different kinds of demands on the state with regards to its regulatory activities and provision of public goods, and whose relative political power and productivity will have different implications for achieving structural transformation and (more broadly) inclusive development.[4]

The shifting economic fortunes of each sector are explored in greater depth in Bukenya et al. (Forthcoming). Here we delve deeper into how the deals

---

[4] See Chapter 1 for a fuller elaboration of these types.

	High-rent	Competitive
Export-oriented	**RENTIERS** e.g. Mineral concessionaires	**MAGICIANS** Exporters of cash crops and agro-processed products; formal manufacturers; informal exporters to neighbouring countries.
Domestic market	**POWERBROKERS** e.g. Large firms in tele-communication, construction, hotels, electricity and water supply, etc.	**WORKHORSES** e.g. Informal manufacturers, wholesale and retail traders, informal-sector businesses, farmers, etc.

Figure 7.9. Structure of Uganda's domestic economy

Source: Based on Pritchett and Werker (2012).

environment plays out in each domain through key informant interviews that were conducted between January and April 2014 with a total of twenty owners, managers, and/or top representatives of firms and associations of business entities in each of the four domains.

7.4.1 *Competitive Export: The Magicians*

Within the competitive export sector, information was gathered from business entities that included a coffee export company and milk processing firm, as well as a review of the literature. The environment for doing business in this sector was described by traders to be laissez-faire, with free entry and exit of firms. Traders can access markets in the neighbouring countries, especially in the East African Community and the new state of South Sudan. Traders also alluded to the political stability that has been created by the NRM in most parts of the country as conducive for regional trade.

Aware of Uganda's unfavourable trade balance, the government has sought to address this anomaly through several export promotion initiatives (Ssewanyana et al., 2011), an increased focus on agro-processing, and export base widening strategies. The government has also created numerous bodies and product-specific agencies to promote exports, such as the Uganda Coffee Development Authority, the Uganda Exports Promotions Board, and the East Africa Dairy Development project. The magicians are also affiliates of private membership associations that ideally 'present a common position of the exporters' to government,[5] including the Uganda Manufacturers' Association (UMA), which was

---

[5] General manager of a coffee-exporting company, 13 February 2014.

formed to further the needs of local manufacturers, irrespective of size. Robinson and Friedman (2007) describe the UMA as one of the most effective policy impact civil society organizations in Uganda. Another influential association is the Private Sector Foundation (PSF). Both UMA and PSF have specialized departments responsible for lobbying, advocacy, and networking. They have regular access to government officials and make submissions on draft legislations (Kangave and Katusiimeh, 2015; Robinson and Friedman, 2007).

However, government agencies and associations are, at times, a source of unnecessary red tape and a barrier to the operation of the free market. For example, traders need a licence to qualify as exporters, but the process of obtaining this is cumbersome: a respondent observed that when one 'wants to get a licence from the Exports Promotions Board, you will be directed to talk to a particular person, who will lead you to the next until when you get to the final person'.[6] Moreover, this sort of gatekeeping is not limited to traders' dealings with government—it extends to their own associations, which ideally exist to promote their interests:

> if you want to obtain a certificate of origin from the National Chamber of Commerce and you want it immediately, you pay some money to the person in charge and you get the certificate in hours. If you do not pay, they tell you to leave your forms behind and then you always go back to check if the certificate was issued and you do not find it, or that the person who is to issue the certificate is out of office, which delays you.[7]

Deals in the magicians sector are stuck in a semi-open setting, since all our respondents suggested that one needs connections to obtain incentives or gain access to lucrative deals. One informant recounts:

> In the coffee exports business, you have to maintain good relations with particular people, so as to be able to access certain markets. If you are to take coffee to the European Union, there is a certain group of people you have to supply your coffee through. These people allow you to supply a quota of your products to the market.[8]

However, the sector is also not fully closed, in that all our key informants indicated that a majority of competitors can access the key powerbrokers in the sector. Most traders suggested that they are confident engaging in long-term capital investment—something that suggests confidence in government, and a pointer that the environment is at least semi-ordered: 'We are confident in investing in machinery and technology, because the demand for coffee is always increasing, which implies that we too have to increase our supply.'[9]

---

[6] General manager of a coffee-exporting company, 13 February 2014.
[7] General manager of a coffee-exporting company, 13 February 2014.
[8] General manager of a coffee-exporting company, 13 February 2014.
[9] General manager of a milk-processing firm, 19 February 2014.

Traders were not worried that a change in personalities would hurt their business, 'because you learn to work with new personalities',[10] suggesting that even informal processes can be relatively ordered.

Large exporters are expected to make political contributions, mostly to the ruling party: 'We make donations to political parties, though only to the NRM, you cannot fund the opposition in Uganda and remain in business. Most businesspeople in Uganda have learnt a simple principle of support *Any Government in Power (AGIP)*.'[11] However, traders indicated that they did not think that 'the donations would lessen the risk of our investment activities in anyway'.[12]

Our informant from the coffee-exporting company expressed concern about the government's policy of banning the cooperatives through which they operated in the 1980s. This observation is significant, as most traders in the competitive export sector are small, with over 50 per cent of Uganda's exports in 2008 coming from small or informal traders (Ssewanyana et al., 2011). Such traders have less bargaining power when they transact business in their individual capacities, rather than as a collective. A case study of the export trade between Uganda and South Sudan illustrates the significance of collective action—and, in its absence, the role of political connectedness—in the export sector.

When security improved in Sudan, following the signing of the Comprehensive Peace Agreement that provided for the creation of the Government of South Sudan in January 2005, a large number of Ugandans flocked into southern Sudan, trading a wide variety of goods for consumption and construction (International Alert, 2014). In 2008, Ugandan exports to South Sudan accounted for 68.9 per cent of total exports (UBOS, 2009). However, from around 2009, trading relations between the two countries developed tensions, which left several Ugandan exporters aggrieved. Stories abounded of how Ugandan traders were being arrested, intimidated, raped, receiving non-payment for goods supplied, and even being killed at the hands of South Sudanese security personnel, with impunity (International Alert, 2014). The situation was aggravated by a civil war that erupted following internal wrangles within the top Sudan People's Liberation Army (SPLA) leadership in December 2013.

According to International Alert (2014), only a few traders were organized into associations, which were also organizationally weak and unable to engage in effective advocacy. When Ugandan traders petitioned their government to intervene on their behalf, as Schomerus and Titeca (2012: 18) report, the

---

[10] General manager of a coffee-exporting company, 13 February 2014.
[11] General manager of a coffee-exporting company, 13 February 2014.
[12] General manager of a milk-processing firm, 19 February, 2014.

government acted 'primarily to protect the interests of large-scale traders, who often work closely with SPLA officials and Ugandan government officials'. These researchers point to the existence of a 'military–commercial nexus', comprising the high-level SPLA officials who determine access to the South Sudanese market, Ugandan officials (mostly from the military circles), and the large-scale Ugandan traders. This implies that the playing field in this nascent market is not balanced, since large-scale traders are better positioned than their small-scale counterparts to trade their goods across the borders.

Besides the example of the South Sudan trade, a closer look at the manner in which government administers incentives to exports also shows favouritism towards some firms and distortion of the playing field. SEATINI-Uganda (2012) estimates that Uganda spends an average of 5 per cent of its current revenue on tax incentives and exemptions, especially on those firms producing for export. However, there have been several cases of the government offering subsidies, loan guarantees, and other incentives to foreign companies, which have subsequently failed to deliver.

7.4.2 Uganda's Workhorses

The workhorses are firms in competitive industries that serve the domestic market. The competitive domestic industry of Uganda comprises a variety of business entities that vary immensely according to size and product specialization. They are mostly wholesale and retail traders of consumer goods (which on average contribute 14–17 per cent of GDP); agricultural businesses (averaging 22 per cent of GDP in the last ten years); and accommodation and food services (4–5 per cent of GDP in the last five years). Although their overall contribution to GDP is significant, the recent Uganda Bureau of Statistics business census revealed that many of these are micro-businesses, with 70 per cent having an annual turnover of less than UGX 5 million (US $2,000) and employing an average of two people (UBOS, 2011). This creates problems, both for collective action and for the state to make systematic interventions to develop the sector as a whole. Currently, SMEs are registered with a variety of government ministries, with no overall body coordinating them. Several analysts observe that, in return, government policies towards the private/business sector have been either non-existent or ad hoc, with variations discernible within sub-sectors aimed at particular enterprises whose political support is deemed important (Kjær and Katusiimeh, 2012; Kjær et al., 2012a).

The environment for business in the competitive domestic sector is best described as semi-ordered and largely open. Although government regulation and interference is not so onerous as to stop firms from entering the market or conducting their business, government–small business communication channels are not particularly effective, and the government seems to lack the will to make the kinds of investment in state capacity that would help the sector reach its potential. Over 90 per cent of the workhorse firms are not members of any association (UBOS, 2011). However, some traders, especially in major towns, are organized in relatively influential associations that are able to engage government to improve the business environment. The Kampala City Traders Association (KACITA) was formed as a pressure group against high taxes, and has achieved a degree of influence over government.

Generally, the process of setting up a business in Uganda is complicated and extremely costly. One needs to interact with at least five government agencies, namely: the Uganda Investment Authority (UIA); the Uganda Revenue Authority (URA); local councils; the National Environmental Management Authority; and the Uganda National Bureau of Standards. The majority of our key informants indicated that, apart from the UIA (which issues investment certificates which are crucial for accessing other agencies), the rest of the agencies are not supportive. In the words of one respondent, other agencies 'are actually a bigger part of your cost',[13] since government officials that occupy them are more interested in 'filling their stomachs' than rendering a public service to the businesses.

All government agencies mentioned above require one to undergo rigorous documentation procedures. Interviews with a businessman who is in the advanced stages of establishing a plumbing factory revealed that, whereas building permits for his 3,000 m^2 factory would officially cost UGX 2.5 million, he paid UGX 1 million extra, while the environmental impact assessment certificate, which officially goes for UGX 2 million, in reality cost him UGX 9 million. He claimed that extra costs went to 'consultants' and bribes to various officials to 'facilitate' the process.[14] These observations are corroborated by a recent World Bank (2016) *Doing Business* report, which showed that the ease of obtaining a construction permit has worsened in Uganda, currently standing at 161, down from 143 in 2013, in the ranking of 189 economies.

As in the competitive export sector, political connections matter a great deal with regard to the profitability of businesses within the workhorse sector. In this sector, influential businessmen have particularistic relationships with the ruling elite and therefore receive preferential treatment from government as individuals, rather than as a sector. Whereas some businesspeople are usually helped by government, the same government has turned a blind eye to independent companies that require its support. One key informant noted that '[while those] close to people in government easily receive money to bail them out of their troubles, a company like Nkima has been begging the

---

[13] Interview with the director of a manufacturing company, 3 March 2014.
[14] Interview with the director of a manufacturing company, 3 March 2014.

government for years to bail it out of its financial troubles, and government is taking forever to respond'.[15]

Even among importers, key informants agreed unanimously that profitability depends on one's connections to URA officials, who assess and declare the nature of goods being imported and therefore how much tax is to be paid. It was observed, however, that not all traders have easy access to these officials. The new entrants in the sector rely on the brokerage services of the clearing and forward agents, who are private business firms certified by the URA to process imports. Those who are senior in the business usually have superior contacts, in the form of links with the supervisors of URA assessors. And, with such contacts, they can ensure that they are designated their preferred official to process their consignments:

> Sometimes I call directly, other times I go through the clearing and forwarding agents to mention my preferred assessor to the supervisor. So this means that when I pay money informally to URA to influence my tax assessment, even the supervisors get their share.[16]

This sector also has a host of politicians-turned-businessmen. Key informants claimed that such politicians are well connected in the URA, because they influence the recruitment process to have their relatives within the tax agency. It is these officials who then facilitate the processing of goods for their 'patrons' (Robinson, 2006). It is alleged that this explains why goods of politicians usually receive priority at customs over those of ordinary traders.[17] For instance, a senior NRM officer and cabinet minister imported a lot of sugar from Kenya during 2011, when there were shortages in Uganda's domestic supply chain. When his sugar reached customs at Malaba, 'everyone else who had sugar was put on hold until his consignment was cleared'.[18] People who know powerful people in the government are also at an advantage. One respondent gave examples of how connections have helped him through troubles, such as when his small fishing nets were confiscated. He claimed that his in-laws contacted a powerful member of the first family, who exerted influence and had the fishing nets 'released unconditionally'.[19]

These observations are corroborated by independent analyses on the workings of the URA. As stated by Robinson (2006), one of the main expected benefits of the URA's semi-autonomous status was that the agency would be

---

[15] Interview with a traders' association representative, 12 February 2014; Nkima is a pseudonym.
[16] Interview with stationery importers, 18 February 2014.
[17] Interview with merchandise importer, 21 February 2014; interview with stationery importers, 18 February 2014.
[18] Interview with merchandise importer, 21 February 2014.
[19] Interview with merchandise importer, 21 February 2014.

insulated from political interests. However, after a honeymoon period, it became clear that:

> There is evidence of systematic political involvement in URA affairs, especially in the form of influence over the recruitment, promotion, and transfer of staff. Ministers, family members with political connections, and political advisers in State House (Office of the President) have all sought to exert influence in this manner. (Robinson, 2006: 23)

Robinson cites one anonymous source who alleged that the majority of URA appointments were more strategic. In particular, the customs and excise department was favoured in view of its critical role in determining levies on imports: 'Politically appointed staff would be in a position to waive or reduce duty requirements or undervalue shipping consignments for patrons with influence and leverage' (Robinson, 2006: 24).

Due to the above, there was a feeling among key informants that the playing field in the workhorse sector is not level. One key informant claimed that: 'lots of other enterprises of a magnitude similar to mine get some incentives from government, e.g. tax holidays from corporate tax, but for us we were not given'.[20] The government is accused of not establishing clear procedures for firms to know what they are entitled to and the processes to follow to access the incentives. Such grey areas create opportunities for corruption. Indeed, our key informants noted that the current situation is that for one to get the incentives, 'you need to know key people in the Ministry of Finance'.

Government capacity to regulate and support this sector is mixed. For example, recent research into economic productivity in Uganda shows how political dynamics have resulted in different sub-sectors within the same ministry (in this case agriculture) being governed in very different ways (Kjær, 2015). Despite the fact that the fisheries sector was an important foreign exchange earner in the 1990s, the ruling elite was generally not keen on strengthening it, because powerful actors within the ruling coalition, particularly ex-NRA militants and fishermen, were opposed to reforms for improving this sub-sector, with subsequent declines in productivity (Kjær et al., 2012a: 18). In contrast, reforms aimed at improving productivity in the dairy sector have been implemented much more effectively, Kjær argues, because the most important part of the ruling elite and NRM's main support base comes from the south-western part of the country, which is Uganda's leading milk-producing region. The dairy sector appears to have achieved a significant degree of orderliness and is generally an open sector, at least within the western part of the country, where farmers' organizations representing dairy farmers and traders, such as cooperatives, are functional and strong (Kjær et al., 2012b).

---

[20] Interview with director of a manufacturing company, 3 March 2014.

7.4.3 Rentiers

According to Pritchett and Werker (2012: 53), 'Rentiers are the high-rent firms that sell their products abroad'. An influential body of research suggests that the availability of revenues from this sector may be the most damaging in governance terms, as it can offer political elites rents in return for little effort, and therefore reduces levels of accountability and the incentive to invest in more developmental sectors. In Uganda, the high-rent export sector is mainly comprised of mineral concessionaires dealing in gold and oil, both of which are relatively new to the country. The mining sector's contribution to GDP has until recently been insignificant; between 2008 and 2013 it averaged 0.3 per cent of GDP (UBOS, 2014) and it had 0.2 per cent of the total number of businesses in 2011 (UBOS, 2011). Moreover, these statistics are inclusive of quarrying stone, and the mining of sand and clay, which are mostly consumed in the domestic market. However, the sector's prospects are bright following the 2006 discovery of commercially viable quantities of oil and gas. Although production is not expected before 2019, the current estimated petroleum reserve capacity for Uganda is approximately 6.5 billion barrels, with the projected recoverable standing at c.1.7 billion barrels (see Hickey et al., 2015).

The two sub-sectors, gold and oil, have contrasting business environments. On the one hand, the business environment in the gold sub-sector is visibly closed, disordered, and lacks a level playing field. This is for historical reasons, stemming from Uganda's unregulated trade links with its war-prone neighbour, the Democratic Republic of the Congo. In 2007, the UN Security Council imposed sanctions on Uganda's major gold exporters following accusations that they were dealing in so-called 'blood gold' (Mthembu-Salter, 2015). Since then, the country's official gold trade has declined. Dealing in gold in Uganda is, therefore, mainly an underground business, save for the few companies involved in small-scale mining in the Busia and Moroto districts.

Less surprising, the sole key informant interview obtained in the gold trade opined that firms/businesspeople dealing in gold have to be connected with officials, 'both in the Congolese army and the Uganda security services, mostly the Uganda People's Defence Force and the police'.[21] Deals in such an environment are very fragile, as actors are unable to guarantee that officials will deliver on their sides of the bargain. 'These relations are very sensitive, any slight mishap can lead to the collapse of the entire business', the key informant reported.[22]

---

[21] Interview with former employee at Drito Global Cooperation, 4 March 2014.
[22] Interview with former employee at Drito Global Cooperation, 4 March 2014.

On the other hand, the oil sub-sector is now best described as closed, moderately ordered, and with some degree of fairness in the playing field. The capacity of the state to regulate Uganda's oil industry, in which investments have been somewhat sporadic since 1986, when the NRM came into government, is now touted as representing a further pocket of effectiveness within Uganda's bureaucracy (Hickey et al., 2015). In 2006, when commercially viable quantities of oil and gas were announced in Uganda, the government suspended the deal-making process with oil companies, in order to put in place the National Oil and Gas Policy. This provided the basis from which more comprehensive legislation would be prepared and passed in 2012, namely the Petroleum Exploration, Development, and Production Bill, and the Petroleum Refining, Gas Processing and Conversion, Transportation, and Storage Bill. The Public Finance Bill, to consolidate existing public finance management laws and address the management of oil revenues, was passed in November 2014. Acknowledging the need to establish this legal and institutional basis before moving to production, the government has delayed the production process and foregone the short-term benefits of securing quick deals. There is a significantly informal element to the current governance of oil in Uganda, with the president taking a strong personal interest in the negotiations with oil companies and, as with gold, the military also playing a key role. Despite this, the 'closed ordered' deals delivered so far around oil seem to be in the national interest, not least because the president has proved capable of controlling (or at least centralizing) rent-seeking activities in the sector, and willing to enable high-capacity oil technocrats to operate with significant levels of autonomy. However, the prevailing dynamics within the political settlement suggest that it may be difficult to sustain this level of commitment and capacity once oil starts to flow (Hickey and Izama, 2017).

7.4.4 Powerbrokers

Powerbrokers are 'the high-rent firms that serve the domestic market' (Pritchett and Werker, 2012: 53). In Uganda this sector comprises the big firms dealing in transport and communication (whose contribution to GDP has averaged around 5 per cent over the last five years), financial intermediation operators such as banks and insurance companies (3–4 per cent of GDP), and construction companies (12–13 per cent of GDP).[23] To this list, we can add beer and soft beverage manufacturers, cement producers, power-generating companies, and water supply enterprises, among others.

---

[23] UBOS statistical abstracts.

The business environment in the high-rent domestic sector is largely semi-ordered and semi-open: it is mainly those with political connections who get to make deals, and they are only assured that government officers will deliver as long as these officers know they are still in office and are happy with the commission (kickback) provided by businesspeople. Interviewees dealing in building and construction and hotel operation confessed that a lot of people must be 'fed' for one to get 'juicy contracts' from government. Before and after winning government contracts, several people have to be 'fed' (given commissions) on the awarded contracts. According to the manager of a medium-sized hotel in the suburbs of Kampala, 'we currently host most of the KCCA [Kampala Capital City Authority] workshops, but to get such a business, we had to feed a lot of people'. Although a change in personality within government agencies can significantly affect the businesspeople in this sector, there are opportunities for existing firms to connect easily with new officials. This is captured by the CEO of a major building and construction company with connections to the Ministry of Education:

> Yes, in my line of business, a change in personalities can affect my business. For instance, if there is a new permanent secretary, new commissioner in charge of planning, or minister, it can hurt my business, especially if I do not get to establish a good working relationship with the new people [fast enough]. Because this would imply that instead of awarding contracts to my company, the contract would go to some other company.[24]

A similar message was conveyed by the hotel manager.[25] Alternatively, Booth et al. (2014) argue that powerbrokers have had to enlist politicians and other high-ranking government officials into joint ventures to secure their businesses, while the latter are assured of enjoying dividends in case the businesses break even.

The playing field in the powerbroker rents space is visibly uneven. Among the many cases of favouritism we uncovered is that of a Ugandan businessman who previously held an important position in the NRM's Entrepreneurs' League. He is said to fund the party and helps it to forge links with the business and Muslim communities. In return, his companies receive government favours in the form of loans, bailouts, and tax waivers (Golooba-Mutebi and Hickey, 2013; Kiiza, 2011). However, despite the closed nature of deal-making, business actors expressed confidence about investing in machinery and costly technologies, as long as their 'scope of work continues growing', mainly through getting contracts from government agencies. Building and construction firms and hotels make donations to political parties, especially to the

---

[24] Interview with the CEO of a construction company, 10 February 2014.
[25] Interview with hotel manager, 17 February 2014.

ruling NRM. They indicate that 'we do this to avoid being frustrated now and in the future. For instance, if they send someone asking for your contribution and you do not pay, the next day you will receive visitors from URA, who will start asking for so many unnecessary receipts.'[26] Donations to political parties are perceived to lessen the risk of their investment activities. Similarly, firms cannot be seen with members of the opposition: 'If you want to stay in business, you cannot be seen to oppose the ruling government; the moment you start opposing the government then your troubles will begin immediately.'[27]

The other sub-sector that we investigated within high-rent production for the domestic market was telecommunications, specifically the mobile phone network operators (MPNOs). In comparison with building and construction, the business environment for MPNOs is slightly more ordered and also more open. Actors in this rents space consider the policies that guide the sector to be largely neutral,[28] as opposed to within building and construction, where government regulation and interference were onerous enough to stop firms from entering the market or conducting their business. However, it is important to understand certain trends here. From 1993 up to the mid-2000s, the telecommunications sector was closed and semi-ordered. In an interview with one of the newest telecommunications companies in Uganda, it was revealed that each of the three pioneering telecoms companies in Uganda (Celtel, 1994; MTN, 1998; and UTL, 2001) 'enjoyed protected telephony services and tax holidays for five years'.[29] At one point, these three collectively lobbied government to restrict new entrants to the market, without success. Since 2007, however, Uganda has opened up the sector to competition, and hence companies currently operate on a free entry and exit principle. At the time of our fieldwork there were seven MPNOs, namely, MTN, Airtel, Uganda Telecom, Orange, Smile, K2, and Smart.

In this liberalized market, the Uganda Communication Commission enhances competition by preventing the misuse of market power, ensuring non-discriminatory access to essential facilities, and providing for interconnection. For instance, since July 2010, all network operators in Uganda are obliged to interconnect with other operators at a uniform interconnection fee of UGX 131.[30] However, and despite the introduction of competition, fixed line penetration in Uganda remains very low, with two operators—MTN Uganda Limited and United Telecoms Limited (UTL)—providing the fixed lines services. UTL is the dominant operator in this area.

---

[26] Interview with hotel manager, 17 February 2014.
[27] Interview with hotel manager, 17 February 2014.
[28] Interview with hotel manager, 17 February 2014.
[29] Interview with telecom shareholder, 11 February 2014; interview with telecom legal advisor Uganda, 10 February 2014.
[30] Kigambo and Talemwa, 2010.

In general terms, most of the actors we interviewed in this sub-sector claimed that there is a level playing field, 'because all the rules and regulations cut across all mobile network providers', although the three pioneering telecoms companies 'enjoyed tax exemptions and protection for five years', a privilege denied to new entrants.[31] A change in personalities in this sector does not significantly affect the fortunes of players.

However, there are some issues that are still keeping the sector partially closed. For instance, new entrants have to part with some informal 'facilitation' fees for government officials to issue them with a licence. As one key informant put it, in this sort of business,

> you cannot do away with informal payments/facilitation, because you have to keep the people you work with happy to ease your business...if one needs a licence, he/she will have to speak to people in the Uganda Investment Authority or the Ministry of ICT, it is very normal to put in our application with a small envelope, so that the licence comes out fast.[32]

In addition, MPNOs are expected to make donations to political parties, but mostly to the government in power. Some confessed to donating to the opposition, but 'this is much concealed, because we do not want to be known as supporters of the opposition'. However, it is important to note that, whereas in a fully disordered setting payments are central to the survival of the firm, in a semi-ordered one they are not. According to one key informant, facilitations and donations 'do not lessen the risk of our investment activities, but we [give them] to prove our good will [to the ruling regime]'.[33]

7.5 Politics of Growth Maintenance

The different kinds of deals space that exist within and across different economic domains in Uganda reflect the interaction of several factors, most notably the economic and organizational capacity of capitalists in each sector, their relationships with the ruling coalition, the rent-seeking opportunities that each domain offers to political actors, and the state's regulatory capacity. The 'magicians' are able to operate within a fairly open space, within which political connections are not as significant as other sectors—although party donations are expected from large exporters—and where deals are at least semi-ordered. This is perhaps because the government is committed to export promotion, as reflected in its establishment of a greater number of strategies

---

[31] Interview with telecom shareholder, 11 February 2014.
[32] Interview with telecom legal advisor, 10 February 2014.
[33] Interview with telecom legal advisor, 10 February 2014.

and agencies dedicated to this end compared with other domains, but also because magicians have managed to forge relatively influential associations (e.g. UMA, KACITA, and PSF), which has enabled them to secure some policy reforms from government (especially those in line with taxation). In contrast, the much broader range of 'workhorse' businesses lack the collective capacity to protect and promote their interests (as reflected in persistent policy failures to deal with problems highlighted in the *Doing Business* surveys), and are subject to a higher degree of political manipulation, leaving the sector both more closed and disordered than is productive. The sector is also subject to low-level, but still persistent and damaging, rent-seeking behaviour from the regulatory bodies involved, most notably the URA. Within the less-competitive sectors, the level of rent-seeking behaviour is predictably higher, although with an interesting variation. On the one hand, the 'monopolist' sector seems to be running true to form, with high-level political connections a critical factor, leading to a semi-ordered and only semi-open scenario, within which even making significant payments to political parties cannot offer security of contracts. Moreover, there is growing evidence that those gaining huge wealth within this sector (particularly telecommunications) are using this to gain political leverage. However, we find a somewhat surprising and alternative story in the rentier export sector. Leaving aside the highly dis-ordered area of gold mining concessions, it is noticeable that the deals made within the emerging oil sector, while closed, have been both ordered and seemingly aligned with national economic interest. This seems to reflect the higher degree of state capacity and elite (presidential) commitment in this domain (Hickey et al., 2015), which in turn may have a transnational element to it, in that dealing with global oil companies requires the development of much higher levels of technical expertise and bargaining power than is required in most other sectors.

7.6 Conclusion and Recommendations

These findings highlight the importance of undertaking a differentiated ana-lysis of the political economy of development in Uganda, not least as it provides a stronger, more relevant, and more nuanced basis for generating policy recommendations. However, there are also some cross-cutting findings that should be noted. First, each of the deals spaces discussed in this chapter remains closely embedded within, and informed by, the broader political settlement, which establishes not only the generalized patterns of rent-seeking behaviour that we identify in all four sectors, but also the level at which, and ways in which, this plays out vis-à-vis the overall priorities of the regime. This becomes clear when we compare the much higher levels of attention given to ensuring that oil is governed relatively well, as compared with the reluctance to develop regulatory state capacity and promote performance-related pressures in other domains. Second, the organizational strength of Uganda's capitalists remains generally weak, which severely reduces their collective bargaining power and the incentives to transcend state–business relations based on collusive rent-seeking, as opposed to a more generalized and productive basis. This helps to maintain the significance of politicized connections. The government is complicit in this, not least as it offers a means through which it can secure both the finances and promises of political loyalty that it needs to remain in power under multiparty politics. Despite some initially promising efforts, including the Presidential Investors Roundtable and now the Presidential Economic Council, there are few influential spaces within which political elites and leading capitalists can interact and make progress on matters of national economic interest. This situation does not bode well for generating the collective capacity and commitment required for a move towards structural transformation.

The policy implications that flow from this analysis, each of which will need to be nuanced for the four domains, fall into four main categories. The first concerns the need for a rebalancing of Uganda's current political economy of development, which is overly skewed towards services (which has over-strengthened the hand of monopolists in ways that are deepening the clientelistic tendencies of the political settlement) and fairly unproductive forms of agriculture, towards a stronger focus on agricultural modernization and manufacturing. To the extent to which oil wealth does start to emerge, this will clearly have to be well governed in line with current legislation (e.g. through a sovereign wealth fund) and reinvested in these sectors to avoid Dutch Disease effects. This strongly echoes the earlier policy advice of Hausmann et al. (2014), while going further in showing how this supports the kind of capitalists who have been associated not only with economic transformation in the periphery (Henley, 2015; Booth et al., 2015), but also with social and political transformation in terms of developing economic interest groups with sufficient autonomy from political elites to start making wider demands for public goods with progressive spillover effects (Khan, 2010; Sandbrook et al., 2007). Importantly, our analysis here also suggests the need to go further than suggesting policy shifts around economic strategy, towards building the relational and organizational forms of capacity among both producers and the state required to achieve this (Vom Hau, 2012).

Second, then, there is a need not just to invest heavily in these other areas of the economy, but also to build the organizational power of the capitalists operating therein. This has implications for donor strategies around 'private-sector development', which need to be much more attuned to the relative power of different groups of capitalists and directed towards those that have the most pay-offs in political as well as productive terms. The obvious targets for such interventions are the magicians and workhorses.[34] Third, more muscular spaces are required within which to develop more productive forms of relationship between government and business, as appeared to be occurring to some extent within the Presidential Investors Round Table until World Bank funding was withdrawn. Finally, there is a pressing need to maintain and build the regulatory and disciplinary power of the state, in terms of its capacity to govern economic activities effectively within and across the four domains discussed in Section 7.4. This will not be easy, but the history of development successes in Uganda suggests it is essential, particularly in terms of the role played by bureaucratic islands of effectiveness within key sectors. This chapter has drawn particular attention to the need to protect and maintain high levels of autonomy and performance within the technocracies for the macroeconomy (Ministry of Finance, Planning and Economic Development, Bank of Uganda), revenue collection (URA), and oil (Ministry of Energy and Mineral Development), and to start developing it as a matter of urgency in the sectors identified here (e.g. agriculture and manufacturing).

References

Alibaruho, G. 1974. 'Production Structure and Income Generation in Uganda: Pathfinder of the Current Negative Growth Rate in the Economy'. Working Paper 188. Nairobi: Institute for Development Studies, University of Nairobi.

Bategeka, L., and Matovu, J. M. 2011. 'Oil Wealth and Potential Dutch Disease Effects in Uganda'. Economic Policy Research Centre Research Paper No. 81. <http://dspace. africaportal.org/jspui/bitstream/123456789/33952/1/Research%20Series%2081.pdf?1>.

Belshaw, D., Lawrence, P., and Hubbard, M. 1999. 'Agricultural Tradeables and Economic Recovery in Uganda: The Limitations of Structural Adjustment in Practice'. *World Development*, 27(4): 673–90.

Bigsten, A., and Kayizzi-Mugerwa, S. 2001. 'Is Uganda an Emerging Economy? A Report for the OECD Project "Emerging Africa"'. Research Report No.118. Nordiska Afrikainstitutet, Uppsala, Sweden. <http://www.diva-portal.org/smash/get/diva2:248947/ FULLTEXT01.pdf>.

Booth, D., Cooksey, B., Golooba-Mutebi, F., and Kanyinga, K. 2014. *East African Prospects: An Update on the Political Economy of Kenya, Rwanda, Tanzania and Uganda*. London: Overseas Development Institute.

Booth, D., Dietz, A. J., Golooba-Mutebi, F., Fuady, A. H., Henley, D., Kelsall, T., Leliveld, A. H. M., and van Donge, J. K. 2015. *Developmental Regimes in Africa: Initiating and*

---

[34] See King and Hickey (2016) for evidence that supporting the associational capacity of smallholder producer groups in Uganda can have real pay-offs, both in terms of empowering subordinate groups and ensuring more accountable forms of governance.

Sustaining Developmental Regimes in Africa. Synthesis Report. London: Overseas Development Institute.

Brett, E. A. 2006. 'State Failure and Success in Uganda and Zimbabwe: The Logic of Political Decay and Reconstruction in Africa'. Crisis States Programme Working Paper No. 78. London: Crisis States Research Centre, London School of Economics.

Brownbridge, M., and Bwire, T. 2016. 'Structural Change and Economic Growth in Uganda'. Bank of Uganda Working Paper Series, No. 03/2016. Bank of Uganda.

Bukenya, B., Hickey, S., and Sen, K. Forthcoming. 'Dominance and Deals in Africa: How Politics Shapes Uganda's Transition from Growth to Transformation'. ESID Working Paper. Manchester: University of Manchester.

Dijkstra, A., and Van Donge, J. 2001. 'What Does the "Show Case" Show? Evidence of and Lessons from Adjustment in Uganda'. *World Development*, 29(5): 841–64.

Evans, P. 1995. *Embedded Autonomy: States and Industrial Transformation*. Princeton, NJ: Princeton University Press.

Golooba-Mutebi, F. 2008. 'Collapse, War and Reconstruction in Uganda: An Analytical Narrative on State-Making'. CSRC Working Paper No. 27. Crisis States Research Centre. London: London School of Economics.

Golooba-Mutebi, F., and Hickey, S. 2013. 'Investigating the Links between Political Settlements and Inclusive Development in Uganda: Towards a Research Agenda'. ESID Working Paper No. 20. Manchester: University of Manchester.

Gore, C. 2000. 'The Rise and Fall of the Washington Consensus as a Paradigm for Developing Countries'. *World Development*, 28(5): 789–804.

Gukiina, P. M. 1972. *Uganda: A Case Study in African Political Development*. Notre Dame, IN: University of Notre Dame Press.

Hausmann, R., Cunningham, B., Matovu, J., Osire, R., and Wyett, K. 2014. 'How Should Uganda Grow?' ESID Working Paper No. 30. Manchester: University of Manchester.

Henley, D. 2015. *Asia-Africa Development Divergence: A Question of Intent*. London: Zed Books.

Hickey, S. 2013. 'Beyond the Poverty Agenda? Insights from the New Politics of Development in Uganda'. *World Development*, 43: 194–206.

Hickey, S., Bukenya, B., Izama, A., and Kizito, W. 2015. 'The Political Settlement and Oil in Uganda'. ESID Working Paper No. 48. Manchester: University of Manchester.

Hickey, S., and Izama, A. 2017. 'The Politics of Governing Oil in Uganda: Going against the Grain'. *African Affairs*, 116(463): 163–85.

Hundle, A. K. 2013. 'The Politics of (In)security: Reconstructing African–Asian Relations, Citizenship, and Community in Post-Expulsion Uganda'. PhD thesis, University of Michigan.

ICG. 2012. *Uganda: No Resolution to Growing Tensions* (online). International Crisis Group. <http://www.unhcr.org/refworld/docid/4f841ba22.html>.

International Alert. 2014. 'Trading with Neighbours: Understanding Ugandan–South Sudan Business Community Trade Relations'. <http://international-alert.org/sites/default/files/Uganda_UgandaSouthSudanTradeRelations_EN_2014.pdf>.

Kabwegyere, T. B. 1974. *The Politics of State Formation: The Nature and Effects of Colonialism in Uganda*. Kampala: East African Literature Bureau.

Kangave, J., and Katusiimeh, M. W. 2015. *Tax Bargains: Understanding the Role Played by Public and Private Actors in Influencing Tax Policy Reform in Uganda*. Geneva: United Nations Research Institute for Social Development.

Kar, S., Pritchett, L., Raihan, S., and Sen, K. 2013. *The Dynamics of Economic Growth: A Visual Handbook of Growth Rates, Regimes, Transitions and Volatility*. Manchester: The University of Manchester.

Kasfir, N. 1983. 'State, Magendo, and Class Formation in Uganda'. *Journal of Commonwealth Political Studies*, 21: 84–103.

Khan, M. H. 2005. 'Markets, States and Democracy: Patron-Client Networks and the Case for Democracy in Developing Countries'. *Democratization*, 12: 704–24.

Khan, M. H. 2010. 'Political Settlements and the Governance of Growth-Enhancing Institutions'. Mimeo. School of Oriental and African Studies, London.

Kigambo, K., and Talemwa, M. 2010. 'Uniform Inter-Network Fee Drives Call Rates Down'. *Observer*. <http://www.observer.ug/index.php?option=com_content&view=article&id=10316:uniform-inter-network-fee-drives-call-rates-down>. Accessed 12 February 2014.

Kiiza, J. 2011. 'Money Matters: Financing Illiberal Democracy in Uganda'. CMI Working Paper.

King, S., and Hickey, S. 2016. 'Building Democracy from Below: Lessons from Western Uganda'. *Journal of Development Studies* (online), 31 August.

Kiwanuka, M. S. M. 1970. 'Nationality and Nationalism in Africa: The Uganda Case'. *Canadian Journal of African Studies*, 4: 229–47.

Kjær, A. M. 2014. 'From "Good" to "Growth-Enhancing" Governance: Emerging Research Agendas on Africa's Political-Economy'. *Governance in Africa*, 1(1): Art. 2.

Kjær, A. M. 2015. 'Political Settlements and Productive Sector Policies: Understanding Sector Differences in Uganda'. *World Development*, 68, 230–41.

Kjær, A. M., and Katusiimeh, M. 2012. 'Growing but Not Transforming: Fragmented Ruling Coalitions and Economic Developments in Uganda'. DIIS Working Paper 2012:07. Copenhagen: Danish Institute for International Studies.

Kjær, A. M., Katusiimeh, M., Mwebaze, T., and Muhumuza, F. 2012a. 'When Do Ruling Elites Support Productive Sectors? Explaining Policy Initiatives in the Fisheries and Dairy Sectors in Uganda'. DIIS Working Paper 2012:05. Copenhagen: Danish Institute for International Studies.

Kjær, A. M., Muhumuza, F., and Mwebaze, T. 2012b. 'Coalition-Driven Initiatives in the Ugandan Dairy Sector: Elites, Conflict, and Bargaining'. DIIS Working Paper 2012:02. Copenhagen: Danish Institute for International Studies.

Leliveld, A. 2008. *Growth Accelerations in Developing Countries: Uganda and Cambodia Compared*. Leiden, Netherlands: African Studies Centre.

Lindemann, S. 2010. 'Exclusionary Elite Bargains and Civil War Onset'. Development as State-Making, Working Paper 76. London: Crisis States Research Centre, London School of Economics.

Mosley, P. 2012. *The Politics of Poverty Reduction*. Oxford: Oxford University Press.

Mthembu-Salter, G. 2015. 'Baseline Study Four: Gold Trading and Export in Kampala, Uganda'. Paper presented in the 9th Multi-Stakeholder Forum on Responsible Mineral Supply Chains, 4–6 May, Paris, France.

Mutebile, E. T. 2010. 'Institutional and Political Dimensions of Economic Reform'. In *Uganda's Economic Reforms: Insider Accounts*. Edited by Kuteesa, F., Tumusiime-Mutebile, E., Whitworth, A., and Williamson, T. Oxford: Oxford University Press.

Mwenda. A. M. 2014. 'Mutebile's Revelations about 2011 Elections'. *Independent*, 24 November.

Mwenda, A. M., and Tangri, R. 2005. 'Patronage Politics, Donor Reforms, and Regime Consolidation in Uganda'. *African Affairs*, 104(416): 449–67.

Nabuguzi, E. 1995. 'Popular Initiatives in Service Provision in Uganda'. In *Service Provision under Stress in East Africa: The State, NGOs and People's Organizations in Kenya, Tanzania and Uganda*. Edited by Semboja, J., and Therkildsen, O. Kampala: Fountain Publishers.

Obote, A. M. (1969). *The Move to the Left*. Entebbe: Government Printers.

Obote, A. M. (1970). *The Common Man's Charter* (No. 1). Entebbe: Government Printers.

Pritchett, L., and Werker, E. 2012. 'Developing the Guts of a GUT (Grand Unified Theory): Elite Commitment and Inclusive Growth'. ESID Working Paper No. 16. Manchester: University of Manchester.

Republic of Uganda. 2014. *Poverty Status Report: Structural Change and Poverty Reduction in Uganda*. Kampala: Ministry of Finance, Planning, and Economic Development.

Robinson, M. 2006. 'The Political Economy of Governance Reforms in Uganda'. IDS Discussion Paper 386. Institute of Development Studies, Brighton, UK.

Robinson, M., and Friedman, S. 2007. 'Civil Society, Democratization, and Foreign Aid: Civic Engagement and Public Policy in South Africa and Uganda'. *Democratization*, 14(4): 643–68.

Ryan, S. D. 1973. 'Economic Nationalism and Socialism in Uganda'. *Journal of Commonwealth Political Studies*, 11: 140–58.

Sandbrook, R., Edelman, M., Heller, P., and Teichman, J. 2007. *Social Democracy in the Global Periphery*. Cambridge: Cambridge University Press.

Schomerus, M., and Titeca, K. 2012. 'Deals and Dealings: Inconclusive Peace and Treacherous Trade along the South Sudan–Uganda Border'. *Africa Spectrum*, 47(2/3): 5–31.

SEATINI-Uganda. 2012. 'Tax Exemptions Implications on Socio-Economic Development'. Southern and Eastern African Trade Information and Negotiations Institute. <http://www.seatiniuganda.org/publications/annual-reports/27-seatini-report-final-final-3rd-dec-2012/file.html>.

Selassie, A. 2008. 'Beyond Macroeconomic Stability: The Quest for Industrialization in Uganda'. IMF Working Paper 08/231.

Sen, K. 2012. 'The Political Dynamics of Economic Growth'. ESID Working Paper No. 5. Manchester: University of Manchester.

Ssewanyana, S., Matovu, J. M., and Twimukye, E. 2011. 'Building on Growth in Uganda'. In *Yes Africa Can: Success Stories from a Dynamic Continent*. Edited by Chuhan-Pole, P., and Angwafo, M. Washington, DC: World Bank.

Tangri, R. 2015. 'Change and Continuity in the Politics of Government Business Relations in Museveni's Uganda'. Paper given at the Africa Studies Association Conference, San Diego, 19–22 November.

Tripp, A. M. 2010. *Museveni's Uganda: Paradoxes of Power in a Hybrid Regime*. London: Rienner Publishers.

Tumushabe, G. W. 2009. 'Trends in Public Administration Expenditure in Uganda: The Cost of the Executive and its Implications on Poverty Eradication and Governance'. ACODE Policy Research Series, No. 27. Kampala: ACODE.

UBOS. 2009. *Statistical Abstract*. Kampala: Uganda Bureau of Statistics.

UBOS. 2011. *Census of Business Establishments 2010/11*. Kampala: Uganda Bureau of Statistics.

UBOS. 2014. *Statistical Abstract 2014*. Kampala: Uganda Bureau of Statistics.

Vom Hau, M. 2012. 'State Capacity and Inclusive Development: New Challenges and Directions'. ESID Working Paper No. 2. Manchester: University of Manchester.

Whitfield, L., Therkildsen, O., Buur, L., and Mette Kjær, A. 2015. *The Politics of African Industrial Policy: A Comparative Perspective*. Cambridge: Cambridge University Press.

World Bank. 2016. *Doing Business 2016: Understanding Regulations for Small and Medium-Size Enterprises*. Washington, DC: World Bank.

8

The Disorder of 'Miracle Growth' in Rwanda

Understanding the Limitations of Transitions to Open Ordered Development

Pritish Behuria and Tom Goodfellow

8.1 Introduction

In the two decades since 1994, the Rwanda Patriotic Front (RPF) government has achieved growth rates of over 6 per cent every year (with the exception of 2003 and 2013). This has led to praise from diverse groups, ranging from international financial institutions (Tumwebaze, 2014; Lagarde, 2015) to mainstream (Collier, 2015) and heterodox scholars (Kelsall, 2013; Booth et al., 2014).[1] Conventional perspectives on the drivers of economic growth in Rwanda vary, but there are three identifiable narratives, all of which tend to oversimplify the drivers of growth by placing disproportionate emphasis on one particular feature of Rwanda's development trajectory.

The first account focuses on Rwanda's embrace of market reforms, supported by foreign aid, as key to its success. A typical statement in this mould would be that: 'The economic growth in Rwanda has been primarily driven by liberalization in the agricultural sector—mainly coffee and tea, the country's main exports' (Oro and Arias, 2012). This chapter demonstrates that liberalization in these sectors has indeed been significant. However, it has not always had a positive effect on economic growth and has been only one aspect of the growth story in Rwanda since 1994.

---

[1] Rwanda has also been subject to extensive and important criticisms regarding limitations on freedoms and human rights, as well as increased inequality (see for example Reyntjens, 2011; Ansoms and Rostagno, 2012), though there is not space to go into these debates here.

A second narrative focuses on the centrality of 'second-generation reforms'—i.e. issues such as improved education indicators, social protection, and women's empowerment—as key to the growth success (Lagarde, 2015). Whatever their significance for human development, such explanations underplay important political economic factors underpinning economic development in key sectors.

A third narrative takes a heterodox perspective, attributing the country's success largely to the use of party- and military-owned enterprises to intervene in strategic and long-term ways in the economy (Booth and Golooba-Mutebi, 2012). Our analysis in this chapter concurs that these strategic state interventions have been important, but challenges the linear simplicity of the focus on 'long-term centralized rent creation', and seeks to deepen the analysis of Rwanda's economic strategy and state–business relations. Unlike existing analyses, we show how important variations in state–business relationships in specific sectors have influenced Rwanda's developmental trajectory. Even within the same economic sectors, the RPF government has attempted to retain some control over rents by using party- and military-owned enterprises in some sub-sectors, while relying heavily on open deals in others. We argue that the government has employed such strategies to spur overall economic growth while retaining some state control (to ensure a continued emphasis on economic transformation) and also attempting to maintain a stable political settlement.

To explore this in depth, this chapter examines four specific sectors of the economy: coffee, mining, construction, and financial services. Tensions between facilitating rent creation and pursuing an agenda of liberalization play out in different ways in different sectors, with important implications. The strain of attempting to pursue 'open ordered' deals while also maintaining a political settlement has started to show in Rwanda, posing potential threats to future prospects. After describing the growth and structural transformation experience in Rwanda, we explore in detail the rents space and deals environment in the four sectors, before reflecting on feedback loops and how the Rwandan case speaks to the theoretical framework set out in this volume.

8.2 Overview of Growth and Structural Transformation Experience

Rwanda became independent in 1961. In the first few years after independence, growth fluctuated, but between 1965 and 1969 annual growth was high (above 7 per cent). Between 1969 and 1975, growth rates remained relatively low, before picking up again until 1981. Rwanda experienced a large deceleration in growth between 1981 and 1994. However, since 1994, Rwanda has experienced its longest ever acceleration episode (Kar et al., 2013). Unlike the previous growth episodes, Rwanda's post-1994 episode has been strong enough and long enough to constitute a clear case of 'miracle growth'. Indeed,

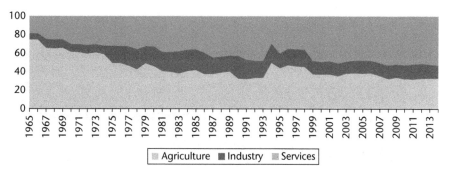

Figure 8.1. Components of GDP in Rwanda by sector, 1965–2014 (% of GDP)
Source: World Bank.

Rwanda was among the top ten fastest growing economies globally in the 2000s (ACET, 2014). It has also experienced some structural transformation. Figure 8.1 shows that agriculture as a proportion of GDP has gradually decreased, falling from 49.7 per cent in 1994 to 33 per cent in 2014. Meanwhile, the services sector contributed 29 per cent of Rwanda's GDP in 1994, compared with 53 per cent in 2014. Figure 8.2 provides a breakdown of GDP composition by activity between 1999 and 2013. In terms of employment, between 2002 and 2011, the percentage of the population employed in agriculture decreased from 87 per cent to 73 per cent, with corresponding increases for the proportion of the population employed in services (from 10 per cent in 2002 to 20 per cent in 2011), and in manufacturing and extractive industries (from 3 per cent in 2002 to 6 per cent in 2011) (NISR, 2012).

Structural transformation remains limited, however. Rwanda is one of the least transformed countries in Africa, ranking eighteen out of twenty-one countries on the African Centre for Economic Transformation (ACET) Index—though this is an improvement from the situation in 2000, when it was ranked last (ACET, 2014: 197). In 2014, Rwanda was ranked eighty-seventh out of 144 countries on the Observatory for Economic Complexity's rankings. It remains a largely rural society, with 70–80 per cent of its population working in the agriculture sector. Coffee, tea, and minerals have accounted for over 90 per cent of Rwanda's exports for most of its history. This has gradually changed during the RPF's rule, and Rwanda has shown marked improvement relative to many other countries in the ACET's ratings on diversification and technological upgrading, despite a lack of progress on measures of export competitiveness and human well-being (ACET, 2014: 33). Figure 8.3 illustrates Rwanda's export space. Some re-exports (petroleum) have recently become increasingly prominent, as have new exports (within the agriculture sector), including wheat and rice. The government has managed to diversify its export base to some degree. However, exports remain concentrated

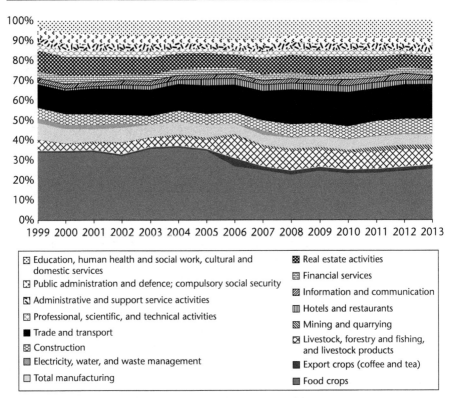

Figure 8.2. GDP by kind of activity
Source: MINECOFIN (2013).

in the agriculture and minerals sectors and there has been no success in developing manufacturing exports.

Lack of attention to manufacturing growth has been a striking feature of development under the RPF so far, barely featuring in the government's Vision 2020 strategy (GoR, 2000). In the Economic Development and Poverty Reduction Strategy 2, the government slightly increased its emphasis on manufacturing, stating an aim of moving 'from an agriculture-based economy to an industry and services-based economy' (MINECOFIN, 2013: 55). Though agriculture grew at a relatively healthy rate between 2000 and 2013, the sector's annual growth rate has remained below the annual GDP growth of Rwanda for most years, while growth in the services sector has been the steadiest (Figure 8.4).

Figure 8.5 demonstrates that construction has been a growing component and the most consistent source of growth in the industry sector. The growth that is implied in industrial sector statistics can also be misleading, given that mining is included within them. As is evident from Figure 8.5, manufacturing

Total: $836 million

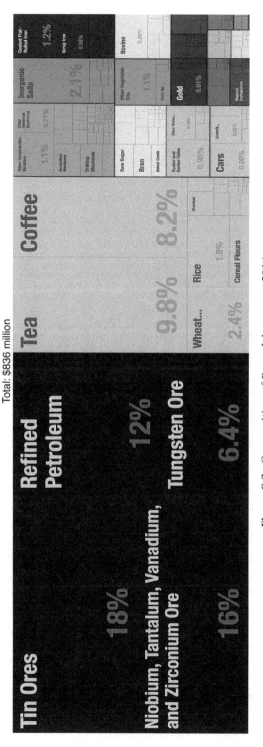

Figure 8.3. Composition of Rwanda's exports, 2014

Source: Atlas of Economic Complexity <http://atlas.cid.harvard.edu>.

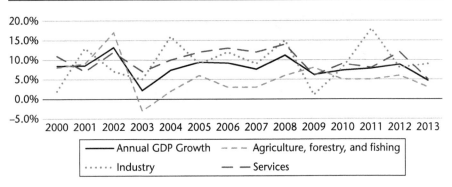

Figure 8.4. Comparison between agriculture, industry, and services sector with annual GDP growth rates for Rwanda, 2000–13
Source: MINECOFIN (2013).

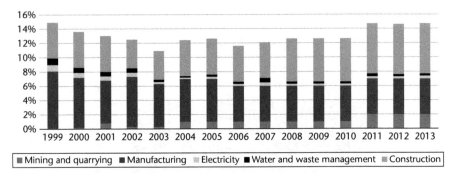

Figure 8.5. Industry as a share of GDP for Rwanda, 1999–2013
Source: MINECOFIN (2013).

has shrunk significantly, while construction and mining have grown. The manufacturing sector is still quite young, given that most companies were destroyed during the genocide. Despite some investment and technology acquisition, several factors inhibit further growth in the sector, including small market size, difficulties in creating supply chains and distribution networks, very high transport costs, inconsistent access to electricity, and problems establishing effective management and production systems.[2]

Growth in services was prioritized after 2000, with the aim of building a knowledge-based economy. Within this sector, finance, real estate, hotels and restaurants, and trading and transport have shown promising growth (Figure 8.6). The government has also launched a Meetings, Incentives, Conferences, and Events (MICE) strategy to augment revenues from the services sector.

---

[2] Various interviews.

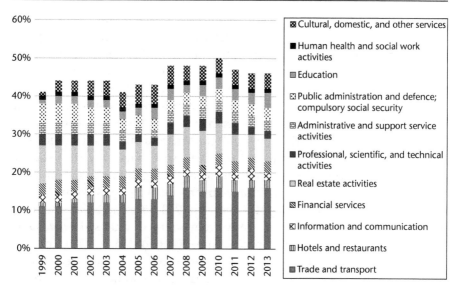

Figure 8.6. Services as share of GDP for Rwanda, 1999–2013
Source: MINECOFIN (2013).

The growth of the construction sector can also be understood in line with such goals. Rwanda Development Board officials claim that revenues from MICE could reach US$150 million by 2015.

8.3 Historical Evolution of Political Settlements in Rwanda

In Rwanda, the dynamic and violent nature of political settlements has been on display since the country became independent in 1962. Before independence, Gregoire Kayibanda—who would later become Rwanda's first president—led his party (MDR-Parmehutu) in organizing the 1959–61 revolution. Kayibanda was a strong advocate of the Hutu Power political movement, and the revolution was mobilized on the basis of ethnic divisions, with the Tutsi monarchy and party (*Union Nationale Rwandaise*) as the targets.

Kayibanda's anti-Tutsi pogroms continued, with the *inyenzi* threat (of returning Tutsis), salient for the early 1960s. However, elite politics during the First Republic were largely contested on a regional basis. Kayibanda relied on Hutus from the southern and central regions for support, while his main threat came from the northern areas of Ruhengeri and Gisenyi. Thus, it could be said that Kayibanda's regime was a 'vulnerable authoritarian coalition' from the start, with significant threats to his power from excluded factions within the majority Hutu ethnic group. Kayibanda continued to control TRAFIPRO (*Travail, Fidélité, Progrès*)—the coffee marketing board—and headquartered it in the south. TRAFIPRO acted as 'the economic arm of the regime' (Verwimp, 2003: 163). Its control over rents led to determined opposition from the north, as southern elites attempted to extend their control across the country. By the early 1960s, Kayibanda's regime moved towards being a 'competitive clientelist' regime. Initially, during the 1960s, there was an opening up of deals space and some new private actors invested in the economy. However, towards the latter half of the 1960s and early 1970s, Kayibanda used state institutions and cooperatives such as TRAFIPRO to monopolize areas of the economy. The deals space gradually shifted from opened to closed, with less private investment during this period.

The army chief of staff, Juvénal Habyarimana, led a group of northern elites within the ruling party to mount a coup in 1973 (Prunier, 1995), the main motivation being to take power away from southern Hutus (Lemarchand, 1995). Habyarimana's Second Republic immediately distanced itself from the racially charged rhetoric of the preceding government. He publicly declared the day of the coup as 'a day of peace and reconciliation' (Verwimp, 2013). However, throughout his reign there were almost no Tutsi *bourgmestres* or *préfets* (Prunier, 1995). The Second Republic enjoyed significant periods of economic growth during the 1970s, as described earlier. During this time, the regime could be classified as a 'strong dominant party'. Until 1981, Habyarimana was largely reliant on elites from his northern support base and was able to manage rivalries between different northern elite groups (Prunier, 1995). Gradually, growth began declining, beginning in 1981. This reflected the beginnings of a commodity crisis, with sharp decreases in global prices of coffee, tea, and tin weakening the Rwandan economy.

Following an attempted coup in 1980, the regime shifted to becoming a 'vulnerable authoritarian coalition' and later, a 'competitive clientelist' regime (particularly once democratic space was opened). Habyarimana became increasingly reliant on a small group commonly referred to as the *akazu* ('little house'). The *akazu* also controlled most positions in the coffee-exporting agency, OCIR-Café, and the national tea regulatory authority, OCIR-Thé, thus dominating control over rents (Verwimp, 2003). As with Kayibanda's reign, Habyarimana did not open the deals environment. Most of the economy remained 'closed' during this period, with the government controlling monopolies in most export sectors (although a limited number of deals were open).

The current RPF government, which took power in 1994 after the devastation of the genocide, has managed severe political pressures, given the fractured society it inherited and the fact that it was the first Rwandan government to be dominated by the minority Tutsi ethnic group. The political settlement that has emerged can be categorized as a 'strong dominant party', in the sense that factions excluded from the ruling coalition are relatively weak, as are lower-level factions within the ruling coalition itself. Some have explicitly classified the RPF government in this way (Lavers and Hickey, 2015), while others have not used the same language but view the government similarly (Booth and Golooba-Mutebi, 2014; Kelsall, 2013; Goodfellow, 2014).

8.4 Studying the Rents Space

The preceding narrative describes how the rents space was dominated by rentiers in the coffee and tea sectors during the Kayibanda and Habyarimana regimes (and powerbrokers in much of the rest of the economy, with a gradual closing up of deals space towards the end of both regimes). This chapter demonstrates that the same is not true today. Figure 8.7 illustrates an attempt at describing the composition of GDP in Rwanda in 2013 in terms of the rents space categories. What this 'radar' chart shows is that overall, despite some success in diversifying exports, GDP is composed largely of activities targeted at the domestic market in the form of workhorses and powerbrokers. Why this is the case and how dynamics operate within our chosen sectors in these categories will be described in Section 8.6.

To undertake the research on the contemporary deals environment, four sectors were selected to cover each of the four key categories in the rents space (Figure 8.8). Given the dynamic nature of reforms in Rwanda, however, the sectors are not a perfect fit in the rents space categories, and choosing sectors to fit these boxes was challenging. There are very few competitive, export-oriented sectors in Rwanda. Since the coffee sector has been liberalized and

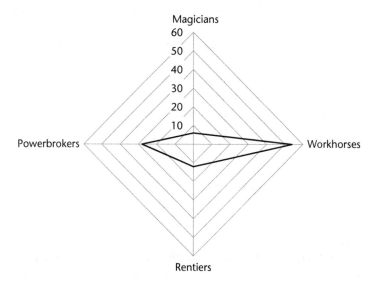

Figure 8.7. Composition of GDP in the rents space in Rwanda

225

	Regulatory rents	Market competition
Export-oriented	RENTIERS Mining	MAGICIANS Coffee
Domestic market	POWERBROKERS Construction	WORKHORSES Financial services

Figure 8.8. Chosen sectors aligned to the rents space in Rwanda

private actors own assets, the coffee sector was chosen as a magician. The mining sector was chosen as a rentier. The construction sector was chosen as a powerbroker, as it is mostly geared towards the domestic market and party- and military-owned investment groups play a significant role. The financial services sector was chosen as a workhorse. The sector has been liberalized, even though the government still has a majority shareholding in the largest bank (Bank of Kigali).

Fresh primary research was conducted for this chapter by both authors in January 2015, building on their existing work in Rwanda. The project focused on interviewing representatives from firms working in the four sectors, as well as government, party, and military officials, where relevant. The two researchers conducted seventy-nine interviews. Some interviews conducted as part of previous research are also used in this chapter. Attempts have been made to triangulate and cross-check data that were presented by respondents. Most private-sector respondents were fairly open in discussions; some respondents had been interviewed previously and the researchers had already established a rapport with these respondents. However, it is possible that many respondents downplayed the degree to which personal connections and corruption might have operated in Rwanda. Judgements regarding deals spaces in different sectors have been made on the basis of interviews with respondents working in the sector. We recognize that such interpretations may not represent the full picture, given the limited database of interviews on which to make generalizations.

8.5 A Characterization of the Deals Space

This section begins with an overview, before turning to four sectors in detail. In all these sectors, the RPF government has faced pressure to embrace market-led reforms, while retaining a preference that domestic firms are able to engage in technology acquisition. In the late 1990s, the IMF pressured the Rwandan government to privatize state-owned enterprises. By 2011, fifty-seven state-owned enterprises had been fully privatized, with a further twenty going through different phases of privatization, though a 2011 consultancy report found only around half of these to be operational. Acknowledging these mixed results, there is recognition among government officials that state regulation and interventions of different forms are required. However, in most sectors, they have been reluctant to pick domestic winners (other than by using investment groups, which we discuss later in this section). Instead, government figures highlight that the state should play a key role in sectors early on and then get out as soon as possible: 'Telecoms represents a good case of how we made investments first and then liberalized. This prepared economic growth, and openness led to innovation in the sector.'[3] They also emphasize that initial government investments are meant to spur private investment that would not otherwise have been forthcoming: 'We invested where no one would invest, like in the tourism sector. It is this model of going in where others will not that has spurred growth in the Rwandan economy.'[4]

The choice of which strategy to embrace in specific sectors depended on a number of factors, including the degree of donor pressure, the nature of domestic competition, and the degree of technology acquisition required. Where no private investor came in, the government invested. Often, investment groups (or party- and military-owned holding companies) were used. These groups have been detailed in the existing literature (Booth and Golooba-Mutebi, 2012; Gokgur, 2012; Behuria, 2015).

Representatives of investment groups likewise claim to follow a strategy of investing in strategic sectors, increasing productivity in those sectors, breaking even, and then eventually leaving. Representatives of Crystal Ventures Ltd (CVL, formerly Tri-Star) attribute the success of many of their firms not just to government backing, but to the philosophy they have 'inherited' from the RPF and their commitment to rebuilding the country. There is also a sense that they have to perform well because everyone is watching.[5] CVL representatives emphasize their commitment to 'crowding in' rather than 'crowding out' domestic private firms and cite some state-owned companies under their umbrella that were allowed to fail.[6]

Investment groups are the largest domestic players in the economy. However, the private sector has also developed an organized platform (with government support and even 'direction'), the Private Sector Federation, which groups together ten professional and promotional chambers. It is now compulsory that for all government policies consultation with relevant private-sector

---

[3] Interview, Emmanuel Hategeka, MINICOM (Ministry of Trade and Industry) permanent secretary.
[4] Interview, MINICOM official.   [5] Interview with foreign advisor, January 2015.
[6] Interview with CVL representative, January 2015.

representatives has taken place. In January 2015, one MINECOFIN official said that parliamentarians sent him back to his office when he presented work on the mining sector that had not been discussed with private-sector representatives.[7] However, despite these efforts to support the private sector, most SMEs struggle and few stay afloat for very long.

This overview is important, because liberalization has, as we show, often been associated with a move towards more open (in the sense of impersonal) deals. However, in these sectors, closed deals are still used for strategic investments and to ensure rents remain under centralized control. The following four subsections briefly describe the trajectory of state–business relationships in four sectors, with explicit reference to the 'deals space' framework. In each case, a brief overview of the sector's history, its current firm structure, and the general evolution of the deals environment will be outlined.[8]

8.5.1 *Coffee (Magician)*

Before 1994, the coffee sector remained in a relatively stagnant 'closed ordered' deals space, with rents centralized under both the Kayibanda and Habyarimana regimes. New exporting companies were sometimes licensed (although they never gained a substantial foothold).[9] However, there is no indication that there were any open deals operating in the sector.

Coffee production in Rwanda has never amounted to even 1 per cent of global production. However, it was Rwanda's leading export before 1994 and it is still counted among Rwanda's top exports today. The volume produced in Rwanda has remained relatively stagnant. In 2015, 20,000 tonnes were produced. In 1995, production was actually slightly higher. In the early 1980s, production was almost double its current amount. Though production has not increased, the value of coffee exports has increased significantly. This can be attributed to an increase in global coffee prices. However, it is also because of the government's prioritization of the production of higher-value-added coffee. Over time, increasing numbers of new investors have entered as exporters and owners of washing stations. Such actors are competing for a relatively unchanged amount of coffee produced in the country. Though an increase in openness has not increased the overall growth of the sector (in terms of production), it has contributed to increased technological change in the sector, which has fuelled growth in terms of the value of coffee

---

[7] Interview, MINECOFIN official.
[8] Greater detail on the dynamics in these sectors can be found in Behuria and Goodfellow (2016).
[9] Interview, National Agriculture Export Board (NAEB) representative, January 2015.

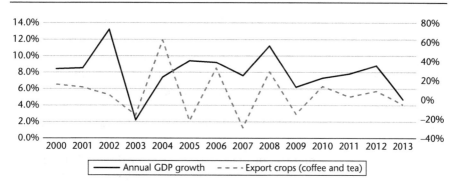

Figure 8.9. Comparison of annual GDP growth and annual export crops growth for Rwanda, 2000–13

Source: MINECOFIN (2013).

produced. Figure 8.9 illustrates how annual GDP growth rates compare with annual export crops growth rates (coffee and tea) between 2000 and 2013.

Immediately after the RPF assumed power, trade and export operations were liberalized. Rwandex—a majority government-owned coffee export agency, which exported most of Rwanda's coffee during Habyarimana's reign—continued to be a prominent exporter, but RPF supporters and prominent businesspeople who had supported the RPF during the war also invested. At this time, government officials claimed that any investors were welcome.[10] Though many individuals who set up companies were closely linked to the RPF, there is no evidence for the claim that the benefits they received would not have been available to other investors. In the 1990s, six new companies entered the sector, two of which went bankrupt after two years (MINAGRI, 2008). Later, other smaller companies that entered in 1994 also went bankrupt (IMF, 2000).

Swiss-based RwaCof, owned by Switzerland-based Sucafina, entered Rwanda in 1995, quickly developed their value chains, and exported large shares of Rwandan coffee (partly because of their foreign contacts).[11] Sucafina had already established a presence in the region through its Uganda-based company, UgaCof. Entering Rwanda was 'a no-brainer' for Sucafina. There was an opportunity, since 'many of the other players here did not have much knowledge of the sector and it was not managed'. RwaCof representatives said that competitors 'learned, but many who started or misbehaved, did not survive'.[12]

RwaCof then gradually competed with Rwandex to become the largest exporting company in Rwanda. Between 2000 and 2002, RwaCof and Rwandex

---

[10] Interview, NAEB representative, January 2015.
[11] RwaCof bought the Gikondo coffee factory in 1997.
[12] Interview, RwaCof representative, January 2015.

collectively held about 65–75 per cent of the domestic market. Agrocoffee (owned by a loyal businessman) and SICAF (owned by the husband of the sister of the president's wife) collectively captured more than 20 per cent of the market. Since 2004, competition in the sector intensified. Several new exporters entered the sector. During this time, the government built an institutional environment to fund the coffee sector and donors had also begun supporting the strategy. In 2009, Rwandex's assets were bought by Scott Ford's Rwanda Trading Company (RTC). The RTC used new innovations in the fully washed coffee chain to capture more of the market. In 2015, sixty-three coffee exporters operated in the country (nearly double the number that existed in 2012).[13]

All respondents in the coffee sector agreed that the government's role in the sector was restricted to regulation and ensuring that it remained productive.[14] Firm representatives also admitted to offering high prices to farmers to capture market share. However, respondents (government officials and private-sector representatives) argued that the liberalized environment in the sector was a challenge. This was primarily because fluctuating international prices forced exporters and washing station owners to speculate, which led to coffee being bought at higher prices and sold at lower prices. Significant challenges faced by most companies related to the lack of skills and the availability of working capital, facilities (such as warehouse space), and logistics.[15]

Today, RTC, RwaCof, and Coffee Business Company dominate trade and export operations. The Nigerian company, Kaizen, entered the sector in 2012 and in five months acquired eight washing stations. The firm's owners initially beat out competition by paying farmers for coffee cherries as soon as they were delivered to washing stations. Kaizen's entrance was marked by increased competition in the sector: 'The days of big traders sitting and waiting for people to bring coffee are going. To survive in the coffee sector, you have to go closer to the source and make your contacts outside.'[16]

The nature of the deals space in the above description may be characterized as open ordered, given the entry of many new firms, and perceptions that government decision-making is relatively predictable. This openness, however, has tended to favour larger operators with access to expertise, international networks, and capital. To facilitate the demands of coffee companies, government officials said they established a Memorandum of Understanding with only the ten largest coffee-exporting companies.[17] Local coffee companies and cooperatives continue to occupy a prominent role in the sector, however. One, Rwashoscco, received significant support

---

[13] Interview, NAEB representative, January 2015.
[14] Interview, NAEB representative, January 2015.
[15] Interview, coffee company representatives, January 2015.
[16] Interview, foreign company representative, January 2015.
[17] Interview, NAEB representative, January 2015.

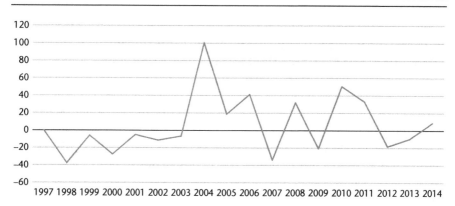

Figure 8.10. Value of Rwanda's coffee exports (annual variation, %)
Source: MINECOFIN (2013).

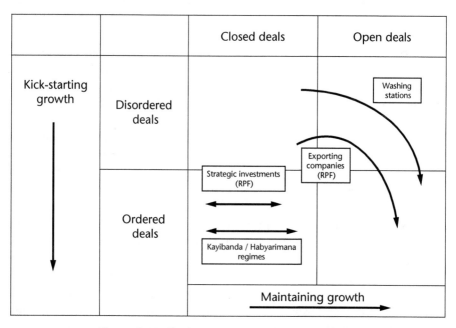

Figure 8.11. Deals space in Rwanda's coffee sector

from USAID and has continued to flourish as a result of the contacts it developed abroad and the expertise gained by local Rwandans working at the cooperative. Rwashoscco's exports multiplied nearly three to four times between 2011 and 2015, with the success attributed to high-quality and efficient management of the supply chain.[18]

---

[18] Interview, Rwashoscco representative, January 2015.

The growth experienced in the coffee sector in the mid to late 2000s led to a resurgence of interest in the sector domestically. The coffee sector turned around in 2004, which was the first year that coffee production volumes matched yearly government targets (Figure 8.10). As a result, 'People started thinking there was money in coffee. However, when they tried, everyone realized it is very difficult because of the competition and small market.'[19] Though foreign investors and donor assistance have contributed to 'transfers of technology' and expertise, some local companies warned that these 'transfers' were not being sustained, as larger players had begun to dominate the market. They argued that heightened competition 'is not good for everyone',[20] and that there was very little protection for local companies: 'It is like a family where you have five children. Two may get PhDs, the other three will not make it to high school.'[21]

Liberalization has been accompanied by the government's choice to prioritize adding value and shifting from the production of semi-washed coffee to fully washed coffee. The number of coffee washing stations in the country increased from two in 2000 to 229 in 2014. Though a large number of washing stations established rapidly, it was on a first-come, first-served basis. For most of the 2000s, washing station owners were making losses, except for those who received support from donors. Though government officials may have facilitated investments, banks and other actors could not support investors. This is borne out by the fact that, of the 229 washing stations constructed in Rwanda, thirty were not in operation and most washing stations operated at 50 per cent capacity (Macchiavello and Morjaria, 2015). Government officials stress that opportunities are open to new investors in this area, but that all operate under strict guidelines with regard to where washing stations are constructed, showing that, despite the problems with washing stations, the government has made substantial efforts to create an 'open ordered' deals environment in this sub-sector.

In contrast, the exports of packaged single-origin Rwandan coffee have been developed through relatively closed but ordered deals. Exporters of packaged coffee included USAID-sponsored Rwashoscco, Kaizen, and coffee brands developed by domestic coffee companies, owned by domestic elites. The government (National Agriculture Export Board and Development Bank of Rwanda (BRD)) has worked with partners, the Clinton Hunter Development Initiative and the Hunter Foundation, to create a coffee company—the Rwandan Farmers' Coffee Company (RFCC)—and invest in a US$3 million coffee processing factory in Kigali. In 2015, the RFCC began operations and will

---

[19] Interview, local coffee company, January 2015.
[20] Interview, local coffee company, January 2015.
[21] Interview, local coffee company, January 2015.

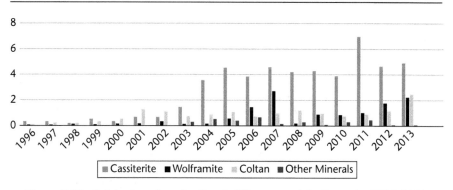

Figure 8.12. Total mineral production (million tonnes) for Rwanda, 1996–2013
Source: MINECOFIN (2013).

produce under the brand 'Gorilla's Coffee', and sell to local, African, Asian, and European markets. The government approached international roasters—Starbucks, Costco, and Rogers Family—to partner specific, local exporting companies and cooperatives.[22] In this deals space for strategic value-addition investments, the government has relied on relatively closed ordered deals, since only certain local firms (with close relationships with the government) are entrusted with risky value-addition attempts. Figure 8.11 details the evolution of the deals space in the coffee sector.

8.5.2 Mining (Rentier)

Figure 8.12 illustrates the turnaround in mineral exports in Rwanda in recent years. Historically, the domestic minerals sector has remained underdeveloped and closely linked with the 'conflict minerals' narrative in the Democratic Republic of the Congo (DRC). During the colonial era, concessions were allocated on a first-come, first-served basis. Pre-1994 governments were unable to incentivize companies to utilize their concessions fully.[23] Figure 8.13 compares annual growth rates in the mineral sector with annual GDP growth rates in Rwanda.

Immediately after 1994, the RPF government showed little interest in rejuvenating the mining sector. Government-owned *Régie d'Exploitation et de Développement des Mines* (REDEMI) controlled all concessions during the 1990s. However, government officials claim that during most of the 1990s, issues of smuggling and theft limited growth in the domestic minerals sector. Some government officials argued that RPF officials and lower-ranked

---

[22] Such companies include RPF cadre Alfred Nkubiri's ENAS.
[23] See Behuria (2015) for a history of Rwanda's minerals sector.

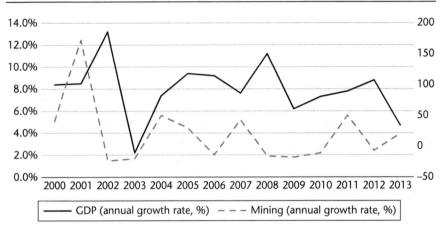

Figure 8.13. Comparison of annual minerals sector growth rates with national growth rates for Rwanda, 2000–13

Source: MINECOFIN (2013).

government officials were the cause of the problem.[24] This showed that there was a 'closed disordered' deals environment in the mining sector at the time:

> Until the genocide, the sector was actually working well. After the genocide, most assets were stolen. Some powerful people also went into concessions and organized stealing minerals. For the government, it was difficult. They traced maybe one or two mining engineers in the country . . . But it was not only because of a lack of skills, it was because of all the procedures that were there in the ministry.[25]

As with the coffee sector, it is important to break down the mining sector into specific sub-sectors or nodes, each of which has a distinctive 'deals environment' under the RPF. These nodes are as follows: links with mineral networks in the DRC; ownership of concessions in Rwanda; the trade and export of minerals from Rwanda; and the organization of artisanal and small-scale mining (ASM). The Rwandan minerals sector has been directly linked with the minerals sector of the Kivus in Eastern DRC for most of its history. Trade networks intensified during Rwandan involvement in the Congo Wars and the RPF's later alleged support of rebel groups. However, even critics (UNSC, 2011) agree that Kigali retained centralized control over mineral networks in the DRC. Though this may have led to individuals gaining access to rents, discipline was strictly administered from Kigali. Thus, rents from minerals networks in the DRC were managed in a 'closed ordered deals' environment, though this centralized control was sometimes threatened.

---

[24] Two interviews, Ministry of Natural Resources (MINIRENA).
[25] Interview, local mining company, January 2015.

Liberalizing trade and export operations picked up pace towards the end of the 2000s. In 2004, one official claimed that REDEMI exported 60 per cent of Rwanda's minerals. The sale of REDEMI's concessions took place rapidly, however: initially REDEMI controlled twenty concessions, but by the end of 2005 only two remained under its control. Many mining companies were registered in the mid-2000s. The Rwanda National Innovation and Competitiveness Report listed fifty-five private companies in the sector in 2005. Most were small *comptoirs*, who exported small quantities of minerals after buying them from artisanal miners. These companies benefited from the rapid privatization that was prioritized ahead of the establishment of a mining law in 2009. Yet government officials admitted that initially they had very little control over the activities of individuals who controlled REDEMI or who managed concessions. In two nodes (ownership of assets, and trade and export operations), the deals environment thus shifted from a 'closed disordered' environment to an 'open disordered' environment, in which the sale of concessions was subject to competitive bidding, though a degree of disorder remained. Trade and export operations operated in a similar way. Disorder was a characteristic of the rapid liberalization in this sector, with many companies operating without licences for several years.[26]

By 2010, thirty-eight large-scale mining licences were granted to (almost entirely) foreign investors: 'Most mining companies said they would invest, but nothing ever came. Because of the way we did privatization, it was difficult to get these companies out after they didn't do what was promised.'[27] Most investors obtained vast concessions at low prices. The government retained shares in the two largest concessions, Gatumba and Rutongo, joint ventures were established, and two companies were created to operate these concessions.

The rapid shift in 'closed' to 'open' deals was not matched by investments in government expertise, which helps to explain the continued disorder. Gradually, the government adapted the mining law in line with achieving government targets. Instances where foreign companies were disciplined are evidence of this, and the government has recently become stricter.[28] Thus, it could be said that there is now a gradual shift to move the deals environment from 'open disordered' to 'open ordered'. However, the openness of deals exposed the 'capability traps' to which the government was vulnerable,[29] and some private-sector operators claimed that the government had not

---

[26] Interviews, local mining companies, January 2015.
[27] Interview, MINIRENA, January 2015.
[28] Interview, MINIRENA official, January 2015.
[29] Capability traps refer to situations where governments adopt reforms to ensure continued flows of external financing, but do not retain the institutions to ensure the functioning of those reforms (Andrews et al., 2013).

delivered on its promises. The government's intent to move towards greater order in the deals environment here has thus not yet been fully realized.

The nature of deals in the sector was also impacted by the Rwandan government's decision to embrace tagging initiatives. The work of advocacy groups, who propagated the 'conflict minerals' narrative, eventually contributed to the inclusion of Section 1502 in the Dodd–Frank Wall Street Reform and Consumer Protection Act of July 2010. Section 1502 directed the US Securities and Exchange Commission (SEC) to promulgate new disclosure rules for SEC-reporting companies that use 'conflict minerals' originating in the DRC or adjoining countries. The Rwandan government was one of the first national governments to adopt tagging initiatives. Some foreign companies then chose to invest in the Rwandan minerals sector, which was previously ignored:

> Earlier, everyone was doing mining from the Congo. People who had concessions here were not using them. Then there was also the minerals ban in the DRC from September 2010 to March 2011, with no export from the DRC. It pushed companies to produce minerals in Rwanda.[30]

Changes in the liberalizing of trade and export operations and the sale of REDEMI's assets are also echoed in changes in the organization of ASM, which was the predominant form of mining in Rwanda for most of the 1990s and 2000s. However, since 2009, there has been a push to formalize ASM operations. By 2013, there were 434 active permits, and by January 2015 more than 700.[31] In the ASM node, government officials affirm that there has been an attempt to bring greater order to the deals environment,[32] though there is some way to go before the government's enforcement capabilities are able to match up to needs.

Fast-paced liberalization has also reduced opportunities for national champions to emerge. The growth of the Fédération des Coopératives Minières au Rwanda (FECOMIRWA) has been limited because of a lack of investment, limited availability of skilled personnel and geologists, and difficulties in dealing with the competitive environment in the domestic minerals sector. Government officials affirm that, despite efforts to help mining cooperatives and small firms, the scale of competition has impeded production increases in this area.[33] It could therefore be argued that the move from 'closed' to 'open' deals has meant increased control of the sector for better-resourced actors. Local operators complained about difficulties in accessing finance, poor recovery of minerals because of inadequate mining equipment, lack of skills, and the high cost of exploration and exploitation. This is true for local operators in

---

[30] Interview, foreign mining investor, January 2015.
[31] Interview, Rwanda Mining Association, January 2015.
[32] Interview, MINIRENA, January 2015.   [33] Interview, FECOMIRWA, January 2015.

trade and export operations and for those who own concessions.[34] Though 70 per cent of companies are still owned by Rwandans, foreigners own most large concessions.[35] The government has realized this, recognizing the importance of agreeing contracts in line with strategic priorities and bolstering enforcement capabilities within government departments.[36]

As with coffee, there is an increasing recognition that strategic initiatives (e.g. value addition, in the form of beneficiation) must take place in a 'closed ordered deals' environment. Rwanda's existing tin smelter was sold to NMC Metallurgie (later renamed Phoenix Metals) in 2003. This occurred in a competitive bidding process, which was open to all investors. Though Phoenix later made significant investments in the smelter, the government has been unable to mobilize the necessary supply of minerals or provide enough electricity, despite guarantees made by the ministry.[37] This trajectory indicates that beneficiation, although a strategic priority, operated in an 'open disordered' deals environment, but this has met with limited success. Attempts are therefore now being made to shift to a 'closed ordered' deals environment, with Phoenix being promised guaranteed supplies of electricity and other benefits (which most other firms in Rwanda would not enjoy). Figure 8.14

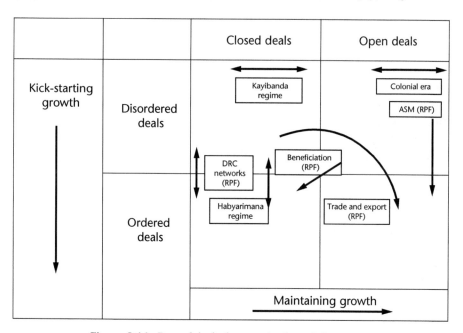

Figure 8.14. Rwanda's deals space in the mining sector
Source: Authors' own data.

---

[34] Interview, local mining exporter, January 2015.
[35] Interview, MINIRENA, January 2015.   [36] Interview, MINIRENA, January 2015.
[37] Interview, Phoenix, January 2015.

illustrates the evolution of the deals space at various nodes in the minerals sector in Rwanda.

8.5.3 Construction (Powerbroker)

Prior to 1994, most major construction projects were undertaken by foreign firms. Some domestic construction firms were also in operation, including a few that have survived to the present day. The deals environment is likely to have been fairly closed and disordered, with a small number of firms with close relations to government, a small amount of activity, and little strategic attention to the sector. At this time, however, construction had nothing like the significance to the economy that it has today.

Figure 8.15 compares Rwanda's annual national GDP growth rates with annual growth rates in the construction sector. Unlike the two sectors discussed in Sections 8.5.1 and 8.5.2, as the graph indicates, growth in construction has regularly equalled or outstripped overall GDP growth since the early 2000s. The growth of the sector in Rwanda since 1994, and especially since 2000, should be understood in relation to the specific demand factors in this period. The devastation caused by the civil war and genocide, followed by the influx of enormous numbers of returnees, international aid, and donor representatives, all contributed to demand for construction services and materials. Physical reconstruction itself necessitated a large amount of building and infrastructure development, and urban real estate projects proliferated to house the new elite. Seizing on construction as a potentially critical sector underpinning the growth of other priority sectors, by the late 2000s the Rwanda Development Board had also introduced very attractive incentives

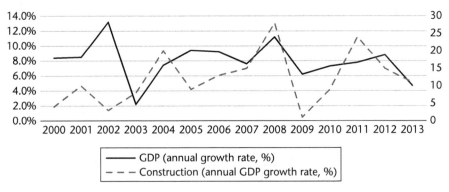

Figure 8.15. Comparison of annual GDP growth rates with annual growth rates in the construction sector for Rwanda

Source: MINECOFIN (2013).

in the sector; for projects over US$1.8 million, there was a flat fee of 10 per cent in place of the usual import duties and other taxes.[38]

This demand spurred the decision to concentrate a significant amount of investment group activity in it. However, different kinds of firms are required for different scales of activity, and the government has been keen to bring in international firms for large-scale projects. Construction differs significantly from the other sectors discussed here, in that much of the work undertaken by firms takes the form of government contracts, often funded by donor money, and generally awarded through processes of competitive tendering. Other forms of construction (i.e. private construction) do operate in a distinctive deals environment of their own, which, while not unproblematic and with some exceptions, can generally be characterized as open and ordered relative to many other developing countries (in terms of the processes of getting building permits and the necessity to adhere to planning and construction regulations).[39] In what follows, however, we concentrate on the large part of construction that occurs through procurement of government contracts, which is a key 'powerbroker' sector in the economy. We distinguish between five key categories of firms: Chinese firms, other foreign firms, state-owned firms, other large domestic firms, and domestic SMEs.

After the genocide, a few new private firms were established to deal with immediate demand. As the government's party- and military-owned investment groups consolidated, several construction companies were also set up under the aegis of Tri-Star/CVL and Horizon. Among these was NPD (Nyarutarama Property Developers), established in 1996. NPD bought the Belgian firm Cotraco in 2008, forming NPD-Cotraco.[40] Meanwhile the military investment group Horizon had its own construction firm, Horizon Construction.

The relationship between the party-owned CVL firms and military-owned Horizon Construction merits some discussion. They are both involved in bidding for infrastructure projects and primarily view each other as competition: 'They complain if we get favoured, they complain if they feel cheated . . . It's normal competition.'[41] They also maintain that they operate in an arena that is open and fair, with a significant degree of consistency and order. In the words of NPD-Cotraco:

We get harshly treated like everybody. We pay our fair share of penalties, we buy our own capital equipment, we pay 18 per cent margins on our loans . . . we are

---

[38] Interview with investment official, June 2014.
[39] See Goodfellow (2013, 2014) for more detail on this.
[40] In 2015, the board of directors decided to rebrand from NPD-COTRACO Ltd to NPD Ltd.
[41] Interview with NPD-Cotraco representative, January 2015.

doing business, just normal business . . . I think the perception that we are favoured was there at the start, but these guys we compete with can't use the excuse that we are favoured any more. Maybe the competition isn't enough, but that's not our fault.[42]

One Horizon representative argued that: 'Some might think we get jobs without competing, but let me assure you that we don't. We always compete and often lose.'[43] This might mean losing out to foreign (usually Chinese) firms, or to small local firms who have a comparative advantage due to lower overhead costs. A number of other large domestic firms also compete with NPD and Horizon, and sometimes win. Domestic firms also work together in some cases, and in joint ventures with foreign ones, and large firms are increasingly encouraged to subcontract to small ones.

The question of how Rwandan firms are treated relative to foreign ones is a source of ongoing tension. The investment groups claim to have sometimes been treated unfavourably. For example, in one case, NPD-Cotraco bid to build a particular road and the tender was cancelled because no foreign company tendered. The tender was subsequently readvertised and awarded to a foreign firm. This caused bewilderment within NPD-Cotraco, which claimed to be unaware of a stipulation that a foreign company was needed for the tendering process to be valid, suggesting a degree of disorder to the deals environment. One investment group representative claimed that 90 per cent of construction in 2014 was undertaken by foreign firms, despite growing local capacity.[44] Some domestic firms even claimed that contracts were given to Chinese firms even when local firms could provide evidence of doing the job more cheaply. They also lamented their lack of knowledge, both of Chinese 'market tricks' and of 'tricks of the so-called consultants', citing the problem that foreign consultants often set the terms and budgets for construction projects before tendering begins, which intrinsically disadvantages locals.[45]

That the government is widely seen as providing preferential access to foreign firms is surprising, given its rhetoric of national rebuilding and the need to cultivate domestic capacity in the sector. The head of one investment group-owned firm complained that:

Rwanda is the only country I know where you can sit on your computer in China and bid for something and win it. Even in Kenya, you would have to have local content, and prove that what you were planning to do can't be done by locals.[46]

---

[42] Interview with NPD-Cotraco representative, January 2015.
[43] Interview with Horizon representative, January 2015.
[44] Interview with head of investment group, January 2015.
[45] Interview with small construction firm, January 2015.
[46] Interview with head of investment group, January 2015.

The foreign firms offered varying perspectives. A key Chinese firm representative suggested that the market was relatively open, if rather small: 'There is no friend or favour . . . by African standards it really is transparent . . . it's not about personal relations.'[47] Yet some other foreign firms believed they lost out due to inconsistent policies and corruption, frequently expressing irritation at the number of contracts awarded to the Chinese and at collusive behaviour among Chinese firms that enabled them to undercut competitors.[48] Some Chinese firms, meanwhile, believed that the government sometimes granted contracts to its own state-owned firms under preferential terms. One claimed that the government gives local firms 'a sort of discount . . . so if we bid for $10 million and a Rwandese firm does too, they consider it more like $9.5 million'. He added that 'there are no rules, it's just certain projects that get that treatment'.[49]

Such claims suggest that the deals space was relatively open, with contracts being allocated across a wide range of providers relative to market size—but also that it was relatively disordered and unpredictable. Consequently, most firms felt discriminated against in some way, not because opportunities were closed to them, but because of the lack of clear rules. Ironically, the state-owned firms feel unfairly treated because they believe that the government's concern to guard against the perception they are always favoured actually loses them some contracts—plus they cannot build as cheaply as the Chinese and do not know the market 'tricks' of the internationals. The non-state-owned domestic firms were actually the least inclined to complain about unfair treatment, though most are too small to compete for the big government tenders.

The openness in the sector is by no means complete, and there are cases in which the allocation of contracts is completely closed. The process of allocating contracts for four new football stadia across the country for the African Nations Championship is a case in point. Originally, the government tendered for these projects and awarded the contract to a large foreign firm. However, amid rising concern about cost, the government performed a U-turn and cancelled this contract, allocating the jobs to three domestic state-owned companies (NPD-Cotraco, Real Contractors, and Horizon) and one foreign firm (Roko).[50] Contracts can also be revoked if firms are not seen to deliver on time; there are several cases where local or international firms were seen to have failed to deliver and the government has brought in the Rwanda Defence Force Engineer Regiment to take over and

---

[47] Interview with foreign construction firm, January 2015.
[48] Interview with foreign construction firm, January 2015.
[49] Interview with Chinese construction firm, January 2015.
[50] Interview with foreign construction firm, January 2015.

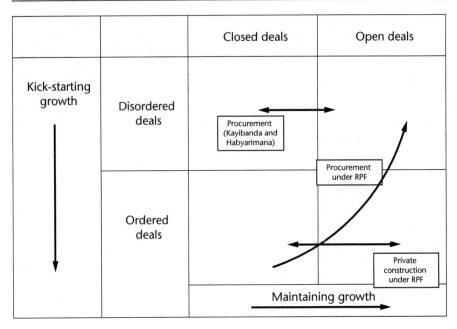

Figure 8.16. Rwanda's deals space in the construction sector

finish the job.[51] Horizon was also sometimes brought in at the last minute for 'crash projects'.[52] Figure 8.16 illustrates the deals space in the construction sector.

8.5.4 *Financial Services*

Preceding governments retained some control over the financial sector. The Banque Commerciale du Rwanda (BCR) was incorporated as the first commercial bank in Rwanda in 1963, partly owned by the Banque Bruxelles Lambert. The government retained 42 per cent of BCR's share capital. The Bank of Kigali (BK) was established in 1966, as a joint venture with Belgolaise SA. Later, the Banque Nationale de Paris and Dresdner Bank also invested in the bank. The government retained 50 per cent of BK's share capital. In 1983, the Banque Continentale du Luxembourg established the Banque Continentale Africaine du Rwanda (BACAR). BCR accounted for 48.4 per cent of commercial bank assets, while BK and BACAR held 36 and 15.6 per cent of total assets, respectively (World Bank, 1991). Figure 8.17 compares Rwanda's annual national GDP growth rates with annual growth rates in the financial services sector.

---

[51] Interview with architect, January 2015; interview with foreign advisor, January 2015.
[52] Interview with Horizon Construction representative, January 2015.

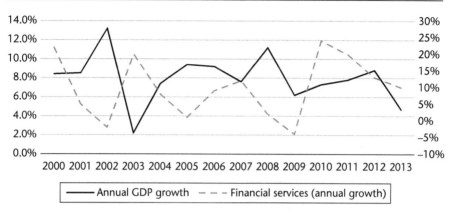

Figure 8.17. Comparison of annual GDP growth rates with annual growth rates in financial services for Rwanda

Source: MINECOFIN (2013).

After the genocide, the local banking sector 'was overburdened with non-performing loans and was not in a position to support the reconstruction of a capital intensive sector in the immediate aftermath of the crisis' (Gathani and Stoelinga, 2013: 22). The government decided to license two new commercial banks—the Bank of Commerce, Development, and Industry (BCDI), and the Banque à la Confiance d'Or (BANCOR). Fick (2002) cites BCDI as an example of entrepreneurial success. BANCOR increased its share capital from RwF 300 million to RwF 1.5 billion between 1995 and 2001 (Emile, 2008). In 1999, more than forty Rwandan investors and state-owned institutions (which owned a minority share) established Cogebanque. Given the way in which these banks were set up, it is clear that the sector was relatively closed until the early 2000s. However, it is unlikely that there was a considerable degree of order in the deals environment. In the mid-2000s, the Chairman of BCDI and a senior BACAR official were both accused of embezzling funds from their banks (Behuria and Goodfellow, 2016). This showed that, for this period, there was some degree of disorder in the deals environment.

The liberalization of the financial sector gradually gathered pace in the early 2000s, with a large number of foreign acquisitions rapidly taking place from 2004 onwards and the entry of a number of international banks into the market, including Ecobank, RABO bank, the Kenya Commercial Bank, the Nigerian-based Access Bank, and the Ugandan Crane Bank.[53] As of 2015, there were ten commercial banks, with the government retaining shares in three. There are also four microfinance banks, one development bank (BRD), and a military savings bank, the Credit Savings Society Zigama.

[53] See Behuria and Goodfellow (2016) for details.

BK has remained Rwanda's largest bank for the last two decades. Despite liberalization, BK's share of the market (by assets) increased from 23 per cent in 2008 to 36 per cent in 2013. In 2013, BK also had a market share of more than 30 per cent in terms of total assets, net loans, customer deposits, and equity. Though the government officially has a minority shareholding in the bank, its total shareholding (including shares owned by the Rwanda Social Security Board) stands at 54 per cent. BK representatives welcomed opening up the sector, arguing that 'there is a lot of room in the market' and that it helped them learn and compete at the regional level.[54] There are also only three banks in which Rwandans retain a majority shareholding (BK, BPR, and Cogebanque).[55] These three banks have retained 50 per cent of the market by assets between 2008 and 2014.

Most representatives of commercial banks agreed that open deals operated in the sector. One banking official said that Rwanda's banking sector was even more open than most countries in Asia, including India, Singapore, and Pakistan.[56] They generally believed that, on balance, an open environment was beneficial, pointing out that each bank has its own niche, so competition is not too damaging, as well as expressing a common belief that: 'without liberalization, complacency sets in, and you don't get innovation'.[57] The managing director of a leading bank claimed that the banking sector:

> has evolved faster than any other industry. There has been a process of leapfrogging on the technological side. We were where Zambia was in 1993. In 2009, we are probably doing more than what Zambia and Kenya have done.[58]

There was a sense that each bank had its own advantages: investment groups were expected to bank with the government-owned BK, while foreign banks benefited from support from their international parent companies, giving them favoured access to corporate international firms. Though representatives from other commercial banks claimed that BK received some deals 'that were allocated without being tendered' and that it was 'patronized', there were few complaints and the same respondent even said there was a 'level playing field'.[59] BK did not receive all government contracts.

The above narrative suggests that, while different banks clearly have preferential access to certain parts of the market, the sector is one in which deals are relatively open and ordered. Most stakeholders stressed predictability and revealed relatively open opportunities to engage in deals. However, the choice to embrace market-led reforms in the sector has been at odds with the need to

---

[54] Interview with BK official.
[55] After Atlas Mara's investments, BPR will no longer have a majority local shareholding.
[56] Interview, BCR official.   [57] Interview, BPR official.
[58] Interview, manager of foreign bank, January 2015.
[59] Interview, foreign bank official, January 2015.

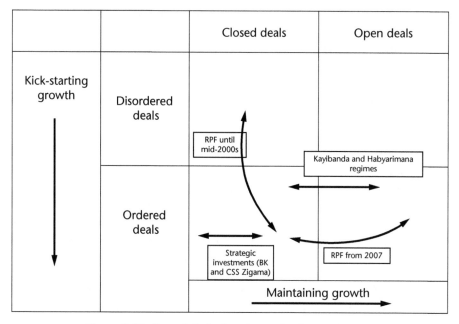

Figure 8.18. Rwanda's deals space in the financial sector

retain control over financing strategic investments. Some representatives of commercial banks were surprised at the government's readiness to open up the financial sector before 'Rwanda can stand on its own two feet'.[60] Figure 8.18 illustrates the evolution of the deals space in the financial sector.

8.6 Conclusion

This account of the dynamics underpinning growth in specific sectors of the economy presents a much more nuanced and finely balanced situation than is offered by the conventional narratives of Rwanda's economic development. Contrary to the idea that Rwanda's growth has been 'primarily driven by liberalization in the agricultural sector', we have shown that in fact liberalization in export crops has not led to much growth, while the importance placed on value addition and strategic investments has spurred transformation in the sector. Such strategic investments have depended on closed deals. Meanwhile, the 'developmental patrimonialism' argument that focuses on the long-term horizons of party- and military-owned firms tells only part of the story, concealing how these operate alongside significant openness in some sub-sector deals environments.

[60] Interview, foreign bank official, January 2015.

245

This openness has at times spurred innovation and facilitated large-scale investments, but also serves to threaten the order that the government has been trying to achieve in the deals environment across the economy as a whole. The increased concern with corruption, and impressive achievements in relation to containing it, can be understood as indicating a shift towards a more ordered deals environment in most sectors. However, donor pressures to embrace market-led reforms alongside the impetus to attract foreign investment have been associated with a move towards more open deals, sometimes prematurely, creating difficulties for the government in retaining control over sectors and empowering national champions. This threatens the order that the government has been trying to create.

The framework presented in this volume posits that the relationship between the political settlement and the rents space is crucial to determining everything else about deals and development. In Rwanda, under the RPF, the 'strong dominant' political settlement—combined with important ideological principles based on self-reliance and domestic ownership—has helped to create a rents space with significant scope for firms serving a domestic market that is substantially funded by foreign aid. As Figure 8.7 shows, GDP is dominated by powerbrokers and even more so (given liberalization) by workhorses. Aid, growth, and investment have helped workhorses (including banking and real estate) to flourish. This nexus between the political settlements and rents space has, however, done little to drive export competitiveness. Rentiers have shifted from being in the coffee sector under previous regimes to activities such as mining, but the liberalization of coffee that precipitated this has not created many magicians. More generally, the effort to create magicians has been difficult, because the government is unable to empower national champions to an extent that gives them the capacity to export in a liberalized domestic environment.

Turning to the deals environment itself, the attempt to pursue growth while maintaining a stable political settlement has led to an effort to push increasingly open deals, but with some space reserved for strategic pockets of closed deals. Government respondents suggested that a key target was to ensure that all sectors eventually operated in an environment of 'open ordered' deals. Yet the pressures caused by moving so rapidly towards this openness have meant that the government sometimes fails to sustain an ordered deals environment, despite the significance it places on policies promoting order. A powerbroker sector, such as construction, which depends on substantial openness due to domestic capacity deficits, exhibits a sort of state-driven open disorder, which fosters growth through openness while allowing the state to retain control through sometimes breaking, revoking, or selectively awarding contracts. Rwanda's growth has thus depended on its ability to manage pragmatically a highly variegated deals environment—one that can appeal to donors and investors, while maintaining a stable (yet always vulnerable) domestic political settlement. The sporadic disorder that results from this is, however, off-putting to investors in some sectors.

As the model predicts, growth and transformation in the economy (primarily towards services) have fed back into the rents space by generating opportunities for workhorses, as well as powerbrokers and rentiers in the mining sector. There have been few successful attempts at creating magicians, with the exports still reliant on primary commodities. The government has also done very little to cultivate the growth of national champions to an extent that they can compete in liberalized competitive export markets. However, it is still relatively early in the country's development trajectory.

Also in line with the model, the Rwandan case shows how transnational factors have affected both the political settlement (for example, through foreign aid effectively supporting the strong dominant position of the current regime and influencing the government to embrace market-led reforms) and the rents space (for example, by generating new mining opportunities in Rwanda, due to the tagging of conflict minerals). However, in contrast with the model, Rwanda also shows how transnational factors can affect the deals environment directly. In construction, for example, there has been a feedback loop between donor funds for contracts and the nature of deals in the sector: the large variety of international actors funding construction has led to a proliferation of different rules and practices in tendering for contracts, causing considerable confusion. In this way, aid-driven construction growth is promoting diverse, poorly integrated institutional processes, which undermines the order of the deals environment. Meanwhile, in struggling traditional export sectors, the recourse to 'closed ordered deals' with loyal capitalist partners (investment groups or local elites) for strategic investments demonstrates a feedback loop between volatile demand in such sectors and the deals environment itself.

In conclusion, though some structural transformation has been achieved since 1994, growth maintenance in the country remains dependent on commodity price fluctuations, access to foreign aid, and the maintenance of a stable political settlement. Rwanda's growth episode continues to be vulnerable to external threats—whether these take the form of international price fluctuations, diminishing donor goodwill, or rival elites who threaten the regime's legitimacy abroad. Yet the nature of its growth in the context of widespread liberalization across sectors also leads to threats to growth maintenance that can be seen as more internal in nature, two of which stand out in particular. The first is that a high degree of openness can result in poorly coordinated economic development without sufficient enforcement capability of the state to discipline firms, so as to promote robust linkages and spillovers in the economy. The second is that growth that is highly dependent on open (and especially foreign) competition results in periodically unpredictable and inconsistent behaviour by the government to keep a balance between foreign and domestic firms and a stable political settlement. This creates negative feedback to the deals environment by creating disorder, which may undermine investor confidence, but also contributes to a situation where the government retains very little capacity to discipline existing foreign investors in line with strategic goals.

References

ACET. 2014. *African Transformation Report 2014: Growth with Depth*. Accra and Washington, DC: African Centre for Economic Transformation.

Andrews, M., Pritchett, L., and Woolcock, M. 2013. 'Escaping Capability Traps through Problem Driven Iterative Adaptation (PDIA)'. *World Development*, 51: 234–44.

Ansoms, A., and Rostagno, D. 2012. 'Rwanda's Vision 2020 Halfway Through: What the Eye Does Not See'. *Review of African Political Economy*, 39(133): 427–50.

Behuria, P. 2015. 'Between Party Capitalism and Market Reforms—Understanding Sector Differences in Rwanda'. *Journal of Modern African Studies*, 53(3): 415–50.

Behuria, P., and Goodfellow, T. 2016. 'The Political Settlement and "Deals Environment" in Rwanda: Unpacking Two Decades of Economic Growth'. ESID Working Paper No. 57. Manchester: University of Manchester.

Booth, D., Cooksey, B., Golooba-Mutebi, F., and Kanyinga, K. 2014. *East African Prospects: An Update on the Political Economy of Kenya, Rwanda, Tanzania, and Uganda*. London: Overseas Development Institute.

Booth, D., and Golooba-Mutebi, F. 2012. 'Developmental Patrimonialism? The Case of Rwanda'. *African Affairs*, 111(444): 379–403.

Booth, D., and Golooba-Mutebi, F. 2014. 'How the International System Hinders the Consolidation of Developmental Regimes in Africa'. Developmental Regimes in Africa Working Paper 4. London: Overseas Development Institute.

Collier, P. 2015. 'Africa: New Opportunities, Old Impediments'. *Economic Affairs*, 35(2): 169–77.

Emile, B. 2008. 'West African Banks Enter Rwandan Market'. *Business Rwanda*, 27 February.

Fick, D. 2002. *Entrepreneurship in Africa: A Study of Successes*. Westport, CT: Quorum Books.

Gathani, S., and Stoelinga, D. 2013. *Understanding Rwanda's Agribusiness and Manufacturing Sectors*. Kigali, Rwanda: International Growth Centre.

Gokgur, N. 2012. 'Rwanda's Ruling Party-Owned Business Enterprises: Do They Enhance or Impede Development?' IOB Discussion Paper. University of Antwerp, Belgium.

Goodfellow, T. 2013. 'Planning and Development Regulation amid Rapid Urban Growth: Explaining Divergent Trajectories in Africa'. *Geoforum*, 48: 83–93.

Goodfellow, T. 2014. 'Rwanda's Political Settlement and the Urban Transition: Expropriation, Construction and Taxation in Kigali'. *Journal of Eastern African Studies*, 8(2): 311–29.

GoR. 2000. *Rwanda Vision 2020*. Kigali, Rwanda: Government of Rwanda.

IMF. 2000. *Rwanda: Recent Economic Developments*. International Monetary Fund Staff Country Report No. 4. Washington, DC: International Monetary Fund.*.

Kar, S., Pritchett, L., Raihan, S., and Sen, K. 2013. *The Dynamics of Economic Growth: A Visual Handbook of Growth Rates, Regimes, Transitions and Volatility*. Manchester: University of Manchester.

Kelsall, T. 2013. *Business, Politics, and the State in Africa: Challenging the Orthodoxies on Growth and Transformation*. London: Zed Books.

Lagarde, C. 2015. 'Rwanda: Taking on the Future, Staying Ahead of the Curve'. Speech made in the Parliament of Rwanda. Kigali, Rwanda.

Lavers, T., and Hickey, S. 2015. 'Investigating the Political Economy of Social Protection Expansion in Africa: At the Intersection of Transnational Ideas and Domestic Politics'. ESID Working Paper No. 47. Manchester: University of Manchester.

Lemarchand, R. 1995. 'Rwanda: The Rationality of Genocide'. *Issue: A Journal of Opinion*, 23(2): 8–11.

Macchiavello, R., and Morjaria, A. 2015. *Fully Washed Coffee Exports in Rwanda: Market Structure and Policy Implications*. London: International Growth Centre.

MINAGRI (Ministry of Agriculture and Animal Husbandry). 2008. *Rwanda Coffee Strategy Update, 2009–2012*. Kigali, Rwanda: Ministry of Agriculture and Animal Husbandry, with Ministry of Trade and Industry.

MINECOFIN (Ministry of Finance and Economic Planning). 2013. *Economic Development and Poverty Reduction Strategy: 2013–2018*. Kigali, Rwanda: Government of Rwanda.

NISR (National Institute of Statistics of Rwanda). 2012. *Fourth Population and Housing Census 2012: Thematic Report*. Kigali, Rwanda: Government of Rwanda.

Oro, Á. M., and Arias, M. B. 2012. 'Rwanda's Economic Success: How Free Markets Are Good for Poor Africans'. Foundation for Economic Education, 27 June. <https://fee.org/articles/rwandas-economic-success-how-free-markets-are-good-for-poor-africans/>.

Prunier, G. 1995. *The Rwanda Crisis: History of a Genocide*. New York: Columbia University Press.

Reyntjens, F. 2011. 'Constructing the Truth, Dealing with Dissent, Domesticating the World: Governance in Post-Genocide Rwanda'. *African Affairs*, 110(438): 1–34.

Tumwebaze, P. 2014. 'World Bank Hails Rwanda's Growth'. *New Times*. 10 April.

UNSC (United Nations Security Council). 2011. 'Report of the Panel of Experts on the Illegal Exploitation of Natural Resources and Other Forms of Wealth of the Democratic Republic of the Congo'. 15 November (S/2011/738).

Verwimp, P. 2003. 'The Political Economy of Coffee, Dictatorship and Genocide'. *European Journal of Political Economy*, 19(2): 161–81.

Verwimp, P. 2013. *Peasants in Power: The Political Economy of Development and Genocide in Rwanda*. London: Springer.

World Bank. 1991. *Rwanda: Financial Sector Review*. World Bank Report No. 8934-RW. Washington, DC: World Bank.

9

The Stroll, the Trot, and the Sprint of the Elephant

Understanding Indian Growth Episodes

Kunal Sen, Sabyasachi Kar, and Jagadish Prasad Sahu

9.1 Introduction

After a prolonged period of low economic growth since independence (famously known as the 'Hindu rate of growth'), India has transitioned to a high growth trajectory since the early 1990s. This trajectory became even steeper during the first decade of the new millennium. Currently, with a slowdown in the Chinese economy, the Indian economy is arguably the fastest growing major economy in the world. This long history of changing growth rates represents a series of growth episodes, rather than deviations from a single steady-state growth path. In this chapter, we identify the distinct 'episodes' of growth for the Indian economy. We analyse the transitions of the economy from each of these growth episodes to the next. We show that these transitions are defined by the interaction of the political settlement, the rents space, and the deals environment in each of these episodes.

It is useful to start by establishing the 'stylized facts' of India's economic growth and structural transformation since its independence. Table 9.1 shows the decadal average of aggregate as well as sectoral GDP per capita growth rates. It clearly shows that economic growth accelerated during the 1990s and 2000s (although there were a few instances of high growth in the 1980s, the momentum did not last for long).

This growth has changed the structure of the economy significantly. Figure 9.1 illustrates the sectoral distribution of total output of the Indian

Table 9.1. Average sectoral GDP per capita growth rates in India (% per annum)

	1951–60	1961–70	1971–80	1981–90	1991–2000	2001–10
Agriculture, forestry, and fishing	1.18	0.31	−0.45	1.35	0.86	1.70
Mining and quarrying	3.70	1.74	2.60	6.26	2.05	3.06
Manufacturing	4.07	3.00	1.76	4.01	4.05	6.66
Electricity, gas, and water supply	8.36	8.81	4.46	6.32	4.75	4.38
Construction	4.75	3.29	0.97	2.51	3.04	8.07
Trade, hotels, and restaurants	3.30	2.52	1.95	3.72	5.40	7.62
Transport, storage, and communication	3.70	3.20	3.78	3.65	6.96	10.38
Financing, insurance, real estate, and business services	1.04	1.17	1.74	6.81	6.08	8.02
Community, social, and personal services	1.70	3.00	1.74	3.71	4.49	4.92
Agriculture	1.18	0.31	−0.45	1.35	0.86	1.70
Industry	4.14	2.97	1.69	3.86	3.53	6.50
Services	2.18	2.43	2.03	4.44	5.49	7.46
Total GDP	1.99	1.49	0.84	3.19	3.69	6.11

Source: *National Accounts Statistics*, Central Statistical Organization (CSO).

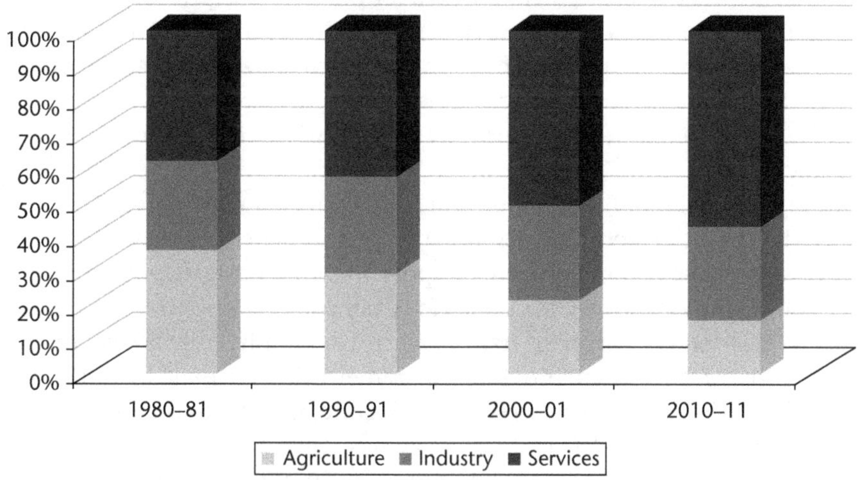

Figure 9.1. Sectoral distribution of GDP in India (% of GDP)
Source: National Accounts Statistics, Central Statistics Office.

economy. The share of agriculture in total GDP has been consistently declining, from 37.2 per cent in 1980–1 to 14.54 per cent in 2010–11. On the other hand, both the industry and services sectors' share of total output have been continuously rising during the same period. While the share of industry has gone up at a relatively slow rate, from 16.9 per cent in 1980–1 to 18.4 per cent in

2010–11, the services sector has undergone a rapid expansion over the years, from 45.8 per cent in 1980–1 to 67.1 per cent in 2010–11.

Several arguments have been put forward that explain India's economic growth in its post-independence era and these have now become the conventional narrative on this issue. The sluggish economic growth from the 1950s to the early 1990s is attributed to a number of factors, such as low productivity growth, low rate of investment, and the dominance of the public sector. The restrictive regime (during this period a large number of industries were reserved for the public sector) and the inward-looking policies (import-substitution strategy) contributed to the inefficiency and poor performance of Indian industries, which resulted in low productivity growth. Moreover, a low level of capital formation, owing to inadequate domestic savings, along with high population growth led to slow growth of income per capita during this period. As discussed earlier, economic growth started accelerating in the early 1990s. The conventional narrative explains this phenomenon as the consequence of the comprehensive economic reforms which India adopted in 1991 (see Bhagwati, 1993; Panagariya, 2008). The economy was liberalized and opened up for the domestic private sector as well as for foreign investors. Liberalized industrial policies, combined with increased openness of the economy, induced domestic firms to become globally competitive. The so-called pro-market strategy led to a rapid increase in investment rate, and raised economy-wide productivity growth, which in turn accelerated economic growth.

The conventional literature on the Indian growth experience does throw some light on the factors underlying this phenomenon. However, the scope of this narrative is limited in two important ways. First, these studies focus on explaining one growth episode (for example, the low growth rate up to the 1970s) or one growth transition (for example, the acceleration in the 1990s), rather than providing a framework that explains all growth episodes and transitions between them. Second, they focus on the proximate determinants of growth, including savings, investments, trade policy, or industrial policy, and ignore the continuously changing face of the deep determinants of growth, namely political factors, institutional factors (deals environment), and the rents space that characterizes the Indian experience from the early years of independence to the current period. As we shall see, it is these changes that have played very significant roles in bringing about the transitions in the Indian economy, moving from one growth episode to the next. In this chapter, we highlight the changes in these three spheres—political space, institutional arrangements, and rents space—and relate them to the three growth episodes in India. To do this, we start by identifying the growth episodes in the Indian economy post-independence.

9.2 Growth Episodes

In order to study the growth episodes in the Indian economy, we first need to periodize these episodes, i.e. establish when the growth accelerations and decelerations occurred. As explained in Chapter 1, we follow Kar et al. (2013a, 2013b), which differs from previous approaches that have attempted to identify the timing of India's growth acceleration. Earlier approaches on periodizing India's economic growth have either been ad hoc, in that they have simply eyeballed the data to establish the timing of the break (such as Sen, 2007), or used a statistical method (Bai and Perron, 1998) mechanistically (such as Balakrishnan and Parameswaran, 2007). Our approach combines the statistical approach with an economic filter to provide a more unified way of establishing breaks in GDP per capita data.[1]

Our procedure identifies 1993 as the beginning of the first growth acceleration episode, and 2002 as the beginning of a second growth acceleration episode. In India, GDP per capita growth accelerated in 1993 to 4.23 per cent per annum (ppa) versus a predicted rate of 2.34 ppa and then accelerated again in 2002 to 6.29 ppa versus a predicted rate of 2.91 ppa. The net present value (NPV) (at a 5 per cent discount rate) of the additional output from the 2002 growth acceleration was US$2.65 trillion in purchasing power parity (PPP) (see Pritchett et al. (2016)). The NPV of output gained from the 1993 acceleration was US$1.05 trillion. Therefore, the total NPV gained from growth accelerations since 1993 was US$3.7 trillion. Taken together, India's two growth accelerations added about US$4,000 in PPP terms to the average Indian's income, as compared with the counterfactual of what the income would have been without the two growth accelerations.

We plot India's real GDP per capita and its growth rate in Figure 9.2. It clearly shows that economic growth has increased steadily since 1993, and at a higher rate since 2002. Based on our periodization, the economic growth experience of India since independence can best be viewed as three distinct growth episodes. These are: (i) a period of low growth from 1950 to 1992 (though there were growth spurts in the late 1980s, they did not last long enough to be considered as a genuine break in trend growth); (ii) a growth acceleration since 1993; and (iii) a period of high growth since 2002. We follow this periodization throughout the subsequent analysis.

---

[1] The question of timing of turning points in India's economic growth is a controversial issue (see Ghate and Wright, 2012). Most previous studies on structural breaks in growth rates in India find evidence of breaks in the late 1970s. Our procedure shows a possible growth break in 1979, but this break is not significant enough statistically.

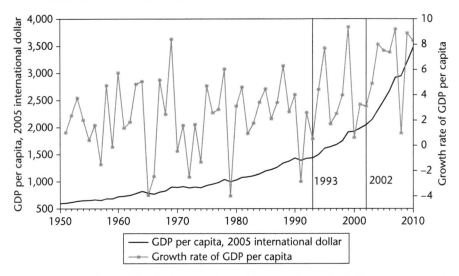

Figure 9.2. GDP per capita and its growth rate in India
Source: Penn World Tables 7.1 <http://pwt.econ.upenn.edu/>.

9.3 Explaining the Growth Episodes

In this section, we analyse the nature of the three growth episodes in India, as well as the deep determinants that drove the economy from one episode to the next. In order to understand the defining characteristics of each episode, we start by looking at the sources of growth in these three episodes. Next, we take up each episode and discuss the political settlement, the rents space, and the deals environment that defined each of them, as well as the critical role they played in the transition of the economy to the next episode.

What are the sources of growth across the three different growth episodes? We find that agriculture has shown a lack of dynamism across all three growth regimes (Table 9.2). The primary sector (agriculture and allied activities, plus mining and quarrying) as a whole has experienced a similar trend. In general, the primary sector has witnessed stagnation over the entire period. However, the mining sector data during the last episode have been grossly underreported (see Shah Commission, 2012). The manufacturing sector has experienced growth acceleration during both the second and the third episodes, although within this sector, registered manufacturing grew faster than unregistered manufacturing. The construction sector grew rapidly during the third episode, with an average growth rate of 8.57 per cent in 2002–10, as compared with 5.61 per cent in 1993–2001. The trade, hotels, and restaurants sector showed strong growth in both the second and third episodes. The communication sector witnessed a surge in growth in 1993–2001, with an average growth rate of

Table 9.2. Regime-wise average sectoral GDP per capita growth rates in India (% per annum)

Sl. No.	Sector name	1951–92	1993–2001	2002–10
1	Agriculture, forestry, and fishing	0.59	1.30	1.46
1.1	Agriculture, incl. livestock	0.75	1.30	1.59
1.2	Forestry and logging	−1.42	−0.07	0.20
1.3	Fishing	2.33	2.88	2.42
2	Mining and quarrying	3.41	2.21	3.42
3	Manufacturing	2.98	4.87	7.38
3.1	Registered	3.95	5.61	8.57
3.2	Unregistered	1.86	3.52	5.07
4	Electricity, gas, and water supply	6.95	3.87	4.89
5	Construction	2.78	3.41	8.75
6	Trade, hotels, and restaurants	2.80	6.54	7.64
6.1	Trade	2.78	6.36	7.69
6.2	Hotels and restaurants	2.94	8.66	7.30
7	Transport, storage, and communication	3.58	7.42	11.05
7.1	Railways	1.95	2.02	6.17
7.2	Transport by other means	4.17	5.32	7.52
7.3	Storage	2.40	0.39	5.82
7.4	Communication	4.44	15.73	23.07
8	Financing, insurance, real estate, and business services	2.85	5.86	8.46
8.1	Banking and insurance	5.69	7.37	11.17
8.2	Real estate, ownership of dwellings, and business services	2.10	4.89	6.48
9	Community, social, and personal services	2.53	4.68	5.25
9.1	Public administration and defence	3.83	4.35	5.30
9.2	Other services	1.68	4.95	5.31
10	Primary (1 + 2)	0.75	1.38	1.68
11	Tertiary (6 + 8)	2.81	6.18	8.04
12	Infrastructure (4 + 7)	4.17	6.46	9.85
13	Agriculture (1)	0.59	1.30	1.46
14	Industry (2 + 3 + 4 + 5)	3.00	4.02	7.17
15	Services (6 + 7 + 8 + 9)	2.79	5.88	7.79
16	Total GDP (13 + 14 + 15)	1.86	4.15	6.42

Source: National Accounts Statistics, CSO.

15.73 per cent during this period, compared with an average growth of 4.44 per cent in 1951–92 (this growth momentum was maintained in 2002–10). The finance, insurance, real estate, and business services sectors also witnessed strong growth in 1993–2001 and 2002–10, driven mostly by growth in the banking and insurance sector and in business services (mostly ICT). Overall, the growth accelerations of 1993–2001 and 2002–10 were mostly due to growth in tradeable sectors, such as manufacturing and business services, and non-tradeable sectors, such as trade, hotels and restaurants, communication, and finance.

Table 9.3 depicts the industrial structure of the economy over the period 1981–2007. It is evident that the average shares of food, beverages, tobacco, textiles and apparel, and machinery in total manufacturing real gross value added have declined over the period. The share of food, beverages, and tobacco has declined from an average value of 15.3 per cent in 1981–92 to

Table 9.3. Average share in real gross value added of total manufacturing in India

Average	Food, beverages, and tobacco	Textiles and apparel	Refined petroleum products	Chemicals	Metals	Non-metallic minerals	Machinery	Motor vehicles and accessories	Others
1981–92	15.33	12.12	6.19	17.68	15.72	4.43	8.62	3.42	16.49
1993–2001	13.80	11.28	5.60	20.59	16.18	4.82	7.93	3.63	16.18
2002–7	11.09	9.96	13.03	17.83	17.27	4.80	7.62	3.50	14.90

Source: Authors' calculations based on data from *Annual Survey of Industries*.

13.8 per cent in 1993–2001 and to 11.1 per cent in 2002–7. Machinery share has declined from 8.62 per cent to 7.93 per cent and further declined to 7.62 per cent over the corresponding period. The share of textiles and apparel has witnessed a similar trend and reached 9.96 per cent during 2002–7, from 12.12 per cent during 1981–92. On the other hand, the shares of refined petroleum products, chemicals, and metals have increased over the period. Although the refined petroleum products share declined from 6.2 per cent during 1981–92 to 5.6 per cent during 1993–2001, thereafter it has shown a rapid increase during 2002–7.

The subgroup, namely 'metals', has experienced a relatively slow but continuous increase in the share in total manufacturing gross valued added over the entire period. Sectors such as non-metallic minerals, and motor vehicles and accessories, have maintained a roughly constant share during the period.

To sum up, Table 9.3 demonstrates that the resource-based sectors (except chemicals) have seen an increase at the expense of labour-intensive and human capital-intensive sectors. In other words, while the share of high-rent sectors (natural resource-based sectors), such as petroleum refinery and metals, has seen an increase during the third growth episode, the share of labour-intensive sectors—such as food, beverages, and textiles and apparel—has decreased during the same period.

9.3.1 *Fixed Capital Formation and Its Components*

For more than half a century, fixed investment rates have steadily gone up in India (Table 9.4). This has been driven mostly by fixed investment by the private sector (both the corporate and household sectors), and also shows an upward trend over the entire period. It recorded high growth in the second period and even higher in the third. However, public sector fixed investment has fallen after a peak in the mid-1980s. There was a sharp fall in private corporate fixed investment in the latter half of the 2002–10 growth episode.

Table 9.4. Fixed investment rates in India (period averages)

Period	Gross fixed investment	Public fixed investment	Private corporate fixed investment	Household fixed investment
1950–1 to 1992–3	17.07	8.17	2.46	6.44
1993–4 to 2001–2	25.35	8.42	7.50	9.43
2002–3 to 2010–11	32.05	8.18	10.85	13.02

Source: Authors' calculations, from the *National Accounts Statistics*, CSO.

9.3.2 *The First Growth Episode (1950–1 to 1992–3)*

POLITICAL SETTLEMENT

India became an independent nation on 15 August 1947 and a sovereign, democratic republic after its constitution came into effect on 26 January 1950. A federal parliamentary system was adopted and the first elections were held in 1952. The Indian National Congress (INC) won 364 out of 489 seats in the national parliament, and Jawaharlal Nehru became the first prime minister of independent India, an office that he held continuously till his death in 1964. During much of his lifetime, the INC was overwhelmingly the dominant political party (Joshi and Little, 1994). National elections were held in 1967, and though the INC won the elections again, for the fourth time in succession, its share in total seats fell from 73.1 per cent in 1962 to 53.4 per cent. Following her election as prime minister, Indira Gandhi turned towards more populist policies, with the nationalization of domestically owned commercial banks in 1969, and the adoption of the Monopolies and Restrictive Trade Practices Act, regulating closely the activities of Indian business houses.

In the general elections in 1971, Indira Gandhi and the Congress won a landslide victory, and secured a clear two-thirds majority in parliament. This strong political position of the Congress Party was, however, weakened in the next few years as the economy was hit by a macroeconomic crisis in 1973 and 1974, with a sharp increase in oil prices and worsening inflation. There was increasing unrest in the country, with food riots, student unrest, and industrial disputes, culminating in 1974 in a threatened strike by two million railway employees in the public sector, which was the first political challenge to the national government by a trade union since independence. In 1975, Indira Gandhi declared a national emergency, suspending some democratic rights for two years. In 1977, for reasons which remain murky (Kohli, 2012), she rescinded the emergency and called for new elections. This time, the Congress Party was comprehensively beaten, and a new anti-Indira coalition, led by the Janata Party, came to power. However, this new government was riven with factionalism and power struggles between individuals, leading to its collapse in 1979. Fresh elections were called, and Indira Gandhi returned to power in 1980.

In the early 1980s, there was growing centre–state conflict and communal problems, particularly the separatist (and terrorist) problem among a section of Sikhs in Punjab (Joshi and Little, 1994). In order to quell the separatist problem, Indira Gandhi launched an assault on the Golden Temple, the religious centre of the Sikh religion, which had been taken over by terrorists. In revenge, she was assassinated by her bodyguards in 1984, and her son Rajiv Gandhi became the prime minister and called for new elections. The Congress Party won the 1984 elections with an overwhelming majority, riding on a huge wave of sympathy among the electorate for Rajiv Gandhi. However, the earlier support for the Congress dissipated over time, with growing regional and ethnic assertiveness, and allegations of corruption. An anti-Congress political front began to emerge, and in the 1989 general elections the Congress suffered an embarrassing defeat. A coalition of parties, led by the Janata Dal, formed a minority government with outside support from the Hindu nationalist party, the Bharatiya Janata Party (BJP). This government did not last for very long, however, as the BJP withdrew its support and new elections were held in 1991, and the Congress came back to power.

In the political space, this long episode represents a period when Indian democracy really established its roots. It underwent a transition from its infancy after the country's independence, when the polity was defined by a single party, to a multiparty system. In other words, India's political settlement decisively moved away from a dominant party settlement, when the Congress Party was hegemonic for the first four decades after independence, towards a more competitive political settlement.

RENTS SPACE

In Chapter 1, the rents space was characterized by four kinds of economic sector, i.e. the rentiers, powerbrokers, magicians, and workhorses. The defining characteristics of these sectors are their capacity to generate rents through discretionary regulation or other government actions (as opposed to leaving the firms open to market competition) and whether the main market is international (i.e. exports, as opposed to a domestic market). Thus the export-oriented discretionary rent-driven sectors are rentiers, while the internationally competitive exporting sectors are magicians. Likewise, we define the monopolistic or oligopolistic domestic market-oriented or non-tradeable sectors that generate high rents as powerbrokers, while the competitive, domestic market-oriented sectors are workhorses. It may be noted that corresponding to the framework in Chapter 1, all sectors of production that are in the public sector are considered to be generating policy-induced rent. Following this assumption, we characterize these sectors as either rentiers or powerbrokers, depending on whether they cater mostly to international or domestic markets. Also, while most sectors fall under the same classification in all three episodes, a few of them do shift from one classification to another over the episodes, because their defining characteristics change significantly. For example, we categorize the mining sector output for the first two episodes as powerbrokers, since they focus mainly on domestic markets during this period. However, in the third episode, public- and private-sector output from mining etc. is categorized as rentier, since they are mainly concerned with exports of these commodities.[2]

Since the rentiers are mainly the natural resource sectors when they are exporting these commodities, we have no rentiers during the first episode. Similarly, the absence of any significant competitive export sector implies the absence of the magician sector. During this episode, (i) mining, (ii) railways, (iii) banking and insurance, and (iv) public administration are considered to be fully in the public sector and hence categorized as powerbrokers. In fact, the public sector in all other sectors is also included in the powerbroker sector. In the private sector, registered manufacturing (which is non-competitive and non-exporting during this period), electricity, gas, and water supply (which are monopolies), and communication (again monopolies during this period) are also considered to be powerbrokers. The rest of the sectors (including agriculture and unregistered manufacturing) are considered to be workhorses.

The rents space is usefully represented in terms of a diamond (see Chapter 1). In order to capture the rents space over the significantly long first growth episode, we have studied it at two points of time, 1960–1 and 1980–1. These are represented graphically in Figures 9.3 and 9.4. These figures show that, while there were no rentiers and magicians during this episode, the share of workhorses was very large, followed by a significant powerbroker sector that was made up mostly by the public sector. Over the episode, the share of the workhorse sector showed a significantly declining trend, from 83.53 per cent in 1960–1 to 73.06 per cent in 1980–1. Correspondingly, the powerbroker sector's share witnessed a sharp increase, from 16.47 per cent in 1960–1 to 26.94 per cent in 1980–1.

Figures 9.5 and 9.6 shed light on the rents space by depicting the export structure during this period. During the first growth episode, India's export

[2] It should be noted that the categorization we use to classify sectors as rentiers, powerbrokers, magicians, and workhorses are indicative rather than precise. For example, we classify an entire sector as either export-oriented or producing for the domestic market when there may be a mix of export-oriented and domestically oriented activity in the same sector. We do not have sufficiently disaggregated data on the economic sector to allow us to ascertain with any level of confidence which proportion of the sector is export-oriented and which proportion is domestically oriented (some sectoral exports data are available, but they are the total value of exports of these sectors, while the output data are value-added). The only exception is the business services sector, where data are available (for the ICT sector, which is its main component) that has made this disaggregation possible.

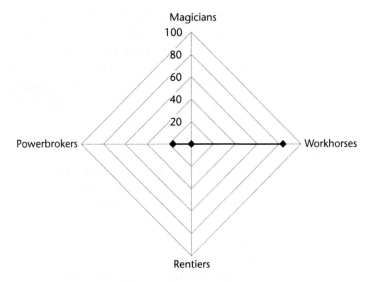

Figure 9.3. India's rents space, 1960–1 (% share)
Source: Authors' calculations based on data from *National Accounts Statistics*, CSO.

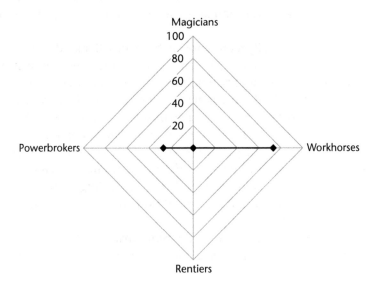

Figure 9.4. India's rents space, 1980–1 (% share)
Source: Authors' calculations based on data from *National Accounts Statistics*, CSO.

structure was dominated by primary products, which are characterized as less complex products, as measured by the Economic Complexity Index (Hidalgo et al., 2007). Agriculture and allied products, and ready-made garments, were the major export earners. Also, ores and minerals were among the largest exporting sectors in this period in the early 1960s. By the 1980s, there were

Total: $1.55 billion

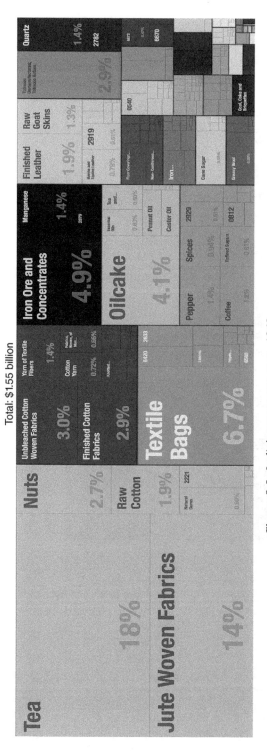

Figure 9.5. India's export structure, 1962

Source: Atlas of Economic Complexity <http://atlas.cid.harvard.edu/>.

Total: $6.88 billion

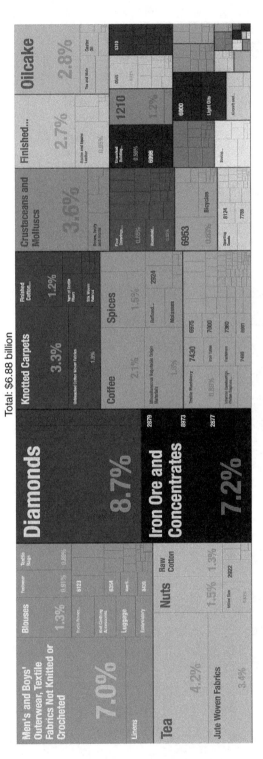

Figure 9.6. India's export structure, 1980
Source: Atlas of Economic Complexity <http://atlas.cid.harvard.edu/>.

a few changes, with diamonds, iron ore, and textiles becoming the major export items.[3]

DEALS ENVIRONMENT

India created one of the most comprehensively controlled and regulated economies in the developing world after independence. As a consequence:

> the Indian elite developed a highly sophisticated mode of discrete lobbying designed to achieve particularistic benefits from the new permit, licence, quota raj. Each major business house established the equivalent of an industrial embassy designed to act as a listening post, liaison office and lobbying agency to deal with political and bureaucratic decision makers. (Kochanek, 1996: 157)

With an almost non-existent magician sector, there was very little mutual confidence between the government and business sector, leading to a lack of trust in any deal that the state might offer. In addition, the nature of the command and control system meant that most of the energies and time of the private sector (including business associations) went into preparing representations to the government demanding changes and modifications in regulatory policies. As Bhagwati (1993: 50) points out:

> the industrial-cum-licensing system . . . had degenerated into a series of arbitrary, indeed inherently arbitrary, decisions where, for instance, one activity would be chosen over another simply because the administering bureaucrats were so empowered, and indeed obligated, to choose.

This led to a disordered deals environment that contributed significantly to low rates of private investment and slow economic growth all through the 1960s and 1970s.

The nature of state–business relations started changing very gradually from the early 1980s. As De Long (2003), Rodrik and Subramanian (2004), and Kohli (2006) have argued, there was a change in the attitudes of the national government under the prime ministership of Indira Gandhi towards the private sector, from being anti-business to being pro-business when she returned to power in 1980. Rodrik and Subramanian (2004: 3) argue that this attitudinal shift 'left little paper trail in actual policies but had an important impact on investors' psychology'. De Long (2003: 203) argues that 'the most important factor that changed in India over the 1980s had more to do with entrepreneurial attitudes and a belief that the rules of the game had changed than with individual policy moves'. Similarly, Kohli (2006: 1255) states that 'Indira Gandhi shifted India's political economy around 1980 in

---

[3] It should be kept in mind that India was a closed economy all through the 1950s to the mid-1980s, with the export to output ratio being less than 15 per cent in this period.

the direction of a state and business alliance for economic growth'. Further, Kohli (2012: 30–1) notes:

> just after coming to power in January 1980, . . . Indira Gandhi let it be known that improving production was now her top priority. In meeting after meeting with private industrialists, she clarified that what the government was most interested in was production.

By the late 1980s, the macro-level deals environment had already become distinctly 'ordered' and more open, with the emergence of new economic elites in both modern sectors and in regions outside the industrial heartlands of Gujarat and Maharashtra. This was reflected in changes in economic policies, such as the half-hearted reforms of industrial and trade policies, especially from the mid-1980s. The shift in the deals environment from disordered in the 1960s to early 1980s, to a relatively ordered one in the late 1980s, was the crucial enabling factor behind the increase in private investment in equipment in the same period, and the subsequent recovery in economic growth.

Interestingly, the disordered deals environment during the first growth episode coincided with a period of India's political history when the Congress Party was dominant. With the dominance that the Congress Party enjoyed, it should have been possible for the ruling political elites to offer deals to the private sector that were ordered. Why did a disordered deals environment result from a dominant party political system such as the one that characterized the Indian polity for much of the first growth episode?

There are two reasons why a disordered deals environment occurred, even with the strong dominance that the Congress Party enjoyed for much of the 1950s to 1980s. First, the nature of the licence raj system and the high levels of discretion accorded to bureaucrats led to a great deal of ad hoc activity in the nature of deals offered. Second, the Soviet inspiration of state-led industrialization played an important role in the development thinking of the day, especially under Nehruvian socialism (Mehta and Walton, 2014; Mukherji, 2014). As a consequence, the ruling political elites believed that the public sector was the key to economic development, and did not have faith in the private corporate sector's ability to play an equal role to the public sector in driving economic growth.[4] This led to a lack of credible commitment on the part of the Congress Party to the deals that might have been offered to the private sector, especially large business houses (in contrast to the manner in which the South Korean political elite offered ordered deals to *chaebols* for much of South Korea's early growth phase).

---

[4] The lack of faith in the private sector was a legacy of the fight against British imperialism during the fight for independence (Mehta and Walton, 2014). In addition, the high growth rates of the Soviet empire during the 1940s and 1950s also led to faith in the model of public sector-driven growth.

Rodrik and Subramanian (2004) note that Indira Gandhi's attitudinal change was primarily grounded in political calculation. As they state, 'Indira's main objective was to counter the perceived threat posed by the Janata Party, which had trounced Congress in the Hindi heartland in the 1977 elections' (2004: 13). Using the terminology introduced in Chapter 1, the vertical distribution of political power became less concentrated in the Congress Party in the early 1980s, with increasing challenge from other political elites (comprising the non-Congress political parties). For Indira Gandhi, a shift from a populist strategy to a more private sector- and growth-oriented strategy became a mechanism of political survival.

Therefore, the shift in the political space that occurred in the early 1980s led to a growing alliance between the political and economic elites (Corbridge and Harriss, 2000; Kohli, 2012; Mehta and Walton, 2014). With the shift in state–business relations from being collusive to being more collaborative, the Indian state clearly signalled to domestic capitalists its intention to commit credibly to an environment where private enterprise would be supported and growth-enhancing policies followed. With the change in the attitude of the state towards the private sector in the 1980s, there was an active encouragement of the state towards peak business associations, such as the Federation of Indian Chambers of Commerce and Industry and the Confederation of Indian Industries, to transform themselves into developmental business associations (Sinha, 2005).

The shift in the relationship between political and economic elites, from one of mutual distrust to a more collaborative and synergistic relationship, was further accentuated with the coming to power of Rajiv Gandhi in 1985. Gandhi took particular interest in modern sectors, such as ICT and engineering, and tried to bring in new economic elites from these emerging sectors into the relationship that the political elite had with the business sector. In addition, with the rise of non-traditional business groups in southern and western India, there was a growing diversification of business ownership, leading to a broadening of the political connectivity of the business elite (Mehta and Walton, 2014).[5]

9.3.3 *The Second Growth Episode (1993–4 to 2001–2)*

POLITICAL SETTLEMENT

We have seen that India's political settlement has decisively moved away from a dominant party settlement during which the Congress Party was hegemonic for the first four decades after independence (except for a brief period in the

---

[5] A more detailed account of the first growth episode is in Kar and Sen (2016). They argue that the deals environment was gradually becoming ordered in the second half of the 1980s. However, as they show, while the increasingly ordered deals environment played a facilitating role in the nascent growth recovery in the 1980s, it is only after 1992 that the average growth rate changes (upward) sufficiently to fulfil the condition for a growth transition.

1970s, when they were in opposition, mostly as a backlash among the electorate due to the emergency). In the 1990s, there was a variety of national-level
political experiments to find a substitute for old Congress Party rule, with the
decline in hegemony of the Congress, especially by the emergence of the
BJP (Kohli, 2001). As a consequence, the country moved to a competitive
political settlement, with two or more political groups jockeying for power,
and where no political party (and its allies) was assured of victory in the
national elections.

During this episode, along with a move to a more competitive political
system, another very important political change took place in the realm of
political thought. This was a shift in the ideas and beliefs of Indian political
elites, from a deep suspicion of the market and the private sector to a more
pro-business orientation. This shift occurred across the political divide.
Among the two dominant political parties, the right-of-centre BJP was more
pro-market than the Congress, but with its nationalist leanings, was suspi-
cious of foreign investors and, therefore, resistant to the easing of restrictions
on foreign direct and portfolio investment. The left-of-centre Congress had
been historically anti-business, but had become markedly pro-market under
the leadership of Narasimha Rao (who was prime minister during 1991–6).
Therefore, while the crisis of 1991 (triggered by the Gulf War) was the immediate reason for the economic reforms that were initiated in the same year,
there were clear signs of gradual changes in the ideas and beliefs of political
elites towards market-oriented economic policies since the early 1980s. As
Mehta and Walton (2014: 30) note, 'the policy changes on de-licensing and
trade liberalization can be seen as a product of the confluence of a changing
cognitive map of state elites, and an evolving, rather than a radical, shift in the
relationship with business interests'.[6]

One important implication of the shift in the ideas and beliefs of political
elites towards a widely held view that market-oriented economic policies are
essential for India's rapid economic development was that economic reforms
were not rolled back whenever a new government took power, whether at the
central or state levels. This meant that deals that were struck with the business
elite by the previous political party, when it was in power, were mostly not
overturned when a new government was elected. Thus, deals remained
ordered, even with the rapid turnover of political parties, both at the central
and state levels in the 1990s and 2000s, and there has been a move to a
competitive political settlement since the early 1990s.

---

[6] A similar point is made by Mukherji (2014), who argues that challenges to old ideas (around
state-driven industrialization) evolved gradually, as these ideas did not deliver desired benefits, till
they reached a tipping point with the 1991 economic reforms.

The shift in the ideas and beliefs of political elites (and hence, in the political space) towards a more pro-business orientation led to a growing diversification of business ownership, along with a widening of the political connectivity that Indian economic elites had with political elites. There were new patterns of entry into business, often from traditionally non-business castes or groups, especially in southern and western India (Damodaran, 2008). There were also examples of new entrepreneurs, who were not from the traditional economic elite, emerging in industries such as pharmaceuticals and ICT, and service sectors such as telecommunications, mutual funds, and banking. For example, 'Sunil Mittal secured licenses for mobile operations in 1992 when cash-rich government companies, the Tata group and Reliance, had not seen much potential in the sector' (Mukherji, 2014: 23). Similar stories of entrepreneurs who were not born into wealth becoming quickly successful in the 1993–2001 growth episode are observed with Sun Pharma and Dr Reddy's Laboratories in pharmaceuticals, and Infosys and Hindustan Computers Ltd in ICT. Thus, in the 1990s, state–business relations became more inclusive, as both new state actors and economic elites came into the fray for the first time.

RENTS SPACE

Since there are no major natural resources exporting sectors during this episode, there are no rentiers during the second episode. Parts of the business services sector (mainly ICT) become an internationally competitive exports sector and hence are characterized as magicians during this episode. Together with business services, the registered manufacturing sector (which becomes increasingly competitive and exporting following the reforms in 1991) is also considered to comprise magicians during this episode. On the other hand, (i) mining, (ii) railways, and (iii) public administration are deemed to be fully in the public sector and hence considered powerbrokers. Banking was in the public and private sectors during this episode. However, even in the private sector, banking is assumed to be a powerbroker sector, due to the oligopolistic nature of this sector. In the private sector (apart from banking), electricity, gas and water supply (monopolies), and communication (again monopolies) are considered to be powerbrokers. The rest of the sectors (including agriculture and unregistered manufacturing) are considered workhorses.

Since this episode is relatively short, we analyse the rents space using a diamond figure for one year, i.e. 1996–7, roughly the mid-term of the episode. As in the first growth episode, there are no rentiers in the second growth episode. The share of magicians goes up considerably (Figure 9.7) compared with the first episode. More specifically, this sector's share in total GDP increased from 0 per cent in 1980–1 to 7.88 per cent in 1996–7. The share of

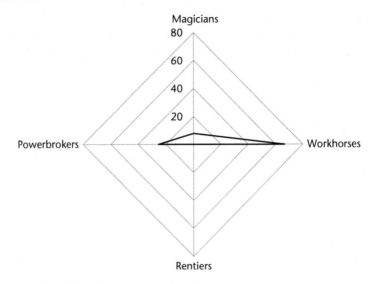

Figure 9.7. India's rents space, 1996–7

Source: Authors' calculations based on data from *National Accounts Statistics*, CSO.

powerbrokers does not change significantly during this period, decreasing very slightly to 25.43 per cent. In contrast, the workhorse sector's share declines (from 73.06 per cent in 1980–1) to 66.68 per cent in 1996–7.

India's export structure changed significantly by the beginning of the second growth episode. Labour-intensive manufactured products, like ready-made garments and footwear, became increasingly important in India's export mix. Over time, agriculture and allied products have become less important, while diamonds and lubricating petroleum have become major sectors for exports during this episode (see Figure 9.8).

Hidalgo et al. (2007) view structural transformation as the upgrading of products in a country's economic structure such that firms in that country move over time to more complex products. They also view high-rent extractive sectors as less complex on the product space. Following this view, and using data on product complexity from the *Atlas of Economic Complexity*,[7] we plot the five-year moving average of product complexity for India between 1993–4 and 2007–8 in Figure 9.9. We find that structural transformation (as captured by increasing product complexity) mostly increased during the 1993–2002 growth episode.

---

[7] Online resource: <http://atlas.cid.harvard.edu/>.

Total: $35.5 billion

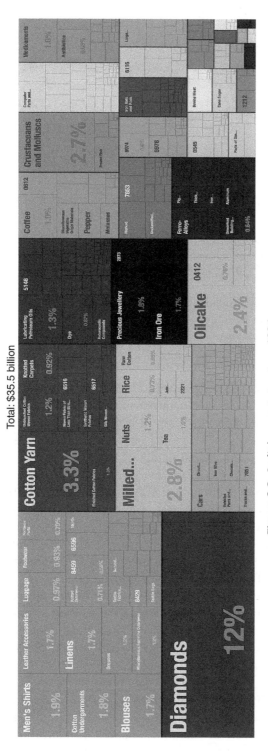

Figure 9.8. India's export structure, 1996
Source: Atlas of Economic Complexity <http://atlas.cid.harvard.edu/>.

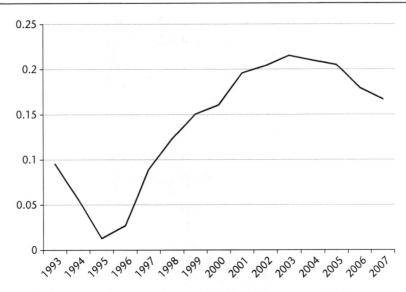

Figure 9.9. Measure of structural transformation (Hausmann–Hidalgo measure of product complexity), five-year moving average for India

Source: Authors' calculations, from *Atlas of Economic Complexity* <http://atlas.cid.harvard.edu/>.

DEALS ENVIRONMENT

As we discussed in Section 9.3.2, there was already a shift to ordered deals by the late 1980s, and a more collaborative relationship between the state and business, with an attitudinal change from anti-business to pro-business on the part of the Indian ruling elite. Two further developments in the early 1990s led to a strengthening of the ordered nature of the deals environment, particularly at the micro level.

First, the dismantling of the industrial licensing system in 1991 removed an important source of 'disorder' in the deals environment at the micro level. This development ensured that the approval of applications that firms made for their expansion, or that new firms made to enter the industrial sector during the previous licensing regime, no longer depended on the whims and fancies of individual bureaucrats in the government.

Second, the removal of the import licensing system in the early 1990s for most commodities also meant that the highly discretionary and case-by-case nature of goods that were allowed to be imported was done away with. The growth acceleration of 1993 was in great part due to the 'ordered deals' environment that had already taken shape in the 1980s and was enhanced by the dismantling of the industrial-cum-trade licensing system in 1991. These deals were largely open, as barriers to entry to many industries were removed. This was reflected in the entry of new firms in manufacturing and services, and especially in pharmaceuticals and ICT (Alfaro and Chari, 2009).

At the same time, the Indian state's collusive relationship with certain sections of the business elite in the pre-reform period remained, and may have been accentuated by the rise of increasingly powerful regional business groups that were closely connected with regional political elites. Thus, during the 1990s, closed deals existed side by side with open deals and, consequently, many traditional industries (such as consumer durables) were still dominated by entrenched business groups that had emerged in the licence raj (Alfaro and Chari, 2009).

Our argument on the role of the ordering of deals in contributing to India's growth acceleration differs from conventional accounts of the rise in India's economic growth, such as Bhagwati (1993) and Panagariya (2008). In their account of India's economic growth, Bhagwati and Panagariya give primacy to the change in the rules environment as reflected in the economic reforms of 1991. Thus, in their argument, changes in rules (or formal institutions) made it easier for firms to invest and expand their production. While formal institutional change would certainly have contributed to the increase in economic growth, in our view what was more important was the change in the deals environment, which is essentially due to informal institutional change—that is, the informal interactions between economic actors and the political and bureaucratic elite. Therefore, among the gamut of economic reforms that occurred in the early 1990s, the ones that mattered for the first growth acceleration were the delicensing reforms (since they cut down drastically on bureaucratic arbitrariness, making deals much less disordered), along with the changes to the manner in which political elites interacted with the business sector. This led to an ordering of the deals environment that contributed to the greater confidence that the private sector had in the credibility of these deals, leading to an upsurge in corporate investment and, consequently, economic growth.

Furthermore, there is evidence from detailed firm-level analysis of the 1990s of significant opening up of the deals environment, particularly in the corporate sector in this period. Harrison et al. (2012) find a large allocation of market share from less productive firms to more productive firms in the first half of the 1990s, but not in subsequent years. Mody et al. (2011) find significant entry of new firms in virtually all industrial sectors in the early-to-mid-1990s, which stops in the late 1990s, with very little new firm entry in the 2000s.[8] Kathuria et al. (2010) show that improvement in productivity performance in the manufacturing sector in the 1990s was not confined to the formal sector, but encompassed the informal sector as well.

---

[8] However, as Goldberg et al. (2010) show, much of the product churning in the 1990s was due to product additions rather than product shedding. In this sense, India's experience of the 1990s with 'creative destruction' was more 'creative' and less 'destruction'.

The opening up of the deals space that one observes in the private sector in the 1990s is also reflected in indicators of growth, as we noted in Sections 9.1 and 9.2. Thus, in the 1993–2002 growth acceleration phase, economic growth was mostly driven by magicians (ICT and chemicals) and workhorses (hotels and restaurants). Such a growth strategy, driven by magicians and workhorses, should have led to a further opening up of the deals space. As we will see in the Section 9.3.4, this did not occur in the next growth episode, due to changes in the rents space and in the political space.

9.3.4 The Third Growth Episode (2002–3 to 2010–11)

POLITICAL SETTLEMENT

We have already observed that India's political system became increasingly fragmented in the 1990s. The level of political fractionalization increased sharply in the 1990s, and continued at this high level in the 2000s (Figure 9.10).[9] Along with this, there was a decreasing share of seats of the majority party (no matter which party won the elections). This is because of the rise of regional parties, such as the Dravida Munnetra Kazhagam and All India Anna Dravida Munnetra Kazhagam in Tamil Nadu, Shiv Sena in

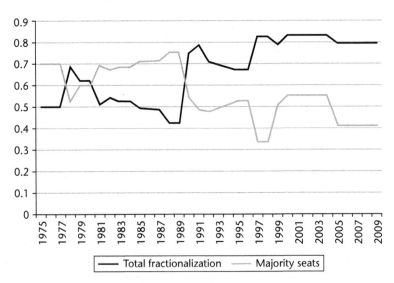

Figure 9.10. Measures of total fractionalization and proportion of seats won by the majority party, national elections in India, 1975–2009

Source: The Quality of Government Data <http://qog.pol.gu.se/data>.

---

[9] We measure fractionalization by the probability that two randomly drawn members of parliament are from the same political party.

Table 9.5. Seats held by political parties in national elections in India, 1952–2009

Year	INC	BJP	Left	JD + BLD	Others	Share of ruling party in total seats (%)	Share of others (%)	Ruling party
1952	364	0	16	0	21	90.8	5.2	INC
1957	371	0	27	0	5	92.1	1.2	INC
1962	361	0	29	0	104	73.1	21.1	INC
1967	283	0	42	0	215	52.4	39.8	INC
1971	352	0	48	0	118	68.0	22.8	INC
1977	154	0	29	295	65	54.3	12.0	JP
1980	353	0	47	72	71	65.0	13.1	INC
1984	415	2	28	10	88	76.4	16.2	INC
1989	197	85	45	143	73	26.3	13.4	JD-led coalition
1991	244	120	49	59	71	44.9	13.1	INC, minority govt
1996	140	161	44	46	152	8.5	28.0	JD-led coalition
1998	141	182	41	0	179	29.7	33.0	BJP +
1999	114	182	37	0	210	33.5	38.7	BJP +
2004	145	138	53	0	207	26.7	38.1	INC +
2009	206	116	20	0	201	37.9	37.0	INC +

Source: Election Commission of India.

Notes: INC: Indian National Congress; BJP: Bharatiya Janata Party; JP: Janata Party; BLD: Bharatiya Lok Dal; JD: Janata Dal. Party name followed by + indicates alliances centred around that party.

Maharashtra, the Janata Dal-U in Bihar, the Biju Janata Dal in Odisha, and Trinamul Congress in West Bengal (Table 9.5). No ruling party had more than 40 per cent of the seats in the Lok Sabha in the first decade of the 2000s. At the same time, there was a frequent change of the ruling party at the centre, with the BJP and the Congress both being in power in the period 2002–10 (Table 9.5).

The regional parties became important components of the ruling coalition in the 2000s, and exerted a significant influence on what the main ruling party (whether the Congress or the BJP) could or could not do. Thus, unlike the classic competitive political settlements that characterize political systems in many parts of the world (such as Bangladesh and Ghana), India's political system became multipolar, rather than bipolar (Varshney, 1999). As a consequence, the number of regional parties officially recognized in the national elections increased from 11 in 1957 to 30 in 2009, and the total number of recognized parties increased from fifteen in 1957 to 230 in 2009.

These changes in the political space had two specific effects on the deals environment. First, given the veto power exerted by numerically small but powerful groups of politicians in regional parties that comprised ruling coalitions in the 2000s, the deals that economic elites had to strike with political elites increasingly accommodated the interests of these parties, with implications for the open nature of these deals. With the increased fractionalization of the political system at the national level, and the growing importance of regional political elites in the coalition governments of the 2000s, 'closed deals' between these elites and powerful economic interests, both at the national and regional levels, become more prevalent in the post-2002 period. This was accentuated by the rapid turnover of governments and closely contested elections, both at the national and regional levels, which led to a shortening of the time horizon of political elites, who were more interested in finding ways to extract rents to finance elections that they would have to fight in the immediate future. Second, again due to the increased fractionalization, election campaigns became increasingly expensive, as political parties in the competitive Indian political system tried to outspend each other to attract voters with various inducements. Reforms in Indian election expenditure laws in 1975 and 2003 put the expenditures of parties and supporters of individual candidates outside the purview of the expenditure limits on these candidates and banned corporate donations. This led to increased informal financing of election campaigns, and a greater reliance on informal deals to finance costly election campaigns. This was also reflected in the increasing participation of criminals in electoral politics, as political parties preferred wealthy candidates with 'deep pockets' to finance their own campaigns. The growing reliance of informal private funding in the absence of state funding also meant that parties and politicians raised funds from businesses informally in return for discretionary contracts and regulatory favours (Gowda and Sridharan, 2012).

RENTS SPACE

In the third episode, natural resources become an exporting sector and hence, this is considered to be a rentier sector. Business services (mainly ICT) and the registered manufacturing sector continue to be considered as magicians. Railways and public administration are still fully in the public sector and hence considered to be powerbrokers. Mining and banking are both in private and public sectors during this episode. As mentioned earlier, in the private sector, mining is considered to be a rentier sector, while banking is assumed to be a powerbroker sector. In the private sector, apart from banking, electricity, gas and water supply, and communication, the construction and real estate sectors enter the powerbroker sector due to the entry of large established firms that get significant incentives from the government (which are rent-generating) in order to develop these sectors. The remaining sectors are workhorses.

Like the second episode, the third episode is also relatively short, and hence we analyse the rents space using a diamond figure for one year, i.e. 2005–6—roughly the mid-term of this episode (Figure 9.11). In the third growth episode, the rentier sector makes an entry in the rents space of the Indian economy, although its share in GDP is quite modest, at 2.64 per cent. During this episode, both magicians and powerbrokers increase their share at the cost of the workhorse sector. In particular, the magician sector increases its

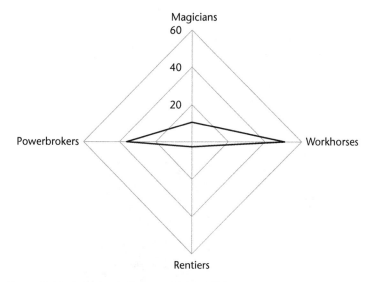

Figure 9.11. India's rents space, 2005–6 (%)
Source: Authors' calculations, based on data from *National Accounts Statistics*, CSO.

share from 7.88 per cent in 1996–7 (the second episode) to 10.61 in 2005–6. During that same period, the powerbroker sector increases its share from 25.43 per cent to 36.13 per cent. Conversely, by 2005–6, the workhorse sector's share has declined to 50.59 per cent.

As evident from Figure 9.12, in the third regime, engineering goods (cars, etc.) have become a larger export earner, while diamonds (cutting), chemicals, and related products have also remained important. However, the share of petroleum products in total merchandise exports increased significantly in this period. There was a sharp increase in the share of exports from the rentier sector, such as iron ore, and a decrease in the share of exports from magician sectors, such as textiles and garments.

To sum up, the share of workhorses has declined, whereas magicians' share has increased consistently in all the growth episodes. Furthermore, the share of powerbrokers has gone up considerably. Unlike the previous growth regimes, rentiers are present in the third episode, though their share is small.

What happened to structural transformation during this period? Figure 9.9 shows that it fell during the 2002–10 episode, indicating a move away from complex products. The move away from more complex products in the 2002–10 period was also obvious in India's export structure. In the early 1990s, before the reforms, agriculture and allied products, gems and jewellery, and ready-made garments were the biggest merchandise export earners (Table 9.6). Over time, agriculture and allied products and ready-made garments have become less important for the exports sector, while gems and

Total: $99.7 billion

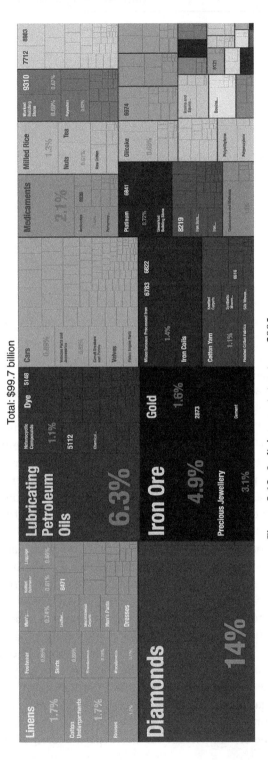

Figure 9.12. India's export structure, 2005

Source: Atlas of Economic Complexity <http://atlas.cid.harvard.edu/>.

Table 9.6. India's merchandise exports, 1990–2010 (% of total exports in commodities)

	1990–1	2000–1	2010–11
Agricultural products	14.57	9.66	6.36
Ores and minerals	4.21	1.87	2.27
Petroleum products	2.27	3.02	10.89
Leather	6.29	3.15	1.03
Chemicals	7.50	9.52	7.59
Engineering goods	9.77	11.03	15.29
Machinery and instruments	3.02	2.56	3.11
Transport equipment	3.02	2.56	3.11
Textiles	5.08	5.60	1.52
Garments	9.71	9.01	3.05
Gems and jewellery	12.70	11.94	10.64
Other commodities	21.85	30.09	35.13
Natural resource exports	21.04	14.55	19.53
Non-natural resource exports	78.96	85.45	80.47

Source: Reserve Bank of India, authors' calculations.

Note: Natural resource exports = agricultural products + ores and minerals + petroleum products.

jewellery have remained a major sector. During the same period, engineering goods have become a major export earner, while chemicals and related products have also remained important. However, since 2000–1, the share of petroleum products in total merchandise exports has increased significantly. As Figure 9.12 makes clear, there was a sharp increase in the share of exports from the rentier sector, such as refined petroleum, and a decrease in the share of exports from magician sectors, such as pharmaceuticals.

DEALS ENVIRONMENT

There was a shift in the deals environment in this period, from relatively open to much more closed deals. This was most evident in the increasing level of 'crony capitalist' deals that political elites struck with economic elites in 'high-rent' natural resource sectors, such as bauxite, coal, iron ore, manganese ore, and natural gas, at both national and regional levels. In various ore-rich states, such as Jharkhand, Karnataka, Goa, and Odisha, influential, politically connected business elites systematically underpaid mining royalties to state agencies (along with extracting iron and bauxite in excess of the amounts stipulated by the leases that the private mining firms held with the state governments). There was a succession of such scams, highlighted by the media. In 2010, the central government constituted a commission to investigate irregularities in the extraction, trade, and transportation of iron ore and manganese ore across the country. It was headed by Justice M. B. Shah of the Supreme Court of India. The Shah Commission found evidence of 'enormous and large-scale multi-stage illegal mining of iron ore and manganese ore running into thousands of crores of rupees every year' (Shah Commission,

2012: 1). The commission also found clear evidence of collusion between ruling politicians at the state and national level and private mining firms, stating that 'the State has "gifted" property of thousands of crores in the hands of private companies/firms/individuals' (Shah Commission, 2012: 604). There were similar concerns over the allocation of licences for coal deposit blocks to private firms by central government in the period 2004–11, which was done preferentially at lower than market rates, instead of via a competitive bidding process, according to investigations on the nature of the allocation process by the Comptroller and Auditor General (CAG).

The existence of 'closed deals' was not confined only to natural resource sectors; it was also evident in an infrastructural sector such as telecommunications. The latter witnessed impressive growth in the 1993–2002 growth episode, driven by high demand for mobile phones among a rapidly expanding middle class. In 2008, the Department of Telecommunications (DoT) decided to allocate second-generation (2G) spectrum licences to mobile phone operators on a first-come, first-served basis at a price significantly below the market price. Later investigation by the CAG found clear evidence of insider information being passed to selected private firms on the timing of the first-come, first-served announcement, as well as the very short time given to submit the applications (Guha Thakurta and Kaushal, 2010). The CAG (2011) also found irregularities in the selective interpretation by the DoT of the recommendation of the telecommunications regulator, the Telecom Regulatory Authority of India, which led it not to conduct a competitive bidding process for the award of the 2G licences. The CAG estimated the loss to the Indian exchequer due to the under-pricing of 2G licences at over US$26 billion.

There were two economic factors behind the emergence of a closed deals environment in the post-2002 growth episode, as compared with a more open deals environment in the earlier growth episode. First, with increased Chinese demand for minerals, there was a sharp increase in commodity prices in the early-to-mid-2000s. Consequently, increasing rents could be extracted in natural resource sectors, where the state had the power to allocate licences for production to private firms. In contrast, after the 1991 economic reforms, licences were no longer required to start operations in manufacturing or services sectors such as ICT. Therefore, there were clear incentives for political elites to allocate these licences preferentially to selected economic elites on terms that were not transparent, or the most economically competitive, in return for extra-legal monetary rewards. Second, as rapid economic growth in the previous growth episode spurred an increase in demand for the services of infrastructural sectors such as telecommunications (naturally oligopolistic and characteristically high rent), political elites entered into rent-sharing arrangements with business groups that were awarded contracts to operate in these sectors. Strong private-sector growth fuelled a similar surge in demand

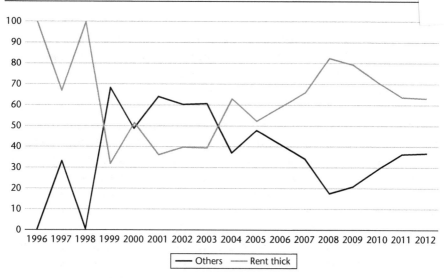

Figure 9.13. Distribution of wealth of billionaires by sources of wealth, India, 1996–2012 (%)

Source: Gandhi and Walton (2012).

for commercial real estate, and there were increasing signs of 'closed deals' between political elites and real estate developers in the allocation of land for commercial real estate (Nagaraj, 2013).

The evidence for closed deals is clear from Figure 9.13, where one observes a clear increase in the proportion of wealth of Indian billionaires originating in rentier and powerbroker sectors (primarily real estate, construction, mining, and infrastructure), as compared with the magician sector (manufacturing, ICT), from 2002.

9.4 Conclusion

After decades of slow growth, when India achieved its first growth acceleration in 1993, analysts dubbed it the 'elephant economy'. The idea was that, like the elephant, the Indian economy had been taking a slow stroll for some time, but when it chose to move faster, others had to sit up and take notice. Stretching that imagery for the three growth episodes that we have described in this chapter, it is insightful to see them as the stroll, the trot, and finally the sprint of the elephant.

The characterization of the last episode as a sprint is also appropriate for another reason, namely that it describes running at full speed, but only over a short distance. In a sense, this is what happened during the third episode, which gave rise to very high growth rates for a time, but which, by 2010, started slowing down. The figures for growth corresponding to this period are available partly from sources based on an old definition of GDP and partly from a new definition of GDP. According to the old definition, which is available till 2014–15, there was a significant slowdown post-2010–11, with the GDP growth rates falling from close to 9 per cent in that year to a low of less than 5 per cent in 2013–14. The figures based on the new definition are available from 2012–13 onwards, and these seem to suggest that there has been a partial recovery from 2014–15 onwards. Irrespective of the definition chosen, there is a clear slowdown in the growth rates after 2010–11.

An analysis of this growth slowdown shows how 'feedback effects' that are generated as a part of the growth process lead to changes in the deals environment, and this in turn can affect the growth process itself. We described in Section 9.3.4 how the nature of exogenous growth stimuli and the effects of the growth in the second episode led to a 'closing up' of the deals space during the third episode. This led to 'crony capitalistic' outcomes and cases of corruption involving the political and the business elites during this episode.

The negative political feedback from this on the deals space was immediate. As media accounts of corruption became widespread, and there was growing popular discontent at the flagrantly excessive levels of rents that were shared between political and economic elites in these deals, state legitimacy was being gradually eroded towards the end of the 2002–10 growth episode. There was also strong social and political mobilization of the masses against attempts by the political elite in states such as Odisha and West Bengal to obtain land through extra-legal and often coercive means for mining or for providing land to large business groups to set up manufacturing plants. In addition, there was strong pushback from accountability institutions, such as a ban on iron ore exports by the Indian Supreme Court, and the investigations of corruption in the allocation of 2G and coal block licences by the CAG of India. All these developments made the 'closed deals' environment unsustainable towards the end of the first decade of the 2000s. In addition, with the increasing uncertainty on the nature of deals, and where the ruling party at the centre lacked the authority to commit credibly to new deals in the face of both popular and legal challenges, deals became increasingly disordered as well. The result of all these was the slowdown of investment and growth rates.[10]

---

[10] The slowdown in India's economic growth coincided with an overall slowdown in economic activity globally. However, while the global slowdown and the resultant recessionary expectations are definitely important factors behind India's growth slowdown since 2010, the IMF (2014) found that two-thirds of India's slowdown was due to internal problems, and not to a worsening external environment. As Kar and Sen (2016) argue, the slowdown in growth in India was mostly due to a shift from ordered to disordered deals, and the resultant decrease in private investment with the increased uncertainty among investors, as the government lacked the authority to commit credibly to new deals in the face of both popular and legal challenges.

The gradual loss of credibility of the United Progressive Alliance (led by the Congress), the paralysis in the institutional arrangements, and the slowdown in growth all prepared the background for a historical election in 2014. After an intense electoral battle, Indian voters gave a decisive mandate for a new government under the National Democratic Alliance (led by the BJP).

With this new beginning, the pertinent question is whether the growth rates of the economy will revive and be sustained in the medium run. The answer will lie in the interactions between future political settlements and rents spaces and their effect on the deals environment. We have seen that, over time, the political settlement in India has moved increasingly towards fragmentation and competitive clientelism. This usually interacts with a rising and dominant powerbroker sector, as we find in India, to give rise to closed and 'crony capitalistic' deals spaces. This might lead to growth accelerations for a short period, but these will definitely not be sustainable over the long term. The positive development in this context is that in the last elections, the emergence of a single party with a majority in parliament implies a weakening of both fragmentation and competitive clientelism. This has the potential to interact with the rising magicians sector in India that can lead to an 'open and ordered' deals space, resulting in growth acceleration that is also sustainable. If this indeed happens, then the elephant will trot again.

Three implications can be drawn from the Indian experience with growth episodes for the overall framework presented in Chapter 1. First, the shifting ideas and beliefs of elites played a key causal role in explaining why India was stuck in a low-growth trap till 1992, and then witnessed rapid growth acceleration subsequently. In spite of a dominant political settlement for much of the first growth episode, which according to our framework should have been conducive to growth by providing a long-enough time horizon for political elites, the socialist ideology of political elites and their mistrust of the private sector was a major constraint on growth. On the other hand, the shift to a pro-business ideology that was shared by the two main political parties—the INC and BJP—was key to the ordered deals that occurred in the 1990s and 2000s, leading to high rates of growth in these two decades. Second, as the framework of Chapter 1 suggests, it was interaction of the political settlement with the rents space that can explain the movements from one episode to another. While the political settlement had turned decisively competitive by the 1990s, the difference in the deals environment in the second growth episode (which was open ordered) and the third growth episode (which was closed ordered) was the growth of the rentier and powerbroker sectors in the third growth episode that led to the creation of high rents in the economy. Thus, in the third growth episode, the twin forces of high rent creation and political compulsions to raise funds to finance costly elections combined to bring about an increasingly crony capitalist tendency in the Indian economy in the first decade of the 2000s, which had not been evident in the 1990s. The final implication of the Indian experience is that political feedback loops from growth to institutions can turn negative in a fairly short period of time in established democracies such as India, with high deconcentration of vertical power and strong political mobilization by non-elites, as occurred from 2010 onwards. This had the consequence of creating a disordered deals environment, with negative consequences for economic growth. The Indian experience suggests that while a closed ordered deals environment may bring about rapid growth for some time, sustaining such a deals environment in societies with a strong civil society presence and powerful rule-of-law institutions (such as the Indian Supreme Court) can be politically difficult and prone to reversal.

References

Alfaro, L., and Chari, A. 2009. 'India Transformed? Insights from the Firm Level 1988–2005'. NBER Working Papers 15448. Cambridge, MA: National Bureau of Economic Research, Inc.

Bai, J., and Perron, P. 1998. 'Estimating and Testing Linear Models with Multiple Structural Change'. *Econometrica*, 66(1): 47–78.

Balakrishnan, P., and Parameswaran, M. 2007. 'Understanding Economic Growth in India: A Prerequisite'. *Economic and Political Weekly*, 14 July, 43(27–8): 2915–21.

Bhagwati, J. 1993. *India in Transition: Freeing the Economy*. Oxford: Oxford University Press.

CAG (Comptroller and Auditor General). 2011. 'Report No. 19 of 2010–11 for the Period Ended March 2010'. Performance Audit of Issue of Licences and Allocation of 2G Spectrum by the Department of Telecommunications (Ministry of Communications and Information Technology). <http://www.cag.gov.in/sites/default/files/audit_report_files/Union_Performance_Civil_Allocation_2G_Spectrum_19_2010.pdf>.

Corbridge, S., and Harriss, J. 2000. *Reinventing India: Liberalization, Hindu Nationalism and Popular Democracy*. London: Polity Press.

Damodaran, H. 2008. *India's New Capitalists: Caste, Business and Industry in a Modern Nation*. New Delhi: Permanent Black.

De Long, J. B. 2003. 'India since Independence: An Analytical Growth Narrative'. In *In Search of Prosperity: Analytical Narratives on Economic Growth*. Edited by Rodrik, D. Princeton, NJ: Princeton University Press.

Gandhi, A., and Walton, M. 2012. 'Where Do India's Billionaires Get Their Wealth?' *Economic and Political Weekly*, 6 October, 47(40): 1–15.

Ghate, C., and Wright, S. 2012. 'The "V-factor": Distribution, Timing and Correlates of the Great Indian Growth Turnaround'. *Journal of Development Economics*, 99(1): 58–67.

Goldberg, P., Khandelwal, A., Pavnik, N., and Topalova, P. 2010. 'Multi-Product and Product Turnover in the Developing World: Evidence from India'. *Review of Economics and Statistics*, 92(4): 1042–9.

Gowda, R., and Sridharan, E. 2012. 'Reforming India's Party Financing and Election Expenditure Laws'. *Election Law Journal*, 11(2): 226–40.

Guha Thakurta, P., and Kaushal, A. (2010). 'Underbelly of the Great Indian Telecom Revolution'. *Economic and Political Weekly*, 4 December, 45(49): 49–55.

Harrison, A., Martin, L. A., and Nataraj, S. 2012. 'Learning Versus Stealing: How Important are Market-Share Reallocations to India's Productivity Growth?' *World Bank Economic Review*, 27(1): 2012–228.

Hidalgo, C., Klinger, L., Barabasi, A.-L., and Hausmann, R. 2007. 'The Product Space Conditions the Development of Nations'. *Science*, 307: 482–7.

IMF (International Monetary Fund). 2014. 'India: Article IV Consultation'. IMF Country Report No. 14/57. <https://www.imf.org/external/pubs/ft/scr/2014/cr1457.pdf>.

Joshi, V., and Little, I. M. D. 1994. *India: Macroeconomics and Political Economy, 1964–1991*. Delhi: Oxford University Press.

Kar, S., Pritchett, L., Raihan, S., and Sen, K. 2013a. *The Dynamics of Economic Growth: A Visual Handbook of Growth Rates, Regimes, Transitions and Volatility*. Manchester: University of Manchester.

Kar, S., Pritchett, L., Raihan, S., and Sen, K. 2013b. 'Looking for a Break: Identifying Transitions in Growth Regimes'. *Journal of Macroeconomics*, 38: 151–66.

Kar, S., and Sen, K. 2016. *The Political Economy of India's Growth Episodes*. London: Palgrave Macmillan.

Kathuria, V., Raj, R. S. N., and Sen, K. 2010. 'Organised versus Unorganized Manufacturing Performance in the Post-Reform Period'. *Economic and Political Weekly*, 15(24): 55–64.

Kochanek, S. 1996. 'Liberalisation and Business Lobbying in India'. *Journal of Commonwealth and Comparative Politics*, 34(3): 155–93.

Kohli, A. (ed.). 2001. *The Success of India's Democracy*. Cambridge: Cambridge University Press.

Kohli, A. 2006. 'Politics of Economic Growth in India: 1980–2005'. *Economic and Political Weekly*, 61(1): 1251–9.

Kohli, A. 2012. *Poverty amid Plenty in the New India*. Cambridge: Cambridge University Press.

Mehta, P. B., and Walton, M. 2014. 'Ideas, Interests and the Politics of Development Change in India'. ESID Working Paper No. 36. Manchester: University of Manchester.

Mody, A., Nath, A., and Walton, M. 2011. 'Sources of Corporate Profits in India: Business Dynamism or Advantages of Entrenchment?' In *India Policy Forum 2010–2011*. Edited by Bery, S., Bosworth, B., and Panagariya A. Washington, DC: Brookings Institute.

Mukherji, R. 2014. *Political Economy of Reforms in India*. Delhi: Oxford University Press.

Nagaraj, R. 2013. 'India's Dream Run, 2003–2008: Understanding the Boom and Its Aftermath'. *Economic and Political Weekly*, 18 May, 48(20): 10–18.

Panagariya, A. 2008. *India: The Emerging Giant*. New York: Oxford University Press.

Pritchett, L., Sen, K., Kar, S., and Raihan, S. 2016. 'Trillions Gained and Lost: Estimating the Magnitude of Growth Episodes'. *Economic Modelling*, 55: 279–91.

Rodrik, D., and Subramanian, A. 2004. 'From Hindu Growth to Productivity Surge: The Myth of the Indian Growth Transition'. NBER Working Paper No. W10376. Cambridge, MA: National Bureau of Economic Research, Inc.

Sen, K. 2007. 'Why Did the Elephant Start to Trot? India's Growth Acceleration Reexamined'. *Economic and Political Weekly*, 27 October, 42(43): 37–49.

Shah Commission. 2012. 'Final Report on Illegal Mining in the State of Goa, Government of India'.

Sinha, A. 2005. *The Regional Roots of Developmental Politics in India: A Divided Leviathan*. Bloomington, IN: Indiana University Press.

Varshney, A. 1999. 'Mass Politics or Elite Politics: India's Reforms in Comparative Perspective'. In *India in the Era of Economic Reforms*. Edited by Sachs, J. D., Varshney, A., and Bajpai, N. Delhi: Oxford University Press.

10

The Politics of Structural (De)Transformation

The Unravelling of Malaysia and Thailand's Dualistic Deals Strategies

Kunal Sen and Matthew Tyce

10.1 Introduction

In the early 1990s, Malaysia and Thailand looked set to join South Korea, Singapore, and Taiwan among the few developing countries which have successfully made the transition from low-income status to high-income status. During the 1950s to the early 1990s, both countries had growth rates that were among the highest in the world in that period, driven in large part by the rapid growth of an export-oriented manufacturing sector. This growth acceleration phase was accompanied by significant structural transformation, as measured by manufacturing value added as a share of GDP and the product complexity of exports. Outside the East Asian miracle economies, there were few other countries in this period that had such impressive rates of structural transformation.

However, with the onset of the Asian financial crisis (AFC) in 1997, economic growth plummeted in these two countries, as in other countries that had seen rapid growth till that point, such as Indonesia and South Korea. The AFC was itself the result of both external factors (contagion driven by outflows of short-term portfolio capital, leading to a currency crisis) and internal factors (overly optimistic investments in real estate and infrastructure, and the inability of the financial system to monitor these investments) (Jomo, 1998; Lauridsen, 1998; Wade, 1998; Kaminsky and Reinhart, 2000). It was widely believed that the recession caused by the AFC would be short-lived and that economic growth would return to Malaysia and Thailand once stabilization and reform measures that were undertaken in these two countries in the aftermath of the crisis had a positive effect on economic activity. This has not happened, with economic growth in the two decades since the crisis significantly below the rates that were achieved in the growth acceleration phase. The growth deceleration episode from the mid-1990s to date has been accompanied by an investment collapse, stagnating manufacturing exports, and slowing or stagnant rates of structural transformation. Two decades after the AFC, it is clear that the slowdown in economic growth since the AFC is a secular phenomenon and not a short-term outcome of the crisis.

A large literature has studied the growth successes of Malaysia and Thailand prior to the AFC (see Ariff, 1991; Bruton, 1992; Warr, 1993; Agarwal et al., 1995; Agarwal et al., 2000). The conventional narrative in this literature is that Malaysia's and Thailand's superior growth performances are due to the open trading regime and liberal economic policies that these two countries followed, which allowed them to succeed in export-oriented industrialization (see Ariff (1991) for Malaysia, and Warr (1993) for Thailand). However, the conventional narrative that lays emphasis on economic factors does not pay sufficient attention to the fact that relatively closed patronage-based networks and mechanisms between political and economic elites were also important during the rapid growth phases observed in the two countries till the mid-1990s. The conventional narrative is also unable to explain why Malaysia and Thailand underwent prolonged growth slowdown since the AFC (while South Korea recovered quickly from the AFC and returned to rapid growth).

In this chapter, we provide a political economy explanation of Malaysia and Thailand's growth experiences, both of their rapid growth phases prior to the AFC and the subsequent growth slowdown. Using the conceptual framework of Chapter 1, we show that the core explanatory variables—the political settlement, the rents space, the deals space, and feedback loops—can provide a unifying explanation of why growth accelerated in the two countries prior to the mid-1990s, and then subsequently decelerated.

We argue that political elites in these two countries followed a dualistic deals environment in the first growth phase (that is, from the 1960s to the AFC), where they offered open ordered deals to magicians—that is, firms in the export-oriented manufacturing sector—and at the same time offered closed ordered deals to powerbrokers: mostly domestic firms operating in non-tradeable sectors or in manufacturing sectors that were protected to a large extent from foreign competition (and, in the case of Malaysia, to rentiers as well). In the case of Malaysia, the dualistic deals environment was an outcome of the strong dominant party political settlement which attempted to balance the need for political stability (through rents that were created for powerful Malay groups in society via the closed deals with powerbrokers) with the need for high rates of growth that occurred from the open ordered deals offered to magicians. In the case of Thailand, the dualistic deals environment was more a result of a shift to a competitive clientelist political settlement in the 1970s, as well as the means of securing the support of the military and monarchy for the growth strategy followed by Thai political elites.

The dualistic deals environments served Malaysia and Thailand well in the first growth phase, as high growth and fast rates of structural transformation ensued with the rapid expansion of the export-oriented manufacturing sector. However, towards the mid-1990s, negative feedback loops were observed in both countries, with the political settlement in Malaysia moving from strong dominant party to a vulnerable authoritarian political settlement after the AFC, and the competitive clientelist political settlement in Thailand becoming increasingly virulent, culminating in a shift to a vulnerable authoritarian political settlement in the 2000s. In the case of Malaysia, the closed ordered deals that were offered to Malay entrepreneurs, as a means of countering the power of the country's Chinese capitalist class, had largely failed to create a dynamic Malay capitalist class that could compete effectively in world markets. This led to a dualistic industrial structure, with multinationals operating in the export-oriented manufacturing sector and globally uncompetitive Malay conglomerates in the domestically oriented manufacturing and service sectors. In Thailand, local content requirements in the automobiles and electronics sectors had created a large number of Thai companies which successfully became supplier firms to the multinationals operating in these sectors. As a consequence, Thailand observed higher rates of structural transformation, though not at the same pace as in the pre-AFC phase, than Malaysia in their respective growth deceleration episodes. In both countries, the dualistic deals environments had increasingly become patronage-based after the AFC (and, in the case of Malaysia, increasingly disordered), and as a consequence, limited the possibility of high growth returning to Malaysia and Thailand after the economic downturn caused by the AFC.

The chapter is organized as follows. Section 10.2 briefly describes the growth and structural transformation experience of Malaysia and Thailand. We then describe the evolution of the political settlement, the rents space, the deals space, and feedback loops in Malaysia and Thailand in the growth acceleration phase. We then follow the same structure in our discussion of the growth deceleration phase in the two countries. Finally, we present some concluding remarks.

10.2 Economic Growth and Structural Transformation in Malaysia and Thailand

As Figure 10.1 makes clear, both Malaysia and Thailand have had extended growth acceleration periods, both starting in the 1950s and ending in the mid-1990s (1997 in the case of Malaysia and 1996 in the case of Thailand; see

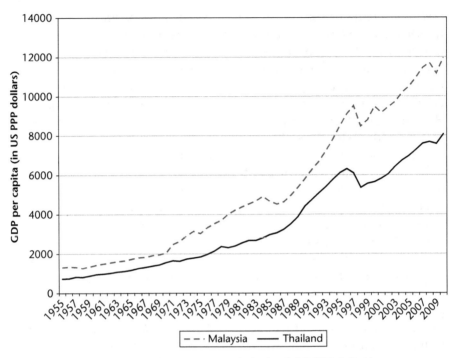

Figure 10.1. Per capita GDP for Malaysia and Thailand (US PPP dollars)
Source: World Bank, *World Development Indicators*.

Kar et al., 2013). In the growth acceleration phase, the annual average growth rate of GDP per capita was 4.9 per cent for Malaysia and 5.7 per cent for Thailand.[1] Beginning in 1997 for Malaysia and 1996 for Thailand, both countries went into a growth deceleration phase, which has lasted to the present day. The growth rate for Malaysia in 1997–2010 was 1.9 per cent, a drop of three percentage points from the previous growth rate. The growth rate for Thailand was 2 per cent, a drop of 3.7 percentage points from the previous growth rate.

Annual growth rates show similar trajectories, with major dips occurring largely as a result of exogenous factors, such as the crash in commodity prices during the early 1970s and early 1980s (both of which hit Malaysia hardest, due to its reliance on oil exports), the 1997 AFC, and the global financial crisis of 2007–8 (Figure 10.2).

A proximate cause of the fall in economic growth since the AFC was the decline in the investment rate in the two countries. Investment as a ratio of GDP rose steadily during the 1960s and 1970s in Malaysia and Thailand, before a surge in the mid-1980s (Figure 10.3). However, investment rates fell

---

[1] Based on ordinary least squares growth rates; see Kar et al. (2013) for more details.

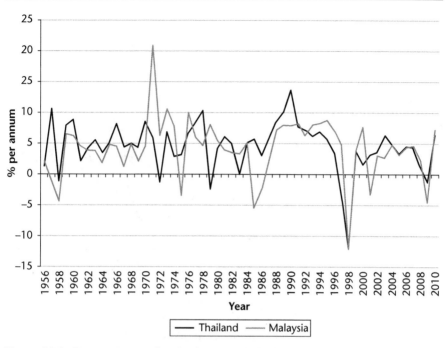

Figure 10.2. Economic growth in Malaysia and Thailand, 1956–2010
Source: World Bank, *World Development Indicators*.

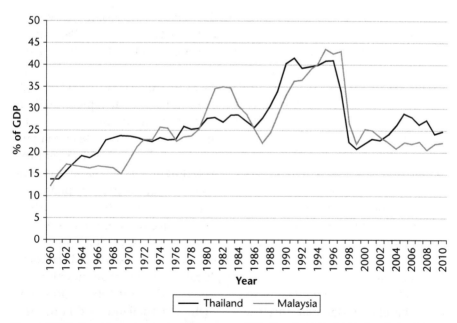

Figure 10.3. Investment rates in Malaysia and Thailand, 1960–2010 (% of GDP)
Source: World Bank, *World Development Indicators*.

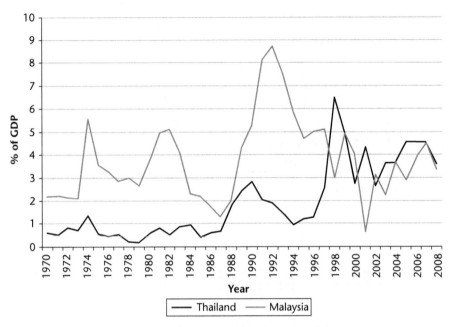

Figure 10.4. FDI in Malaysia and Thailand, 1970–2008 (% of GDP)
Source: World Bank, *World Development Indicators*.

sharply from a high of over 40 per cent in the mid-1990s to around 25 per cent in the two countries in the 2000s, following the AFC. We see a similar pattern with FDI as a ratio of GDP, though the increase as well as the fall has been much more pronounced in Malaysia (Figure 10.4).

A feature of Malaysia and Thailand's growth experience has been the high rates of structural transformation that has accompanied the rapid growth in these two countries. This is evident from the sustained increase in manufacturing value added as a percentage of GDP since the 1960s in Malaysia and Thailand (Figure 10.5). The trend was broken at the turn of the century, however, as Malaysia experienced a clear decline, while Thailand has continued to rise steadily, though at a slower rate than in the pre-AFC phase.

A similar picture emerges from the exporting behaviour of the two countries (see Figure 10.6). Both have followed similar trajectories, though Malaysia enjoyed—and has maintained—a higher starting point, possibly as a result of the legacy of colonialism, which left it with a relatively advanced economy that was far more connected to the global economy than uncolonized Thailand. However, manufacturing exports as a share of total exports has fallen sharply for Malaysia since the AFC, while in Thailand we do not see a similar fall (though manufacturing exports as a share of exports seems to have plateaued for Thailand in the 2000s) (Figure 10.7).

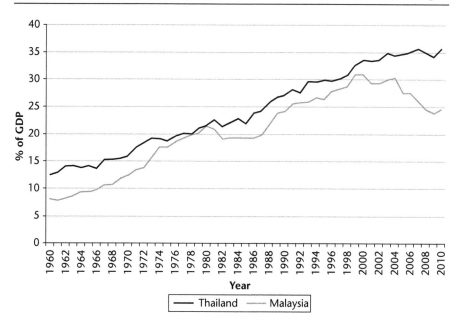

Figure 10.5. Manufacturing value added in Malaysia and Thailand, 1960–2010 (% of GDP)

Source: World Bank, *World Development Indicators*.

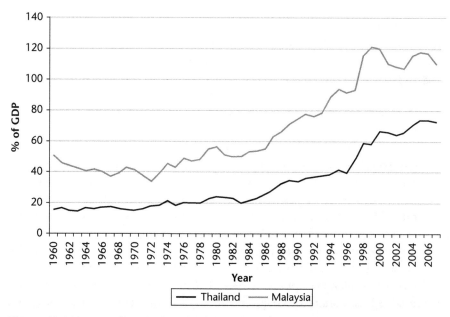

Figure 10.6. Exports from Malaysia and Thailand, 1960–2008 (% of GDP)

Source: World Bank, *World Development Indicators*.

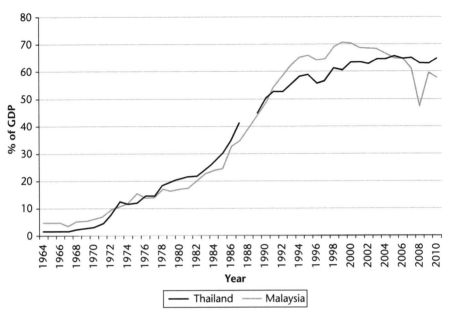

Figure 10.7. Manufactured exports from Malaysia and Thailand, 1964–2010 (% of GDP)

Source: World Bank, *World Development Indicators*.

Finally, examining the movement in the Hausmann–Hidalgo measure (Hausmann et al., 2013) of product complexity, we see a sustained increase in this measure for both Malaysia and Thailand from the early 1970s (see Figure 10.8). This increase was observed till the early 2000s. Beyond this date, there has been no improvement in the product complexity measure for Malaysia, but a further increase for Thailand during the 2000s, though at a lower rate of increase.

Overall, we find that both Malaysia and Thailand have had very similar growth experiences, in that both countries witnessed a prolonged period of rapid growth from the 1960s to the mid-1990s, before the onset of the AFC. Both these countries have seen a noticeable growth deceleration phase since the mid-1990s. This has been reflected in surges in investment rates till the mid-1990s and then a sharp fall. Much of the growth in the pre-AFC phase in these two countries has been driven by the export-oriented manufacturing sector. Both these countries have seen significant structural transformation in the growth acceleration phase, as reflected in an increase in manufacturing value added as a share of GDP, and in the product complexity of exports. However, where these countries have parted ways has been in the nature of structural transformation in the growth deceleration phase. In Malaysia, there

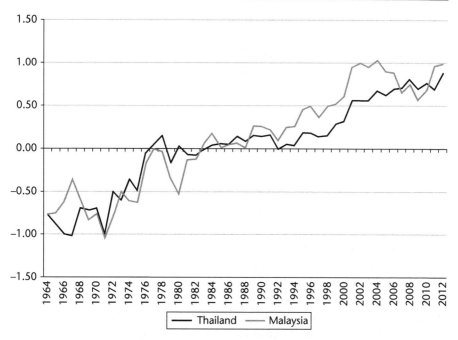

Figure 10.8. Hausmann–Hidalgo measure of economic complexity, Malaysia and Thailand, 1964–2013

Source: *The Atlas of Economic Complexity* <http://atlas.cid.harvard.edu/>.

has been a slowdown and possible regress in structural transformation.[2] This has not happened in Thailand to the same degree, with both indicators of structural transformation—manufacturing value added as a share of GDP and the Hausmann–Hidalgo measure—showing an improvement over time in the post-AFC phase, though the rate of improvement was not as impressive as that observed in the growth acceleration phase.

In Sections 10.3 and 10.4, we analyse the growth acceleration and deceleration episodes in turn, using our conceptual framework to understand why there was rapid growth in the first episode in Malaysia and Thailand, followed by a growth slowdown in the second episode.

---

[2] Most countries show a decline in manufacturing value added as a share of GDP at high levels of per capita income as the share of manufacturing in total output shows an inverted U-shaped curve over the course of development (Rodrik, 2016). However, as Tan (2014: 160) notes, 'the turning point for manufacturing at around US$4,000 GDP per capita in 2000 indicates that (Malaysia's) deindustrialisation is premature'. The regress in structural transformation in the case of Malaysia is also indicated by the decline in the product complexity measure, as well as the decline in manufacturing output and productivity growth in the 2000s (Tan, 2014).

10.3 The Growth Acceleration Episodes in Malaysia and Thailand

We begin by analysing the political causes of Malaysia's growth acceleration. We do this by discussing the political settlement, rents space, deals space, and feedback loops in Malaysia in turn. We then follow the same structure while discussing Thailand's growth acceleration episode.

10.3.1 *Malaysia*

MALAYSIA'S POLITICAL SETTLEMENT

Malaysia possessed a strong dominant party throughout its growth acceleration episode, though the structure of the ruling coalition shifted significantly during that time (see Figure 10.9). At independence, Malaysia's political settlement was based on a power-sharing agreement between its three major ethnic groups. Referred to as 'the bargain', it represented an understanding that Malays would dominate the political system, due to their status as the original inhabitants of the Malay Peninsula, but that the sizeable and economically powerful Chinese and Indian communities would remain unmolested by the state (Gomez, 2004). This distribution of power was reflected in both the new constitution, particularly Article 153, which offered non-Malays full citizenship in exchange for acknowledging the 'special position of the Malays', and in the configuration of the tripartite ruling coalition called the Alliance

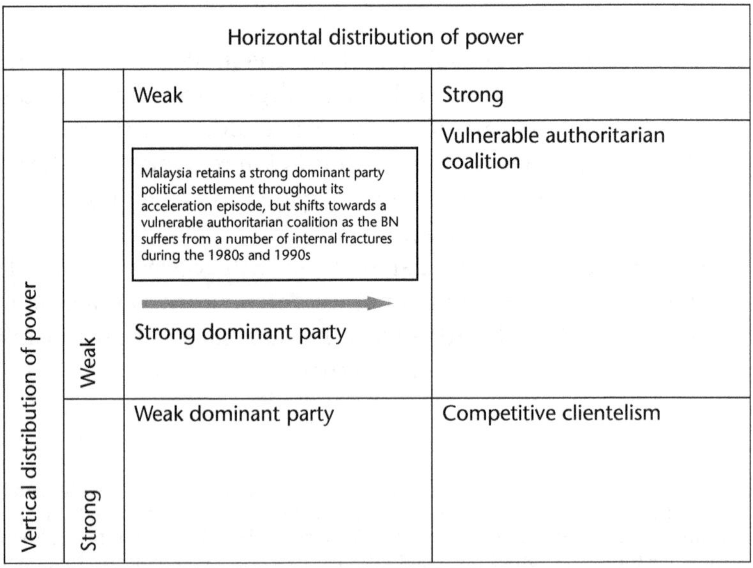

Figure 10.9. Malaysia's political settlement during its acceleration episode
Source: Authors' illustration.

(Milner et al., 2014: 25). Led by the Malay prime minister, Tunku Rahman, it was comprised of Malaysia's three biggest ethnically based parties—the United Malays National Organization (UMNO), the Malaysian Chinese Association (MCA), and the Malaysian Indian Congress—but was dominated by UMNO, as per the power-sharing formula. Nonetheless, the MCA enjoyed a significant degree of influence, as its links with Chinese apex organizations such as the Chambers of Commerce ensured a stream of donations from Chinese firms. Reliant on the MCA for financial support, UMNO elites ceded control of the Finance, Commerce, and Industry Ministries to the latter (Jesudason, 1990). From there, it blocked policies encroaching on Chinese commercial dominance, instead advocating a laissez-faire approach that favoured non-Malay commercial and industrial interests (Thirkell-White, 2006).

As a result, extreme socio-economic inequalities from the colonial period became more accentuated, also taking on an ethnic dimension as poor Malays blamed the 'ubiquitous Chinese businessman' (Gomez and Jomo, 1997: 21).[3] Ethnic tensions became increasingly divisive, escalating in 1969 during the aftermath of an election that saw Chinese voters desert the Alliance en masse to support a new opposition party demanding an end to Malay special status (Jesudason, 1990). Rioting began in Kuala Lumpur and spread across Malaysia, realigning the balance of power within its political settlement. After two years of martial law, the Alliance reinvented itself as the Barisan Nasional (National Front, BN), enlarging its roster to incorporate a number of small Malay opposition parties. The effect of this political restructuring was twofold: on the one hand, it brought competing Malay groups into a unified structure; on the other, it reduced the MCA's influence, giving Malay elites dominance over Chinese interests (Jesudason, 1990). These changes also cemented UMNO's status as the dominant force in Malaysian politics. Where coalition partners previously held important posts, they now contented themselves with token seats, while the 'power portfolios' went to the UMNO (Pepinsky, 2007: 115).

With this control over Malaysian politics—and Chinese interests in particular—the BN, led by newly elected prime minister, Tun Razak, embarked in 1971 on an assertively pro-Malay stance called the New Economic Policy (NEP). Funded by taxing Malaysia's now politically isolated Chinese capitalists, the twenty-year NEP aimed to foster national unity and racial harmony, henceforth the guiding principles of Malaysian politics, through two mechanisms: first, by eradicating poverty regardless of race; second, by restructuring society to achieve socio-economic parity between Malay Bumiputera ('sons of the soil') and predominantly Chinese non-Bumiputera (Gomez et al., 2013). The former would be achieved through an export-oriented industrialization

---

[3] As Thillainathan and Cheong (2016) note, the Gini coefficients on income for all ethnic groups increased during 1957–70, with the fastest increase in inequality among the Malays.

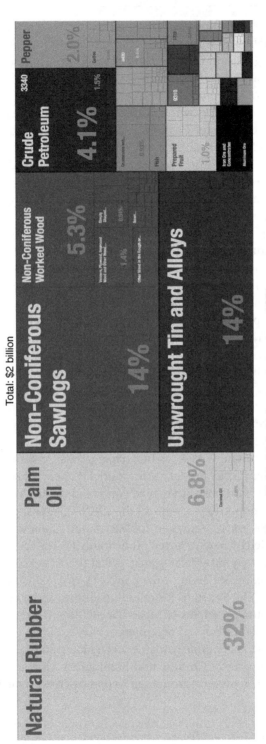

Total: $2 billion

Figure 10.10. Malaysia's export structure, 1971

Source: Atlas of Economic Complexity <http://atlas.cid.harvard.edu/>.

Total: $14.2 billion

Figure 10.11. Malaysia's export structure, 1981

Source: Atlas of Economic Complexity <http://atlas.cid.harvard.edu/>.

strategy that would yield high growth rates and raise income levels for all, while the latter would be brought about through affirmative action; the most ambitious target was increasing Bumiputera corporate ownership from 1.9 per cent in 1970 to 30 per cent in 1990 (Gomez et al., 2013). Recognizing that a Malay business class would not emerge overnight, however, the BN created a plethora of state enterprises and trust agencies, mandating them with acquiring assets and holding them in trust until such time as they could be taken over.

Mahathir bin Mohamad became prime minister in 1981, marking a turning point in Malaysian politics. Inspired by South Korean strongman, Park Chung-Hee, he centralized power within the executive and utilized his control over state organs to enforce a major shift in development policy (Gomez, 2004). Long critical of the NEP for encouraging a 'subsidy mentality' among Malays (Mahathir, 1982: 40), Mahathir felt vindicated when escalating public spending combined with plunging commodity prices to tip the economy into recession in 1985 (Gomez, 2002). Claiming that the NEP had become unsustainable, Mahathir significantly narrowed the range of beneficiaries, switching from a broader goal of interethnic parity to fostering an elite entrepreneurial class that could symbolize Malay prosperity. This would be done through an intensive focus on heavy industry, which Mahathir saw as a powerful expression of Malay nationalism. Pointing to South Korea as the model to emulate, Mahathir sought to create Bumiputera businesses of international repute. Enormous conglomerates soon emerged as he pressed ahead with a 'Look East' approach that emphasized rapid industrialization (Nyanjom, 2013).

MALAYSIA'S RENTS SPACE

Before the launch of the NEP, Malaysia's rents space was dominated by rentiers, with primary commodities such as rubber and palm oil, both of which were grown on large-scale plantations, as well as timber and tin, driving growth (Figure 10.10). Rentiers were predominantly foreign mining and plantation firms, the exceptions being wealthy Malaysian Chinese business people who had started as rubber and tin dealers during the colonial period before diversifying backwards into owning plantations (Jesudason, 1990). The limited numbers of manufacturing firms were either magicians involved in basic agro-processing or powerbrokers assembling imported components for sale in the protected domestic market, with Chinese capitalists dominating both these activities (Cho, 1990).

Ten years after the launch of the NEP, Malaysia's rents space had changed quite dramatically. Rentiers remained influential, with declines in tin and rubber offset by a surge in petroleum exports following the founding of Petronas, Malaysia's national oil company, in 1974 (Figure 10.11). However, the most significant shift was the rise of Malaysia's magicians, to the extent that they held the second largest share of GDP after the powerbrokers in 1987

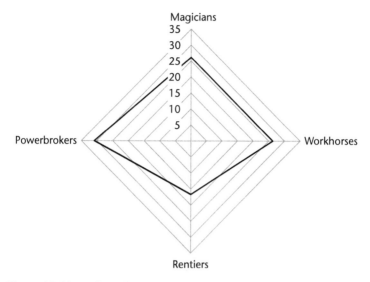

Figure 10.12. Malaysia's rents space, 1987

Source: Department of Statistics, Government of Malaysia, authors' calculations.

Note: Percentage share.

(Figure 10.12).[4] Major emergent industries were textiles and basic electronics, both of which were promoted under the BN's export-oriented industrialization strategy (Hobday, 1999).

By the end of the acceleration episode, Malaysia's economy had undergone a structural shift from being resource-based to one centred on manufacturing and services, demonstrated by reductions in the workhorse and rentier sectors and the continued growth of magicians (see Figure 10.13). Not only did magicians continue to grow, they also moved into increasingly complex products, with electronics and electrical goods growing sixfold during the 1980s, to comprise half of Malaysia's exports structure (Figure 10.14; Hobday,

---

[4] We construct the rents space diamond for Malaysia and Thailand by classifying manufacturing as magicians; agriculture, wholesale trade, and hotels and restaurants as workhorses; construction, utilities, and transport and communications as powerbrokers; and mining as rentiers. Unfortunately, the national income accounts for Malaysia are not disaggregated enough for the agricultural sector, which did not allow us to classify rubber and palm oil within agriculture as rentiers. Note also that not all of agriculture will be producing for the domestic market, with a large proportion of agricultural produce (at least in Thailand) sold in the export market. However, the national income accounts for Malaysia and Thailand do now allow us to differentiate between export-oriented and domestically oriented agriculture (so between that part of agriculture which should be included in the magician sector, and not in the workhorse sector, as in the current classification). Finally, we do not include community services, education, and health in the calculation of the rents space diamonds, as most of these are in the public sector (and the national income accounts data do not make clear which of the services outputs originate in the private sector). Given the coarse assumptions we need to make to generate the rents diamonds, our calculation of the economic contribution of magicians, workhorses, rentiers, and powerbrokers needs to be treated with some caution.

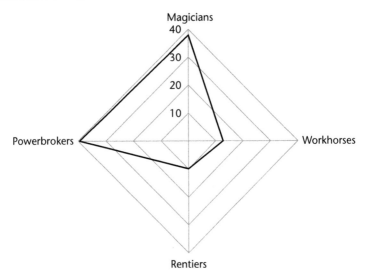

Figure 10.13. Malaysia's rents space, 1996

Source: Department of Statistics, Government of Malaysia, our calculations.

Note: Percentage share.

1999). An even more dramatic shift was the rise of Malaysia's powerbrokers, to the extent that they held the largest share of GDP by 1996. Much of this can be attributed to Mahathir's industrialization strategy, which entailed a second round of import-substituting industrialization involving state-led investment in heavy industry to create linkages between magicians and the rest of Malaysia's economy (Lee, 2012).

MALAYSIA'S DEALS SPACE

Deals were ordered throughout the acceleration episode, owing not just to the fact that there was a managed handover of power to a stable ruling coalition in 1957, but also because that same coalition, albeit with significant shifts in its structure and orientation, remained in power for the duration (Jomo, 1997). However, the extent to which deals were open or closed differed greatly across the acceleration episode, as well as within different rents space domains. Due to the structure of the rents space and the power-sharing system inherited at independence, deals were extremely closed until 1969, with business opportunities going to foreign or Chinese rentiers with the resources to 'assiduously lobby' the Alliance, particularly the MCA elites running the Ministries of Finance, Industry, and Commerce (Jomo, 1997: 96). The ability of Chinese capitalists to secure deals was also boosted by the domination of Chinese banks within Malaysia's financial sector, which allowed them to source credit and financial guarantees on highly preferential terms (Jesudason, 1990).

Total: $80.7 billion

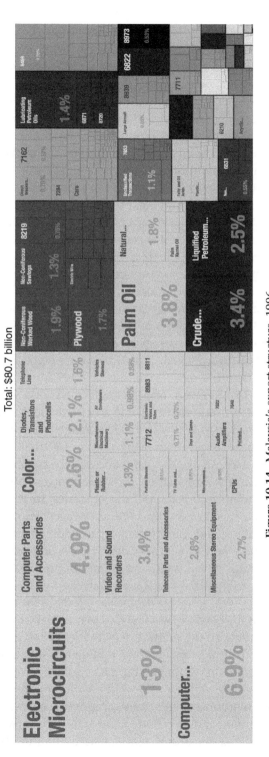

Figure 10.14. Malaysia's export structure, 1996

Source: Atlas of Economic Complexity <http://atlas.cid.harvard.edu/>.

The nature of deals changed significantly following the NEP's launch. Driven by the goals of sustaining growth and restructuring society, the BN presided over a dualistic deals strategy, whereby closed ordered deals were offered to certain domains while open ordered deals were offered to others. Closed deals went to rentiers and powerbrokers, where the relative ease of shielding them from competition allowed the BN to advance its restructuring goals (Cho, 1990). In industries requiring little capital and technological expertise, and where it had control over licences and contracts—notably in construction, logging, rubber dealing, trade, and transport—the BN heavily favoured Malays through newly created agencies, such as the Majlis Amanah Rakyat (People's Trust Council) and Urban Development Authority, which provided loans, credit, and advisory services (Jesudason, 1990). The flow of funds to Malays was also boosted by stringent lending targets set by the Central Bank, with commercial and development banks facing punitive charges for not complying. As a result, Bumiputeras were receiving 20.6 per cent of loans by 1980, up from 4 per cent in 1968 (Jesudason, 1990).

The BN pursued a different strategy in capital-intensive powerbroker and rentier industries. Backed by enormous funds and regulatory power, trust agencies accumulated assets on behalf of Bumiputeras (Jesudason, 1990). The principal agencies incorporated for this task were Perbadanan Nasional Bhd (National Corporation, Pernas), established in 1969 and controlled by the Ministry of Finance Incorporated, and Permodlan Nasional Bhd (National Equity Corporation, PNB), founded in 1978 to accelerate the Bumiputerization of strategic sectors. Their role was to purchase foreign (often ailing) plantation and mining firms, notable acquisitions being London Tin (the largest producer in the world) in 1975, Sime Darby (the plantation-based conglomerate) in 1976 and British-owned Guthrie Corporation (Malaysia's largest plantation company, with 200,000 acres of oil palm and rubber estates) in 1981 (Jesudason, 1990). Such was their success that, by 1982, these agencies controlled over 60 per cent of plantation and mining activity, in addition to having made inroads into powerbroker sectors such as cement, hotels, property, and finance. Divestments were limited at this stage, and did not begin in earnest until the mid-1980s, but went to politicians, ex-bureaucrats, and well-connected business persons whenever they did occur (Gomez and Jomo, 1997).

Open ordered deals, by contrast, were offered to magicians to foster growth and employment. Owing to the political sensitivities of relying on Chinese firms, the BN sought to attract foreign firms, leading to a situation whereby it was reducing the dominance of foreign capital in some sectors, but increasingly reliant on it in others (Ritchie, 2005). In addition to providing a stable political and fiscal environment, generous incentives were offered through the Investment Incentives and Free Trade Zone Acts, both unveiled in 1971. The former provided tax relief and pioneer status to industries such as electronics and textiles, while the latter offered tariff and customs exemptions, as well as infrastructural support to firms in export-processing zones (EPZs) (Bowie and Unger, 1997). There was also a willingness to reform ministries and agencies to meet investor demands. While most of the bureaucracy remained subsumed by ethno-political interests, 'pockets of effectiveness' were carved out within the Ministry of Finance, Ministry of Trade and Industry, and the Malaysian Industrial Development Authority, the latter becoming a 'competent and supportive' one-stop investment authority (Leutert and Sudhoff, 1999: 263).

This dualistic deals strategy became even more pronounced under Mahathir. Retaining open ordered deals for magicians—and even opening them further with the 1986 Investments Promotion Act, which provided ten-year tax holidays and relaxed foreign equity restrictions for firms in priority sectors (Gomez, 2013)—Mahathir offered extremely closed deals to powerbrokers and rentiers. To foster his industrial class, Mahathir established the Heavy Industry Corporation of Malaysia (HICOM). Backed by enormous resources, HICOM was to spearhead Malaysia's industrialization by investing in industries such as cement factories, iron and steel works, petrochemical plants, and Proton, the national automobile manufacturer (Lee, 2012). In reality, however, it became little more than a vehicle for dispensing patronage to a 'politically influential minority' (Gomez and Jomo, 1997: 1).

Following the recession and fiscal crisis of 1985, Mahathir gave in to pressure from international finance institutions to initiate privatization reforms. Within a decade, the BN had sold off its state enterprises, including HICOM and Petronas in 1994, shifted to private infrastructure procurement, and divested Pernas' and PNB's enormous assets (Thirkell-White, 2006). Rather than competitive tenders, however, privatization became a political mechanism for fostering Mahathir's industrial elite, with beneficiaries being Bumiputeras with connections to senior UMNO elites, particularly Mahathir, Deputy Prime Minister Anwar Ibrahim, and Finance Minister Daim Zainuddin. This unique brand of privatization showed 'scant regard for relevant experience and expertise', leading to the emergence of huge, ultimately unsustainable, Bumiputera conglomerates (Gomez and Jomo, 1997: 180).

MALAYSIA FEEDBACK LOOPS

Positive and negative feedback loops characterized Malaysia's acceleration episode. Positively, the increasing importance of magicians allowed them to pressure the BN into implementing a number of reforms, notably overhauling the Malaysia Industrial Development Authority, relaxing foreign equity stipulations, and liberalizing the tax code (Ritchie, 2005). The accommodative 1986 Promotion of Investments Act was also implemented on the back of investor demands. However, one should not overstate the positive feedback. Hill (2012: 12), for example, believes Malaysia was 'too open', in that the BN was so reliant on FDI to foster growth and employment that it was unwilling to enforce local content requirements or promote linkage generation. Instead, magicians remained cocooned within EPZs, importing equipment and materials.

Negative feedback was political in nature, stemming from the closed deals offered to rentiers and powerbrokers, particularly under Mahathir. By the late 1980s, Malaysia's most successful businesspeople were all intimately connected with—and owed their continuing success to—senior UMNO elites, with the result that huge groups of interlocking corporate interests cohered around particular politicians. With 'power agglomerated at the top', fractures emerged, as factions jostled to secure preferential access to rents (Jesudason, 1990: 117). Initially, these disputes were contained within the ruling coalition, such as in 1984—when there was a bitterly fought contest for the deputy presidency between Deputy Prime Minister Hitam and Finance Minister Razaleigh—and in 1987, when they united in a failed attempt to unseat Mahathir (Gomez and Jomo, 1997). However, power struggles became increasingly irreconcilable, to the extent that Razaleigh defected to form an opposition party before the 1990 elections, only returning in 1995 with the lure of prominent positions for himself and his supporters. Though these internal machinations did not at this time threaten the BN's longevity, they do provide an important backdrop to the shifts that, as we discuss later, occurred in Malaysia's political settlement during its deceleration episode.

10.3.2 Thailand

THAILAND'S POLITICAL SETTLEMENT
Strong Dominant Party (1957–73)
Our analysis of Thailand's political settlement begins in 1957, the year that Field Marshal Sarit Thanarat launched a coup. Previously, Thailand had been undermined by violence and disorder, as competing military factions jostled for power. Following Sarit's coup, however, rival factions were purged, the constitution was abolished, and political parties were banned, as Sarit established a system of 'despotic paternalism', whereby his Revolutionary Party emphasized order and stability over democracy and Western-style representative institutions (Warr, 1993: 11). To bolster his legitimacy, Sarit rehabilitated the monarchy, which had been reduced to little more than a figurehead following a 1932 coup. While there was no return to absolute rule, the Palace re-emerged as a para-political institution that operated through a web of alliances and proxies, notably the president of the privy council, to influence Thailand's political direction—a modern form of monarchical rule that McCargo (2005) terms 'network monarchy'.

With his First Army command structure arrayed below him, and buttressed by the ideational holding power of a rehabilitated monarchy, Sarit guided Thailand into a period of unprecedented stability (Hewison, 1997). Where no single faction had been able to establish its supremacy, Sarit's systematic elimination of his rivals, coupled with his suppression of political activity, ensured that excluded factions and lower-level actors remained weak, giving Thailand a classic strong dominant party (Khan, 2010). Even when Sarit died unexpectedly in 1963, power transferred smoothly to Generals Thanom Kittikachorn and Prapas Charusathiarana, his deputies, who ensured that the regime continued unabated into the 1970s.

Competitive Clientelism (1973–96)

As in Malaysia, iniquitous distribution of economic opportunities generated unrest. Unlike Malaysia, however, the ensuing riots altered the structure of power so significantly that they overturned the ruling coalition and triggered a shift in Thailand's political settlement. During the early 1970s, a disparate range of actors had become disaffected with military rule, notably student movements, trade unions, and a business community that resented paying informal taxes to generals (Phongpaichit and Baker, 2000). Unrest peaked in 1973, when students were arrested in Bangkok for distributing leaflets demanding an end to military rule. More than 400,000 protesters spilled on to the streets but the police responded in a heavy-handed manner, which left over a hundred dead. Alarmed at escalating unrest as government buildings were ransacked and torched, King Bhumibol ordered Thanom and Prapas into exile, causing the junta to collapse.

Khan (2010) believes the riots initiated a transition to competitive clientelism and in broad terms we agree with this classification, though we stress that Thailand had a hybrid competitive settlement, in which extra-parliamentary actors—the so-called 'unelected' elites, notably the Palace and military—retained significant holding power (Kanchoochat, 2014). Following the riots, Thailand endured a period of upheaval as parties and factions jockeyed for power under a new constitution that adopted the basic tenets of a parliamentary democracy. A number of unstable coalitions came and went as each struggled to find a power balance that worked (Phongpaichit and Baker, 2000). Lower-level actors became increasingly influential within this context, because they were able to play off competing factions against each other, switching sides at will. After years of turbulence and military-instigated no-confidence votes, the constitution was modified in 1978 to allow a stronger military presence in parliament, with generals again allowed to serve in the cabinet and as prime minister. While regressing on the spirit of 1973, this inaugurated a period of relative stability. In 1979, Kukrit Pramoj's Social Action Party won the election and selected General Prem Tinsulanond as prime minister. Prem had the support of the military and of the Palace, while Kukrit represented a plethora of emerging business interests, and the two agreed a power-sharing deal; Prem's allies would control the defence, interior, and finance ministries, while sectoral ministries would be distributed between Kukrit's party and its coalition partners (Wingfield, 2002).

Prem was prime minister for eight years before retiring from frontline politics in 1988, opting to join the privy council and later becoming its president. With Thailand's business and middle classes assertive after years of stability and growth, the resulting election heralded a 'watershed' moment; unprecedented numbers of businesspeople-cum-politicians were elected and there was optimism that Thailand was leaving its military past behind (Wingfield, 2002: 261). Chatichai Choonhavan's incoming coalition mounted an attack on the institutional bases of the military's power, seizing the defence, finance, and interior ministries from Prem's allies, before passing a cut in defence spending, thereby terminating the delicate power-sharing deal that Prem had cultivated (Baker, 2016). To protect its patrimony, the military launched a coup in 1991, remaining in power for a year to oversee the passage of a constitution enshrining its dominance, before handing over to its own Samakkhitham party following discredited elections. Demonstrations started immediately thereafter, prompting the military to wage a brutal Phairi Phinat ('crush the enemy') anti-insurrection strategy (Phongpaichit and Baker, 2000: 359). Intense rioting ensued before the king again intervened to demand that the military step down.

Mirroring events of 1973, Thailand endured a period of upheaval following the dissolution of military rule, as businesspeople-cum-politicians vied with each other now that they were no longer unified against the junta. The country endured three unstable governments between 1992 and 1997, each failing to survive a full term. These years saw the emergence of unrestrained 'money politics', with money becoming vital for bringing parties to power and keeping them there (Hewison, 1997: 2). Elections were won by those who could buy the most votes—a trend established in 1992, when the military ploughed vast sums into buying the previously untapped, but now increasingly engaged, rural vote. Elections became little more than bouts of 'horse-trading', as parties sought not only to purchase the support of voting blocs, but MPs from other parties, signalling the increasing strength of lower-level actors (Maisrikrod and McCargo, 1997: 137). Prior to the 1995 election, for example, MPs could command 'transfer fees' of 20 million baht (Maisrikrod and McCargo, 1997: 138). Once in office, the logic of competitive clientelism then guided politicians; they had to recoup expenses and start building a coalition for the next election by diverting resources to key allies and constituencies (see Figure 10.15 for an evolution of Thailand's political settlement during its growth acceleration episode).

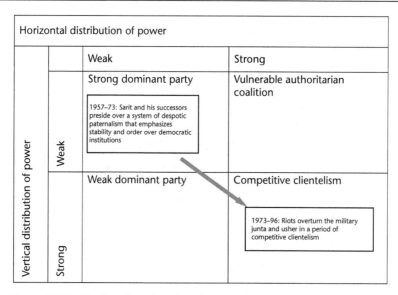

Figure 10.15. Thailand's political settlement during its acceleration episode

THAILAND'S RENTS SPACE

Like Malaysia, Thailand's economy underwent a structural shift from agriculture to manufacturing, with the most significant changes occurring between the advent of competitive clientelism in 1973 and the end of Prem's tenure in 1988. Prior to 1973, Thailand's export structure had been dominated by agricultural commodities, such as rice and rubber (see Figure 10.16). In contrast to Malaysia's plantation-based rentier economy, however, these commodities were produced predominantly by workhorses, as the monarchy had seen smallholder agriculture as a way of stymieing the rise of land barons, who might pose a threat to its rule (Raquiza, 2012). The limited numbers of magicians operated within basic manufacturing sectors, such as textiles and footwear, while the almost non-existent rentier domain reflects Thailand's limited natural resource endowments, save for small reserves of tin that were all but exhausted by the mid-1970s (Dixon, 1999). Indeed, Figure 10.17 illustrates that the most important groups in 1973 were workhorses (agriculture and retail trade), followed by magicians (manufacturing) and powerbrokers (construction, utilities, transport, and communication), owing to the fact that Thailand had a sizeable service sector, as well as a large rice-growing agricultural sector.

By 1988, Thailand's export structure had changed significantly, with labour-intensive manufactured commodities, such as footwear and textiles, becoming increasingly important. In addition, high-technology products, such as electronics and auto parts, had emerged (see Figure 10.18). Taken together,

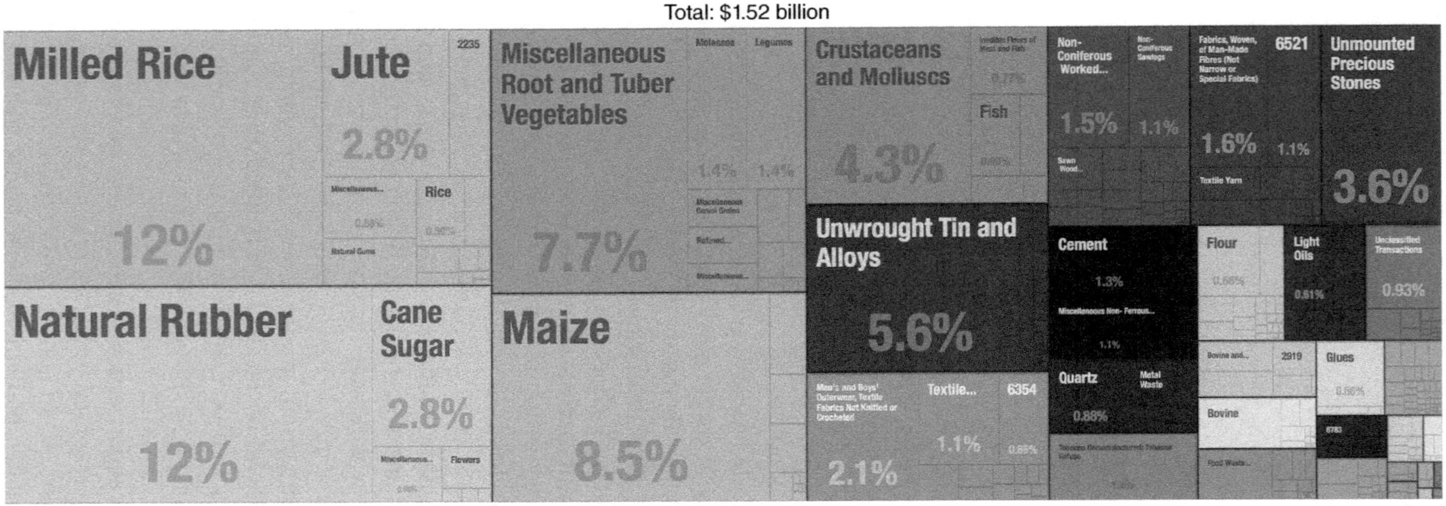

Total: $1.52 billion

Figure 10.16. Thailand's export structure, 1973

Source: Atlas of Economic Complexity <http://atlas.cid.harvard.edu/>.

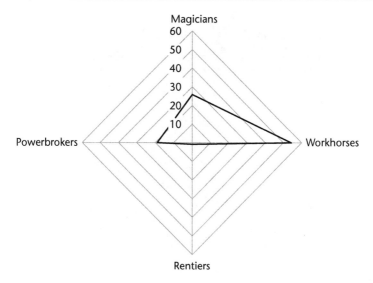

Figure 10.17. Thailand's rents space, 1973

Source: National Economic and Social Development Board, Government of Thailand, authors' calculations.

Note: Percentage share.

magicians increased their share of GDP, with workhorses diminishing in importance. These trends continued throughout the 1990s, with workhorses continuing to lose ground to magicians, who had, by 1996, moved into industries such as computer peripherals and microcircuits, and fertilizer and petrochemicals, respectively (see Figures 10.19 and 10.20).

THAILAND'S DEALS SPACE

Where deals had been disordered, due to intense divisions within the military, Sarit presided over a reorientation of the economy and a transition to orderly deals. Under the tutelage of the USA, which regarded Thailand as a bulwark against communism, his administration developed within a capitalist framework that emphasized private-sector growth (Wingfield, 2002). Concurrent with this vision, Sarit carved out space for the Ministry of Finance and the Bank of Thailand to operate as a pocket of effectiveness, staffing them with Western-educated technocrats, such as Governor Puey Ungpakorn, who imbued the Bank with 'a spirit of fierce integrity' between 1959 and 1979 (Siamwalla, 1997: 70). In so doing, Sarit returned Thailand to a technocratic tradition that had begun in the nineteenth century (Raquiza, 2012). At that time, hemmed in by colonial powers, and resolving that fostering financial stability was the only way to maintain sovereignty, King Chulalongkorn launched a state reform programme that gave birth to a modern technocracy.

Total: $13.4 billion

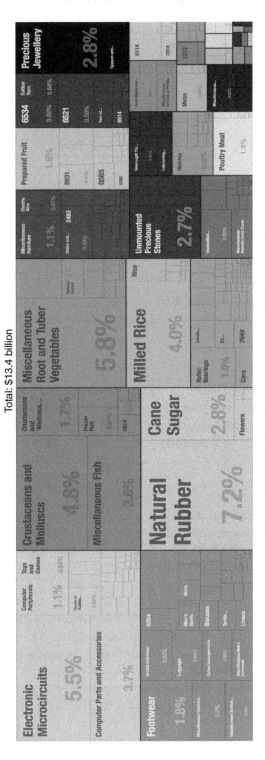

Figure 10.18. Thailand's export structure, 1988
Source: Atlas of Economic Complexity <http://atlas.cid.harvard.edu/>.

Total: $53.3 billion

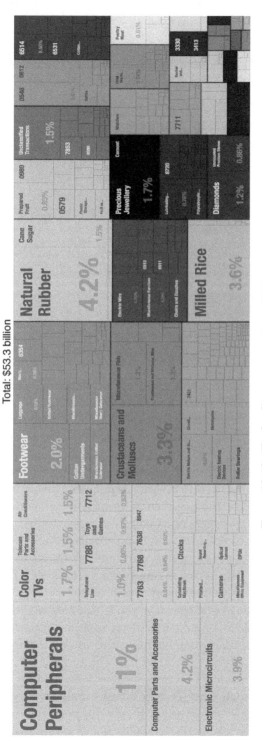

Figure 10.19. Thailand's export structure, 1996
Source: Atlas of Economic Complexity <http://atlas.cid.harvard.edu/>.

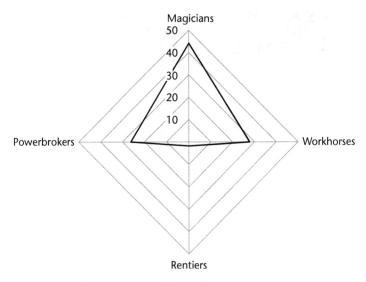

Figure 10.20. Thailand's rents space, 1996

Source: National Economic and Social Development Board, Government of Thailand, authors' calculations.

Note: Percentage share.

As Doner and Ramsay (2000) argue, these reforms have endowed subsequent generations of ruling and bureaucratic elites with strong ideological preferences for macroeconomic stability and fiscal caution, and are instrumental to understanding why Thailand's macroeconomic institutions remained relatively autonomous for much of its acceleration episode.

While ordered, deals were also closed under Sarit, with two groups benefiting particularly. The first were Sino-Thai capitalists, who had dominated Thailand's economy since the nineteenth century, when, concerned about indebtedness and seeking to generate foreign exchange, King Chulalongkorn had entered into a de facto alliance with them (Doner, 2009). In exchange for offering board positions, directors' fees, and other kickbacks to Sarit and his deputies, a handful of Sino-Thai banking families hoovered up government contracts and licences, as well as investment incentives being distributed by the newly created Board of Investment (BOI) (Samudavanija, 1997). This allowed them to establish conglomerates that sprawled across financial services, agri-business, and basic assembly industries, as well as newly promoted industries such as chemicals and automobiles. Indeed, by 1973, nearly 300 firms—and much of Thailand's economy—were controlled by the Lamsam, Rattanarak, Sophonpanich, and Techaphaibun families (Wingfield, 2002). These close relationships with ethnic Chinese businesspeople represent an important and enduring feature of Thai politics, and are also where the story diverges from that of Malaysia. Unlike in Malaysia, Sarit and his successors partnered with Sino-Thai capitalists because the legitimacy of their regime did not hinge on redistribution, but instead on fostering rapid growth, which meant supporting Thailand's most capable business persons (Dixon, 1999).

The second beneficiary was the Palace. In addition to reinstating the political role of the monarchy, Sarit returned the Crown Property Bureau (CPB)— seized during the 1932 coup—into Palace hands. Acting as the monarchy's 'investment arm', the CPB 'became one of the conglomerates at the core of the expanding economy' (Ouyyanont, 2008: 166). Its success rested on three pillars. The first was property, as it owned two-thirds of the land in Bangkok, while the second was Siam Commercial Bank, which grew precipitately, along with Sino-Thai banks. The third was Siam Cement, a company founded by royal decree in 1913, which would become Thailand's largest conglomerate, with a fraction of its income actually coming from cement (Ouyyanont, 2008: 172). The rest came from a plethora of unrelated companies, including Thailand's largest iron and steel foundry, a battery manufacturer, paper producer, and several resource-based companies extracting marble, rubber, and plywood.

As in Malaysia, the political restructuring that followed the riots led to a major reorientation of the deals space, with a dualistic deals environment emerging that was similar to that of Malaysia. However, this was not as distinct, or indeed as deliberate, as Malaysia's. On the one hand, closed deals were offered to powerbrokers and rentiers, because this was critical to the longevity of the political settlement. Following the Sarit years, many of Thailand's senior political and bureaucratic elites had shares with, or were board members of, Sino-Thai conglomerates; thus they had a stake in their continuing success (Raquiza, 2012). As a result, foreign investment laws were introduced in 1973 and 1979 reserving certain industries exclusively for Thais, notably those utilizing natural resources or catering to the domestic market. Examples include rice milling, real estate, retail, and pharmaceuticals (Raquiza, 2012).

On the other hand, open deals were offered to magicians. In contrast to Malaysia, these deals were not initially a conscious decision, but an 'accident' arising from Thailand's shift to a unique type of competitive clientelism (Unger, 1998: 125). Between 1973 and 1978, a rapid turnover of ruling coalitions—and with them the bureaucrats in sectoral ministries, such as agriculture, commerce, and industry—created a system in which 'many centres of state regulatory control and their links to different political factions ensured that no single firm or group of firms could block competition from new entrants' (Unger, 1998: 125). As Doner and Ramsay note (2000: 154), this 'particular type of clientelism tended to expand, rather than restrict, opportunities', particularly in industries not dominated by the CPB and

Sino-Thai conglomerates, such as textiles and electronics. Indeed, entry barriers were so low in textiles that deals verged on being disordered. During the mid-1970s, a glut of firms resulted in overcapacity, prompting the Ministry of Industry to impose a ban on new entrants; however, in a context of political competition and bureaucratic flux, it proved impossible to enforce and illegal entrants were given amnesties, causing even greater saturation (Doner, 2009). Nonetheless, while entry barriers were low, so too were the exit barriers. Owing to the fact that macroeconomic institutions remained insulated from political turbulence, the government refused to bail out large and inefficient firms, instead letting them collapse, despite intense lobbying. The autonomy of the Finance Ministry and the Central Bank also produced a very stable macroeconomic environment, giving firms advantages over exporters in other countries (Doner and Ramsay, 2000).

Initially an accident, offering open ordered deals to magicians became explicit under Prem, as his administration launched an export-led industrialization strategy that responded to shifting global economic conditions and the limits of import-substitution industrialization (Warr, 1993). In addition to key macroeconomic reforms—such as devaluing the baht and implementing a wave of liberalization measures—that made Thailand more attractive to FDI at a time when the surging yen was forcing Japanese firms to relocate overseas, Prem restructured the BOI so that it favoured export-oriented industries, such as electronics, textiles, and automobiles (Raquiza, 2012). As in Malaysia, EPZs also figured prominently; the predominantly foreign firms located in them benefited from relaxed labour laws, tax exemptions, and infrastructural support (Jomo, 1997). Nonetheless, Thailand's dualistic deals strategy remained in place, albeit one that was less marked than Malaysia's at this time. For instance, the CPB was able to capitalize on its links with Prem's regime to diversify Siam Cement into petrochemicals after the discovery of natural gas in the early 1980s; indeed, while it continued to go by the name of a cement company, petrochemicals became Siam Cement's 'largest segment, both in profits and assets' (Jomo, 1997: 177). Similarly, Prem presided over a heavy industry project called the Eastern Seaboard Development Plan. Located on the coastline near Thailand's gas fields, it sought to create capital-intensive import-substituting industries, such as fertilizer and chemical plants, but ultimately favoured Sino-Thai conglomerates (Raquiza, 2012).

THAILAND FEEDBACK LOOPS
Similar to Malaysia's acceleration episode, one can identify positive and negative feedback loops. As Thailand's private sector grew, it also became increasingly organized, with a number of business associations emerging (Doner, 2009). In response to the demands of Thailand's peak association, the Association of Thai Industries, Prem established the Joint Public and Private Sector Consultative

Committee (JPPCC) to foster dialogue between the business community and senior officials from core ministries; Prem chaired its monthly meetings and a number of obstacles to export were remedied (Doner, 2009). Sectoral business associations also successfully lobbied the government. The Thai Garment Manufacturers Association, for example, pressured it into improving the supply and quality of local cotton, and also worked closely with the Department of Export Promotion to identify new export markets that eased overproduction issues and offered potential for higher-value-added production (Doner and Ramsay, 2000). In automobiles and electronics, meanwhile, suppliers formed associations to lobby for local content requirements that were, despite initial resistance from multinational corporations, relatively successful in generating linkages, due to the time-bound targets set by the BOI (Rock, 2000; Natsuda and Thoburn, 2012).

As in Malaysia, negative feedback was political in nature. It stemmed from the advent of money politics in the 1990s, and specifically from the ruptured power balance that Prem's coalition cultivated between military and bureaucratic elites and businesspeople-cum-politicians. Thais tend to characterize the period as a series of 'buffet cabinets', referring to the eagerness with which politicians helped themselves to state resources (Marshall, 2014: 94). So corrosive was the political climate that even macroeconomic cornerstones became subject to political feuding. Technocrats were replaced with politically motivated appointments, resulting in increasingly disordered deals and a 'rapid decline in the management of the economy' (Phongpaichit and Baker, 2000: 23). Where Prem's eight-year tenure saw three finance ministers, the following ten saw thirteen men hold the position. Even the previously incorruptible Central Bank became embroiled in a series of scandals, including the bailout of a politically connected commercial bank that would have been unthinkable previously (Hicken, 2004). Beyond the macroeconomic cornerstones, there was a weakening of Thailand's institutions generally; the National Economic and Social Development Board (NESDB) and BOI were captured by rent-seekers and used to lavish opportunities upon cronies, while the JPPCC stopped meeting and was later dissolved (Doner, 2009).

10.4 Deceleration Episodes in Malaysia and Thailand

10.4.1 *Malaysia*

MALAYSIA'S POLITICAL SETTLEMENT

While power struggles had undermined the BN since the late 1980s, it was only after the AFC—and particularly the sacking, beating, and imprisonment of Deputy Prime Minister Anwar—that an outright rupture occurred. Nominally, differences had arisen over how to deal with the crisis, as Anwar was reluctant to bail out Bumiputera conglomerates and instead favoured an

IMF-style rescue package; while Mahathir, swayed by ethno-political consid-erations, was determined to save them, arguing that failure to do so would jeopardize Bumiputera interests (Balasubramaniam, 2006). Just as import-antly, however, Mahathir believed that Anwar was using the crisis as a pretext to challenge him, as there had been rumours ever since the early-1990s that he was plotting a leadership bid (Abbott, 2004). Either way, the affair triggered an unprecedented backlash, because it revealed the extent to which the police, judiciary, and Attorney General's Office were controlled by Mahathir's inner circle. As the 1999 elections approached, a multi-ethnic multiparty coalition called the Barisan Alternatif (Alternative Front, BA) emerged, led by Anwar's wife, declaring that it would contest on a platform of improving governance, strengthening democratic institutions, and eradicating money politics (Abbott, 2004).

For the first time since independence, Malaysians talked seriously about BN rule coming to an end. The BA transcended ethnic divisions, uniting Chinese voters long resentful of pro-Bumiputera policies with middle-class Malays, who had felt neglected since Mahathir reduced the number of Malays bene-fiting from the state (Gomez, 2004). That the BN held on owed much to the legislative and coercive apparatus at its disposal. In addition to reinstating the colonial-era Internal Security Act to imprison opposition activists without trial, Mahathir tampered with electoral procedures so that 680,000 newly registered young voters thought to favour the BA could not vote, and utilized his control over the media to shut down newspapers and websites and embark on a propaganda campaign that played on the opposition's ethnic and class divisions (Gomez, 2004). Thus, while nearly half of Malays did not vote for the BN—and in two states it lost control completely—the election did not over-turn the ruling coalition.

Yet this was merely a reprieve, as the BN's vote share has declined in each subsequent election (see Figure 10.21). Not only are excluded factions getting stronger, they are also increasingly unified under the new Pakatan Rakyat opposition banner, and hence less easy to play off against each other (Weiss, 2016). The exception was in 2004, when Abduallah Badawi, succeeding Mahathir upon his retirement, lured voters with a reformist agenda. Upon assuming office, however, Abdullah encountered forces resistant to change; stacked with Mahathir's old guard, his cabinet blocked reforms, leading to an unprecedented rejection of the BN in 2008 (Weiss, 2016). Abduallah was succeeded by Najib Razak, a hard-line politician in Mahathir's mould. Exem-plifying Malaysia's new vulnerable authoritarian coalition, he has employed unsavoury measures following another disastrous election in 2013. These include reimprisoning Anwar on exactly the same charges, despite Abdullah ratifying his release (Amnesty International, 2016). Belying Najib's inclusive Malaysia rhetoric, there has also been a disconcerting return to identity

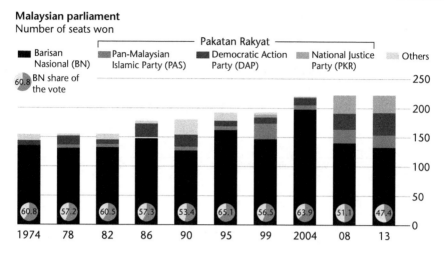

Figure 10.21. Seats in Malaysian parliament
Source: The Economist (2015).

politics, with Najib blaming the 2013 losses on a 'Chinese tsunami', rather than on what would more appropriately be called a middle-class one (Milner et al., 2014).

INCREASING COMPETITIVE CLIENTELIST TENDENCIES
However, while the BN is currently a vulnerable authoritarian coalition, this is not likely to be the case for much longer, as Malaysia's political settlement demonstrates increasing competitive clientelist tendencies (see Figure 10.22). Haemorrhaging middle-class support, the BN is now increasingly reliant on working-class Malays, with the result that lower-level actors—particularly UMNO leaders at divisional and branch levels, as well as non-party brokers—have become influential, due to their importance in distributing patronage and mobilizing voters (Weiss, 2016). More generally, the strength of lower-level actors as voting blocs is also forcing the BN into unveiling a raft of populist measures before elections. Unveiling his 2012 budget, Najib, who now doubles up as finance minister, announced that 1.4 million civil servants would receive a 13 per cent salary increase, that low-income households would be given RM500, and that high-school and university students—the demographic most likely to vote for the opposition—would receive book vouchers worth RM500 (Crisis Group, 2012). Forced into doling out these goodies by Malaysia's shifting political settlement, the BN is increasingly dependent on illicit money for campaigning and vote-buying, which only exacerbates the collusive state–business relations that the middle classes seek to eradicate. This is exemplified by the scandal surrounding the US$681 million that 'mysteriously' appeared in Najib's bank account prior to the 2013 elections, which is rumoured to have

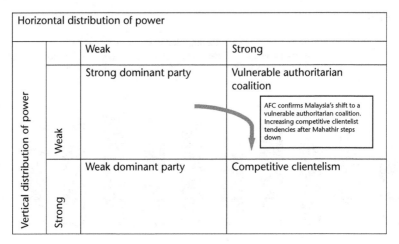

Figure 10.22. Malaysia's political settlement during its deceleration episode
Source: Authors' illustration.

been siphoned off from 1Malaysia Development Berhad, a state investment fund he chairs (*Wall Street Journal*, 2016a).

Such is the increasing strength of lower-level actors, that previously peripheral players have become kingmakers. A prime example is Sarawak's chief minister. The loss of votes in the relatively wealthy, urbanized, and middle-class peninsular Malaysia means that the BN's political base hinges on the less developed and rural Sabah and Sarawak (see Figure 10.23). Following the 2013 elections, the BN had a twenty-one-seat majority; considering Sarawak alone contributed twenty-five MPs, this means it would have collapsed without its votes. This shift in political geography has endowed Sarawak's chief minister with hitherto unimaginable political influence, which long-serving Abdul Taib Mahmud (1981–2014) and Adenan Satem, his brother-in-law and successor (2014–17), have exploited to leverage significant concessions from the federal government (Aeria, 2013). As long as Sarawakians continue to vote for the BN, as they did in the 2016 state elections, which eliminated most of the remaining opposition strongholds, the chief minister has free rein in Malaysia's resource-abundant state.

MALAYSIA'S RENTS SPACE
Two trends characterized Malaysia's rents space during its deceleration episode, both of which are intimately linked to its political settlement. First, Malaysia's magician sector, measured either by share of GDP or export structure, has declined markedly (Figures 10.24 and 10.25). The textiles industry has contracted, with average growth rates of −6.4 per cent between 2000 and 2010, while electronics fared little better, averaging an anaemic 0.9 per cent

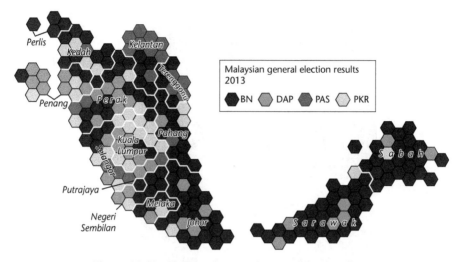

Figure 10.23. Malaysia's general election results, 2013
Source: *The Economist* (2015).

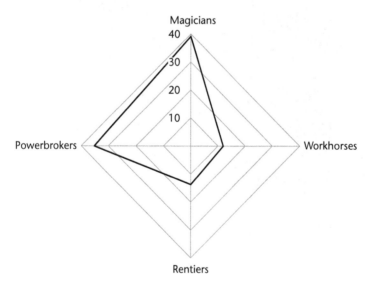

Figure 10.24. Malaysia's rents space, 2011
Source: Department of Statistics, Government of Malaysia, our calculations.
Note: Percentage share.

(Rasiah et al., 2015). While this process accelerated after the AFC, when foreign investors questioned the dynamism of South East Asian economies, it actually started in the late 1980s, when Malaysia entered a 'suffocating structural squeeze' (Ritchie, 2005: 746). On the one hand, rising salaries were prompting multinational corporations to relocate to China and

319

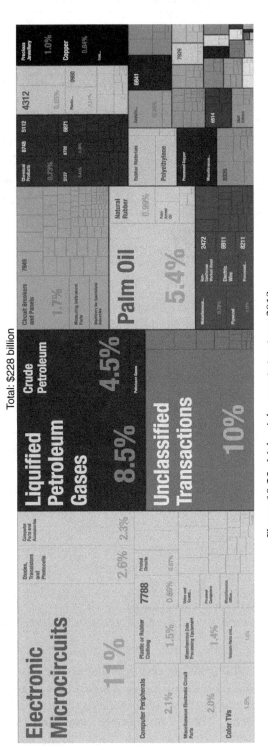

Figure 10.25. Malaysia's export structure, 2013
Source: Atlas of Economic Complexity <http://atlas.cid.harvard.edu/>.

Vietnam, which offered similar export incentives and infrastructure, but lower wages for assembly-based industries; on the other, Malaysia was unable to compete in higher-value-added activities with Singapore and the newly industrialized countries.

An underlying cause of this squeeze was the lack of strong local ancillary industries to foster linkages with foreign magicians, and this is where the links with Malaysia's political settlement come in. Unlike the newly industrialized countries, Malaysia has avoided nurturing indigenous firms through industrial policy because Chinese capitalists would have benefited. As Ritchie (2005: 753) argues, 'the exception that proves this rule is Penang', as the majority of its inhabitants are Chinese, which has allowed the Chinese-dominated state government to foster linkages between local and foreign firms 'without fear of upsetting delicate communal balances', particularly through its much-lauded Penang Development Corporation. Bumiputera suppliers, meanwhile, are almost non-existent, because Malays prefer to operate in highly protected rentier and powerbroker sectors, such as extractives, finance, trading, infrastructure, construction, and property, which offer easy profits (Gomez et al., 2013). The BN tried to remedy this situation in 1988 with its Vendor Development Programme, which sought to increase the share of inputs sourced from SMEs. However, even this succumbed to ethnic politics, as the approved Bumiputera suppliers were wholly uncompetitive, even by Malaysian standards (Capannelli, 1999). The widespread failure of private Malaysian companies after the AFC also led to the state purchasing non-performing loans from these companies through the state asset management company, Danaharta, and the replacement of private managers by state managers. Thus, the post-AFC phase was characterized by 'renationalization and a return to state ownership in the form of government-linked corporations (GLCs) as a proxy for Malay corporate ownership' (Tan, 2014: 160). GLCs accounted for over 50 per cent of the market capitalization of the Kuala Lumpur stock market by the 2000s. As Tan (2011: 171) argues:

> the emergence of GLCs may be seen as a return to proxy ownership of corporate equity by the state on behalf of Malays in the context of the historic failure of numerous high profile Malay entrepreneurs and reflected the failure of domestic companies to move into high technology sectors in the face of increasing competition.

These GLCs were mostly present in powerbroker sectors, such as utilities, transportation, banking, and retail trade, and their dominance led to a crowding out of private investment in these sectors (Menon and Ng, 2013). One important reason for the failure of the Malaysian state to foster the creation of a strong domestic capitalist class was that, unlike South Korea, the subsidies provided to Malay entrepreneurs did not have performance requirements

(Menon and Ng, 2013). Further, the lack of skills and a previous learning base in the Malay entrepreneurial class meant that the government could not address the issue of the lack of absorption of the complex organizational and production processes in the private sector necessary for industrial upgrading (Bruton, 1992; Lall, 1995).[5]

The second and related trend is a resurgence of rentiers. This has resulted in a reversal in structural transformation, with declines in textiles and electronics accompanied by increases in petroleum and palm oil. Palm oil's return is particularly pertinent, because again it is intimately linked to the shifting political settlement. To further its restructuring goals, the BN had tried to turn it into a workhorse sector, using trust agencies to purchase foreign plantations; land was then parcelled out to smallholders through schemes such as the Federal Land Development Agency (FELDA). FELDA was Malaysia's biggest grower by 1990 and was lauded for integrating smallholders into production (Cho, 1990). Since then, however, and in the context of a weakening BN, production has become rentier-dominated. Reliant on private money to bankroll election-related expenditure, Sarawak's chief minister, cooperating closely with top UMNO elites, has granted enormous concessions in Malaysian Borneo to politically connected businessmen (Cramb, 2011). In exchange for receiving long-term leases at well below market prices, or often for free, or 'payment in kind', these businessmen channel donations to the minister's Pesaka Bumiputera Bersatu party, as well as the BN more broadly (Aeria, 2013: 134). By 2011 it was estimated that 198,882 hectares, an area three times the size of Singapore, had been allocated to palm oil plantations. This heralds a 'radical transformation' of the sector since 1990, when 23,000 hectares were cultivated, the majority under FELDA-type schemes (Cramb, 2011: 275).

MALAYSIA'S DEALS SPACE

Up to the AFC, the BN got its dualistic deals strategy more or less right, striking a reasonable balance—albeit less so under Mahathir—between sustaining growth by offering open ordered deals to magicians, while simultaneously restructuring society with closed ordered deals to rentiers and powerbrokers. Owing to recent shifts in Malaysia's political settlement and rents space, however, this strategy is unravelling, with policies and institutions that were once successful in driving growth and fostering ethnic harmony becoming counterproductive (Nelson, 2012). For one, the heady combination of declining magicians, resurgent rentiers, and an increasingly vulnerable authoritarian coalition is making

---

[5] The failure of Malay companies is reflected in the ownership pattern of companies, where seven of the ten largest Malaysian companies in 2008 were state-owned and not a single Malay company featured in the largest twenty companies (Tan, 2011).

Malaysia's deals space more closed. This is exemplified by the shady patronage deals, land leases, and interlocking shareholdings that have transformed palm oil (Cramb, 2011).

Malaysia's automotive industry provides a clear example of how the dualistic deals strategy increasingly became a constraint on growth over time, as powerbrokers were created, even in industries which are usually the domain of magicians. In 1982, Mahathir Mohamad announced that a company called Proton would be established to produce Malaysia's first national car. The national car project was aimed at accelerating Malaysia's heavy industrialization drive, as well as strengthening the economic position of the Bumiputeras and securing their participation in supporting industries (Segawa et al., 2014). Proton was protected not only by the general level of automotive tariffs, but also by a variety of additional measures. In particular, the Malaysian government encouraged the development of component suppliers with a strong bias towards entrepreneurs of Bumiputera origin, which were of poor quality and high costs (Segawa et al., 2014). As a consequence, automobiles made by Proton have been a failure, both in export and domestic markets, and in the first decade of the 2000s, Proton was operating at half of its capacity and making substantial losses (Natsuda et al., 2013). Unlike Thailand's automotive industry, which functioned as a successful magician sector, Malaysia's domestic automotive industry could be characterized as a powerbroker sector, operating under non-competitive market structures and in a closed deals environment, and unable to sell automobiles in export markets.

Of even more concern, the ordered deals that have underpinned Malaysia's growth trajectory are slipping, with disorderly deals becoming increasingly prevalent. Oil is a perfect example. Deals have been closed—extremely so— since the 1974 Petroleum Development Act gave Petronas exclusive rights to exploit Malaysia's reserves, much to the chagrin of foreign companies (Cho, 1990). However, deals were highly ordered, with Petronas earning a reputation as one of the world's best-managed national oil companies, staffed with capable technocrats who secured favourable production-sharing agreements (Jesudason, 1990). Yet the weakening of Malaysia's political settlement has led to increased 'political meddling' (Doraisami, 2015: 102), with Petronas deployed to prop up flagship Bumiputera projects such as Proton, and provide energy subsidies to politically connected firms or even suppress the opposition, with royalty payments to oil-producing regions halted whenever opposition parties are elected (Doraisami, 2015). As the BN has become increasingly reliant on Petronas as a patronage tool, management of the oil sector has concomitantly declined, demonstrated by the BN's disregard of its own National Depletion Policy. Unveiled in 1980 to manage Malaysia's oil reserves, production was meant to be capped at 270,000 barrels per day, a far cry from the 603,000 currently being produced (Doraisami, 2015).

MALAYSIA FEEDBACK LOOPS

Even in the late 1980s, the BN was acutely aware of Malaysia's impending structural squeeze, with Mahathir launching an Industrial Master Plan to stimulate technological upgrading (Rasiah, 2012). Najib is similarly under no illusions, warning that: 'we have become a successful middle-income economy, but we cannot be caught in the middle-income trap; we need to make the shift to a high-income economy or risk losing growth momentum' (World Bank, 2016: 1). The problem is that just when political commitment, state capacity, and effective complementary institutions are needed to implement the deep structural reforms required, negative feedback from Malaysia's shifting political settlement and rents space has caused severe institutional degradation (Gomez, 2012: 79).

There are two forces at play. First, declining political support has led the BN increasingly to dole out prominent public sector jobs to politically influential individuals, resulting in 'revolving door' patronage appointments (Lopez, 2009: 274). Even the previously relatively insulated macroeconomic institutions are under threat. The finance ministry has been compromised ever since Najib took on the dual role of prime minister and finance minister, while the long-serving and internationally lauded Central Bank governor, Zeti Aziz, was due to be replaced by a politically motivated appointee until Najib's recent U-turn (*Wall Street Journal*, 2016b). Second, bureaucratic performance has been undermined by employment quotas, which reportedly require a ratio of 10:2:1 for Malays, Chinese, and Indians (Gomez et al., 2013). UMNO elites accept that these quotas are undermining performance, but will not remove them as they are popular with working-class Malays, on whose support they now depend. It is the same with education, where quotas allow poor Malays to attend university, but exclude talented non-Malay students, who leave Malaysia in search of tertiary education, sometimes never to return (Rasiah, 2012). This is a real concern, given Malaysia's chronic shortage of engineers and researchers, and the urgency with which it needs to implement an upgrading agenda.

10.4.2 Thailand

THAILAND'S POLITICAL SETTLEMENT
Competitive Clientelism (1996–2014)

Thailand retained a competitive clientelist settlement for the majority of its deceleration episode, though the political fissures it generated became increasingly virulent, ultimately triggering a shift to a vulnerable authoritarian coalition. As in Malaysia, the AFC—and particularly the unwieldy six-party ruling coalition's inept response to it, which entailed months of dithering over the terms of an IMF bailout before finally accepting one on even more stringent terms—triggered an outpouring of public anger and the eventual resignation of Prime Minister Chavalit Yongchaiyudh (Freedman, 2006). Spurred on by bringing down Chavalit's administration, an alliance of social forces steered by the middle classes pressured an incoming seven-party coalition led by Chuan Leekpai into appointing a constitution-writing committee stacked with civil society actors. The resulting constitution was radical; informed by notions of good governance, it sought to create a modern political system, where parties would compete through manifestos rather than money (Khan, 2010). The electoral system was altered to favour large parties, election spending was capped, MPs were prevented from defecting before elections, and monitoring bodies were established, notably the Electoral Commission, Constitutional Court, and National Counter Corruption Commission. These provisions, it was hoped, would 'attack money politics on a number of levels' (Wingfield, 2002: 273).

It was within this context that Thaksin Sinawatra, a telecommunications tycoon with interests in the media, transport, and manufacturing sectors, led his Thai-Rak-Thai (TRT) party to success in 2001, the first elections under Thailand's new constitution. Also a first, Thaksin won on the basis of a coherent manifesto that pledged 'new thinking, new ways, for all Thais' (quoted in Hewison, 2004: 511). His policy platform united a remarkably eclectic spectrum of voters, unmatched before or since. The middle classes, new rich, and Sino-Thai capitalists all flocked to Thaksin, because he railed against IMF measures; while he also struck a chord with poor, predominantly rural, voters by promising spending programmes and to channel credit to SMEs (Wingfield, 2002: 278). Another first, he followed through with his pledges, launching the Village and Community Fund, which provided low-interest loans to entrepreneurs and small enterprises in every village, and the Universal Health Scheme, which offered healthcare for 30 baht, within just a year of assuming office (Hewison, 2004). By 2002, these schemes were reaching fifty-two million beneficiaries, and Thaksin was riding a wave of popularity.

Thaksin's stance changed dramatically as he neared his second term. The 'nationalist shibboleth' that had swept him into power was dissipating; his unwieldy coalition had put aside its differences to deal with the crisis, but tensions surfaced as the economy recovered, particularly over escalating rural spending (Hewison, 2004: 512). A political chameleon, Thaksin reinvented the TRT as the 2005 elections approached. Espousal of economic nationalism was dropped for a populist platform that positioned him as a defender of the poor (Khan, 2010). A stunningly successful strategy, it produced the most crushing victory in Thailand's history. Thaksin won 375 of 500 seats, his numbers swelling as smaller parties were corralled into his coalition. Within this context, parliament became a place for the TRT to 'talk shop' and process legislation unopposed, with Thaksin's behaviour becoming increasingly authoritarian as he lavished business opportunities on cronies and placed allies within the clutch of institutions that had been created to provide checks and balances (Hewison, 2010: 123).

Furious at a resurgence of money politics, the middle classes formed the People's Alliance for Democracy, a movement that enjoyed support among the business community, military, and Palace. It launched non-stop street demonstrations during 2006, eroding Thaksin's ability to govern. Finally, on 19 September, claiming to be restoring stability, the military launched a coup. Hurling Thailand back into its 'familiar whirl of coups, constitutions, and elections', the junta rewrote the constitution in ways that unravelled Thaksin's control over the political system and then called another election, to be held in 2007 (Pongsudhirak, 2008: 143). The political tumult that has occurred since is too complex to recount in detail here, but has followed a similar pattern. Broadly speaking, this involved the re-election of Thaksin-linked parties in 2007, 2011, and 2014, the consequent mobilization of the anti-Thaksin yellow shirt movements in 2008, 2011, and 2014, and the over-throw of these Thaksin-linked parties by the courts or military in 2008 and 2014, followed by pro-Thaksin red shirt protests (Crisis Group, 2012). Such are the 'ravine-like political divisions' in Thailand's political settlement that these rifts between yellow/red, rural/urban, for/against Thaksin are now almost unbridgeable, with the result that incoming coalitions struggle to reconcile the interests of business and middle classes, on the one hand, and factions that Thaksin mobilized, on the other (Connors, 2011: 285).

Vulnerable Authoritarian Coalition (2014–Today)
It is in this context that the military launched its third coup since 1996. Declaring that feuding had left Thailand on the brink of civil war, it ousted a government led in Thaksin's absence by his sister Yingluck, which had riled the establishment with an amnesty bill pardoning Thaksin. While coups have been a constant feature of Thailand's trajectory, this had several features that distinguish it from others, leading us to conclude that the political settlement has shifted to a vulnerable authoritarian coalition (see Figure 10.26). In contrast to 2006 and 2008, when the military made relatively minor constitutional amendments before presiding over elections weighted against Thaksin-aligned parties, this time it has systematically restructured the political system in ways that unravel the electoral system and prevent future 'parliamentary dictatorships' (Kanchoochat, 2014). A military-dominated Constitution Committee was tasked with drafting a new constitution. As expected, the draft curbed the authority of elected politicians and parties while enhancing the power of appointed officials, oversight bodies, and a military-dominated upper chamber, all of which were mechanisms for extending military rule.

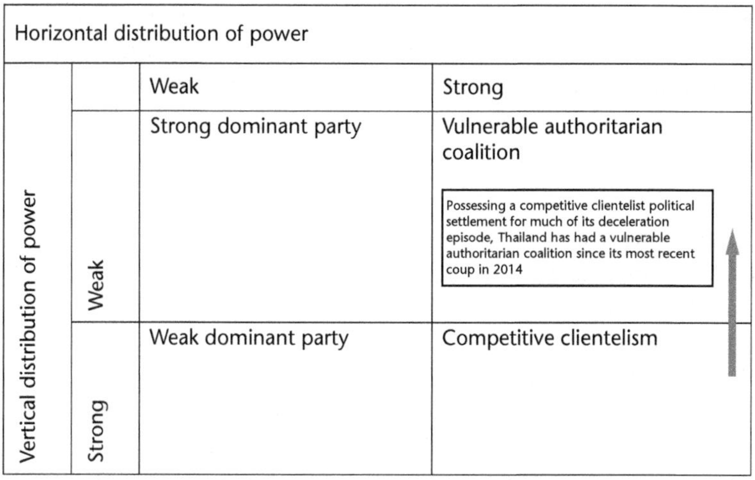

Horizontal distribution of power			
		Weak	Strong
Vertical distribution of power	Weak	Strong dominant party	Vulnerable authoritarian coalition Possessing a competitive clientelist political settlement for much of its deceleration episode, Thailand has had a vulnerable authoritarian coalition since its most recent coup in 2014
	Strong	Weak dominant party	Competitive clientelism

Figure 10.26. Thailand's political settlement during its deceleration episode
Source: Authors' illustration.

The charter caused an outcry, prompting the junta to respond with Orwellian-esque 'attitude adjustment' sessions for critics at remote military bases.

After repeated postponements, a referendum on the charter was held in August 2016. In spite of criticisms from the USA, UN, and European Union that observer groups were prevented from monitoring the process, and that voter turnout was only just over 50 per cent, the junta heralded the vote as a decisive victory and promised elections in 2017 (*Economist*, 2015). Yet King Bhumibol died two months after the referendum, plunging Thailand back into a period of intense uncertainty. A year of national mourning was immediately called by Prime Minister Prayuth, while the junta shelved any discussion of elections to oversee the transition and made increasingly draconian use of *lèse-majesté* to prevent discussion of the succession.

Following a rapprochement of sorts in the months leading up to the King's death, Prayuth announced that Vajiralongkorn would be Thailand's next monarch, but that his accession would be delayed for an unspecified period of time, feeding rumours that the establishment was assessing other options. Despite the constitution stipulating that Vajiralongkorn, the undisputed heir, should have immediately succeeded his father, seven tense weeks passed before the leader of the national assembly finally invited him to take up the throne. The official explanation was that the prince needed time to grieve for his father. In reality, however, the delay was due to intense behind-the-scenes negotiations, as the junta sought guarantees on key issues such as Thaksin's ongoing exile, and the upholding of its new constitution. Vajiralongkorn ultimately accepted the junta's offer and ascended to the throne. However, there remains a significant level of mistrust regarding each other's motives. As such, the junta is even more committed to staying in power than it was before, demonstrated by its reticence to offer even a vague timetable for the elections it proposed before Bhumibol's death.

THAILAND'S RENTS SPACE

Thailand's rents space had shifted towards powerbrokers by 2009 (see Figure 10.27). Like Malaysia, Thailand is increasingly finding itself squeezed between low-wage and high-technology competitors (Doner, 2009). However, there has not been the same exodus of multinational corporations, owing to the (limited) linkages forged with predominantly Sino-Thai suppliers through the various local content policies launched in the 1980s (Rock, 2000). Unlike in Malaysia, where ethno-political considerations have prevented the BN from promoting indigenous firms, Thailand's political settlement has allowed—and even encouraged—ruling elites to nurture Sino-Thai capitalists, both as a means of stimulating growth and as a source of personal enrichment (Raquiza, 2012). Similarly, unhindered by redistributive ethnic concerns, Prem's coalition reacted quickly when it became clear there was a shortage of researchers and engineers in the 1980s, launching a major training programme for science and technology students that was devoid of ethnic quotas

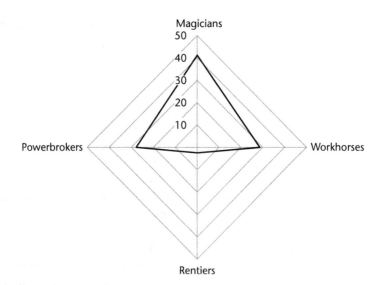

Figure 10.27. Thailand's rents space, 2009

Source: National Economic and Social Development Board, Government of Thailand, authors' calculations.

Note: Percentage share.

as seen in Malaysia (Rock, 2000). This has helped to generate relatively strong linkages with foreign magicians, in turn explaining their continuing—and, in the case of automobiles, increased—presence within Thailand's rents space and export structure (see Figure 10.28). On the other hand, there has not been the resurgence of rentiers witnessed in Malaysia, owing to the fact not just that Thailand has never been as well endowed with natural resources, but that the one resource it did have—land—has been exhausted since the 1980s, in stark contrast to Malaysia's vast land frontier in Sabah and Sarawak.

THAILAND'S DEALS SPACE
Where deals became increasingly disordered during the 1990s, Thaksin reordered the deals space by implementing major reforms within the bureaucracy. Notably this involved strengthening core institutions, such as the Central Bank and Ministries of Finance and Industry, as well as revitalizing the BOI and NESDB after years of neglect (Kanchoochat, 2014). Yet, even here, Thaksin clashed with the old elite, as he also demanded an 'ideational shift' among bureaucrats (Thak, 2007: 72). Thailand's bureaucracy has long been relatively effective, but promotions and advancement have historically been predicated upon seniority rather than ability, whereas Thaksin implemented a rigorous new public management system, whereby high-performing bureaucrats were fast-tracked to the top as 'CEO governors' (Doner, 2009: 131). Some suggest this offered Thaksin a convenient way to transplant allies into the upper echelons of the bureaucracy, while others maintain that he was genuinely committed to reform. Either way, it was yet another arena in which he clashed with the establishment.

Aside from reordering deals, Thaksin retained the broad features of Thailand's dualistic deals strategy, though the beneficiaries of these deals changed significantly in certain domains, offering further insights into why he was overthrown. Consistent with previous administrations, Thaksin offered open ordered deals to magicians, unveiling a comprehensive, cluster-based industrial policy that offered incentives and cheap credit to firms in five priority sectors—automobiles, computers, textiles, food, and tourism (Doner, 2009). Thaksin focused on automobiles, believing Thailand had the potential to become the 'Detroit of Asia' and a regional export hub (Chen, 2014: 71). In 2002, he unveiled a four-year master plan offering tax incentives in exchange for meeting ambitious targets such as producing 1,000,000 cars a year and localization of 60 per cent (Kanchoochat, 2014: 20). These targets were met a year ahead of schedule and several Japanese manufacturers established research and development facilities in the country. Referring to Thailand's structural squeeze as the 'nutcracker effect', Thaksin also helped domestic suppliers to upgrade, establishing a National Committee on Competitiveness,

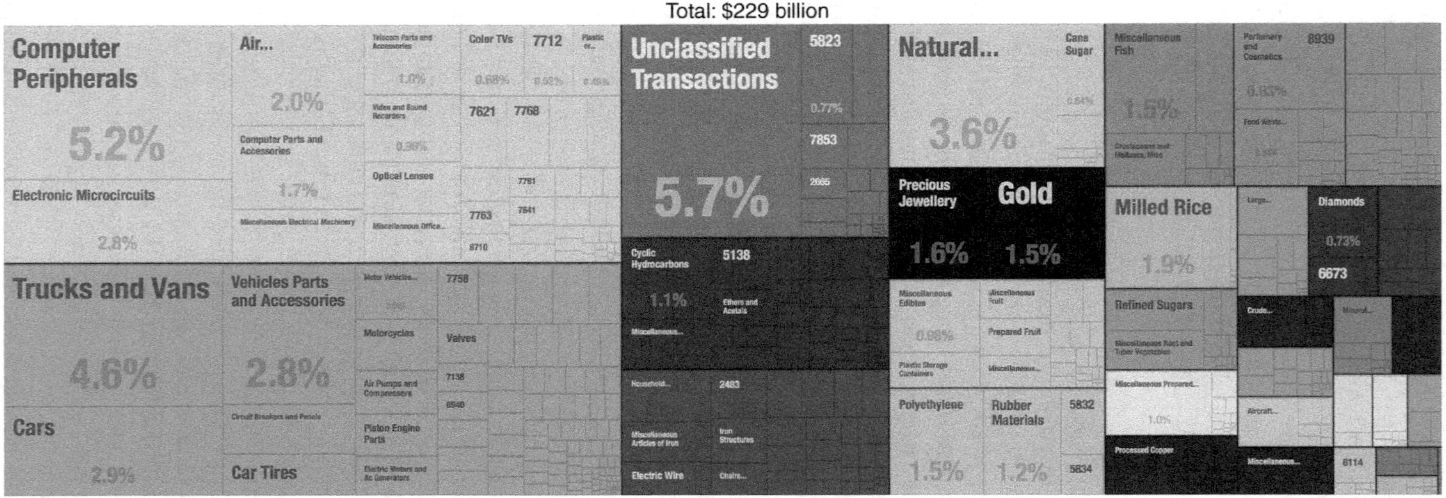

Figure 10.28. Thailand's export structure, 2013

Source: Atlas of Economic Complexity <http://atlas.cid.harvard.edu/>.

as well as instructing the BOI to focus on promoting technology development (quoted in Doner, 2009: 131).[6]

While there was continuity for magicians, a major shift occurred within the rentier and powerbroker domains. Closed ordered deals remained the order of the day, but beneficiaries were no longer establishment-linked firms; instead, deals went to Thaksin's business associates. Thaksin was Thailand's major telecommunications tycoon, while his inner circle had interests across the construction, real estate, media, and retail sectors, all of which have historically been dominated by the 'old oligarchy' (Hewison, 2010: 127). Deals became exceptionally closed within these sectors as Thaksin channelled licences and contracts to 'a small coterie' of TRT-linked businesses, helping them to expand at an unprecedented rate. Pasuk and Baker (2009), for example, estimate that the stock market value of Thaksin's five listed enterprises more than tripled during his first term, with Shin Corp capitalizing particularly to expand into a range of new ventures. Simultaneously, the protection long afforded to establishment-linked conglomerates as a means of sustaining the political settlement was unravelled, particularly privileges given to the CPB, whose 'special status' Thaksin resented (Hewison, 2010: 128). These are critical insights, then, as they reveal the extent to which Thaksin 'was pitted against the "old oligarchy"', and that the coup was ultimately a mechanism for 'preserving the status quo' (Hewison, 2010: 127).

Deals have remained generally ordered following Thaksin's ouster, particularly for magicians, who are cocooned within Thailand's EPZs and largely insulated from political upheaval. Yet this order has been punctuated by pockets of disorder around regime changes. Thailand has had five prime ministers between 2006 and 2014, resulting in 'constant changes on the management level' of ministries and agencies, as each incoming administration rewarded its supporters in a bid to keep itself in power (Chen, 2014: 71). There has been a significant reordering since 2014, however, with the junta presiding over major reforms within the bureaucracy (*Asian Review*, 2016). There has also been a return to a more traditional dualistic deals strategy under the junta's twenty-year 'Thailand 4.0' plan, which aims to transform the country into a 'first world nation' with a value-added economy, and whose provisions will be enshrined in law so that future governments are forced to implement them (*Diplomat*, 2016). Offering incentives to magicians such as automobiles, electronics, and textiles, on the one hand, and powerbroker industries such as petrochemicals, chemicals, and pharmaceuticals, on the

---

[6] In 2010, 53 per cent of the 690 companies that constituted the Tier 1 suppliers to the assemblers were pure Thai or Thai majority firms, while all 1,700 Tier 2 suppliers were Thai firms (Natsuda and Thoburn, 2012).

other, it pointedly removes subsidies from Thaksin-linked industries such as telecoms and roads (BOI, 2016).

THAILAND FEEDBACK LOOPS

The shift to a vulnerable authoritarian coalition since 2014 suggests the possibility of a clear negative feedback loop from the evolving political situation to the deals space that may lead to a disordering of deals in the near future. The increasingly authoritarian nature of the current political regime could lead to pushback from excluded elites (for example, those loyal to the Thaksin family). It is also possible that the pent-up frustration in the countryside, due to the stark regional inequalities in the country, spills over to the streets of Bangkok once again. While magicians have been remarkably resilient during previous periods of electoral turmoil and military coups, the lack of clarity on when new elections will be held in the country, as well as the continuing role of the monarchy as a key source of patronage, may prolong (or worsen) Thailand's current growth deceleration episode for an indefinite period.

10.5 Conclusion

Both Malaysia and Thailand have had strong economic growth since the 1960s, and are among the few developing countries which had seen high rates of structural transformation until recently. However, their growth experiences can be broken down into two phases: one, a growth acceleration phase from the 1960s to the mid-1990s; and two, a growth deceleration phase, from the mid-1990s to date. In this chapter, we have provided a political explanation of why these two countries first witnessed a long period of growth acceleration, followed by an extended period of growth deceleration, which is still ongoing. We have stressed the role of the political settlement interacting with the rents space in influencing the nature of deals that political elites offered to firms in Malaysia and Thailand. We have argued that both these countries witnessed a dualistic deals environment where closed deals were offered to powerbrokers and rentiers and open deals were offered to magicians. The dualistic deals environment facilitated economic growth and, at the same time, preserved rents for powerful groups that maintained political stability. However, the dualistic deals environment increasingly became patronage-based and disordered, especially after the AFC, as the political settlements in Malaysia and Thailand became more vulnerable to challenges from excluded elites, as well as non-elites, over time. In the case of Malaysia, the inability to create a dynamic, outward-oriented Malay capitalist class, who could push for open deals in the sectors of the economy that provided critical inputs to the export-oriented manufacturing sector, was the major impediment for further industrialization and value addition in the manufacturing sector. In the case of Thailand, there was the successful creation of a Sino-Thai entrepreneurial class, which explains the relative success that Thailand has had with structural transformation as compared to Malaysia after the AFC.

The findings of this chapter suggest that a dualistic deals strategy can achieve growth along with political stability for a prolonged period, but also has the potential to act as an impediment to further growth and structural transformation over time. This is particularly true if negative feedback loops lead to further closing of the deals space and if there is not a sufficiently dynamic domestic capitalist class that can push for open deals across the board. In both Malaysia and Thailand, there was a need to move away from the closed deals that were prevalent in large parts of the economy, but this was difficult to do, given the prevailing political settlement.

Our findings also suggest that structural transformation per se may not lead to a movement from deals to rules if the underlying political settlement remains clientelist, and if it is not in the interests of the political elite to embrace rules-based capitalism, which would mean an end to the closed deals that may benefit them. This implies that there is nothing preordained about the movement from middle-income to high-income status, even for countries such as Malaysia and Thailand, which have had remarkable growth success for many years. The 'middle-income trap', as it is sometimes referred to, for countries in this kind of situation (see Eichengreen et al., 2013) may then be a reflection of a type of political equilibrium that prevails in middle-income countries, which may not be conducive to the set of institutional reforms needed for further growth and structural transformation. For Malaysia and Thailand to break out of the middle-income trap, it would be necessary for them to move out of the political equilibrium trap that both countries find themselves in. The outlook for this to happen does not look positive for Malaysia or Thailand in the foreseeable future.[7]

References

Abbott, J. 2004. 'The Internet, Reformasi and Democratisation in Malaysia'. In *The State of Malaysia: Ethnicity, Equity and Reform*. Edited by Gomez, E. Abingdon: Routledge.

Aeria, A. 2013. 'Skewed Economic Development and Inequality: The New Economic Policy in Sarawak'. In *The New Economic Policy in Malaysia*. Edited by Gomez, E., and Saravanamuttu, J. Singapore: Institute of Southeast Asian Studies Publishing.

---

[7] We wish to acknowledge comments from Dr R. Thillainathan, which have considerably strengthened the chapter.

Agarwal, P., Gokarn, S., Mishra, V., Parikh, K., and Sen, K. 1995. *Economic Restructuring in East Asia and India: Perspectives on Policy Reforms*. London: Macmillan.

Agarwal, P., Gokarn, S., Mishra, V., Parikh, K., and Sen, K. 2000. *Policy Regimes and Industrial Competitiveness: A Comparative Study of East Asia and India: Perspectives on Policy Reforms*. London: Macmillan.

Amnesty International. 2016. *Amnesty International Report 2015/16: The State of the World's Human Rights*. London: Amnesty International Ltd.

Ariff, M. 1991. *The Malaysian Economy: Pacific Connections*. Singapore: Oxford University Press.

Asian Review. 2016. 'Corporate Reforms Prompt Rare Praise for Thai Junta'. <http://asia.nikkei.com/Politics-Economy/Economy/Corporate-reforms-prompt-rare-praise-for-Thai-junta?page=2>.

Baker, C. 2016. 'The 2014 Thai Coup and Some Roots of Authoritarianism'. *Journal of Contemporary Asia*, 46(3): 388–404.

Balasubramaniam, V. 2006. 'Embedding Ethnic Politics in Malaysia: Economic Growth, Its Ramifications and Political Popularity'. *Asian Journal of Political Science*, 14(1): 23–39.

BOI. 2016. 'BOI Policy Update'. Presentation by Duangjai Asawachintachit, Deputy Secretary-General Office of the Board of Investment, 1 March. <http://www.boi.go.th/upload/content/Eurochamber_luncheon_Mar2016_57378.pdf>.

Bowie, A., and Unger, D. 1997. *The Politics of Open Economies: Indonesia, Malaysia, the Philippines and Thailand*. Cambridge: Cambridge University Press.

Bruton, H. 1992. *Sri Lanka and Malaysia*. Washington, DC: World Bank.

Capannelli, G. 1999. 'Technology Transfer from Japanese Consumer Electronic Firms via Buyer–Supplier Relations'. In *Industrial Technology Development in Malaysia: Industry and Firm Studies*. Edited by Jomo, K., Felker, G., and Rasiah, R. London: Routledge.

Chen, S. 2014. 'The Political Economy of Industrial Development in Thailand'. *Journal of ASEAN Studies*, 2(2): 62–79.

Cho, G. 1990. *The Malaysian Economy: Spatial Perspectives*. London: Routledge.

Connors, M. 2011. 'Political Reform and the State in Thailand'. In *Politics of Modern South East Asia*. Edited by Hicken, A. London: Routledge.

Cramb, R. 2011. 'Re-inventing Dualism: Policy Narratives and Modes of Oil Palm Expansion in Sarawak, Malaysia'. *Journal of Development Studies*, 47(2): 274–93.

Crisis Group. 2012. *Malaysia's Coming Election: Beyond Communalism?* Brussels: International Crisis Group.

Diplomat. 2016. 'Can Thailand's Junta Reverse Its Economic Decline?' <http://thediplomat.com/2016/03/can-thailands-junta-reverse-its-economic-decline/>.

Dixon, C. 1999. *The Thai Economy: Uneven Development and Internationalisation*. London: Routledge.

Doner, R. 2009. *The Politics of Uneven Development: Thailand's Economic Growth in Comparative Perspective*. New York: Cambridge University Press.

Doner, R., and Ramsay, A. 2000. 'Rent-Seeking and Economic Development in Thailand'. In *Rents, Rent-Seeking and Economic Development: Theory and Evidence in Asia*. Edited by Khan, M., and Jomo, K. Cambridge: Cambridge University Press.

Doraisami, A. 2015. 'Has Malaysia Really Escaped the Resource Curse? A Closer Look at the Political Economy of Oil Revenue Management and Expenditures'. *Resources Policy*, 45: 98–108.

Economist. 2015. 'Economic Malays: A Guide to Malaysia's Politics and Economics in Graphics'. <http://www.economist.com/blogs/graphicdetail/2015/09/malaysia-graphics>.

Eichengreen, B., Park, D., and Shin, K. 2013. 'Growth Slowdowns Redux: New Evidence on the Middle-Income Trap'. NBER Working Paper. Cambridge, MA: NBER.

Freedman, A. 2006. *Political Change and Consolidation: Democracy's Rocky Road in Indonesia, South Korea, and Malaysia*. Gordonsville, VA: Palgrave Macmillan.

Gomez, E. 2002. 'Political Business in Malaysia: Party Functionalism, Corporate Development and Economic Crisis'. In *Political Business in East Asia*. Edited by Gomez, E. London: Routledge.

Gomez, E. 2004. 'Politics, Business and Ethnicity in Malaysia: A State in Transition'. In *The State of Malaysia: Ethnicity, Equity and Reform*. Edited by Gomez, E. Abingdon: Routledge.

Gomez, E. 2012. *Political Business in East Asia*. London: Routledge.

Gomez, E. 2013. 'Nurturing Bumiputera Capital: SMEs, Entrepreneurship and the New Economic Policy'. In *The New Economic Policy in Malaysia*. Edited by Gomez, E., and Saravanamuttu, J. Singapore: Institute of Southeast Asian Studies Publishing.

Gomez, E., and Jomo, K. 1997. *Malaysia's Political Economy: Politics, Patronage and Profits*. Cambridge: Cambridge University Press.

Gomez, E., Saravanamuttu, J., and Mohamad, M. 2013. 'Malaysia's New Economic Policy: Resolving Horizontal Inequalities, Creating Inequities?' In *The New Economic Policy in Malaysia*. Edited by Gomez, E., and Saravanamuttu, J. Singapore: Institute of Southeast Asian Studies Publishing.

Hausmann, R., Hidalgo, C. A., Bustos, S., Cosica, M., Simoes, A., and Yildirim, M. A. 2013. *The Atlas of Economic Complexity: Mapping Paths to Prosperity*. Center for International Development, Harvard University.

Hewison, K. 1997. 'Power, Oppositions and Democratisation'. In *Political Change in Thailand: Democracy and Participation*. Edited by Hewison, K. London: Routledge.

Hewison, K. 2004. 'Crafting Thailand's New Social Contract'. *Pacific Review*, 17(4): 503–22.

Hewison, K. 2010. 'Thaksin Shinawatra and the Reshaping of Thai Politics'. *Contemporary Politics*, 16(2): 119–33.

Hicken, A. 2004. 'The Politics of Economic Reform in Thailand: Crisis and Compromise'. William Davidson Institute Working Paper Number 638. Ann Arbor: University of Michigan.

Hill, H. 2012. 'Malaysian Economic Development: Looking Backward and Forward'. In *Malaysia's Development Challenges: Graduating from the Middle*. Edited by Hill, H., Yean, T., and Zin, R. Abingdon: Routledge.

Hobday, M. 1999. 'Understanding Innovation in Electronics in Malaysia'. In *Industrial Technology Development in Malaysia: Industry and Firm Studies*. Edited by Jomo, K., Felker, G., and Rasiah, R. London: Routledge.

Kaminsky, G. L., and Reinhart, C. 2000. 'On Crises, Contagion and Confusion'. *Journal of International Economics*, 51: 145–68.

Kanchoochat, V. 2014. 'Coalition Politics and Reform Dynamics in Thailand'. GRIPS Discussion Paper 13–26. National Graduate Institute for Policy Studies, Tokyo, Japan.

Kar, S., Pritchett, L., Raihan, S., and Sen, K. 2013. *The Dynamics of Economic Growth: A Visual Handbook of Growth Rates, Regimes, Transitions and Volatility*. Manchester: Effective States and Inclusive Development Research Centre. <http://www.effective-states.org/wp-content/uploads/other_publications/final-pdfs/handbook.pdf>.

Khan, M. 2010. 'Political Settlements and the Governance of Growth-Enhancing Institutions'. Mimeo.

Jesudason, J. 1990. *Ethnicity and the Economy: The State, Chinese Business, and Multinationals in Malaysia*. Oxford: Oxford University Press.

Jomo, K. 1997. *South East Asia's Misunderstood Miracle: Industrial Policy and Economic Development in Thailand, Malaysia and Indonesia*. Oxford: Westview.

Jomo, K. S. 1998. 'Financial Liberalization, Crises and Malaysian Policy Responses'. *World Development*, 26(8): 1563–74.

Lall, S. 1995. 'Malaysia: Industrial Success and the Role of the Government'. In *The Economic Development of South East Asia*, Volume 4. Edited by Hill, H. Cheltenham: Edward Elgar.

Lauridsen, L. 1998. 'The Financial Crisis in Thailand: Causes, Conduct and Consequences'. *World Development*, 26(8): 1575–91.

Lee, C. 2012. 'Microeconomic Reform in Malaysia'. In *Malaysia's Development Challenges: Graduating from the Middle*. Edited by Hill, H., Yean, T., and Zin, R. Abingdon: Routledge.

Leutert, H., and Sudhoff, R. 1999. 'Technology Capacity Building in the Malaysian Automotive Industry'. In *Industrial Technology Development in Malaysia: Industry and Firm Studies*. Edited by Jomo, K., Felker, G., and Rasiah, R. London: Routledge.

Lopez, G. 2009. 'Country Report: Malaysia'. In *Global Corruption Report*. Edited by Transparency International. Berlin: Transparency International.

Mahathir, M. 1982. *The Malay Dilemma*. Kuala Lumpur: Federal Publications.

Maisrikrod, S., and McCargo, D. 1997. 'Electoral Politics: Commercialisation and Exclusion'. In *Political Change in Thailand: Democracy and Participation*. Edited by Hewison, K. London: Routledge.

Marshall, A. 2014. *A Kingdom in Crisis: Thailand's Struggle for Democracy in the Twenty-First Century*. London: Zed Books.

McCargo, D. 2005. 'Network Monarchy and Legitimacy Crises in Thailand'. *Pacific Review*, 4: 499–519.

Menon, J., and Ng, T. H. 2013. 'Are Government Linked Companies Crowding Out Private Investment in Malaysia?' Asian Development Bank Working Paper Series, No. 345.

Milner, A., Embong, A., and Yean, T. 2014. *Transforming Malaysia: Dominant and Competing Paradigms*. Singapore: Institute of South East Asian Studies.

Natsuda, K., Segawa, N., and Thoburn, J. 2013. 'Liberalization, Industry Nationalism and the Malaysian Automotive Industry'. *Global Economic Review*, 42(2): 113–34.

Natsuda, K., and Thoburn, J. 2012. 'Industrial Policy and the Development of the Automotive Industry in Thailand'. *Journal of the Asia Pacific Economy*, 18(3): 1–25.

Nelson, J. 2012. 'Political Challenges in Economic Upgrading: Malaysia Compared with South Korea and Taiwan'. In *Malaysia's Development Challenges: Graduating from the Middle*. Edited by Hill, H., Yean, T., and Zin, R. Abingdon: Routledge.

Nyanjom, O. 2013. 'The Politics of Poverty for Poverty Reduction: Comparing Malaysia with Kenya'. In *Asian Tigers, African Lions: Comparing the Development Performance of South East Asia and Africa*. Edited by Berendsen, B., Dietz, T., Nordholt, H., and van der Veen, R. Leiden: Brill NV.

Ouyyanont, P. 2008. 'The Crown Property Bureau in Thailand and the Crisis of 1997'. *Journal of Contemporary Asia*, V38(1): 166–89.

Pasuk, P., and Baker, C. 2009. *Thaksin*. Chiang Mai: Silkworm Books.

Pepinsky, T. 2007. 'Malaysia: Turnover without Change'. *Journal of Democracy*, 18(1): 113–27.

Phongpaichit, P., and Baker, C. 2000. *Thailand: Economy and Politics*. Oxford: Oxford University Press.

Pongsudhirak, T. 2008. 'Thailand Since the Coup'. *Journal of Democracy*, 19(4): 140–53.

Raquiza, A. 2012. *State Structure, Policy Formation and Economic Development in South East Asia: The Political Economy of Thailand and the Philippines*. Abingdon: Routledge.

Rasiah, R. 2012. 'Is Malaysia's Electronics Industry Moving Up the Value Chain?' In *Malaysia's Development Challenges: Graduating from the Middle*. Edited by Hill, H., Yean, T., and Zin, R. Abingdon: Routledge.

Rasiah, R., Crinis, V., and Lee, H. 2015. 'Industrialization and Labour in Malaysia'. *Journal of the Asia Pacific Economy*, 20(1): 77–99.

Ritchie, B. 2005. 'Coalitional Politics, Economic Reform, and Technological Upgrading in Malaysia'. *World Development*, 33(5): 745–61.

Rock, M. 2000. 'Thailand's Old Bureaucratic Polity and Its New Semi-Democracy'. In *Rents, Rent-Seeking and Economic Development: Theory and Evidence in Asia*. Edited by Khan, M., and Jomo, K. Cambridge: Cambridge University Press.

Rodrik, D. 2016. 'Premature Deindustrialization'. *Journal of Economic Growth*, 21: 1–33.

Samudavanija, C. 1997. 'Old Soldiers Never Die, They Are Just Bypassed: The Military, Bureaucracy and Globalisation'. In *Political Change in Thailand: Democracy and Participation*. Edited by Hewison, K. London: Routledge.

Segawa, N., Natsuda, K., and Thoburn, J. 2014. 'Affirmative Action and Economic Liberalisation: The Dilemmas of the Malaysian Automotive Industry'. *Asian Studies Review*, 38(3): 422–41.

Siamwalla, A. 1997. 'Can a Developing Democracy Manage Its Macroeconomy? The Case of Thailand'. In *Thailand's Boom and Bust*. Bangkok: Thailand Development Research Institute.

Tan, J. 2011. *Privatization in Malaysia: Regulation, Rent Seeking and Policy Failure*. London: Routledge.

Tan, J. 2014. 'Running out of Steam? Manufacturing in Malaysia'. *Cambridge Journal of Economics*, 38: 153–80.

Thak, C. 2007. 'Distinctions with a Difference: The Despotic Paternalism of Sarit Thanarat and the Demagogic Authoritarianism of Thaksin Shinawatra'. *Crossroads: An Interdisciplinary Journal of South East Asian Studies*, 19(1): 50–94.

Thillainathan, R., and Cheong, K. 2016. 'Malaysia's New Economic Policy, Growth and Distribution: Revisiting the Debate'. *Malaysian Journal of Economic Studies*, 51(1): 51–68.

Thirkell-White, B. 2006. 'Political Islam and Malaysian Democracy'. *Democratization*, 13(3): 421–41.

Unger, D. 1998. *Building Social Capital in Thailand: Fibres, Finance and Infrastructure.* New York: Cambridge University Press.

Wade, R. 1998. 'The Asian Debt and Development Crisis, 1997–? Causes and Consequences'. *World Development*, 26(8): 1535–53.

Wall Street Journal. 2016a. 'Malaysia Prime Minister Najib Razak Says He Isn't a "Crook"'. <http://www.wsj.com/articles/malaysia-prime-minister-najib-razak-says-he-isnt-a-crook-1458550120>.

Wall Street Journal. 2016b. 'Malaysia's Najib Razak Rains Largess on Jungle State Ahead of Vote'. <http://www.wsj.com/articles/malaysias-najib-razak-rains-largesse-on-jungle-state-ahead-of-vote-1462458587>.

Warr, P. 1993. *The Thai Economy in Transition.* Cambridge: Cambridge University Press.

Weiss, M. 2016. 'Payoffs, Parties, or Policies: "Money Politics" and Electoral Authoritarian Resilience'. *Critical Asian Studies*, 48(1): 77–99.

Wingfield, T. 2002. 'Democratisation and Economic Crisis in Thailand: Political Business and the Changing Thai State'. In *Political Business in East Asia.* Edited by Gomez, E. London: Routledge.

World Bank. 2016. *The Middle-Income Trap: Myth or Reality?* Edited by Larson, G., Loayza, N., and Woolcock, M. Kuala Lumpur: World Bank.

11

Searching for a 'Recipe' for Episodic Development

Lant Pritchett, Kunal Sen, and Eric Werker

11.1 Introduction

Economic growth in developing countries is highly episodic. Many countries in Asia, Africa, and Latin America often attain the 'miracle' growth rates of countries such as South Korea and Taiwan, but only for a few years, after which their per capita incomes decline or stagnate. In this book, we propose a theoretical framework (see Chapter 1) which can explain such patterns of 'boom and bust' episodic growth. We argue that any theory of economic growth must speak not just to long-run and 'steady-state' growth differences, but also to the episodic nature of economic growth in most of today's so-called developing countries. Any realistic strategy for generating sustained development must recognize the political economy dynamics of growth episodes and have a pragmatic approach to navigate them.

We then apply the framework to ten countries in the developing world—Bangladesh, Cambodia, Ghana, India, Liberia, Malawi, Malaysia, Rwanda, Thailand, and Uganda. Each case study (from Chapters 2 to 10) examines the country's growth experience using the theoretical framework of Chapter 1.

In this chapter, we summarize what our country case studies say about the two big questions that we posed in the opening chapter: (a) what ignites growth, and (b) why is growth so difficult to maintain, once ignited? We then circle back to our theoretical framework to see what we have learnt from the case studies that speaks to the core arguments of our framework. We end this chapter with some reflections on what our findings imply for development thinking and policy.

11.2 What Ignites Economic Growth?

We summarize the main findings of the ten country case studies in Table 11.1. Our country case studies show the various paths of how developing countries launch into growth accelerations that are not predetermined by history or slowly evolving 'institutions'. When Sarit Thanarat came to power in Thailand in 1957, or the United Malays National Organization (as part of the Alliance) in Malaysia in 1959, or Hastings Banda in Malawi in 1964, or Jerry Rawlings in Ghana in 1981, or Yoweri Museveni and the National Resistance Movement in Uganda in 1986, or Hun Sen and the Cambodian People's Party in Cambodia in 1993, or the Rwandan Patriotic Front (RPF) in 1994, economic growth accelerated in these countries from previous periods of stagnation or collapse. The common element in all these growth accelerations was a shift from an unstable political settlement which underpinned a disordered deals environment, to a stable political settlement in dominant party settings, leading to an ordered deals environment that kick-started growth. Key to growth accelerations in several of these countries was the pro-growth ideology of the ruling coalitions, which was in part shaped by the economic collapse and unstable political settlements associated with periods of conflict prior to the emergence of these coalitions. Ruling elites in these countries viewed a growth-oriented strategy as a mechanism to legitimize the regime and prevent a return to political instability and economic chaos; they used their dominance in the political system to offer ordered deals to selected economic actors. Typically, these closed ordered deals were offered to rentiers and power-brokers, leading to a rapid increase in incomes within a short time in our case study countries.

Not all growth accelerations occurred in dominant party settlements—one of the largest accelerations in economic growth (measured by net present value of the cumulative change in GDP per capita) occurred in India in 1993 after four decades of economic stagnation, when India had already moved decisively from a strong dominant party (under the Congress from independence till the early 1980s) to a competitive clientelist political settlement. The shift from an anti-business to a pro-business ideology among ruling elites from the mid-1980s led to an ordering of deals from the late 1980s onwards, with the pro-business ideology broadly shared among two major political parties, Congress and the Bharatiya Janata Party (BJP). This meant that a commitment to growth-oriented policies remained in place, irrespective of the election results. A similar phenomenon was observed in Bangladesh, where the two parties that alternated in power (the Awami League and the Bangladesh National Party) shared a commitment to ordered deals for the major growth sectors in the economy (such as ready-made garments). Here, ordered deals were maintained to magicians—exporters in competitive sectors—through a process of rent-sharing across the political divide, no matter which political

Table 11.1. Causal pathways to growth acceleration, maintenance, or collapse

Country	Growth episode	Growth outcome	Political settlement	Rents space: influence of economic actors	Nature of deals
Bangladesh	1972–82	Deceleration	Dominant party (1972–early 1975); vulnerable authoritarianism (late 1975–8); dominant party (1979–81)	Strong presence of powerbrokers; emergence of workhorses and their relative consolidation	Closed, disordered (1972–early 1975); moving to increasingly open and ordered (1976–82)
	1982–95	Weak acceleration	Vulnerable authoritarianism (1982–6); dominant party (late 1986–90); competitive clientelism (1991–5)	Rise of magicians (garments); further consolidation of workhorses; emergence and consolidation of new powerbrokers (private banks)	Gradually open and ordered; some closed/ordered deals (private banks)
	1996–	Rapid acceleration, with some ST	Competitive clientelism (1996–2013), very brief period of vulnerable authoritarianism (2007–8), dominant party (2014–)	Economic and political consolidation of magicians (garments) powerbrokers (power sector, private banks) and workhorses (real estate); emergence and gradual consolidation of other magicians (electronics, leather, drug manufacturers, export)	Semi-open ordered for magicians (garments), closed/ordered for powerbrokers (power sectors, private banks)
Cambodia	1971–82	Collapse	Vulnerable authoritarian	Large presence of workhorses with weak political power	Disordered
	1982–98	Weak acceleration	Vulnerable authoritarian	Emergence of magicians and rentiers	Closed ordered, with increasing open deals in magician sectors
	1998–	Rapid acceleration, some ST	Weak dominant	Consolidation of magicians as well as rentier, strong presence of powerbrokers	Closed ordered to rentiers, semi-open ordered to magicians and workhorses, open and disordered to some powerbrokers (telecoms)
Ghana	1957–66	Stagnation	Dominant party	Power held by powerbrokers and workhorses	Weakly ordered
	1966–74	Weak acceleration	Vulnerable authoritarian	Power held by powerbrokers	Some order, gradually disordered
	1974–83	Growth collapse	Vulnerable authoritarian	Power held by rentiers and powerbrokers	Disordered

(continued)

Table 11.1. Continued

Country	Growth episode	Growth outcome	Political settlement	Rents space: influence of economic actors	Nature of deals
	1983–	Rapid acceleration initially, slowing growth in the 2000s, limited ST	Strong dominant, then competitive clientelist from 1992	Power increasingly held by rentiers (oil), magicians marginal	Closed ordered
India	1950–92	Stagnation	Dominant party (weak from 1980s)	Political power held by powerbrokers (mostly public sector enterprises)	Disordered in most part, gradually ordered in 1980s
	1993–2002	Acceleration, with some ST	Competitive clientelist	Rise of magicians (ICT, pharma) and workhorses (retail trade)	Ordered, mostly open with some closed deals in traditional industries
	2002–	Further acceleration, structural regress, with some hint of a slowdown since 2010	Competitive clientelist	Increasing importance of rentiers (mining) and powerbrokers (telecom)	Largely closed ordered, disordered after 2010
Liberia	1960–71	Weak acceleration	Strong dominant	Strong presence of rentiers and powerbrokers	Open ordered for rentiers, closed ordered for powerbrokers, open disordered for workhorses
	1971–80	Deceleration	Vulnerable authoritarian	Increasing importance of powerbrokers	Increasingly disordered
	1980–90	Collapse	Vulnerable authoritarian	All sectors contracting	Disordered
	1990–2005	See-saw	Competitive clientelist, warlordism	All sectors contracting	Hyper-closed and disordered
	2005–	Rapid acceleration, no ST	Competitive clientelist	Re-emergence of rentiers and powerbrokers	Disordered, except for large foreign and well-connected firms
Malawi	1964–78	Acceleration	Strong dominant party	Strong presence of rentiers (tobacco estates) and powerbrokers (Banda's Press Holdings)	Closed ordered
	1978–2002	Deceleration (sharp)	Weak authoritarian, multiparty elections from 1994	Strong role of powerbrokers	Disordered
	2002–	Acceleration (weak), no ST	Competitive clientelist	Political elite tied to powerbrokers, magicians and workhorses marginal	Weakly ordered

Country	Period	Growth	Political settlement	Dominant actors/sectors	Deals/ordering
Malaysia	1955–97	Rapid acceleration, with increasing ST	Strong dominant, moving to vulnerable authoritarian	Rentiers omnipresent (plantation economy) initially, rise of magicians (textiles and electronics) in 1980s	Closed ordered till 1969, dualistic after the launch of the New Economic Policy in 1971, with some closed ordered to rentiers and powerbrokers, and open ordered to magicians
	1996–	Deceleration, limited ST	Vulnerable authoritarian, moving to competitive clientelist	Re-emergence of rentiers, increasing strength of powerbrokers	Increasingly closed deals to powerbrokers and rentiers, with signs of disorder
Rwanda	1962–81	Positive growth	Vulnerable authoritarian coalition to competitive clientelist coalition	Rentiers and powerbrokers are dominant	Open initially and then movement towards closed/disordered
	1981–94	Rapid deceleration	Move to vulnerable authoritarian coalition and then competitive clientelist	Rentiers and powerbrokers are dominant	Deals are mostly closed (although some openness) and disordered
	1994–	Strong growth, with some ST	Strong dominant (with threats from rival elites pressuring moves to vulnerable authoritarian)	Mostly workhorses and powerbrokers; some rentiers and very few magicians	Deals mostly moving towards open ordered, but with closed deals for strategic investments and creeping disorder in some sectors due to pressures of liberalized environment
Thailand	1955–96	Strong acceleration, with increasing ST	Strong dominant till 1973, then competitive clientelist	Increasing importance of magicians (garments, electronics)	Closed ordered to powerbrokers, open ordered to magicians
	1996–	Deceleration, some ST	Competitive clientelist, moving to vulnerable authoritarian	New magicians emerge (autos), but powerbrokers (Crown companies) become important, workhorses influential under Thaksin	Some disorder in 1990, reordered under Thaksin; increasing uncertainty of deals after 2014 military coup
Uganda	1962–70	Rapid acceleration	Strong dominant	Mostly workhorses (subsistence agriculture)	Ordered, closed
	1972–88	Collapse, followed by stagnation	Vulnerable authoritarian	Mostly powerbrokers and workhorses	Hyper-disordered
	1988–	Rapid acceleration initially, limited ST	Strong dominant party initially, moving to weak dominant party	Emergence of magicians (coffee), followed by rentiers (oil)	Semi-open semi-ordered for magicians and powerbrokers, semi-ordered and slightly open for workhorses, closed and ordered for rentiers

Note: ST = structural transformation.

party was in power. In Liberia, a growth acceleration occurred from the mid-2000s as regional powers, backed by the United States and the international financial institutions, and buoyed by favourable commodity prices, brokered and enforced a peace that ended some three decades of instability, war, and economic decline. This shows the potential of external actors to reverse home-grown negative feedback loops, even in a competitive clientelist settlement.

11.3 Why is Maintaining Growth a Challenge?

No country in our case studies has shown uninterrupted rapid growth accompanied by robust structural transformation and improving institutions. Even for the two South East Asian countries (our 'mature' growers, Malaysia and Thailand)—which had growth acceleration episodes with rapid growth for over three decades from the 1950s to the late 1990s, accompanied by structural transformation—growth decelerated following the 1997 Asian financial crisis and has not recovered to its previous rapid levels in the twenty years since the onset of the crisis. For the other countries in our case studies that, at the final year of data analysed, still remained in growth acceleration episodes that were two decades and counting, such as Bangladesh, Cambodia, Ghana, India, Rwanda, and Uganda, economic growth has not been as rapid as had been observed in the miracle growth countries. In all these countries, economic growth remains vulnerable to reversal, as growth has not been accompanied by high rates of structural transformation and/or unequivocal movement from closed to open deals (much less credibly institutionalized rules).

For several of these countries, the growth acceleration episodes were underpinned by a closed ordered deals environment that became increasingly vulnerable to challenges from non-elites as well as excluded elites, and political delegitimation of the growth process (such as in Ghana, Cambodia, India, and Uganda).[1] In addition, the persistence of closed ordered deals led to the increasing possibility of the deals environment becoming disordered, and acted as a constraint to structural transformation and for growth to be 'locked in'. The persistence of closed ordered deals was itself an outcome of the relative political importance of rentiers and powerbrokers in the political settlement, and the marginalization of magicians and workhorses, which generally prevented any real improvement of political and inclusive institutions alongside the economic growth realized. Not all movement to open

---

[1] However, not all closed ordered deals in the rentier and powerbroker sectors were seen as politically delegitimate—as in the case of the oil industry (a key emerging rentier sector) in Uganda, where these deals were seen as being in the national interest, and where Museveni has so far been capable of controlling rent-seeking arrangements in this sector and willing to enable high-capacity oil technocrats to operate with significant levels of autonomy.

ordered deals has been benign, however. In the case of Rwanda, premature opening up of the deals space in key sectors without prior investment in state capacity has led to a state-driven open disorder, with negative implications for the ability of the RPF regime to meet its strategic goals of state-led structural transformation.

The most successful episodes of rapid economic growth that were maintained for a reasonably long time along with structural transformation were seen in Cambodia, Malaysia, and Thailand. Ruling elites in these three countries followed 'dualist' strategies with respect to deals, offering open ordered deals to magician firms, and maintaining closed ordered deals to rentier and powerbroker firms. In Cambodia, the ruling CPP used closed deals to generate large rents from rentier and powerbroker sectors (land and mineral concessions, and large-scale urban development), a significant proportion of which was ploughed back into rural communities in the form of patronage spending. In Malaysia, the ruling UNMO offered closed deals to Bumiputera companies in powerbroker sectors as a mechanism to generate rents for themselves, as well as to maintain political stability. In Thailand, where the onset of democracy in the late 1980s did not seem to reduce the holding power of the monarchy and the army, closed deals were offered to powerbroker companies owned by the monarchy as a way of maintaining the stability of the political settlement (this settlement was effectively challenged by the rise of Thaksin Shinawatra in the 2000s, culminating in a military coup and a return to autocracy in 2014). These dualistic deals strategies could be seen as maintaining the stability of the prevailing political settlement (or, in North et al.'s (2009) terminology, a mechanism of sharing rents among elites), and at the same time ensuring a shared commitment among elites to ordered deals for the magician sector.

However, while dualistic deals strategies *could and did* deliver growth for quite a long while, these strategies had their 'sell-by date'. This was mostly clearly seen in the case of Malaysia and Thailand, with their prolonged growth deceleration after the Asian crisis, when the ineffectiveness of the dualistic deals strategy followed by ruling elites was increasingly evident in the 2000s, with negative implications for future growth and institutional development. In both these countries, the clientelist nature of the prevailing political settlement, even with impressive levels of structural transformation (as compared with other developing countries), acted as a constraining factor in the transition from deals capitalism to rules capitalism. Open ordered deals in the magician space could not indefinitely compensate for a lack of policy coherence and open order provided to workhorse firms, as well as the negative spillover effects originating from the closed deals offered to rentiers and powerbrokers.

At the other end of the spectrum of growth experiences in our case studies were Liberia and Malawi, where the busts dominated the booms, and an increase in standards of living was not generated over time. In Malawi, economic growth initially occurred in a dominant party political settlement under Hastings Banda in 1964–78, but as Banda became increasingly predatory, growth collapsed from 1978 onwards. The shift to a competitive political settlement in 1994, and frequent changes in the ruling coalition, led to short-termism among political elites. In conjunction with a rents space where rentiers and powerbrokers dominated, this situation has led to a weak acceleration in economic growth since 2002 and very limited prospects for structural transformation. Liberia, too, entered the dataset under the relatively prosperous dominant party settlement of William Tubman, which cultivated open ordered deals for foreign investors in the rentier sector and redistributed the rents through domestic powerbrokers. But its legitimacy depended on the logic of an ever-expanding patronage network, which the rentier sector alone could not generate—particularly during the terms of trade shock that struck many oil importers in the 1970s. Subsequent negative feedback loops pulled the economy into an abyss of instability and disorder through a coup and brutal civil war.

11.4 Political Settlements, Rents, and Deals

As suggested by our framework, the interaction of the political settlement with the rents space determined in large part the deals that were offered to economic actors by political/economic elites. The nature of deals—whether they were closed or open, disordered or ordered—then explained whether growth accelerated from a period of stagnation or collapse, and whether growth was maintained. In all the case studies, the nature of deals differed across sectors, with deals being offered to firms in a sector depending on the political power of the firms in the sector, and how elites viewed the sector within the prevailing political settlement. Closed ordered deals were likely to be offered to firms in the sector if the sector was a mechanism of rent extraction or creation (typically, these were rentier and powerbroker sectors), with open deals more likely if the sector was politically salient in the growth process (typically, these were magician sectors). The Rwanda case study also showed that there could be variation in the deals environment even *within* the same sector, in large part due to the nature of the political settlement. For example, in the case of coffee—an important export for the Rwandan economy—the ruling elite allowed for an open deals environment for parts of the sector which were not important strategically (the low-value-added segment of semi-washed coffee), while maintaining closed ordered deals for segments of the sector where they saw a strategic interest (the high-value-added segment of fully washed coffee).

11.5 Feedback Loops

Both positive and negative feedback loops were evident in our case studies. Positive feedback loops were observed in two ways. First, with the increase in the number of magician firms in countries with large export-oriented manufacturing sectors (such as Bangladesh, Cambodia, and Thailand), there was an increasing ability of these firms, through the associations that represented them, to lobby for economic policies that could benefit these firms to compete effectively in world markets. What these firms typically asked for was not specific deals that benefited them individually, but public inputs that had positive spillover effects on other magician firms in the same or cognate industries (such as tax concessions in Bangladesh, simplifying procedures for exporting in Cambodia, and local content requirements in the case of Thailand). Second, with the rise of the middle class and their participation in more productive workhorse firms in several of the countries that witnessed positive growth (such as Ghana, India, and Malaysia), there was increased demand for more transparency in state–business relations and for open deals.

Negative feedback loops were also twofold. First, negative electoral feedback loops occurred when closed ordered deals that underpinned the growth acceleration phase were seen as politically delegitimate, and there was pushback from non-elites or from rule-of-law institutions, as in the case of Cambodia, India, and Malaysia. In the case of India, the negative political feedback effect from these mechanisms contributed to a disordered deals environment that led to a slowing of economic growth in 2010–14.[2]

In the case of Malaysia, the pushback from excluded elites as well as non-elites was an important contributory factor behind the shift in the political settlement from strong dominance to vulnerable authoritarianism to potentially competitive clientelist.

Negative feedback loops were also evident when rentier and powerbroker firms had stronger political power relative to magicians and workhorses. In general, powerbroker and rentier firms made different demands of the state as compared with magician firms, preferring weak state capacity to regulate and enforce. This implied that where rentier and powerbroker firms were politically important, weak state capacity in the area of industrial policy was likely to occur. The absence of magician firms in some country contexts (such as in Ghana, Liberia, Malawi, and Uganda) implied that there was little pressure on ruling elites to build better state capacity for productivity-increasing industrial policy, making it more difficult for the economy to diversify away from commodity exports.

---

[2] More recent GDP data suggests a partial recovery, following the election of the BJP under the prime ministership of Narendra Modi in 2014, with a commanding majority in the Indian parliament.

11.6 Transnational Factors

Four sets of transnational factors mattered for understanding the initiation and end-of-growth episodes through the role they played in influencing the political settlement and the rents space:

(a) *Commodity price movements*: While the direct effect of surges or collapses in commodity prices on growth outcomes has been well documented in the literature, our research also identified the mechanisms by which commodity price movements affected growth outcomes by either interacting with or changing the prevailing political settlement. Commodity price booms were not necessarily beneficial to the maintenance of growth, as they strengthened rentiers at the expense of magicians/workhorses, as in the case of India in the first decade of the 2000s, shifting the deals space from open ordered towards closed ordered deals. Commodity price collapses often precipitated a change in the prevailing political settlement that was already unstable, as in the case of Malawi, with a move from a dominant party to a competitive settlement in the early 1990s.

(b) *Foreign aid and the role of donors*: The effect of an aid surge in post-conflict economies (such as Cambodia, Liberia, and Rwanda) on growth outcomes was intermediated by the prevailing political settlement and the manner in which the additional resources from foreign aid were used for the purposes of growth. In Cambodia and Rwanda, the surge in aid provided additional economic opportunities to the ruling elite, who had a long-term vision for economic development. In contrast, in 1980s Liberia, foreign aid provided appropriable and transferable resources to the ruling elite to maintain otherwise weakening patronage networks, with negative implications for growth and stability. Similarly, the role of donors was not necessarily benign on the deals environment, as in the case of Rwanda, where donors influenced the RPF regime to open up the deals environment in sectors such as mining, leading to disordered open deals, with the state not possessing the necessary enforcement capabilities to monitor and regulate firms in this sector.

(c) *Foreign direct investment (FDI)*: Similar to foreign aid, the prevailing political settlement influenced in large part which types of foreign firms were allowed to enter the country, and the nature of the deals that were offered to these firms. In Cambodia, Malaysia, and Thailand, where the growth strategy was predicated on a strongly growing magician sector, first in labour-intensive products such as garments and then in electronics, open deals that were relatively ordered were offered to foreign firms, along with state capacity that was 'cocooned' to export-processing zones. There was some attempt to develop local firm capabilities, but this was largely unsuccessful in the case of Malaysia, with negative implications for future economic growth and further structural transformation. In Liberia and Rwanda, with large natural resource endowments, FDI entry was mostly in the rentier sector, along with the entry of Chinese firms in the powerbroker sector in the case of Rwanda and post-war Liberia.

(d) *Neighbourhood effects*: These were strongly evident in the South East Asian case studies—the inflow of investors into Malaysia and Thailand first, and then Cambodia later, was driven in some part by regional trade agreements with purchaser countries that fostered growth in exporting sectors, as well as the ability of policymakers in these countries to learn from the experiences of other East Asian countries in providing a stable deals environment for foreign firms.

11.7 What Do Our Findings Imply for Development Thinking and Policy?

The study of political economy and institutions, and their standing on top of the podium of potential contenders capable of explaining the long-run wealth of nations (Rodrik et al., 2004), has prompted aid organizations to attempt to bring the new insights into the practice of development. Yet the leading theoretical accounts of the role of political economy in determining the health of institutions, and from there, economic prosperity (Acemoglu and Robinson, 2008; Acemoglu and Robinson, 2011; North et al., 2009), are based primarily on events that in some cases occurred centuries ago. The main advice to policymakers today that follows from this evidence is to have better institutions, which the World Bank and others have been dutifully trying to bring about (World Bank, 2002) (a slightly more jaundiced take is that the not-so-helpful advice is that we should have had better institutions a hundred years ago). But what these attempts miss out on, as we argued in Chapter 1, is that the economic growth for most countries that actually need it (in order to escape from poverty) is not a linear process, but proceeds in booms and busts. Moreover, 'improving institutions' cannot be the key to generating economic growth in any meaningful time frame, as institutions take decades to improve, and on top of that, any measured improvement in indices of institutions has effectively zero correlation with improvements in GDP per capita over contemporaneous periods (as we noted in Chapter 1).

But development practitioners are correct to search for political economy explanations. After all, there are usually good technocratic answers to many problems of low economic development. Got natural resource-induced economic volatility? Consider a sovereign wealth fund, a stabilization rule, or at least counter-cyclical fiscal policy. Got pockets of rural poverty? Consider conditional cash transfers, or even unconditional cash transfers. No electricity provision, even as billions of dollars in capital search for opportunities to 'Power Africa'? Set up reforms to the power sector, allowing for a competitive market for power production, a well-managed state-owned grid, and private but well-regulated distribution companies. As will be obvious to any reader, the problem with these examples is not a lack of technical solutions—even technical solutions that in other contexts have proven successful—rather, it is getting the politics right in order to adopt the reform in the first place and then ensuring its successful implementation.

We have put forward a framework that offers insights about when the political economy is favourable to growth-enhancing reforms and when it is not. Our intended audience certainly includes the global community of scholars seeking to understand the political economy of economic development. But our intention is also to write for those policymakers and practitioners who seek ways to operationalize cutting-edge development thinking into context-specific situations.

For these policymakers and development practitioners, the framework highlights three forces:

1. *Constituencies for reform.* In our framework, the rents space describes how to think about the economic interest of different industries. Interests drive the 'asks' of government, which then drives economic policies.

2. *Stable coalitions of power.* The political settlement concept recognizes that for any given set of underlying constituencies and their economic interests characterizing a country, there could be a multitude of different realizations of the ruling elite, with implications for the actual policies that they choose to focus on and implement.

3. *Dynamics between economic performance and constituencies.* The political economy of policy implementation is not a one-off event. Whatever economic policies are in place, via the deals space, will help determine the rate and character of economic growth and transformation. This in turn will raise and lower the fortunes of different constituencies in the rents space and potentially influence the political settlement.

There is no perfect algorithm to determine how these forces interact in a given country. This puts the burden on the analyst to think hard about the specifics of the situation and context, but still gives them a 'road map' to do that. In a sense, the framework employed by this book is more like Michael Porter's five forces (1979) or Hausmann et al.'s (2008) growth diagnostics. These frameworks do not tell firms whether to enter an industry or tell governments which problems to focus on first, but rather they allow for a focused and analytical conversation that will ensure that investors or policymakers are having a productive discussion. Likewise, as the country case studies made clear, our framework is not designed to give all the answers, but rather it supplies the questions to ensure that a team of analysts can navigate the chaotic levels of facts and anecdotes in any national context.

Nor do we have the evidence to say with certainty whether all of the features of this framework have prescriptive power or are merely descriptive. But for finance ministers, development planners, and aid agency analysts looking to boost a country's chances at generating sustained, inclusive growth in the medium run, our framework suggests a manageable goal as well as a number of levers of potential intervention.

Goal The goal of a policymaker trying to improve people's lives in a developing country should be twofold: one, to sustain economic growth over the medium run or, if economic growth is absent, to accelerate it; and two, to improve the probability that the growth dynamics bring about increased strength of those constituencies who favour pro-(inclusive) growth policies.

Levers of intervention We describe potential policy levers of policy interventions corresponding to the different variables of the framework (as in Figure 11.1).

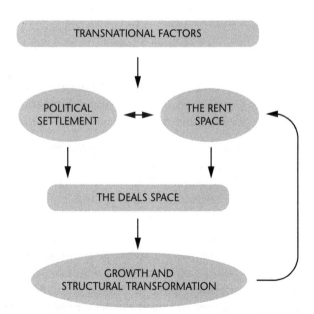

Figure 11.1. Interrelationships between political settlements, the rents space, and the deals space

Transnational factors Global policymakers and change-makers seeking to improve the likelihood of widespread inclusive growth could invest in:

1. *Disruptive technology.* New technologies like smartphones and Twitter have the ability to change the relative strength of existing constituencies by giving less organized ones a stronger ability to mobilize. Targeted investments could leverage the potential of existing technologies to generate these outcomes.

2. *Factor price changes.* Oil and mining rents have the power to cause growth accelerations, but also to sustain political settlements that invest in exclusive, rent-hoarding governance that is unlikely to bring about improvements in governance and economic policy. Climate change policy, including targeted global subsidies to renewables, could influence the political dynamics inside countries reliant on rentiers.

Political settlement Voters, heads of state, political party operators, and aid agency analysts hoping to tip the balance towards a 'good' political settlement (that is still consistent with underlying holding power) could consider seeking to bring about:

3. *Inclusive or pro-growth political settlements.* Not all constituencies end up with proportional representation in the ruling administration or with direct access to its channels of influence. An inclusive or pro-growth settlement means that constituencies interested in broad-based growth get a seat at the table. Strategic appointments, technical assistance, or budgeting could influence the character of the political settlement, at least at the margin.

Rents space Sector developers and economic policymakers interested in creating the conditions for the strongest, most capacious industries that favour a fair, productive, and open business environment could push for:

4. *Cluster-building activities in magician and workhorse industries.* High-potential industries could be targeted for investment that would improve the chances for globally integrated firms to succeed. Along the way, the political demands of these firms would improve the country's overall chance of success and achieving structural transformation.

5. *Better-organized magician and workhorse industries.* Often, when the government interfaces with the private sector, only those industries used to lobbying show up to talk. Powerbroker firms derive a greater benefit from lobbying, since they earn direct rents. So magicians and powerbrokers, with their more disparate interests, will need a lower cost of organizing, in order to get their voice as loudly heard.

6. *Expose bad rents to competition.* When rents, as in powerbroker industries, are divided between producers and consumers, firms will do their best to hide the presence of their advantage. Governments and watchdog organizations can bring transparency, if not effective anti-trust regulation and enforcement, to show consumers the prices they pay relative to other countries in key powerbroker industries.

Deals space Since not all deals are personal, policymakers can influence the deals environment and increase the odds that deals will be open and ordered.

7. *Go for de facto policy initiatives rather than de jure policy reform.* Wholesale reforms that improve the national 'investment climate' or aim to create a 'level playing field' are unlikely to work in deals-based economies. There is huge variation in the deals environment for firms within the same country, which suggests that instead of just looking at the overall national investment 'climate', we should look at how microclimates for different kinds of firms are created and to what extent they can enable ordered deals to happen. For the policymaker, it might be better to concentrate on initiatives that may have minimal impact on de jure policy, but which signal a decisive shift in policy implementation. Such a shift may have substantial impacts on investor expectations and initiate an acceleration of growth.

8. *Get the big deals right.* Some investments, like a big mining or infrastructure project, are enough single-handedly to jump-start a country's growth acceleration. It is important that these deals are ordered and transparent and that their benefits flow to the right constituencies.

Feedback loops Constituencies, holding power, and deals can bring about growth patterns with positive or negative feedback loops. Reformers, particularly outside the system, should think about where these loops might use a nudge or a reset.

9. *Punish rights-violating cronies.* When a country's negative feedback loops result in business leaders accumulating so much power that they are able to abet the regime's violation of human rights at the same time as ensuring protected monopolies for themselves, targeting the power that their businesses earn from the country's growth process (via sanctions, for example) can reduce the rights violations at the same time as changing the arc of the country's growth feedback loops.

10. *Protect incremental improvements in moves towards open deals.* Often successful policies emerge as the consolidation of emergent practices that muddle or struggle their way into existence rather than as 'big bang' strategic efforts.

11.8 Future Research

This book is not meant to offer a definitive account of episodic growth. Rather, it endeavours to put forward a political economy framework capable of explaining the dynamics of growth episodes and then subject that framework to country case studies in all of their complexity. The case studies have shown both the potential and limitations of the framework. The policy implications in Section 11.7 suggest the potential for further projects and research, rather than a fully vetted book of recipes for keen policymakers.

We see a number of avenues for future research, including further investigation into measurement and hypothesis testing, smaller fields of observation, and effective policymaking. For example, how can the variables in the framework be better measured, and subject to additional methodologies of research? What are the dynamics inside decisive industries that lead to structural transformation in the broader economy? And, going from descriptive to prescriptive, under what conditions can industries be given more political clout, and under what conditions can that change the deals environment for others?

References

Acemoglu, D., and Robinson, J. 2008. 'The Role of Institutions in Growth and Development', Working Paper No. 10. Washington, DC: Commission for Growth and Development.

Acemoglu, D., and Robinson, J. 2011. 'Why Nations Fail: Based on *Why Nations Fail: The Origins of Power, Prosperity and Poverty* by Acemoglu, D. and Robinson, J. A.' MIT Presentation. <http://economics.mit.edu/files/6699>.

Hausmann, R., Rodrik, D., and Velasco, A. 2008. 'Growth Diagnostics. The Washington Consensus Reconsidered: Towards a New Global Governance'. In *The Washington Consensus Reconsidered*. Edited by Serra, N., Stiglitz, and J. Oxford: Oxford University Press.

North, D. C., Wallis, J. J., and Weingast, B. R. 2009. *Violence and Social Orders: A Conceptual Framework for Interpreting Recorded Human History*. New York: Cambridge University Press.

Porter, M. 1979. 'How Competitive Forces Shape Strategy'. *Harvard Business Review*, 57(2): 21–38.

Rodrik, D., Subramanian, A., and Trebbi, F. 2004. 'Institutions Rule: The Primacy of Institutions over Geography and Integration in Economic Development'. *Journal of Economic Growth*, 9(2): 131–65.

World Bank 2002. *World Development Report: Building Institutions for Markets*. Washington, DC: World Bank.

Index